D1332727

ON HIS MAJESTY'S SERVICE

For sale by the Superintendent of Documents, U.S. Government Printing Office, Washington, D.C. 20402

NAVAL WAR COLLEGE
HISTORICAL MONOGRAPH SERIES
No. 5

The Historical Monograph Series consists of book-length studies on the history of naval warfare which are based, wholly or in part, on source materials in the College's Naval Historical Collection. Publication is by the Naval War College Press and printing and distribution by the Superintendent of Documents, Washington, DC.

Financial support for research projects leading to publication and for printing is provided in part by the Naval War College Foundation, Inc. Information about the Series is available from the President, Naval War College, Newport, RI 02840 (tel. (401) 841-4052).

Other monographs in the Series are:

No. 1. *The Writings of Stephen B. Luce* edited by John B. Hayes and John B. Hattendorf (1975). GPO Stock No. 008-047-0022-5. Price $2.80 softcover.

No. 2. *Charleston Blockade: The Journals of John B. Marchand, U.S. Navy, 1861-1862*, edited by Craig L. Symonds (1976). GPO Stock No. 008-047-00201-7. Price $3.00 softcover.

No. 3. *The Naval War College and the Development of the Naval Profession* by Ronald Spector (1977). GPO Stock No. 008-047-00212-2. Price $2.75 softcover.

No. 4. *The Blue Sword: The Naval War College and the American Mission, 1919-1941* by Michael Vlahos (1980). GPO Stock No. 008-047-00325-1. Price $5.50 softcover.

U.S. Naval War College, Newport, R.I. 02841
First Edition

Joseph Harold Wellings
Lieut. Commander United States Navy

Assistant Naval Attaché
American Embassy
London

ON HIS MAJESTY'S SERVICE:

OBSERVATIONS OF THE BRITISH HOME FLEET
FROM THE
DIARY, REPORTS, AND LETTERS OF
JOSEPH H. WELLINGS
ASSISTANT U.S. NAVAL ATTACHÉ
LONDON, 1940-41

edited by

JOHN B. HATTENDORF

Naval War College Press
Newport, Rhode Island
1983

Cover: A reprint of C.E. Turner's painting of the sinking of the *Bismarck*. Courtesy, *The Illustrated London News* Picture Library.

Library of Congress Cataloging in Publication Data

Wellings, Joseph H. (Joseph Harold), 1903-
   On His Majesty's service.

   (Naval War College historical monograph series; no. 5)
   Includes bibliographical references and index.
   1. World War, 1939-1945—Naval operations, British. 2.
Wellings, Joseph H. (Joseph Harold), 1903-   . 3. World War,
1939-1945—Personal narratives, American. 4. Great Britain. Royal
Navy—History—World War, 1939-1945. 5. United States. Navy—
Biography. 6. Military attachés, American—Great Britain—Biog-
raphy. I. Hattendorf, John B. II. Title. III. Series: Historical
monograph series (Naval War College (U.S.)); no. 5
D771.W36   940.54'5941   82-6416
                                          AACR2

TABLE OF CONTENTS

LIST OF ILLUSTRATIONS

PREFACE

Documents are materials for the historian to use as source materials. Not all of them deserve publication, but some have an intrinsic value as well as serving as sources. Others provide information from depositories that are distant from the main collections that pertain to a subject.

The documents in this volume serve all these functions. They have been selected from the papers of Rear Admiral Joseph H. Wellings, U.S. Navy (retired), deposited in the Naval Historical Collection at the Naval War College by the Naval War College Foundation. The documents printed here have been selected, edited and arranged to form a coherent, firsthand account of the experiences of an assistant naval attaché and observer of the Royal Navy between September 1940 and June 1941.

The papers consist of personal letters, a diary, memorabilia, notes, photographs, charts, copies of official reports and a typescript volume of reminiscences. The latter two items were finished pieces of writing, but the remainder were often written in haste, under adverse conditions and certainly not intended to be read by others. However, in printing these materials I have used the normal rules of editing historical manuscripts and followed the originals in spelling, capitalization and punctuation. In places where an obvious mistake has been made in the choice of words, I have discussed the intent and meaning with Admiral Wellings and placed the correction within square brackets. I have put other comments and clarifications in the footnotes at the bottom of each page.

I am grateful to a large number of individuals for their help and assistance in the preparation of this volume.

At the Naval War College, I am grateful to Capt. Thomas J. McEnaney, Jr. His invitation to participate in a panel discussion on the sinking of *Bismarck* led me to Admiral Wellings and to look seriously at the Wellings Collection. Mr. Anthony S. Nicolosi, director of the Naval Historical Collection, has been most helpful in his enthusiastic support of this project while Cdr. W.R. Pettyjohn has made the book possible through his own interest in the subject and his editorial skill. Tony Sarro was extremely helpful in providing the assistance of the Graphic Arts and Photographic Sections. The deposit of the Wellings Collection was skillfully handled by Capt. Walter B. Woodson, Jr., USN (ret.), Executive-Director of the Naval War College Foundation. Finally, a special word of thanks must be given to Cdr. Noël Unsworth, RN, who endured a barrage of trivial questions about the Royal Navy.

In other places, I am grateful for information and advice from the office of the Historian, State Department, and the Naval Historical Center, in Washington, D.C.; the Military History Research Institute at Carlisle Barracks, Pennsylvania. In particular, Roselyn C. Lilleniit of the Canadian National Defence Headquarters Library, Ottawa, went to great lengths to provide me with data from volumes of *The Navy List* that were not available in the United States.

The Department of Photographs at the Imperial War Museum gave permission to use a number of photographs in their collections. VAdm Ronald J. Hays, Commander iv

in Chief, U.S. Naval Forces, Europe, obtained permission from the present owners of "New Pipers" to photograph the house and his staff provided the photograph in a timely fashion.

Gunnar Sundell gave me great encouragement and sound advice in the early stages of the work that saw me through to its completion. Grace Garth did an excellent job in turning my difficult handwriting and transcriptions into an accurate and readable typescript.

RAdm and Mrs. Joseph H. Wellings have made the entire project possible by their great generosity in donating their naval papers to the Naval War College Foundation. Their unstinting assistance and constructive criticism have been tremendously valuable. I am particularly grateful to Mrs. Wellings for preserving and giving me permission to use all the personal letters that her husband wrote to her during the months he was with the Royal Navy.

My deepest thanks go to my wife, Berit, and to my three daughters, Kristina, Ingrid and Anna. The ladies of my house have had extraordinary patience with a husband and father who spent so many long winter weekends with J.H. Wellings and the Royal Navy, forty years past.

J.B.H.

Portsmouth, R.I.
May 1981

EDITOR'S INTRODUCTION

During the period between the outbreak of World War II in September 1939 and the attack on Pearl Harbor in December 1941, American leaders found themselves in a difficult position. They were becoming increasingly interested in providing assistance to Britain in the war against Hitler, but at the same time they wished to steer clear of any direct participation in the war.

The United States became involved in a number of activities to assist Britain, short of war. The most widely known aspects of this assistance were Lend-Lease, the destroyers for bases agreement, and the Neutrality patrol. In addition, there were other aspects that were not so widely known. One of these was the exchange of technical information between the Royal Navy and the United States Navy.

The separate, technical and professional development of the two navies in the period since the First World War had created two complementary bodies of experience and knowledge. Naval leaders in the two countries were well aware that an exchange of technical and operational information could be profitable, but the grounds upon which such an exchange could take place grew slowly and hesitantly, at first.[1]

By the summer of 1940, however, a firm basis had been established for a valuable and substantive exchange of information. At first these matters were handled directly by the U.S. naval attaché in London with the technical departments of the Admiralty. This arrangement was not satisfactory as it involved technical matters in a wide variety of special subjects. In order to profit more effectively from British knowledge and experience, American naval officers with competence in specific areas were sent to London to examine matters within their area. Officers sent on this duty were usually sent for a short period of time, several months, and then returned to duty in the United States.

The first additional officer to be sent from the United States to London to deal directly with technical matters was Lcdr. J.N. Opie III, USN. He arrived in London in June 1940 to look into the question of minesweeping and to report back to the Bureau of Ships on the subject.[2] He was followed by a number of other officers who had assignments to deal with specific areas.

Joseph H. Wellings was the first of the group to go to London and to concentrate on fleet operations and tactics. His assignment was to observe the fleet at sea and to examine shipboard practices in convoy operations, gunnery and fleet maneuvers and to report back to the Fleet Training Division in the Office of the Chief of Naval Operations.

---

[1]For a general study of this period, see Stephen Roskill, *Naval Policy Between the Wars* (London: Collins, 1968 & 1976). On the broad aspects behind these exchanges, see James R. Leutze, *Bargaining for Supremacy: Anglo-American Naval Collaboration, 1937-1941* (Chapel Hill: University of North Carolina Press, 1977) and a forthcoming study by Malcolm H. Murfett based on his 1980 Oxford D. Phil. thesis: "Anglo-American Relations in the Period of the Chamberlain Premiership, May 1937-May 1940: the Relationship between Naval Strategy and Foreign Policy."

[2]Naval History Center, Washington, D.C.: Typescript Administrative History. Europe Naval Forces, "Office of the United States Naval Attaché, American Embassy, London, England, 1939-46," (1946) p. 45.

Wellings had seen the potential value of the exchanges that the technical bureaus had initiated and he proposed that the procedure be extended into the operational sphere.

The American naval officers who were sent to London at this time were among the very best officers in the service. Their quality is perhaps best illustrated by noting that a very high percentage of them were later promoted to flag rank. From 1940 to 1942, the officers assigned to this duty were given the title "Assistant Naval Attaché" and ordered to observe the Royal Navy. In 1942, officers who were on this duty in London had their titles changed to "Naval Observer."

U.S. Naval Officers

Assigned to the Office of Naval Attaché[3]

Dates	Naval Attaché Naval Air Attaché Assistant Naval Attaché	Special Naval Observers	Naval Observers	Others
Dec. 1939-30 June 40	6		5	
1 July 1940-30 Dec. 40	38		4	
1 Jan. 1941-31 Dec. 41	79	60	91	10
1 Jan. 1942-31 Dec. 42	17		110	26

The work of these officers in dealing with the technical and professional aspects of Anglo-American naval relations has received little attention from historians. As the table indicates, there was a significant number of officers assigned to this duty. Most of the officers were on short-term assignments and performed a specific function. Few of them seem to have stayed as long as the 10 months that Wellings spent with the Royal Navy.

The Wellings collection contains some material of unusual interest for the historian on this subject. The combination of personal and official documents creates a rare record that presents a rounded view of a naval officer's life at midcareer. Professional concerns at sea are balanced by a deep concern for family at home. Even at sea, naval tactics and operations are seen in the context of wardroom social life and the daily routine in an officer's life. Beyond the purely naval aspects, one can see here a broader cultural aspect in an American's first reaction to British life. Certainly, his mixed feelings of awe, wonder and exasperation have been echoed by many an American traveler to England.

As a middle-grade professional naval officer, Wellings was in an ideal position to view the entire range of the British naval hierarchy. He could cast a sharp professional eye on operations while being able to discuss technical issues with the ratings as well as the admirals. Wellings' letters and reports record for us some of the differences in the social life between American and British wardroom officers. At the same time, one can learn about varying practices in the two services, see some of the operational procedures in convoy operations and examine the quality of gunnery training and antisubmarine warfare procedures. In these years there were many overly high expectations for the use

[3]From table: "Personnel of Joint Naval Establishment, London, 1940-45" in *ibid.*, p. 24.

of both sonar (asdic) and radar. Wellings' reports give a great deal of perspective on actual capabilities at the time and show some of the real problems that needed to be faced.

Although the documents largely express Wellings' critique of British procedures, one can see some areas where he was able to introduce some standard American procedures to his British friends. For example, we learn of the American sight reduction tables and maneuvering board diagrams put to use in H.M.S. *Hood* and the *Blue Jacket's Manual* being used by Rear Admiral, Scapa.

The final chapter of this volume documents one of the most famous naval battles of the century: the sinking of the German battleship *Bismarck*. The documents printed here record the view that Wellings saw as an operating officer in the battleship H.M.S. *Rodney*. They give some details of the search and the engagement that have not been previously published. Aside from a new perspective found in printing the British message traffic, one learns more particularly about the aviators from their own reports, especially from Ensign Smith's narrative on the sighting of *Bismarck* and the details of the damage to *Rodney* in the engagement. The report from H.M.S. *Tartar* fills in the gap in the descriptions of the battle that usually end with *Bismarck*'s sinking.

This volume of documents illustrates only one aspect of a long and varied career in the U.S. Navy. Joseph Harold Wellings was born on 23 April 1903 in Boston, Massachusetts, the son of John A. and Bridget S. Wellings. He was the third youngest of their four sons, all of whom became rear admirals in the Navy. Before his appointment to the Naval Academy in 1921, young Wellings attended Samuel Adams School, Boston Latin School and English High School in Boston. As a midshipman at Annapolis, he participated in several sports including football, boxing, baseball and sailing. For his ability in practical seamanship he earned the Daughters of the American Revolution Sword. He was graduated from the Naval Academy and commissioned Ensign on 4 June 1925.

Wellings' first assignment was to the battleship U.S.S. *Utah*, operating with Division Two, Battleship Divisions, Scouting Fleet. In September 1926 he received orders to another battleship in the same division. U.S.S. *Florida*, and served in her until May 1929. Following duty in the destroyers U.S.S. *King* and U.S.S. *Tillman* attached to the Training Squadron, Scouting Force, Wellings was appointed an instructor with the Naval Reserve Officer Training Corps Unit at Harvard University. In 1933 while at Harvard, he enrolled as a special student at the Harvard Law School.

In 1935 Vice Admiral William D. Leahy selected Wellings to be his aide and flag lieutenant as Commander, Battleships, Battle Force. Wellings continued as Leahy's aide when the Admiral was promoted and took command of the Battle Force. Following a brief assignment on temporary duty in the Navy Department, Washington, D.C., Wellings returned briefly to Massachusetts where he married Dorothea Kirstine Bertelsen of Boston in January 1937. He was then ordered to the Battle Force as the secondary battery officer and senior watch officer in the battleship U.S.S. *California*. In April 1938 he returned to Washington where he was assigned as tactical officer in the Division of Fleet Training of the Office of the Chief of Naval Operations. While in Washington, the Wellings' daughter, Anne, was born. In the summer of 1940 Wellings was ordered to take command of the destroyer *Hopkins* in Hawaii. En route, his orders were abruptly cancelled and he was sent as an assistant naval attaché and an observer of the Royal Navy.

Upon his return from Britain in June 1941, Wellings returned to the Fleet Training Division and then, in February 1942, he was assigned for three months to the Headquarters, Commander in Chief, as an antisubmarine and tactical officer. In both these positions he applied his experiences with the Royal Navy in developing tactical doctrine and antisubmarine doctrine for convoy operations and gunnery.

In June 1942 Wellings reported to Bath Iron Works at Bath, Maine for fitting out the destroyer *Strong* (DD-467), then under construction. He took command of *Strong* upon her commissioning on 7 August 1942. After her shakedown cruise she participated in convoy operations in the Caribbean, Eastern Atlantic and in North African waters, including the Casablanca invasion. In late 1942, *Strong* was ordered to the Pacific where she saw her first combat operations at Noumea on 30 January 1943. In May, Wellings earned the Bronze Star medal for action in the Solomon Islands. He was cited

> For meritorious achievement . . . during combined minelaying expeditions and bombardment missions in the enemy Japanese-held Kolombangara and New Georgia Areas, Solomon Islands, the nights of May 7 and 13, 1943. Skillful maneuvering through poorly charted waters under cover of darkness, [he] carried out his assigned duties courageously and with unwavering determination, delivering his devastating bombardments against these heavily fortified strong-holds and successfully mining areas used extensively by Japanese surface forces, subsequently bringing his ship through without damage following each decisive action . . . .

Later that summer, *Strong* was sunk and Wellings was awarded the Silver Star Medal,

> For conspicuous gallantry and intrepidity . . . in action against enemy Japanese forces in the Solomon Islands on July 4-5, 1943. As part of a task force in close support of the landings . . . at Rice Anchorage on New Georgia Island, [he] skillfully maneuvered his ship through restricted submarine infested waters and effectively bombarded enemy shore batteries and installations in the face of intense Japanese opposition until the STRONG was struck by an enemy torpedo. Calmly and efficiently [he] directed the abandonment of his sinking ship, heroically remaining aboard as she went down. The explosion of her depth charges threw him, seriously injured, into the sea, and several hours later he was rescued . . . .

Following the sinking of *Strong*, Wellings was hospitalized until January 1944 when he reported for temporary duty with the Anti-Submarine Warfare Unit, Fleet Operational Training Command, Atlantic Fleet. In March 1944 he took command of Destroyer Division ONE HUNDRED TWO and from November 1944 to March 1945, held additional responsibility as Commander, Destroyer Squadron TWO. For his services in these positions he received Gold Stars in lieu of his second and third Bronze Star Medals. He was cited particularly for his performance as Commander, Attack Group Screen, Blue Beach, at Lingayen Gulf, Philippine Islands between 9-16 January 1945 and for escort and fast carrier task group screening duties in the Western Pacific and Philippine Islands area.

In March 1945 he returned to Washington for duty in the Bureau of Personnel where he was responsible for developing plans and general policy for the postwar transfer of reserve officers to the regular navy and also policy for the postwar Naval Reserve. In 1946-47, he attended the course at the National War College and following his graduation he remained as a member of the faculty for a year as an instructor in international relations. Upon completion of this assignment he became Assistant Chief of Staff for plans on the staff of Adm. DeWitt Ramsey and later, Adm. Arthur W. Radford, Commander in Chief, U.S. Pacific Fleet. In July 1950 he took command of the heavy cruiser, U.S.S. *Columbus*, flagship of Adms. Richard L. Conolly and Robert B. Carney, successive Commanders of U.S. Naval Forces Eastern Atlantic and Mediterranean.

Returning to Washington in 1952, Wellings served in the Office of the Assistant Secretary of Defense (Manpower and Personnel). While in that assignment he was selected for Rear Admiral to rank from 1 May 1953. Following his promotion ceremony in Washington, which was attended by the first admiral on whose staff he had served, Fleet Admiral William D. Leahy, Wellings took command of the Naval Base, Newport, Rhode Island. From June 1954 to September 1955 he held additional duty as Commandant of the First Naval District.

His next assignment was Deputy for Navy to the Commander, Joint Task Force Seven and Commander, Task Group Seven Point Three. Joint Task Force Seven was comprised of elements from the Army, Navy and Air Force working in conjunction with civilian scientists from the Atomic Energy Commission and conducting thermonuclear tests under the code name "Operation Redwing" at the Pacific Proving Grounds at Eniwetok and Bikini Atolls in the Marshall Islands. For his service in this position, Wellings was commended by the Secretary of the Navy:

> As Commander of the Naval Task Group, Admiral Wellings was primarily responsible for the accomplishment of the mission assigned that Group. This mission included, but was not limited to, providing air and surface security patrols for the area, providing living accommodations for large numbers of task group personnel during certain phases of the tests, maintaining an emergency evacuation capacity for all personnel in the Pacific Proving Ground, supplying facilities for the afloat phases of the scientific program and providing intra-atoll air and surface transportation. Due to the nature of the operation, extreme flexibility in the utilization of the forces assigned was required. That the Task Group was able to expeditiously fulfill, with marked success, all the many complex requirements placed on it with the limited forces available attests to Admiral Wellings' effective planning and direction, and contributed materially to the accomplishments of the Task Force. Admiral Wellings' foresight, effective leadership and outstanding professional efficiency in the discharge of his responsibilities were major factors in the success of Operation REDWING . . . .

In September 1957 RADM Wellings was appointed Assistant Chief of Naval Operations (Plans and Policy). While in that assignment he served as Head of the U.S. delegation for the negotiation of United States Base Lease Agreements with the West Indies Federation concerning the naval base at Chaguaramas in Trinidad. After a year in this position, Wellings became Deputy Director of the Joint Staff, Joint Chiefs of Staff. His title was later changed to Vice Director, and he continued to be concerned with the Chaguaramas negotiations in addition to his other duties that took him to a number of political-military conferences, mainly in Southeast Asia.

Following this duty Rear Admiral Wellings was appointed Commandant of the First Naval District with headquarters in his birthplace, Boston, Massachusetts. He also served additionally as Commander of the Naval Base at Boston and at Portsmouth, New Hampshire. Following a stroke, he retired in August 1963 and moved to Newport, Rhode Island.

In December 1980 Rear Admiral and Mrs. Wellings donated their personal papers relating to the Admiral's 40 years of active service in the United States Navy to the Naval War College Foundation. This collection has been placed on deposit in the Naval Historical Collection at the Naval War College for the use of naval scholars.

CHAPTER ONE

ASSIGNMENT TO LONDON
31 July - 16 September 1940

Reminiscences, 31 July - 1 September 1940[1]
"Wellings, your orders to command the Destroyer *Hopkins*[2] are cancelled. New orders are being issued to proceed to London, England. Return to Washington immediately for further instructions." This startling news came on 31 July 1940 from the communications watch officer at the Boston Navy Yard as Mrs. Wellings and I sat in the garden of her parents' home in Boston, Massachusetts, enjoying a cocktail before dinner. We were in a turmoil that evening as bags were repacked and plans made for the long drive to Washington early the next morning with my wife, Dolly, and our two year old daughter, Anne. I had left my assignment in the Office of Fleet Training in Washington[3] only five days earlier, and had planned to leave for Honolulu, not Washington, that morning.

I suspected that Rear Admiral H. Fairfax Leary,[4] the Director of Fleet Training, and Captain Willis A. Lee,[5] the Assistant Director, were responsible for my change in orders. After returning to Washington my first stop was to check in with my two former superior officers. Admiral Leary said, "Wellings, you are going to work your way across the Atlantic as an operations officer of a Halifax to Liverpool convoy. Your official orders will assign you as an Assistant Naval Attaché in the American Embassy in London. However, after your experience as tactical officer for Admiral Leahy, and your two years work here revising our regular tactical and convoy instructions, you will be of more value to our Navy by confining your duties to that of an observer in the British

---

[1]This is an edited version of J.H. Wellings' reminiscences entitled "On His Majesty's Service," pp. 1-4, written about 1968-1973. Hereinafter referred to as "JHW, *MS. Reminiscences.*"

[2]The Destroyer *Hopkins* (DD-249) was assigned to the Pacific Fleet. She would shortly be converted to a destroyer, minesweeper, at Pearl Harbor Naval Shipyard.

[3]The Division of Fleet Training was a part of the Chief of Naval Operations' Staff (Op. 22). Its major responsibility was tactical training of the fleet for war.

[4]Herbert Fairfax Leary (1885-1957). U.S. Naval Academy, 1905; Naval War College 1932-33; Director Fleet Training 1936-37, 1939-41; Rear Admiral, 1938; later Commander, Cruisers, Battle Force, 1941; Vice Admiral 1942; Commander, Naval Forces, Southwest Pacific, 1942; Superintendent, New York State Maritime College, 1949-51.

[5]Willis Augustus Lee, Jr. (1888-1945). U.S. Naval Academy, 1908; Naval War College, 1928-29; Division of Fleet Training, Washington, 1930-31; Head, Gunnery Section 1933-35, Head, Tactical Section 1935-36; Assistant Director 1939-41; later Director 1941-42; Rear Admiral 1942; Commander, Task Force 64, at Guadalcanal 1942; Commander Battleships, Pacific Fleet.

ships of the Home Fleet based at Scapa Flow. We will inform Captain Kirk,[6] our Naval Attaché in London, accordingly."

Captain Lee, with whom I had worked very closely in Fleet Training, was finally able to break into the conversation and said, "Gus, you talked so much about the desirability of having U.S. Naval observers in the British Fleet, we had your orders to *Hopkins* cancelled. Send us all the information you think of value to the Navy in regard to tactics, convoy operations, antisubmarine warfare, and the practical aspects of their shipboard radar." Admiral Leary wound up the conversation in his customary forceful manner by saying, "Damnit, we are not going to fight the British. Tell them everything you know and get as much information out of them as you can. Let's make this 100 percent exchange of information effective."

After receiving my official orders as Assistant Naval Attaché in our Embassy in London, and my verbal instructions to be an observer in the British ships of the Home Fleet based at Scapa Flow, I was eager to get underway as quickly as possible. I was silently pleased with my change in orders although I would miss being with my family. My impatience to get started had to be curbed when my superiors informed me that it would be two to three weeks before my briefings were completed and clearance obtained from the British for me to act as an observer in their combatant ships. Captain Willis A. Lee arranged for me to obtain the following Navy equipment for my wartime service with the Royal Navy in the cold, rough and cruel North Atlantic Ocean:

An aviator's hollow canvas life jacket called a "Mae West" which could be instantaneously inflated by pulling two toggles that released the contents of two carbon dioxide cartridges (CO_2).

An aviator's leather wool-lined jacket with a large leather collar and the words "U.S. Navy" stamped on the left breast pocket.

A long heavy leather wool-lined bridge coat with a fur collar and belt.

One pair of wool-lined knee-length boots, one marine helmet, and one gas mask.

Two navy blue woolen shirts with small anchors stamped on the buttons called "Chief Petty Officer shirts."

Mrs. Wellings was most surprised and suspicious when she saw all of this equipment, especially when I demonstrated the life jacket and gas mask. "I thought you were going to London," she said. "I am," I replied, "but anything can happen on the way over, and the Germans are bombing London every night." My assignment was a secret one and I could not tell her my primary duty would be as an observer in ships of the British Home Fleet based at Scapa Flow.

Upon completion of my briefings in Washington, which included tactics, antisubmarine warfare, carrier operations, radar, I obtained my clearance from the British Admiralty and I proceeded to Halifax, Nova Scotia where I reported to the Canadian naval authorities at the naval dock yard. Everyone was grand to me. I had lunch with Rear Admiral R.A. Plowden, R.N.[7] and his staff and read some reports. Late that

---

[6]Alan Goodrich Kirk (1888-1963). U.S. Naval Academy, 1909; Naval War College, student and later staff, 1928-31; Naval Attaché, London, 1 February 1939-23 January 1941; later Rear Admiral, 1941; Commander, Amphibious Forces, U.S. Atlantic Fleet, 1942; Commander, Task Force at invasion of Sicily, July 1943; Commander, Task Force at Normandy, 1944; Vice Admiral, 1944; Commander, U.S. Naval Forces, France September 1944; Admiral and retired list 1946; U.S. Ambassador to Belgium and Minister to Luxembourg, March 1946; Ambassador to U.S.S.R., 1949-1952; Ambassador to Republic of China, 1962-63.

[7]Richard Anthony Aston Plowden (-1941). Served in World War I, mentioned in despatches, DSO 1919; Captain (D) of the Nore Destroyer Flotilla, 1926-28; Captain of the Dockyard, Malta, 1928-30; Commanded H.M.S. *Centurion*, 1931-32; Rear Admiral and retired list, 1933; Died 24 February 1941.

evening I wrote my wife, Dolly, "I wish you could have listened in on some of the reports today. If they are anywhere near correct I will have a grand vacation. My big boss wanted to know how good I was at deck golf and shuffle board. He said it was a grand way to while away the time."[8]

The following day I attended the Departure Conference for a 42-ship convoy which was to sail that day, 1 September 1940, for Liverpool, England.

The Halifax Naval Control Service Officer was in charge of the conference. The captains of all ships in the convoy, plus the captain of the ocean escort, and the convoy commodore attended this conference. Each captain was given a copy of the sailing orders, a copy of the convoy formation, and a copy of the pamphlet titled "Pamphlet of Instructions for the Conduct of Convoys," short title "Consigs." The Naval Control Service Officer explained these instructions, and questions were asked of a few captains to insure they understood their orders. The Naval Control Service Officer also explained the methods used by the convoy to change course and other maneuvers.

The Commodore of the convoy, Rear Admiral Plowden, made a few brief remarks that information had been received that the Germans were using magnetic pistols in their torpedoes which would explode the torpedo as it passed under the ship. All ships were urged to use their degaussing device, which neutralizes the magnetism in the ship, all the way across the Atlantic. When one of the captains asked about the use of fog signals, the convoy commodore stated that the odd-numbered column leaders would sound the Morse equivalent of their column number every half hour. All other vessels were to use their fog whistles only in an emergency. All captains were informed that each ship should be prepared to stream and tow a fog buoy[9] with 300 yards of towline when ordered by the convoy commodore.

The captain of the Ocean Escort, H.M.S. *Montclaire*,[10] a converted merchantman, said he carried seven 5.5-inch guns and promised that his ship could take care of any raiders, even a pocket-battleship. He said in the latter case there probably would not be much left of *Montclaire* but that most of the ships would escape. I suddenly thought of *Rawalpindi*'s engagement with a pocket-battleship[11] and decided perhaps it would be better if we didn't see a pocket-battleship. However, I admired his courage.

At the end of the conference each captain received his sealed envelopes containing the secret routing instructions. The conference lasted about 45 minutes and the convoy sailed 1½ hours later.

At the same time the captains were attending the departure conference, the radio operators were assembled in another room and given their instructions about watches, frequencies "to guard," and to listen for messages on designated frequencies and the importance of maintaining radio silence.

Immediately after the conference I went on board the commodore's flagship, the merchantman *Hilary*.

---

[8]Letter to Mrs. Wellings, 31 July 1940.

[9]Fog buoys are strong casks or especially designed position buoys that churn up the water in the wake of a ship, thereby helping the ship astern to remain on station.

[10]H.M.S. *Montclare*; launched 18 December 1921, Clydebank; length overall 570', beam 70'; draft 27¾'; speed 16 knots; displacement 21,550 tons; armament 4-4" AA (2x2) 32-2 pdr AA (4x8), 19-20mm. AA (19x1) Armed Merchant Cruiser, later Depot ship for submarines with the Pacific Fleet, 1944-45. Pennant number F. 85. Scrapped 1958.

[11]H.M.S. *Rawalpindi*, an armed merchant cruiser of 16,697 gross tons, was sunk by *Scharnhorst* on 27 November 1939.

HILARY, c.1942

Launched in 1932 by Cammell, Laird & Co., Birkenhead; length 424'; beam 56'; draft 24.8'; gross tonnage 7,403; speed 15 knots. Owned by Booth S.S. Co., Liverpool. Before the war, she ran a passenger service between Liverpool and Brazil, including a 1,000-mile trip up the Amazon River. Requisitioned by the Royal Navy, 1940, as an Ocean Boarding Vessel, Pennant Number F. 22; converted to Landing Ships Headquarters, LSH(L), in 1943 and served as Rear Admiral Sir Philip Vian's flagship at the landings in Sicily and Commodore G.N. Oliver's flagship at Salerno, 1943; returned to owner 1946; sold for breaking up in 1958. (Photo: Imperial War Museum A9626).

Personal Diary, 1 September 1940[12]
. . . Underway at 2:00 p.m. Fog outside harbor . . . . Trunks brought to room, unpacked and everything all set for a quick departure including life jacket handy with cartridges inserted.

Official Diary, 1 September 1940[13]
SORTIE - No time was set for each ship to get underway. Instead a time was given to pass one of the control stations, in the inner harbor. Ships were to pass this station at 5-minute intervals, in a designated order . . . . All ships were ordered the day before to be ready to get underway at a definite time. They did not know the exact sailing time until the conference. (Actual sailing time was two hours after steam was up.) All ships sortied on time except two which were delayed about 2 hours and later rejoined. Cause of delay unknown.

Submarine nets are located at entrance of harbor. Double row of nets on each side of channel. Two gate vessels marked the limits of the channel at the nets, port vessel painted red, starboard vessel black. These vessels looked like large size fishing trawlers. A small size tug was used to open the gate. Two small vessels which also appeared to be converted trawlers were lying to about two miles from the harbor entrance. They were apparently minesweepers but I did not see any mine sweeping.

FORMING THE CONVOY - After passing a special buoy about 4 miles from the harbor entrance, the convoy flagship changed to the designated formation course and slowed to allow ships astern to form the convoy formation. At this time the convoy commander made his first signal meaning to form the convoy as shown. If this signal is not made all ships as they turn the buoy change to the designated course and speed. After about 3 out of the 19 ships had formed, heavy fog set in and continued for about 3 hours. About 2 hours before dark the fog lifted and by darkness all but the 2 ships which were delayed in getting underway had taken station in formation. The commodore made his second signal (all signals by flag hoist) just before dark "increase speed to 6 knots."

LOCAL ESCORTS - One large Canadian destroyer and one large patrol boat, both zigzagging ahead of the convoy. Guns were trained 0-180° and not manned. Several men were on the platform above bridge of the destroyer, apparently lookouts. These ships were not present at daylight the following morning. One twin motor plane acted as inner air patrol during the afternoon of the first day.

OCEAN ESCORT - H.M.S. MONTCLARE arrived on station about one hour before dark. The interval between column 4 and 5 is supposed to be 6 cables to allow the Ocean Escort to steam between the columns.

DARKENED SHIP - Naturally all ships were darkened at sunset. However, attention had to be called to three vessels which showed lights.

Letter to Mrs. Wellings, "Second Day Out"
I reported on board ship as per schedule. The ship is quite large and I have very comfortable quarters. My stateroom is very large and has accommodations for three passengers, but of course I am the sole occupant. One bunk is a double decker but the top one folds up against the bulkhead. I have a table, dresser, big closet, wash basin, two

---

[12]The following entries labeled "Personal Diary" are taken from a diary written in pencil covering the period 29 August 1940 to 12 June 1941.

[13]The following entries labeled "Official Diary" are taken from the official reports that Wellings submitted as an Assistant Naval Attaché. The entries relating to this convoy are from Enclosure F to his report serial 1100 dated 21 September 1940.

6

DIAGRAM #1

42 – SHIP CONVOY FORMATION – HALIFAX TO LIVERPOOL – 1 SEPT. 1940

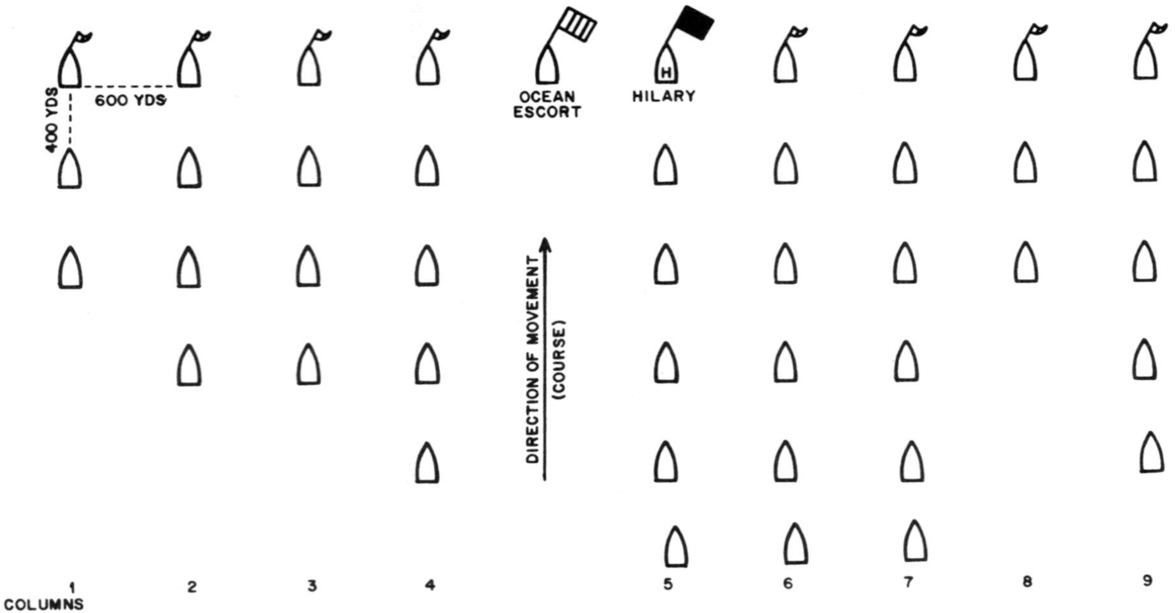

OCEAN ESCORT

HILARY

DIRECTION OF MOVEMENT (COURSE)

600 YDS

400 YDS

COLUMNS

1 2 3 4 5 6 7 8 9

The convoy was formed in nine columns. The leading ships of each column in line. Ships in each column astern of each other. Distance between ships in each column 400 yards. Distance is measured from stem to stern. (Interval between columns 4 and 5 was 1,200 yards in order to allow the ocean escort to take station between columns 4 and 5.) Interval between columns 600 yards. Ships arranged within convoy according to destination, not according to type of cargo or armament. This arrangement permits an orderly dispersal of ships whose destinations are not in the same general area. (Note: Destination of 15 ships changed en route which required some change in stations.) Number of ships in each column left to right, 3, 4, 4, 5, 6, 6, 6, 3, 5. Prior to entering North Channel the formation was changed from 9 to 3 columns. [Official report of 21 Sept. 1940, p. 2]

rugs & two big windows. It is on the A deck and is a corner room. I have a steward to myself he take go[od] care of me. For example, my bunk is now turned back—that is the bed clothes are [out] and my pajamas and slippers laid out. This morning he had my bath all ready—with the water at the correct temperature. Such service! I am afraid I will be spoiled.

I eat at the captain's table—on his left with the commodore on his right. Everyone is unusually kind to me. I have complete freedom of the ship, and of course spend most of my time on the bridge.

We sailed according to schedule. So far the sea has been very calm. However the ship looks as though she will ride well and I hope I don't have to . . . report a case of sea sickness. Today we ran into fog.

Personal Diary, 2 September 1940

Food somewhat different, but O.K. Coffee poor. I have all kinds of service. A room steward all to myself—bath ready at designated time. Tea brought to my room at 4:00 p.m. and 9:00 p.m. Dinner is at 1230, high tea at six . . . . Fog whistle kept me awake until 2300.

Official Diary, 2 September 1940, Second Day

Speed 7 knots. Heavy fog set in about 0300 and cleared at 1100. During this period each column leader sounded the morse equivalent to his column number every half hour on the whistle. No other fog whistles were blown except when ships thought they were unusually close to one another, one long blast was sounded. When the fog lifted the convoy was scattered everywhere. Only 5 of the 9 column leaders were anywhere near on station. The number two's in each column (those that were still anywhere near in column) were anywhere from about 1500 yards to 4 miles astern. The column leaders are numbered from left to right in the direction of movement. One of the ships which was late in clearing port came up through the formation and was approximately in position for No. 4 column leader, and close aboard to this ship was the ship which was supposed to be astern of us—our station is 51. No. 82 was missing and did not rejoin by the end of the day. Three of the eight ships supposed to be on our starboard beam were on our port side—anywhere from the quarter to a little forward of the beam. By 1400 all except two ships were again on station (No. 82 was still unaccounted for). The commodore took advantage of the clear weather and made a change of course signal for 1715. This change was a 43° change of course to the left. At about 1400 the fog set in again. The commodore sounded the fog whistle every 15 minutes instead of every half hour.

At 1715 course was changed 43° to the left by wheeling. The procedure was as follows. Convoy flagship sounded 4 long blasts on whistle. Column leaders repeated the 4 blasts. After commodore thought he heard all column leaders (very difficult to hear leeward leaders), course was changed 20° to the left. After waiting about 5 minutes the same procedure was repeated. About 5 minutes later the commodore's flagship spelled out on the whistle course zero seven three. Escort repeated signal but made numerals instead of spelling out the numerals. Course was then changed the additional three degrees to 073. Fog continued to be very thick. Commodore decided to make his fog signals every five minutes. We could only hear the column leaders to windward. Believe it or not the column leader next adjacent to up to starboard (No. 61) dropped back, crossed our stern, came up the port side, apparently passed close to the escort as indicated by frequent single blasts, crossed ahead and dropped back into position again, all in about 2 hours time. We positively identified the ship as she made numeral 6 on her whistle every five minutes. About 2300 the fog lifted sufficiently to enable us to see about ¾ of a mile.

Note: After dark the commodore's flagship turned on her masthead light, side lights and a large cargo light at the stern.

Personal Diary, 3 September 1940

. . . Worked on making Mercator chart & studying signals and blinker. Napped from 4:30 to 5:30. Listened to British news broadcast after high tea. (U.S. turned over 50 DD's[14] today in exchange for British bases.) Have to be diplomatic about comments on war. Talked over certain points of our work with captain and commodore until time for tea at 9:00 p.m. Worked on report, blinker & signal flags—turned in at 11:30.

Official Diary, 3 September 1940 Third Day

Fog closed in again about 0300 but began to clear about 0600. At 0630 visibility was about 4 miles. No. 82 was still missing. Of the ten ships supposed to be to port only five were in sight. The ship supposed to be astern of us also was not in sight. One of the ships whose station was on the port beam (No. 32) was on our starboard beam outboard of the 9th column. As the visibility increased more ships appeared and by 0900 all ships but two were accounted for, No. 82 which was missing since yesterday and No. 93 who went astray during the night. Supposed to be at rendezvous with Sydney group at 0900 but will not arrive until 1130. *Note:* Sydney rendezvous position is 20 miles north of ours. Sydney group must change course to next position at its rendezvous if our convoy is not sighted. In clear weather commodore of Halifax group would arrive at his rendezvous ahead of time and continue on to meet the Sydney convoy. Changed course at 1135 to head for next position. Have not sighted Sydney convoy. All ships except two missing ships arrived on station at 1200. Station keeping is far from being 600 yards between columns and 400 yards between ships in column. Estimate columns to be about 1000 to 1500 yards apart and ships in column to be about 1000 to 1500 yards. Excellent weather all afternoon, sea calm. MONTCLAIRE (ocean escort) informed commodore that she would use DF[15] transmissions in afternoon in order to allow stragglers to get bearings. (Note—all ships have been informed of time of DF transmissions), twice in A.M. and P.M.—ten minutes apart. The Ocean Escort before dark said she would leave convoy at daylight and search for Sydney convoy which has not joined the Halifax group.

Letter to Mrs. Wellings, describing the third day[16]

The fog lifted . . . about daylight and ever since the weather has been really wonderful. A grand cool breeze, scarcely a cloud in the sky and so little sea that the ship just rolls the very smallest amount. Really the weather is such that passengers would delight in strolling the decks, inhaling the clean, fresh sea air with occasional rest periods to sit quietly in a steamer chair and read a good book. Weather like this is what makes land lubbers want to go to sea for a rest.

. . . I was up at 0530 in order to look around at daylight. Shortly afterwards the fog lifted and the scenery was very interesting. I was on the bridge all morning except for an hour at breakfast time 0800.

Prior to *dinner* at 1230 the big boss and the captain came to my room and invited me to have a cocktail. My first impulse was to politely decline but while I was thinking it over

---

[14]Destroyers. On 2 September Secretary of State Cordell Hull and Lord Lothian, the British Ambassador to the United States, completed the destroyer-for-bases transaction with an exchange of letters. On 3 September President Roosevelt transmitted the executive agreement to Congress for its information.

[15]Radio Direction Finder.

[16]Dated "Fourth Day."

my lips said, "Yes sir, I will be delighted to join you." After all I am a passenger with no duties, which eased my conscience. We had the entire cocktail lounge to ourselves. I must say the *one* (yes only one) martini was very refreshing.

After lunch I again went up to the bridge and fooled around with some charts and reading on navigation. My tea was waiting for me at 4:00 p.m. (incidentally we also had tea on the bridge at 0600). Afterwards I took a nap for an hour before dinner. After dinner we listened to a news broadcast from England. The broadcaster announced the transfer of our American destroyers. Needless to say they all were pleased. About an hour on the bridge plus about an hour or two of reading completed the days work. I was turned in by 1130 and was soon off to slumberland. Such was my schedule for a quiet day at sea.

Personal Diary, 4 September 1940

Up at 0730, steward had bath ready. Excellent weather on bridge most of the morning, practiced signals . . . . Had a glass of sherry before dinner with the Commodore and Captain. On the bridge all afternoon except for an hour of studying. Listened to British news broadcast after dinner plus Lord Haw Haw. Left the bridge at 9:00 p.m. Listening to stories by the Commodore and Captain. Tea. Wrote notes for the day. Beautiful sky tonight. The heavens are literally clustered with stars which appear to be so close that one could reach them with a ladder. Northern lights a beautiful sight. To bed at 1030 as I will be up at 0500.

Official Diary, 4 September Fourth Day

Patches of fog during the early morning but clear at daylight, and for remainder of day. Light winds, sea smooth. Ocean escort left convoy about an hour after daylight, searched ahead on port bow about 10 miles for the Sydney convoy, then changed course and searched as far as the starboard quarter to distance of about 10 miles. Upon return she reported no contact. She also reported that she sent a radio to the flagship of the Sydney convoy asking her to transmit at 1100 in order that the ocean escort could take D/F bearings. We also took bearings which indicated that the Sydney convoy was 10° on the starboard bow. The Ocean Escort reported that the D/F bearings indicated that the Sydney convoy was about 10° on the port quarter but maybe on the starboard bow. A plot of her track if she carried out her instructions and was on time definitely placed the convoy on the starboard bow. Our radio operator was sure of his bearings. About a half hour later the Ocean Escort asked if the commodore thought it worthwhile to search 10° on the starboard bow. After an affirmative she left the convoy and did not return until 1730. She reported the Sydney convoy 10° on the starboard bow, distance 28 miles, with its course and speed. (If the Ocean Escort had taken station on either beam about 4 to 5 miles before the D/F bearings were taken, we could have used this distance as a base line and could have cut the convoy in.) On our existing course and speed we hope to meet the Sydney convoy at daylight.

Station keeping improved today, but the second ship in each continues to remain about 1000 to 2000 yards instead of 400 as required. One of the missing ships appeared on the horizon at daylight and joined the convoy at noon.

Personal Diary, 5 September 1940

Up at 0300 to look things over. Turned in again from 0600 to 0800. On the bridge all morning. Heavy rain squalls. Glass of sherry with Captain and Commodore before dinner. Have to cut down on the food—eating too much. On bridge most of the afternoon but took time out to write home . . . . Did considerable professional reading at night. Turned in at 2400.

Official Diary, 5 September, Fifth Day
Steaming as before—speed 8.5. At 0241 sighted Sydney convoy. 0400 Sydney convoy abeam. 0500 changed course 40° to starboard when ahead of Sydney convoy (in two steps by wheeling method in order to head in direction of rendezvous with Bermuda convoy set for 0900), course and speed sent to Vice Commodore of Sydney convoy. 0730 one aircraft from ocean escort of Bermuda convoy made several runs over our ocean escort giving bearing, distance, course and speed of Bermuda convoy. Aldis lamp was used by plane for signalling. 0800 Sydney convoy formed astern and part of Halifax convoy. 0830 sighted Bermuda convoy. 0930 Halifax ocean escort left convoy and returned to Halifax (after lying to off Bermuda ocean escort and exchanging information). Sydney convoy had no escort. Ocean escort for entire convoy is now the HMS EMERALD,[17] a light cruiser. 1200 Bermuda convoy now in formation. The commodore in charge of the Halifax convoy is in charge of the entire convoy. The vice commodores who were in charge of the Bermuda and Sydney convoys now have no authority whatsoever. Heavy rain squalls all afternoon. Continued on present course, speed 8.5 remainder of day.

Letter to Mrs. Wellings "Sixth day at sea"
. . . Yesterday we had heavy rain squalls off and on all day. However, the sea wasn't rough and I feel grand. This morning it is overcast, very damp but no rain. The sea has increased a little and I can feel the motion of the ship; but I still feel fine so *perhaps* I have retained my sea legs.

I am getting to be an expert in finding my way around at night in the dark. At first I had considerable trouble in not being able to miss the stanchions, lockers etc. Now I can find my way around like a blind man who has a sixth sense in aiding him to "see" where he is going . . . .

Personal Diary, 6 September 1940
. . . Up at 0730, bath ready, on bridge most of morning, practiced sending radio & blinker, did a little reading . . . glass of sherry before dinner at 1230 with captain & commodore . . . tea at 1600. High tea at 1830 listened to British news broadcast.

Official Diary, 6 September, Sixth Day
Steaming as before. Sky overcast, wind about 15 knots, moderate sea. One Greek ship was separated from convoy during the night, did not rejoin, total number of ships now 40. Station keeping improving due to signals to several ships calling their attention to being out of station. Escort ship informed commodore that oscillations could be heard from a ship of the convoy on 500 kcs. Commodore informed convoy. Escort slowed and allowed convoy to pass in an attempt to locate ship. No result. Held abandon ship and fire drills in afternoon.

Personal Diary, 7 September 1940
. . . Up at 0720, bath ready . . . On bridge most of morning, practiced blinker. Studied a few hours. Usual glass of sherry before dinner. Listened to the Commodore & Captain spin yarns. Entered navy as a midshipman 19 years ago today. Celebrated by asking captain & commodore to have a high ball before high tea. Found out this

---

[17]H.M.S. *Emerald*. E. Class Cruiser. Launched 19 May 1920 by Armstrong. Wallsend; completed at Chatham, 1926; length overall: 570'; beam: 54'; draft: 16'; speed: 33 knots; displacement: 7,550 tons; armament: 7-6", 3-4" AA, 2-2 pdr AA, 16-21" (4x4) torpedo tubes; 1-aircraft; served as Atlantic escort 1939-40, East Indies 1941-42, Eastern Fleet 1942-44, Home Fleet 1944, Reserve 1945; sold for breaking up 1948.

morning that bath tub is filled with salt water and that one is supposed to soak in it and try to wash with salt water soap and then rinse off with pan of fresh water about size of Anne's baby bath tub. Quite a joke on me. Sent laundry.

Official Diary, 7 September, Seventh Day

Steaming as before. Weather cleared during the night, sea smooth. In morning ocean escort slowed and apparently cut in position of all ships in convoy. She reported the average distance between ships in column was 1100 yards. Commodore again informed several ships that they were not on station. Station keeping improved in afternoon. At dusk there is a tendency to increase distance.

Personal Diary, 8 September 1940

Up at 0800. Usual bath—a little better now that I know about the salt water. Beautiful day . . . . On bridge most of A.M. Usual sherry before lunch. Studied on bridge in afternoon . . . . A good hour's promenade in afternoon followed by more sunshine on the bridge. Listened to the British broadcast after high tea. (It takes about an hour—the captain, commodore and I listened to the broadcast in the captain's cabin.) More writing at night after about a half hour on bridge. Turned in at 1030.

Official Diary, 8 September, Eighth Day

Steaming as before. Weather clear, sea smooth. Ocean escort received a report from the Admiralty that six planes had attacked a steamer and gave latitude and longitude. This position was about *300 miles* off the west coast of Ireland. Ocean escort also received latest report on location of U-boats in general area through which we will pass. Three ships temporarily had casualties which forced them to drop astern, average time out of station about one-half hour. Practiced emergency turns (40° to starboard and port). At one time in afternoon counted 21 ships making smoke, 12 of which were smoking badly. (About three quarters of the ships burn coal.) Sighted two steamers almost simultaneously in afternoon on opposite course. Ocean escort investigated one of them. These are the first ships sighted since leaving port.

Letter to Mrs. Wellings, Eighth Day

. . . Yesterday and today have been remarkably good days as far as the weather is concerned. One would think we were in Boston harbor. I only hope it continues for awhile, however a little later on one or two bad days will be welcomed.

I don't believe I have told you about the food. Every meal, including breakfast has about four courses. They certainly have plenty to eat. After a day or two I decided to follow as closely as possible my American routine. As a result I have an orange or grapefruit, toast and coffee for breakfast. The coffee is terrible, however, I am getting used to it. They put about a half of cup of milk in the cup with coffee. After the first meal I ordered only a demi-tasse, so that I could have it without milk and also not to have too much coffee. I am saving your special brand but I believe I will be forced to open a can before we reach port.

The big meal of the day is at 1230. At this meal one can have soup, any or all of the three heavy courses plus a pudding followed by fruit or crackers and cheese. Of course I can't eat all this food but I swear the Chief Engineer and doctor who eat at the same table as I do eat two out of three main courses every day and once or twice they ate all three. Yes, they show it. At night they have almost a repetition of the noon meal except everyone has a large cup of tea. The food is seasoned altogether different from ours. However it is [not] too bad. I just take what I think is O.K. and let it go at that. I feel fine so don't worry. We have a fine promenade deck—12 laps to the mile—and I make a point to walk at least an hour a day.

Personal Diary, 9 September 1940
. . . Usual routine including sherry before lunch and the British broadcast. Did considerable reading and writing (professional), Rec'd laundry—one of the stewards did 4 shirts, two pair of socks and two suits of underwear for 3 and 6 (how does that sound) about 56 cents. Worked until 0030 . . . .

Official Diary, 9 September, Ninth Day
Steaming as before. Fog set in at 0600 and continued intermittently until noon. Overcast remainder of day. Ships continue to smoke badly. One ship broken down for about 20 minutes. Quiet day. Twelve ships had their destination changed by Admiralty.

Letter to Mrs. Wellings, Ninth Day
. . . today has been another quiet day except for several periods of fog. The first one set in around 0600. I awoke with the first sound of the whistle, got dressed and went up to the bridge to see what was doing. I stayed up *all day* and here I am writing to my darling before doing a little more reading and then to bed.

Everything has been running so smoothly the past three or four days that the daily routine is getting to be standardize[d]. Now that I have the key on how to take a bath I get along very well. Everyone continues to be exceedingly nice to me. I get all kinds of service. The Captain, Commodore and myself get along splendidly. They have given freely of their experiences . . . .

Personal Diary, 10 September 1940
. . . Usual routine. Chief Engineer had some good stories at dinner. Felt fine . . . . Did some walking for a good hour. Have to be careful not to eat to[o] much . . . .

Official Diary, 10 September, Tenth Day
Steaming as before. Fog set in again at 0530, burned off by 0700 but set in again from 1700 to about 2000. Practiced zigzagging from 0800 to 1700. Convoy is limited to three zigzag plans due to foreign ships not having British publications—the three plans were given to foreign ships at Naval Control Service Office. At start of zigzag one large ship dropped out of formation. Commodore guessed that they were not ready to zigzag. Ships carried out zigzag very well. However, distances increased considerably. Doubt if much of an attempt is made at station keeping during zigzags. Was amazed at how easy and without excitement they carry out the zigzag plan. The helmsman is alone in the pilot house, he can not see ahead due to the slots in the concrete forward of the wheel being closed by shutters. The slats let in too much light through such a small opening which has the effect of blinding the helmsman. The zigzag clock rings, he looks at his blackboard and automatically comes to the next course. He informs the O.O.D. when he is on the new course. The O.O.D. stays on the wings of the bridge and is not in the pilot house over two minutes of every hour. One ship dropped out of convoy and did not return, total now in convoy 39. Ocean escort reported one of the ships as oscillating its radio. She gave the number of the ship. Apparently no difficulty in cutting the ship in by R.D. bearings. Had a long talk with the Captain and Commodore about the manner in which the Admiralty runs British shipping in time of war. If we plan similar action, my only thought was that we have considerable work to do.

Letter to Mrs. Wellings, Tenth Day
Another quiet day is about over. Everything is running according to schedule and I must say running very smoothly.

We had fog again early this morning but by eight o'clock the sun burned it off, and from that time up to 5:00 p.m. the weather was grand. At 5:00 fog again set in and lasted for about three hours. It has again cleared and I hope it remains so because it takes me almost an hour to get used to the fog whistle. You know I don't like my sleep to be disturbed . . . .

Personal Diary, 11 September 1940

. . . Up at 0730 for a change. Sea and wind increasing but still moderate. Fog later part of the morning but clear in p.m. Usual routine. Listened to Churchill's speech at 1500.[18] London is apparently being bombed quite heavily. Poor Dolly is probably worrying about me being in London and here I am in the broad Atlantic, cool calm and collective.

Official Diary, 11 September, Eleventh Day

Steaming as before. Commenced zigzagging at daylight. Shortly afterwards ocean escort informed commodores that a submarine was patrolling north of Lat. 56 between 28° and 25° west. Also stated that report was 24 hours old due to dispatch being sent to the *Montclare* (the ocean escort which left us on the fifth day and returned to Halifax). Also stated that 4 submarines were operating in western approaches giving position of two. Ocean escort said she would not return to Halifax at dark on the *12th* as originally planned but would continue with us. (Original plan called for her leaving at dark, the convoy proceeding alone that night and picking up the local escort at daylight.) Ocean escort reported two ships sunk last night at 0140 in Lat. 55-30 N, Long. 16-00 W. Our course would have taken us about 10 miles from the eastern limit of submarine on patrol reported above. Commodore and Captain of ocean escort decided to change course 40° to the eastward. Ceased zigzagging and steamed on this course from 0600 to 1100 then returned to original course. I hope the patrolling submarine has not shifted to the eastward while the dispatch was being handled on the *Montclare*.

Sea moderate, fog at 0700 with visibility about one mile. At 1110 ocean escort received message from Admiralty ordering convoy to change course 30° to the left at 2100, stay on this course for 3 hours and then take a course which would take us to our next designated position. Some doubt in Commodore's mind whether time referred to was local or G.M.T.,[19] also whether we should return to our original track as the Admiralty did not know we changed course 40° to the eastward to avoid patrolling submarine. After an exchange of messages with ocean escort Commodore decided to steer the present course (which is parallel and about 25 miles to the eastward of our original track) until 2100 local time, then change course 30° to the left for three hours, followed by a 20° change of course to the right and remain on this course until daylight when he plans to set a course for our next designated position. Note: Ocean escort believed Admiralty's order to change course was a desire to have the convoy change course after dark in order to avoid any trailing submarine and not to avoid any particular submarine. His assumption was based on another convoy to the northeast of us also receiving orders to make a similar change of course. The Commodore and the Admiralty have a series of noon positions. The convoy endeavors to be approximately at these noon positions, therefore the Admiralty at all times knows the approximate location of the convoy.

---

[18]"Every Man to his Post" speech. Text published in W.S. Churchill, *Blood, Sweat, and Tears* (New York: Putnam, 1941), pp. 367-69.

[19]Greenwich Mean Time.

Weather cleared at 1300, commenced zigzagging. It is interesting to note that practically a straight line joins the eastern limit of the patrolling submarine, an R.D. report of another submarine, and the position where two ships were torpedoed this morning. Distance between points about 150 miles. At 1435 ocean escort informed Commodore that he had received orders to leave the convoy. With a farewell and good luck he was off in a southeast direction, speed about 20 and zigzagging. I wonder what caused his orders to be changed. We now have no escort of any kind and will not meet the local escort until daylight the 13th (about 38 hours from now). Listened to Churchill's speech at 1500. He warned the people about the invasion which may occur at any time. Maybe this has something to do with the departure of ocean escort. The crew did not like to see the ocean escort leave. England must be very short of ships or is planning a large scale operation to leave 40 ships completely unprotected just as they enter the submarine zone.[20]

1830, Ceased zigzagging. 1900 changed course 30° to the left by "wheeling." Only signal was too short blasts (convoy was informed of this and the next change of course by flag hoists earlier in the day). 2200 changed course by "wheeling" 20° to the right. Wind and sea increasing, sky overcast, moon covered by clouds (thank the Lord)— passed across submarine line at 2100.

Personal Diary, 12 September 1940
. . . Up at 0530, wind strong, sea rough. Regular routine as far as practical. Ship rolled considerably but not too uncomfortable . . . .

Official Diary, 12 September, Twelfth Day
Wind increased during night. Sky overcast, fresh southwest winds at daylight. 0500 changed course 22° to the right. This places us on original track. Check up of convoy indicates one more ship missing. Inquiry of ship astern indicated engine casualty—it was our largest ship, 10,254 gross tons. Ships now remaining in convoy—38. Commenced zigzagging at 0530 but after about an hour had to stop due to increased wind and sea. Wind now about 35 knots with heavy sea. Ship rolling badly. Strong winds and sea continued all day. Ships widely separated but convoy intact. At 2000 another ship showed breakdown lights and dropped astern. Total in convoy now 37. At 2300 changed course 40° to right. Wind and sea now almost astern. Expect to rendezvous with local escort at 0500. However, if local escort had to head into this sea to arrive at rendezvous it is doubtful if he (I hope it's *they*) will meet the convoy until later in the day.

Letter to Mrs. Wellings, Twelfth Day
. . . Why the pencil? I don't dare attempt to use a pen. Yesterday afternoon the wind and sea increased, and continued to do so. Right now we have what is called strong winds with heavy sea. The wind is a little abaft the port beam (get it?) and the ship is rolling heavily. I didn't get much sleep last night and I doubt if tonight will be much better. You should hear the wind howling through the rigging. It is a cold wind. So much so that I have my heavy golf socks on plus my camel's hair sweater and my light aviation jacket. No, I am not outside but in my room. Guess they don't know what steam heat is on this ship. Of course having an outside room on the upper deck does not make the room any warmer.

---

[20]"Commodore Plowden was, of course, an expert in convoy operations with the usual British proclivity for understatement. He exhibited to a very high degree the British trait of accepting conditions as they were without any outward manifestations of worry and concern. 'Certainly,' he often said, 'we should have more and better escorts, but they are not available, so we will do the best we can with what escorts are available and trust in God.'" JHW, *MS. Reminiscences.* p. 9.

With the exception of a fairly good roll the ship is riding like Dorthea used to ride horseback—smooth and even. No, I haven't been the least bit sick. Perhaps I have (wow a big roll), as I was saying, perhaps I have retained my sea legs. However, I am not boasting.

Yesterday I couldn't stand the ship's coffee any longer so I "broke out" the small can of coffee you so thoughtfully packed for me. The coffee was excellent and next to my darling's [blotch] (sorry) it was almost as good as I have ever—just grabbed the ash tray—tasted.

I guess I had better stop before there is a casualty . . . .

Personal Diary, 13 September 1940

Up at *0810*—due to being up late. Sea still rough & wind strong. However, barometer is rising very slowly. Usual routine. On bridge most of day. However, we all took time out for our sherry. Weather started to moderate in afternoon (very slightly). Ship continues to roll considerably. Guess I have my sea legs as I have not been sick.

Official Diary, 13 September, Thirteenth Day

. . . Wind and sea same as last night. Naturally the distance between ships and columns was large at daylight due to the strong wind and sea, but the convoy was at least in formation. The ships deserve great credit. 0600 (daylight) arrived at rendezvous and much to our surprise 3 destroyers, 1 sloop, and 2 corvettes were waiting for the convoy. They took stations as follows: 2 DD's and 1 sloop in line about 1 mile ahead of convoy, 1 corvette on each side of convoy opposite the leading ship in each outer column. 1 DD patrolling astern. The escort vessels ahead did not zigzag but did patrol their stations very slowly. Local escort commander informed Commodore to change course 20° to the left to avoid a submarine whose RD[21] yesterday was on line about 80 miles ahead of our present position. 0930 received despatch from Commander Western Approaches to change course 40° to starboard immediately and to pass south of a certain point. Course immediately changed and ten minutes later changed course 10° more to the right to pass well clear of above mentioned point.

1015, one four motor flying boat was sighted and joined local escort as inner air patrol. Distance from nearest land 350 miles, ceiling about 3000 ft., wind about 30 knots, sea very rough. I doubt if the plane could have sighted a periscope under the weather conditions which existed. Plane left convoy at 1610.

1115 Informed by commander local escort that new route instructions had been received. As a result course altered 23° more to starboard in order to pass through the first of our new positions. Weather commenced to moderate in late afternoon. However, sea is still quite rough. 1900 (almost dark) arrived at first position. Changed course 36° to port and headed for next position.

Personal Diary, 14 September 1940

. . . Up at 0430 to see the scenery . . . . Usual routine except no bath for past two days—due to bad weather. Weather clear in p.m. beautiful night. Big moon N'everything—oh for my sweetie.

Official Diary, 14 September, Fourteenth Day

. . . Wind and sea moderated during night. Intermittent rain squalls until 0800. Commenced zigzagging at beginning of morning twilight. (A display of lights used for signal.) Increased speed 1/2 knot. 0700 one aircraft arrived and began inner air patrol.

---

[21]Radiobeacon, *i.e.*, the submarine's position as indicated by her radio transmissions.

(A twin motor land plane.) The ship that failed to join convoy off Halifax reported being bombed and machine gunned, giving her position. We will arrive at approximately this position at daylight tomorrow. 1015 ceased zigzagging in order to close up formation, reduced speed 1/2 knot. The sloop in local escort reported an acute case of appendicitis on board, asked if our doctor could operate. Reply was negative—no facilities. Just as well. I doubt if I would permit him to operate on me. (If I could help it.)

1130 Escort sloop reported man getting worse requested permission to perform operation on convoy flagship. Sloop to provide doctor and all instruments. Doctor on board convoy flagship required only to give anaesthesia. Commodore answer affirmative. Convoy flagship hoisted "disregard my movements" but the ship next astern insisted on following the flagship. The entire convoy slowed with the flagship. Finally after considerable difficulty in trying to have the convoy continue, the commodore suggested hoisting the two black balls (out of control). This produced results, the convoy flagship dropped astern and the patient was transferred from the sloop, while the rear guard destroyer circled the flagship. As soon as patient was on board, the captain of the flagship lost no time in going full speed ahead (14 knots). His face looked more cheerful when the ship rejoined the formation. The sloop carried one 4" double purpose forward and one aft. I counted 35 depth charges on the stern (all but 10 in racks). There were two depth charge throwers. The sloop used a loud speaker when close aboard the convoy flagship. The speaker was very effective at about the 250 yards the ships were separated. Total number of ships now in convoy—36.

1330 Sighted a ship escorted by three trawlers. Ship proved to be one of the three which were separated from convoy night before last. Ship rejoined the formation. Trawlers plus 1 additional corvette acted as additional escorts. Escorts now total 10, (3 destroyers, 1 sloop, 3 corvettes (about the size of our 165' PC's),[22] 3 trawlers). Wind and sea continued to improve all day. Late in afternoon another of our ships which lost the convoy two nights ago rejoined. However, one of the ships which lost the convoy three nights ago reported just before dark that she was being attacked by submarine. Changed course 10° at end of evening twilight and 40° more at 2230 at which time one section of convoy left for its final destination. Weather now excellent—bright moonlight night. Operation on patient was successful.

Letter to Mrs. Wellings, 14th Day, At Sea

I hope you will forgive me for not writing so often the last few days. Between the storm and other interesting events I honestly have had very little time to myself . . . .

Everything is running along very smoothly, so far, and I feel confident that it will continue. The weather moderated today so that right now it is a beautiful clear night with an even more beautiful moon . . . .

Personal Diary, 15 September 1940

Up at 0430 in order to see some excitement at daylight. I figured that this was the day. I was not disappointed, but it was minor. Otherwise usual routine.

Official Diary, 15 September, Fifteenth Day

. . . 0400 changed course after sighting lighthouse, approaching entrance of North channel. 0530 sighted land on port bow. 0545 sighted one plane which circled escorts ahead, close aboard and departed apparently friendly. 0600 commodore ordered columns 7, 8 and 9 to take station astern of columns 4, 5, and 6 respectively. 0615 while columns were changing station an enemy bomber appeared on port quarter of flagship, at extreme end of convoy, crossing from port to starboard. Bomber dived

---

[22]Submarine chasers.

bombed at an approximate angle of 30° and released three bombs, two landed in the water and one hit a tanker, carrying gasoline, on its starboard quarter near extreme end of ship. A fire broke out on tanker. Bomber continued across end of convoy, altitude about 2000 feet. A corvette of the local escort opened fire with a pom-pom as bomber passed. Bomber returned over the same route, flew over the ship she bombed, again circled and flew over the same ship and then flew away from convoy. Last seen on relative bearing about 160. The tanker reported the fire under control and only minor damage. If the bomb had landed about 150 ft. forward, on the gasoline storage, the ship undoubtedly would have been lost. (Net tonnage of tanker 2,638, nationality Latvian.) The bomb must have been small not to have done more damage. The explosion was too loud for an incendiary bomb.

When the explosion occurred the officer on watch on the flagship sounded an old hand type automobile klaxon, with no apparent results. After much commotion and five minutes of valuable time, the one 12-pounder was manned.

The bombing occurred in practically the same position as a ship was bombed yesterday and within 15 minutes of the same time.

0645 three British fighters arrived, circled convoy for about a half hour and then departed.

0915 passed a merchant ship in channel which had also been bombed with more serious results. The bomb hit the ship about 75 feet from the stern, tearing a huge hole in the deck and topside about half way to the water line. The gun platform and gun was hanging vertically over the stern. The ship was heavily loaded. The crew were still aboard. Five trawlers were circling the ship, apparently the hull was watertight as the ship was not sinking and preparations were being made to take the ship in tow. The funnel indicated that steam was on the boilers. The rudder was over hard left and apparently jammed.

0915 convoy now in three long columns as the ships pass through the channel.

During the remainder of the day ships left the convoy and proceeded independently to their final destinations.

Beautiful calm and moonlight night (full moon). Perfect for an air raid. Only 3 escorts remain. At 2000 received information that navigation lights were ordered extinguished at Liverpool about sixty air miles away. At midnight sky became overcast which lessens danger from air raid.

Official Diary, 16 September 1940

Only Liverpool ships now with convoy. 0700 anchored 12 miles from Liverpool as harbor is closed. 1130 underway proceeding into harbor. 1430 anchored in Liverpool harbor.

Official Report[23]

SYNOPSIS. The convoy consisted of a total of 42 ships. 19 ships sailed from Halifax, 11 from Sydney, Nova Scotia, and 12 from Bermuda. The ships from the above three ports rendezvous four and one half days after the Halifax ships sailed and formed a single convoy. Speed of convoy 9 knots. Twelve days after leaving Halifax the convoy rendezvous with the local escort from England, just outside the submarine danger zone (supposedly) as determined by the latest reports of the British Admiralty. Ships bound for the Methil (east coast Scotland), the Clyde, Belfast, Milford Haven, etc., were released as prearranged positions. The Liverpool ships, a total of 15, arrived on 16 September.

---

[23]Report serial 1100 of 21 September 1940.

STATISTICS. Total number of ships which sailed from Halifax, Sydney, and
  Bermuda.. 42
Number of British ships in convoy..................................... 23
Total number of ships from other nations 19
  (7 Norwegian, 4 Greek, 2 Danish, 1 Swedish, 1 Dutch, 1 Finish, 1 Latvian, 1 Polish,
  1 French (according to Lloyds))
  Number of ships separated from convoy due to rough weather,
  fog or breakdown 7
  Number of ships which rejoined convoy after separation 2
  Number of ships in convoy at end of passage......................... 37
  Total gross tonnage (37 ships) 186607
  Total net tonnage (37 ships) 112960
  Tonnage of largest ship, ... gross 10,042, net 6,060
  Tonnage of smallest ship, ... gross 1,123, net 631
  Average tonnage, ... gross 5,043, net 3,053
  Maximum speed of convoy .... 9 knots
  Cruising speed of convoy....................................... 8 knots
  Number of ships bombed (up to the time convoy separated in
  small groups)—Only minor damage 1
  Number of ships attacked by submarines 0
Only one ship of the 19 which sailed from Halifax had a gyro compass. About three
quarters of the ships burned coal.

STATION KEEPING. For the first two and three days station keeping was very
poor. Unfortunately during this period there was considerable fog. Each time the fog
lifted the ships were scattered everywhere. The commodore stated that we were
fortunate in not having a collision . . . . Later on station keeping improved tremendously and ships kept fairly well closed up even during fog. Consideration should be
given to the fact that about three fourths of the ships were coal burners which makes
control of the steam pressure more difficult especially when hauling fires. Sextant angles
are used in measuring distances. The after masthead heights are known to all
ships . . . and a table is provided showing the number of yards equivalent to various
angles for various heights of mast. I tried using sextant angles and consider it practical.
However, it is by no means as easy or as rapid as a stadiometer. I believe that most of
the ships use the "seamans eye" which has been so weather beaten that it approaches
Nelson's bad eye as far as station keeping is concerned. There is the usual tendency of
opening out at night. Even when ships are closed up the distance is greater than 400
yards and the interval greater than 600 yards. At these times the distance is about 600
yards and interval from 700 to 800 yards. Ships at the end of each column have a
tendency to increase distance. When one considers the many types of ships with
radically different characteristics, the lack of equipment, and the many different
nationalities, the station keeping should be considered excellent.

MANEUVERS. The maneuver instructions and signals, plus all other necessary
information, are contained in one 41 page book called "Pamphlet of Instructions and
Signals for the Conduct of Convoys." (Short title "CONSIGS.") Maneuvers are
restricted to head of column and turn movements, the latter for emergency use only.
Head of column movements may be executed by two different methods: one is the same
as our division head of column movement and the other is by "wheeling." In the former
line is again formed upon completion of the maneuver. If sufficient time is available the
line of bearing may be changed before the change of course so that upon completion of

the latter the formation is in line. When the "Wheeling" method is used the leader of the center column changes to the new course and reduces speed 1 knot.

Column leaders in the direction toward which the change of course is made, change course so as to maintain their relative bearing and distance from the leader of the center column and reduce speed 2 knots. Column leaders away from the direction toward which the change of course is made change course so as to maintain their relative bearing and distance from the leader of the center column and increase speed 1 knot. Each column leader takes the speed of the center column leader when on station. Then the commodore makes a signal to the entire convoy to change speed to a definite number of knots. (Same speed as before the maneuver.) Ships astern of the column leaders use follow the leader tactics, changing speed without signal. What actually happens is that each column changes speed in accordance with the above and the column leaders ease out or in according to the direction of turn until they arrive on station. The division head of column movement was not used during the entire passage. I was informed that it is seldom used by any convoy. The "wheeling" method is described in detail because it is believed to be well suited for our use. See Recommendations.

The signals for changes of course during darkness should be made during daylight if practicable. If in area where fog is prevalent these signals should be made at the first opportunity during clear weather. The commodore of the convoy stressed this point. He did it many times to good advantage. At night in clear weather two horizontal red lights are displayed to indicate that a change of course is about to begin. The signal of execution is the turning off of the two red lights. In addition the convoy flagship (not required) usually sounds one or two short blasts on the whistle. (One blast for changing course to starboard and two to port.) Each column leader repeats the whistle signal but does not diplay the lights. At the execution of the signal the maneuver is performed by wheeling in 20° increments. (Note: No provision is made to change course other than an even 20° by using red lights.) In a fog 4 long blasts are substituted for the red lights in the above maneuver. Column leaders repeat the 4 long blasts.

An emergency turn at night is indicated by one 15 second blast on the whistle, repeated by the column leaders, followed by one or two short blasts depending upon the direction of the change of course (repeated by all column leaders) upon hearing the one or two short blasts *all* ships of the convoy *turn 40°* in the direction indicated. A 40° turn is the only emergency turn provided. Simultaneous turns during daylight are made in the same manner as in our instructions. I was pleasantly surprised at the way the convoy maneuvered and the virgin halyards made me realize I was in another navy.

ZIGZAGGING. Convoys zigzag in areas where submarines may be located. Two days before entering the possible submarine area the convoy zigzagged during daylight hours for practice. Convoys also zigzag on unusually clear or moonlight nights. In daylight flag signals are used to commence and cease zigzagging. At night the signal to commence zigzagging is three vertical lights (red, green, red). When these lights are turned off the convoy starts zigzagging in accordance with the zigzag plan last used by the convoy. The commodore stated ships had no trouble remembering the number of the last plan. If the convoy is zigzagging the above signal means to cease zigzagging and resume the base course. A whistle signal is provided to cease zigzagging if fog is encountered.

Ten zigzag plans are provided in the confidential appendix A to Defence of Merchant Shipping Part I. Since foreign ships do not have this publication three of these plans are mimeographed and given to all foreign ships by the Naval Control Service Officer. As a

A North Atlantic Convoy making a Turn Movement to Port
[Photo: Imperial War Museum C3263]

result the convoy is limited to the use of these plans. (Note: Only one plan was used during the entire passage.)

The zigzag plans in Appendix A referred to above look very similar to the zigzag plans in Instructions for Naval Transportation & U.S. Merchant Vessels Part II *before* the first revision in December 1939. The first course to be steered is always that course corresponding to 0 minutes on the diagram regardless of the number of minutes passed the last exact hour that the signal was executed. I believe this method is easier for the merchantmen than our present system, but I believe our system will be satisfactory. (I tried it out on the Third Officer.)

Ships are equipped with zigzag clocks. These are large face clocks (about 9″ in diameter) with a number of movable contacts around the outer edge which can be set at the time of the course changes for the zigzag plan in use (good for 1 hour). A bell rings when the minute hand touches these contacts and the helmsman turns to the next course.

A blackboard is kept in the pilot house showing the times of changes of course, amount to turn, new course by gyro and p.s.c. The officer of the deck seldom enters the pilot house. The helmsman comes to the new course every time the bell rings.

The ships have a tendency to open out while zigzagging. I doubt if much of an effort is made to keep correct station. The flagship drops a time ball at the end of every hour while the ships are zigzagging.

SIGNALS. All signals are taken from the "Pamphlet of Instructions and Signals for the Conduct of Convoys" (CONSIGS). All maneuvering signals (except whistle signals) were made by flag hoist. The signals may be sent by radio but strict radio silence is observed. A provision is made to use flashing light for maneuvers but it was not used as the commodore said it was impracticable, in which I concur. (Ships have no yardarm blinker lights—only portable aldis lamps are provided.) All maneuvering signals contain one letter followed by one, two or three numerals. These signals are made without a call—similar to our "all ships" signal. (The instructions provide for using the third repeater to indicate the signal meaning as in CONSIGS but it was never used.) "Don't need it. Why use an extra flag and tack line on these short halyards" said the Chief Signalman. I concur. Visual responsibility is similar to ours. However, it is not carried out. The signalmen on the flagship check up on all ships. Signals are immediately two-blocked. The whistle signals are not sounded by the column leaders in order which causes a little uncertainty but did not worry the commodore.

RADIO . . . . Strict radio silence is observed and is only broken in an emergency. Maneuvering signals are not but can be sent by radio. Radio operator has ship's position for each half hour in case of use in an emergency. Radio silence was not broken by convoy during entire passage . . . .

FOG. The convoy encountered about three full days of fog. Position buoys with 300 yards of tow line are supposed to be used. I was in a position to observe five ships, but never saw more than three position buoys when the fog lifted. A strong cask or a specially designed position buoy is used . . . . Speed was not reduced, however, speed was only 8.0 knots. The commodore stated they do not reduce speed in a fog except perhaps one knot to insure all ships being able to keep station. Fog whistles were used sparingly. Ships astern of column leaders do not sound fog signal except in an emergency. Column leaders are guided by the commodore. When sounded the column leaders make the morse equivalent of their column number on the whistle. The commodore in charge of this convoy had only the odd numbered column leaders sound the whistle following his motions. Time interval between whistles varied from 30 to five minutes. Ordinarily navigation lights not used if ships can see the next ahead and the ships on either side. In thick fog navigational lights are optional for each captain. A large cluster of lights are used on the stern and on each quarter (showing abeam) in thick fog. Ships do not keep closed up in fog. . . .

ESCORTS . . . . The type and number of ocean escorts naturally depends upon the enemy opposition expected plus the types and numbers of own ships available for such duty. I believe a converted merchantman a poor type of ship for an ocean escort for a convoy of 42 ships. A converted merchantman with high freeboard and probably not much protection would be no match for any vessel except a vessel of similar type. The light cruiser, of course, is a better type but one vessel of this type is not sufficient for a convoy of 42 ships . . . .

SUBMARINES. The Admiralty by means of broadcasts informs all ships of the location of submarines. Naturally routes for convoys and ships sailing independently are continually being changed to avoid submarines. On this passage course was changed twice by the commodore to avoid submarine areas, and twice by the Admiralty. The last of these course changes by the Admiralty was followed by new route instructions for the last four hundred miles, which varied considerably from the original route ordered by the Admiralty. From Admiralty reports five submarines were operating west of England, however, none were observed and no attacks were made by local escorts. One of the submarines which caused the Admiralty to change the convoy route later attacked one of the ships which left the convoy formation two nights previously . . . .

DISTINGUISHING MARKS OF SHIPS. Merchant vessels had no distinguishing marks. Combatant ships—Sides and superstructure painted a very dark gray which approached black in color. The H.M.S. EMERALD's three funnels were painted a very light gray. The foremast of the same ship was painted white above the fire control station. The destroyers had various combinations of wide and narrow red horizontal stripes around each funnel. The funnels were painted with the same very dark gray as the sides. In addition the barrels of the forward and after guns on some of the destroyers were painted either red or very light gray. About half of the destroyers had a white wave painted on each side of the bow . . . .

ARMAMENT OF MERCHANT VESSELS. Convoy flagship had one 4.7" surface gun and one 12-pounder antiaircraft gun. No machine guns although it is understood that they are being provided to ocean going vessels as quickly as possible. Other British ships had what appeared to be the same type of guns. Twenty rounds of ammunition in ready box at each gun. I was informed that 80 rounds for each gun were stowed below. No rangefinder on board. Range is estimated by gun captain. Fuses set to burst at between 1200 and 1500 yards.

Armed guard consisted of one retired chief gunners mate, one gunners mate second class, active and two stewards assigned to this duty by the ship. Chief gunners mate on watch during daylight hours, the others stood a straight watch in three. Balance of gun crews taken from ships personnel of watch when attack takes place.

Due to mainmast and rigging antiaircraft gun could not bear more than 20° forward of the beam on either side. As was indicated by the air attack on the convoy, the enemy bombers know this fact and therefore attack merchant vessels from ahead. It is strongly recommended that an antiaircraft gun be placed forward as well as astern on U.S. merchant vessels.

RECOMMENDATIONS.

(a) Determine to what extent the Navy will take control over the sailing and routing of all U.S. merchantmen in time of war. In order to properly safeguard American merchant vessels and to insure uninterrupted seaborne traffic, particularly for strategic materials, it is recommended that the Navy take complete control over the sailing and routing of all U.S. merchant shipping . . . .

(b) Make preparations to establish Naval Control Service Offices in the principal ports of the United States and at focal points of sea-borne commerce in possession of the United States outside its continental limits. A Naval Control Service representative should be located at minor ports.

(c) Designate the officers who will act as Naval Control Service Officers. Send as many as possible of these officers to Halifax to observe the operations of a Naval Control Service Office in order that they may be able to function efficiently at the very beginning of hostilities.

(d) Set up an organization which will function as a central Naval Control Service Office. This office should inform the local Naval Control Service Offices of the best route for all ships sailing from the various ports and change the routing as may be necessary when the ships are at sea. One office should control the routing of all shipping in the North Atlantic. A similar office should be established on the west coast of the United States. Due to the large areas involved, it would probably be advisable to have the Naval Control Service Officers at Panama, Hawaii and the Philippines handle this work within their respective areas. In order to efficiently perform this work it is essential that the maximum coordination exist between these offices and the communication sections which handle the network of radio direction finder stations and the reports from ships at sea pertaining to attacks of various kinds of the sighting of enemy ships.

(e) Select the officers who will be assigned as convoy commanders. Active or recently retired commanders or captains are recommended for this duty. The officers selected should be in good physical condition, have the reputation for being good seamen and, above all, they should have PATIENCE. While it is true that the British use retired admirals for this duty, the average age of these officers is considerably younger than retired admirals in the U.S. Navy. With very few exceptions, it is doubted if the retired admirals in our service could stand the physical and mental strain of convoy duty. The officers selected should be informed of their prospective duty in order that they may study the publications used in convoys and be ready at the outbreak of war. In this connection, the British convoy commodores received one week's instruction at Plymouth prior to being assigned to duty. Their instruction included the reading of "Merchantmen at Arms" by Captain J. Bone, R.N. . . .

(f) Be prepared to detail the enlisted men who will serve as the convoy commanders staff. The entire staff of a 42-ship convoy . . . consisted of the commodore, one chief radioman, one chief signalman and three seamen signalmen. The radioman was on active duty at the outbreak of the war; the chief signalman had been retired for three years; the seamen signalmen enlisted at the start of the war and received only six weeks of instruction prior to being assigned to convoy duty. The above is stated in detail because it is believed that a liaison group is not required on each vessel which sails in a convoy. However, arrangements should be made with the Maritime Commission and ship owners to insure that each merchant marine officer is proficient in flag and flashing light signals . . . .

(g) The maneuvering section and the appendix on signals in "Instructions for Naval Transportation and U.S. Merchant Vessels in Time of War, Part II," should be revised. The following specific changes are recommended . . . .

(1) Eliminate all reference to interval and call the distance between adjacent guides the distance between columns. Interval is too complicated for merchant marine officers.

(2) Change standard distance to 500 yards and the distance between columns to 700 yards. It is believed that 400 yards for distance between ships and 600 yards for distance between columns (as used by the British) is a little too close, provided the ships keep their proper distance, whereas 500 and 700 yards for distance between ships and columns respectively are practicable even if the ships are on station. The importance of keeping the convoy closed up in order to facilitate signaling, and maneuvering in addition to affording greater protection to the convoy as a whole, cannot be over-emphasized. If a convoy should consist of large, fast ships the distance between ships and columns should naturally be increased.

(3) The senior officer of the escort should be in complete charge of the convoy regardless of the rank of the convoy commander . . . .

(4) Adopt the wheeling method of changing course. It is simple, practical and only requires the one basic signal . . . .

(5) Adopt the two horizontal red lights for changing course at night by wheeling. At present we have no method of signaling a change of course at night except by flashing light or radio, which are not recommended . . . . The 4 long blasts as a substitute for the two red lights during a fog should also be adopted. This signal should be repeated by all column leaders and, in addition, they should sound one or two blasts on the execution of the signal.

(6) Adopt the emergency turn signal for day and night. At present we have no emergency turn signal at night except by radio, which should be used only in extreme emergencies. . . .

(7) Adopt a light signal for zigzagging at night . . . .

(8) Increase the number of signals using "Pamphlet of Instructions and Signals for the Conduct of Convoys" as a guide . . . . Only about one per cent of the signals were taken from the "International Code of Signals."

(9) Delete all reference to submarine danger zones as they are impractical for merchant ship use. Suggest using submarine or wake of torpedo sighted to starboard, port, ahead or astern. Three numerals may be added to indicate true bearings.

(h) A large and well-coordinated organization both afloat and ashore will be required to efficiently control the sailing and routing of U.S. merchant vessels in time of war. Detail[ed] plans should therefore be made while the opportunity permits to insure that such an organization will be able to function at the outbreak of war.

CHAPTER TWO

THE BATTLE OF BRITAIN
16 September-7 October 1940

Personal Diary, 17[16] September 1940
. . . Tremendous amount of shipping at anchor and a[t] piers. No apparent damage to docks and shipping. Cleared by customs—did not look at my luggage. 1630 Ashore with Commodore Plowden. Took luggage to railroad station. 1700 air raid—went in an air raid shelter for first time. In air raid shelter at railway station there were about 150 children ages 5-14 who had just arrived from southeast England. They had been travelling since 0700. They are bound for Canada.[1] The group of children were well taken care of by women. The children were cheerful—they played with dolls and various games. However, I could not help but feeling sorry for them. My first reaction was how I would hate to have my Anne in a similar position. Also that War is hell even for civilians & thank God our country has escaped such a life—so far. One remark from a woman of about 45 impressed me. She said "why should I go to America at a time when I might be some use to my country." She was one of the escorts for the children.[2] All clear at 1800. Saw for the first time a blackout in a city . . . . Called at the Naval Control Service Office, paid my respects, then checked in at Adelphi Hotel for the night. Met Commodore Plowden again—he is taking the 2400 train to Plymouth, had a farewell drink with the Commodore. Four more air raids during night. Secured from last one at 0200. Went down to hotel air raid shelter which was the billard room and bar in basement. Other people were in adjacent rooms.

Letter to Mrs. Wellings, 16th Day, NOT at Sea
Well darling here I am safe and sound in an English port a long way from the area which is receiving most of Hitler's attention.
I have just finished dinner and the time is 9:15. I have made all preparations to leave for London at 0800 tomorrow. From the radio I would judge that London is having plenty of attention these days. I don't see how it can continue at the present rate of losing planes, however no one really knows and therefore it is foolish to make a prediction.
I have a single room on the second floor of the best hotel in town. Which incidentally is not so hot based on our standards. They have signs and instructions about air raid shelters and you may rest assured that I will not take any unnecessary chances. The

---

[1]On the following evening, Tuesday 17 September at 10 p.m., the *City of Benares* was torpedoed and sunk about 600 miles off the coast. She was carrying 90 similar children with their nine escorts to Canada under the evacuation plan of the Children's Overseas Reception Board. They were the first casualties in a scheme that had transported, by this date, nearly 3,000 children to wartime homes in the overseas dominion. *The Times*, 23, 27 September 1940.

[2]The section describing the children in the air raid shelter has been transposed from the end of the entry in order to maintain a chronological narrative. *Ed.*

people in the city and in the hotel seem to carry on as usual. The elevator boy had several remarks to make (one arm man) and he wound up by saying that they could take [it] and I believe them . . . .

Personal Diary, 18[17] September 1940

Breakfast in hotel room at 0645 due to dining room not opened. Checked out at 0715, went to station to ensure baggage would be on my train. Excess baggage 12 shillings to ship. Man in charge asked me if I could keep my council. After trying to figure out what he meant with no result I said "yes." He then charged me 6 shillings & I gave him a 2½ shilling tip—what a country if they run it this way. Train left at 0815 and arrived at London at 1330—a 200 mile run. Normally it is a 4 hour ride. No evidence of war enroute—only saw one soldier along the road . . . .

Checked baggage at station then took cab to embassy. Everyone out to lunch except 2 reserve ensigns. One of them took me to Selfridges where Count Austin[3] and MacDonald[4] were having lunch. Seemed good to see someone you know after 17 days. Report to Captain Kirk at 1600 also saw Ad. Ghormley,[5] Savvy Forest[6] and rest of officers.

Left town at 1800 with Comdr. Hitchcock[7] for Virginia Waters where Capt. Kirk has taken a house for the officers in order not to be in London at night. Severe night bombing has been going on for a week. After listening to the boys' stories I am glad I decided to go to the country—30 miles west of London. House is a very nice English home with 9 bedrooms, a huge living room and a game room. Turned in at 2400 (talked with Bill Ammon[8]—Boys seem to be jittery—I guess the strain of no families, the bombing, and work has been getting them down).

Personal Diary, 19[18] September 1940

Up at 0700 drove in to town with Comdr. Hitchcock at 0845 arrived 0945. Lunch at Simonds around corner from Embassy. Left for home with Comdr. Hitchcock at 1730. Worked on report during the day after listening to all the stories. Name of house at Virginia Waters is New Pipers. The lawn and gardens are very pretty. Vaughn Bailey[9]

---

[3]Bernard Lige Austin (1902-1979). U.S. Naval Academy, 1924. Flag Lieutenant to Rear Admiral R.L. Ghormley, USN, Special Naval Observer in London. Later, Vice Admiral, Deputy Chief of Naval Operations (Plans and Policy), 1959-60; President, Naval War College, 1960-64.

[4]Donald John MacDonald (1908-   ). U.S. Naval Academy, 1931. Staff of Rear Admiral R.L. Ghormley, later, Rear Admiral. Retired 1959.

[5]Robert Lee Ghormley (1883-1958). U.S. Naval Academy, 1906; Naval War College, 1938; from August 1940 to 1942 Special Naval Observer in London, coordinated Anglo-American naval relations. Later assigned additional duty as Special Naval Observer while serving as Commander U.S. Naval Forces in Europe. Vice Admiral. Retired 1946.

[6]Francis Xavier Forest (1904-   ). U.S. Naval Academy, 1926. Assistant Naval Attaché, London. Later, Captain. Retired 1954.

[7]Norman Ridgeway Hitchcock (1896-1978). U.S. Naval Academy, 1920. Assistant Naval Attaché for Air, May 1939-May 1941. Later Captain. Retired 1947.

[8]William Bronley Ammon (1902-   ). U.S. Naval Academy, 1923. Assistant Naval Attaché, London, in charge of naval communications. Later, Rear Admiral.

[9]Vaughn Bailey (1895-1979). U.S. Naval Academy, 1918. Assistant Naval Attaché, London. Later, Captain.

NEW PIPERS
Gorse Hill Road, Virginia Water, Surrey
[Photo 1981, Courtesy Commander in Chief, U.S. Naval Forces, Europe.]

28

also staying there. After dinner the nightly excitement is to go out on the lawn and watch the bombing of London. Every few minutes searchlights jab the sky and the burst of anti-aircraft fire can be seen. They look like stars in the sky. Every now and then a huge flash can be seen. The boys argue whether it is AA[10] fire or a bomb. Planes can be heard overhead every few minutes.

Letter to Mrs. Wellings, 18 September 1940

Well sweet here I am in dear old London. What a fine time I picked to see the largest city in the world. Oh well! It is still London and there is plenty to see.

I arrived yesterday afternoon at two p.m., after quite a ride thru the country. Believe it or not there was not one single evidence of bombing all the way down on the train. The English countryside is really beautiful . . . .

Now as for London. There is some bombing but most of it takes place at night. They have the air raid warnings down to a science so that the people have plenty of opportunity to see[k] shelter. In the daytime there is practically no bombing. We work in the office just like we would at home although the hours are not so long.

Now what do you suppose happens at night? Well the boys have a fine English country home about 30 miles from London where we go after working hours. It is fully equipped in every way. A real English country home. Last night was a revelation to me. I slept in a grand bed plenty of fresh air and didn't know a thing until 0700 this morning when my alarm went off. After a good breakfast we set off for town with no trouble whatsoever. Some of the boys who have engagements for dinner (with English officers) stay in town all night at the Embassy which has a fine air raid shelter. If I stay in town you may be sure that I will stay at the Embassy. All in all sweet, the actual goings on is not so bad as one would believe in reading the newspapers at home. I don't mean to say that there has been no damage because there has been damage. But life seems to go on as usual. Shops are open and the people go about their work as usual.

Yesterday I had lunch at 1430 in Selfridges—the big department store corresponding to Filenes at home. Business was going on as usual. Today was the same, so please don't worry. Of course there is some danger but not one hundredth as much as one would believe who has not been there.

Personal Diary, 20[19] September 1940

Drove in with Capt. Kirk (he is staying with Comdr. Hitchcock at "Englemead" house which is about 2 miles from New Pipers). Continued work on report. Back to New Pipers at 1900, Dinner watch air raid on London and to bed.

Personal Diary, 21[20] September 1940

Drove in with Capt. Kirk—worked on report of convoys, lunch and home to New Pipers with Comdr. Hitchcock—very pleasant getting a ride both ways. Air raid on London more violent last night. Inspected damage down in south east London caused by a magnetic mine dropped from a plane—Damage was considerable—glass knocked out of all buildings for a block on either side, roofs of over 20 houses demolished. Fortunately only 2 people missing.

Letter to Mrs. Wellings, 20[21] September 1940

. . . It rained all last night and today it is very cloudy . . . . What am I doing out in the country, well we shifted some of our gear out here in order to be prepared to continue operations in case the bombing gets considerably more intense. One officer stays here

---

[10]Antiaircraft.

each day to keep an eye on things and today it is my turn to stay here. The other boys drove in at the usual time.

Yesterday I had lunch with MacDonald at one of the big clubs in town. The name was the United Services Club and one of the best clubs in the city. The English certainly know how to run a club. Incidentally, I have been granted all the privileges of this club and about four other clubs in town.[11]

Yesterday afternoon I made my calls at the Admiralty. Captain Kirk escorted me around to meet all the high officers. This is the usual procedure for new officers. Believe it or not they were conducting business in the usual way and were pleased to take time out to chat for a few minutes. Incidentally they make a regular schedule for your calls; 10 minutes here, 5 minutes there, etc. A secretary politely informs you when the time is up, if you do not adhere to the schedule. All the officers were unusually pleasant and did not appear to be worried in any way. I believe this reflects the British point of view. They realize they are up against a difficult opponent, but they believe they can hold out and win in the end. This is particularly true of the common people who say "We can take it."

Last night we left the office at the usual time—5:00 p.m. and arrived out here at 6:00 p.m. Everything was very quiet all night so that after a few games of ping pong I turned in at 11:00 p.m. and slept soundly until seven in the morning.

This estate is certainly a lovely place which of course dates back for years and years. Originally it included all area for miles around but of course now it is cut up into a number of smaller estates. The flower gardens are perfectly beautiful, which I understand is characteristic of all English country homes. Really living out here is like being in another world. Absolutely no indication of war except the sound of a few planes every once in awhile.

Letter to Mrs. Wellings, 22 September 1940

. . . We really have a very comfortable house and all the help that one could ask for. So I really haven't one single complaint to make about living conditions. We have plenty of food and an excellent cook, but of course she can't compare with a little girl I know. The food is the same as is given to everyone else. In other words, we have not used any diplomatic privileges to get additional food.

Last week my daily schedule ran like this. Up at 0700, bathe, shaved, dress and breakfast at 0745. At 0815 we take a cab down the road two miles where the captain and exec. are living. It is the same house the exec. had when his wife was here. The captain is staying with him. The Captain and exec. both have cars (the captain's a fine black *Buick* 7 passenger sedan plus chauffeur, an official car). We drive into town with them arriving about 0930. People here go to lunch about 1:30 to 3:30 p.m. However, we generally go to one of the clubs near the Embassy and are away from the office about an hour and a half. At between 5:00 and 6:00 p.m., we drive home, which takes about an hour. Have a cocktail before dinner which is served about 8:00 p.m. At 10:30 to 11:00 at the latest we turn in. Our favorite outdoor sport is to walk about 100 yards from the house and look toward London. You can see the flash of anti-aircraft shells, and the stabbing beams of search lights in the sky every now and then . . . . So you see we are not spending the evenings dodging bombs and huddled in a shelter as you probably think . . . .

Tonight we are going to the ambassador's house to see a movie. I understand they are regular Sunday night . . . features. He lives in a fine estate (so I am told) about 6 miles

---

[11]Junior United Service Club, Charles Street, St. James; Army Navy Club, 26 Pall Mall; United Service Club, 116 Pall Mall; Naval and Military Club, 94 Piccadilly.

from us. I will have my first opportunity to meet him tonight as he has been unusually busy the past week . . . .

Personal Diary, 22 September 1940

. . . At night went to St. Leonard's and Ambassador's house at 2110 to see movies. Met Ambassador[12]—quite pleasant—he wore a light blue lounging suit—quite something. Went outside afterwards to see air raids. Beautiful clear night. Driving to and from New Pipers which is outside Windsor was my first experience at driving at night in a blackout. No so good. Capt. Kirk drove us (the Dr.—Norman)[13] home at 1230.

Personal Diary, 23 September 1940

Taxied as usual over to Comdr. Hitchcock's house. Six new officers arrived yesterday—Capt. Cockran[14], Comdr. Mills[15], Lt. Comdrs. Huffman[16], and Eller[17] plus two reserve Lt. Comdrs., Scott and Hodgson. They stayed at Comdr. Hitchcock's. We all drove in Capt. Kirk and Comdr. Hitchcock's cars. Lunch with Comdr. Hitchcock, Eller and Huffman at Le Coq d'Or—some fancy place to eat and quite expensive. Returned to country at 1830. Address of house in country—New Pipers, Gorse Hill Road, Wentworth Estate, Virginia Waters, England—Some address.

Personal Diary, 24 September 1940

Duty in country today—duty necessary due to confidential publications at country house which will be used if Embassy is bombed. Very quiet day.

Letter to Mrs. Wellings, 25 September 1940

. . . A day out here removes all thoughts of war except for a few planes which fly overhead every now and then (Friendly planes). It has been a beautiful day with the sun shining and only a few scattered white clouds . . . . One would never dream that the greatest war in history is being waged.

---

[12]Joseph Patrick Kennedy (1888-1969). Ambassador to the Court of St. James, 1937 to November 1940. Father of President John F. Kennedy. "The Ambassador was very friendly and was kind enough to inquire about my mother and father. Before the Kennedy family became well known, they and the Wellings were neighbors in East Boston, Mass." JHW, *MS. Reminiscences,* p. 21.

[13]Irwin Louis Vincent Norman (1903-1965). Assistant Naval Attaché, London July 1940-May 1941; Senior Medical Officer for Army and Navy personnel at the Embassy. Surgeon. Entered Naval Medical Corps, 1927. Later, Rear Admiral, Medical Corps, 1954. Retired 1959.

[14]Edward Lull Cockrane (1892-1959). U.S. Naval Academy, 1914; Naval War College 1940. Sent as Assistant Naval Attaché, London, to study British ship construction. Later, Vice Admiral; Chief, Bureau of Ships, 1942-46; Chief, Material Division, Navy Department, 1946-47; Chairman, Federal Maritime Board and Maritime Administration, 1950-52; Dean, Engineering, Massachusetts Institute of Technology, 1952-54.

[15]Earle Watkins Mills (1896-1968). U.S. Naval Academy, 1918; sent as Assistant Naval Attaché, London, to observe battle damage and means of repairing damage from mines and bombs. Later, Vice Admiral; Chief, Bureau of Ships, 1946-49; President and Chairman of the Board, Foster-Wheeler Corporation, 1949-58.

[16]Leon Joseph Huffman (1898-1974). U.S. Naval Academy, 1922. Assistant Naval Attaché, London. Later, Rear Admiral. Retired 1957.

[17]Ernest McNeill Eller (1903-   ). U.S. Naval Academy, 1925; sent as Assistant Naval Attaché, London, to observe British gunnery. Later, Rear Admiral; Director of Naval History, 1956-1971.

The general situation in London is the same as last week. Business as usual in the daytime, air raids at night. I have yet to stay in town after dark and do not intend to because I am perfectly contented to enjoy a good night's sleep.

Six officers arrived Sunday night so that our country estate is rapidly becoming a country club . . . .

Personal Diary, 25-27 September 1940

25 Sept.—Duty in country again today. Very quiet during day. Extremely heavy bombing of London and two towns within 5 miles of us. Enemy planes came over every 3 to 5 minutes from 2130 to 2400. About 20 bombs rocked the house, heard one whistle, we all dropped to the lawn—we were watching bombing from lawn. Enemy planes flew right over the house all night.

26 Sept.—Drove in town with Captain. Finished convoy report. Talked operations with Austin. Discussed with Captain arrangements for contacts with Admiralty. Captain informed Admiralty that I am ready to go to sea. Where will I go??—Drove home with Comdr. Hitchcock—Quiet in country compared with last night.

27 Sept.—Drove in town with Captain. Usual day in office—still no information as to where I will go—Read reports in office—can't do much work when one arrives at 1000, 2 hours for lunch and leave at 1700. Guess I had better take it easy while I can and not worry.

Letter to Mrs. Wellings, 28 September 1940

Today is Saturday and a holiday for us. The embassy is closed all day Saturday but usually the navy contingent continues to work until 1300. However yesterday Captain Kirk decided we would have Saturday off which means a real weekend in the country.

This morning after a nine o'clock breakfast we played ping pong and walked around the lawn getting some real sunshine. However, at 1200 we decided to take a walk before lunch and started out to walk to the inn which is about a 25 minute walk. We continue[d] past the inn and then returned by another road. The result was a grand hour and a quarters walk over the English countryside. This afternoon Franny Forest, Capt. Cockran and I walked to the railroad station (15 min.) and took a train to a town called Stain[e]s about 8 miles away. We walked up one side of the main drag and down the other looking in all the stores. We spent most of our time rummaging thru Woolworth's 5 & 10. Oh! it seemed grand to see something that looked like an American store. I bought some toothpaste, face cloths, shoe polish (for the boy—not for me—although they don't know how to shine shoes) ink, spirits of camphor (no I don't need it now—just a precaution) . . . .

We arrived back to New Pipers at 1715—just in time for tea. I am writing this letter up in my room sitting by the window. I hope to finish before dinner and the blackout.

All the curtains in the house have been backed by special blackout cloth. The curtains were very heavy before—now they weigh a ton. At the tops and sides special additional material must be placed to insure a complete blackout. Believe me it is quite a job to effectively blackout a house. We go outside and inspect after dark. If we didn't and a light showed the local air raid warden would soon be ringing the bell. You have no idea how thoroughly each area is patrolled and inspected.

Well Darling, what do you think?? I have bought your liberty "bell" velvet.[18] I took yesterday afternoon off and did some shopping for two reasons. First there is a 12½% *increase* in the sales tax on 1 October. The second is that I thought I had better buy it

---

[18]Purchased at Liberty's, the well known store in Regent Street.

while the store was still intact (the front windows on the *ground* floor only have been broken due to the bomb blast—not hit). I bought 5 yards. There was no choice as the man said they only had standard black velvet suitable for a suit—their regular brand—they never had more than one.

The cost was 24s. and 6d. a yard which is just about $5.00 figuring the pound at $4.00 . . . .

There is no change in the general situation in London. Work goes on without interruption during the daytime with the air raids at night. I believe the people are standing up under the strain of nightly bombing very well. I doubt if the Germans can break the people's morale.

A number of the bombs do fall in the residential and business districts which seems a crime because they are definitely not military objectives. Personally, I think the Germans are wasting their time bombing London, even if they are eventually able to stop all business in the city . . . .

Personal Diary, 28 September–1 October 1940

28 Sept.—Saturday . . . Understand the Embassy staff never work on Saturday but quite unusual for Navy contingent to take day off . . . . Had a long talk with Comdr. Mills and Bill Ammon at night—we discussed the navy in general.

29 Sept.—Sunday, up at 0830, went to mass with Savy Huffman at Englemead about a twenty-five minute walk from house. In p.m. walked for an hour. Aircraft quite lively overhead at night . . . .

30 Sept.—Monday. Duty in country. Very quiet day. Saw three flights of English planes. Rather interesting to see their formation. Capt. Cochran, Comdr. Mills and Savvy Forest left for Bath. Bill Ammon had duty. Savy Huffman, Miss Ziegler[19] and I only ones for dinner. During dinner had one bomb land which rattled windows quite severely. I jumped from chair.

1 Oct. Tuesday. Duty again in country. Last night a bomb landed in field about 500 yards from Ranleigh, our other house. Mrs. Ripman,[20] Miss Ziegler, Bill, Savvy and I for dinner. Mrs. Ripman is quite a problem. She is really the "duchess." Can't understand how she gets away with the things she does. Dad's birthday—sent him a cable.

Letter to Mrs. Wellings, 2 October 1940

. . . Since the cable was sent from London I knew it would let you know that I am still around watching the show. As a matter of fact even now I have no information as to when—and where I will go. I am getting tired of hanging around here because I figure that the quicker I get started the quicker I will get home. These British certainly work slowly. If they plan their war operations as slowly as they plan my trip I hate to think of the final outcome. Nothing seems to worry them. They carry on—as they always have, including time out for tea. I can't figure them out at all. Perhaps it is me wanting to get started . . . .

I suppose you think London is about in ruins by now. We do have bombings each night and once in awhile in the daytime. However, the daytime bombings are negligible and everyone not out[on] the streets continue their work. I have not been in London after

---

[19]Miss L.D. Ziegler, an American civilian employed as clerk-stenographer in the Attaché's office.

[20]Mrs. M.G. Ripman, an American civilian employed as Principal stenographer in the Attaché's office. Later transferred to the Office of Naval Intelligence.

dark and still have no desire to go in to dinner or to watch the show. There is as much danger from the British schrapnel as from the German bombs . . . .

Personal Diary, 2-4 October 1940

2 Oct. Wednesday. In office all day. Attended meeting of Admiral Bailey's committee.[21] Admiral Ghormley, Count Austin, Date Clark[22] and myself. Home at 1800.

3 Oct. Thursday. In office all day. Gear I sent to *Hopkins* arrived including six suits of whites. What a surprise. In country at night.

4 Oct. Friday. In office during day—arriving as usual at 1000 and leaving at 1700—lunch at Claridges Causerie. Quite nice. In country at night.

Letter to Mrs. Wellings, 4 October 1940

Yesterday was a quiet day both in town and in the country. The weather was what we have been led to believe was typical London weather. Rain and fog were everywhere. It is damp rain and I can now see what they mean by London fog. Today, however, it has been cleared considerably but so far the sun has not been in evidence. I guess the German bombers have difficulty locating their positions in days like yesterday and today.

The nightly raids continue but the Germans apparently have been prevented from reaching the area around the Embassy because I can see no evidence of recent bombings. I still think the Germans are wrong in bombing London—at least the residential sections. Of course one has to consider that at night it is difficult to locate a definite objective and therefore some of the bombs are just errors in judgment when they land in residential areas. All in all I think the British are and can take it.

Personal Diary, 5-6 October 1940

5 Oct. Saturday. Holiday. Comdr. Mills and I walked to station for a paper. Met Scottie and Hodgson. Walked back to Ranleigh—inspected bomb crater nearby and then back to New Pipers. At 1300 Bill Ammon, who had duty called & said I was to pack and come to town immediately as I was on my way. Carried out orders arrived at Embassy at 1600. Called at Admiralty and received all the information. Took baggage to Houston station[23] in order to avoid bothering with baggage during blackout. Dinner with Bill, & Mr. & Mrs. Alcock at Claridges. Returned to Embassy immediately afterwards & then set sail for Houston station at 2120. Train due to leave at 2255. This

---

[21]Admiral Sir Sidney R. Bailey, K.B.E.,C.B.,D.S.O.,R.N. (1882-1942). Served as Chairman of an Admiralty committee established in 1940 that acted as a clearing house for requests from the Navy Department and the U.S. Naval Attaché in London as well as from the Admiralty and the British Naval Attaché in Washington.

"The discussions at the eleventh joint meeting, 2 October 1940, were largely technical, covering the various aspects of gunnery dealt with in Section XI of the Bailey Committee Report . . . . Particular emphasis was given to anti-aircraft gunnery. The officers of the Admiralty summarized their own experiences in the operations in the North Sea and Channel in the Spring of 1940. They strongly urged that the United States develop as large a production as possible of anti-aircraft guns and give special attention to tactics and to the training of personnel of the anti-aircraft batteries." [Tracy Kittredge] COMNAVEU Historical Monograph *U.S. British Naval Relations 1939-1942*, p. 226. Naval War College Archives, RG 23, Box 47, item B.

[22]Augustus Dayton Clark (1900-   ). U.S. Naval Academy, 1922. Assistant Naval Attaché, London. Later, Captain. Retired 1945.

[23]Euston Station serving the Midlands, Wales, Northeast England and Scotland via the west coast.

is my first night in town and I can't say that I enjoy it very much. The AA guns, planes overhead, plus the blackout just do not tend towards having any peace of mind. I was afraid I would have to walk to station—about a 30 minute walk—which did not appeal to me. After walking one block I decided to try to get a cab at Claridges—one block away—It is almost impossible to get a cab at night—I had good luck however and paid the cab driver one pound for a 2½ shilling ride. It was worth it. I just don't like dodging shrapnel at night—or at any other time for that matter. The R.T.O.[24] at station arranged for baggage to be put aboard train—very courteous officer. Train was 20 minutes late in leaving. Was glad to feel train pull out because a railroad station is not a healthy place to be during an air raid. Had sleeper accommodations and turned in immediately.

Sunday 6—October. Enroute to Scapa Flow. Train 5 hours late arriving at Perth (1500) transferred to train for Inverness. Train had dining car so that I was at last able to get some food. Arrived Inverness at 2000 where I stayed for night at the Station hotel. Dinner at 2100 & turned in at 2300.

Letter to Mrs. Wellings, 6 October 1940

. . . Please excuse the paper and writing. I am sitting in an arm chair which is not good for my Palmer method . . . .

I am now in a hotel having just come up from dinner. The time is 2230 and when I finish this note I must be to bed . . . . Tomorrow I will be up at 0530 and at 0640 underway again. I hope to reach my destination tomorrow afternoon . . . .

Darling please don't even think of worrying about me. This trip is nothing at all. Perhaps safer than being in London. As I said before I am looking forward to it with eager anticipation. You should have seen the hills and farms I passed today. It reminded me of New Hampshire. The fields were as green as could be and the air crisp and cool but not cold. I know now where the Scotch girls get their color . . . .

Personal Diary, 7 October 1940

Monday . . . . Left Inverness on 0640 train to Thurso, arriving at 1500 (1½ hours late). No boat today; consequently stayed overnight at Royal Hotel. Called on Captain Newcombe (RN)[25], Naval Control Officer at Thurso. He was extremely pleasant. Took Comdr. Halloran (RN)[26] and myself for drive in country. Saw Scottish Hills at first hand. Had a marvelous 4 hours with him. (One legged man who was more active than either Halloran or myself.) Almost shot a grouse, went walking through the heather.

---

[24]Railroad Transportation Officer.

[25]Percy Frederic Newcombe. naval Officer in Charge, Thurso. Retired 1927. Recalled to service.

[26]Charles Francis George Thomas Hallaran. Commander; retired.

CHAPTER THREE

DESTROYER DUTY: HMS *ESKIMO*
8 October-17 November 1940

Personal Diary, 8-12 October 1940
Tuesday, 8 October. Left Thurso by boat at 0930 arrived at Scapa Flo at 1230. Everyone was marvelous to me. Lunch with Rear Admiral of the Destroyer.[1] Reported on board *Eskimo* at 1500 when she returned to port. Comdr. Micklewaite (the C.O.)[2] very pleasant. Met all officers—a very fine group of men. Called on Capt. Caslon,[3] the flotilla commander and met Commanding Officers of other Tribals in port.

Wednesday, 9 Oct. U.W. [underway] screening *Furious*[4] 0800-1630, fueled upon arrival—on ½ notice until 2000 then on 1 hour notice, no luck in operations due to weather. Dinner with Captain, plus Capt. Lean[5] of the *Punjabi*[6].

Thursday, 10 October. A.A.[7] until 1745—then U.W. as guard ship on 15 min. notice. Zed one berth in Flow.

Friday, 11 October. U.W. at 0800 same operations as Wed. Better luck due to weather. On way home called for special duty out all night with two other DD's[8] searching for a submarine—NO LUCK.

Saturday, 12 October. Arrived in port at 1130—fueled, after which went to buoy. U.W. at 1800 acting as screen for *Furious, Norfolk* and *Berwick* on their way to off Tromso, for bombing expedition.

---

[1]Ronald Hamilton Curzon Hallifax (1885-1943). Rear Admiral (D), Commanding Home Fleet Destroyer Flotillas, 1938-41. Later Vice Admiral, 1942. Flag Officer Red Sea and Canal Area.

[2]St. John Aldrich Micklethwaite, D.S.O. with two bars (1901-1977). Later Rear Admiral, 1950; Flag Officer Gibraltar and Admiral Superintendent H.M. Dockyard.

[3]Clifford Caslon, C.B.E. Commander, 6th Destroyer Flotilla.

[4]H.M.S. *Furious. Courageous*-class Aircraft Carrier, former light battle cruiser, built 1916, 22,500 tons. 786' length overall, 90½' beam, 24' draft. Speed 30½ knots. Served in Home Fleet, 1939-44. Scrapped 1948.

[5]John Trevor Lean, D.S.O. (1903-1961). Later, Captain; Assistant Director Naval Equipment, Admiralty 1948; Commanding Officer, H.M.S. *Manxman*, 1951-53; Secretary, Royal Albert Yacht Club, 1954-61.

[6]H.M.S. *Punjabi. Tribal*-class Destroyer, Pennant number F. 21. Rammed and sunk in low visibility by the battleship H.M.S. *King George V* while escorting convoy PQ 15, 1 May 1942.

[7]Antiaircraft defense duty.

[8]Destroyers.

H.M.S. *Eskimo*

377½′ length overall, 36½′ beam, 9′ draft; 1870 tons, 36 knots. Complement 190 men. Armament 8-4.7 in., 4-2 pdr AA, 8-5 inch AA guns; 4-21″ Torpedo tubes Tribal Class Destroyer Pennant number F. 21. Launched 3 September 1937. Scrapped at Troon 27 June 1949. A detailed plan of this vessel has been published in Edgar J. Marsh, *British Destroyers* (London: Seeley, 1966), pp. 324-325.

[Photo: JHW Collection. Autographs of officers serving in *ESKIMO*, 17 November 1940.]

Letter to Mrs. Wellings, 12 October 1940

Today is "Columbus Day" and as I remember it is a holiday in Massachusetts. Please celebrate for me and have a cocktail before dinner and imagine I am with you with my usual greeting "Pretty good Navy . . . . "

How do the Boston papers write up the war these days? I suppose between the papers and the radio one would be lead to believe that London is in ruins and England is approaching desolation. Well Sweet just don't believe it. There has been damage of course but to my mind England is just getting started . . . .

Official Diary, [9] 12-14 October 1940

1800, 12 October, the 4 DD's steamed in column, distance 600 yards., speed 25K, from the fleet anchorage, through the swept channel and gates of the boom defense in order to explode any acoustic mines which may have been in the channel.

Upon clearing gates in defense booms, the 4 DD's took station for screening the 2 CA's [10] and 1 CV.[11] Formation as indicated below, speed 20, entire formation zigzagging.

Just before dark the formation was changed as follows: CV took guide, the DD's retained same screen but formed on CV, 1 CA took station 5 miles on starboard beam of CV, other CA took corresponding station on port beam of CV. Speed 20, cont. to zigzag, using a different plan. Weather conditions: sky overcast, visibility fair (just able to see silhouette of CV, distance about 3600 yds.). Sea on port quarter—destroyer rolled considerably.

13 October. At daylight unable to see the CA stationed on our port beam (visibility about 4 mi., sky overcast, heavy mist, low ceiling). On orders from O.T.C.,[12] the DD on port bow of CV made the collective call for the Raiding Force on 20" searchlight from port quarter to port bow; no answer. At 0700 speed changed to 15K. At 0800 received orders to search on port beam for missing CA. Searched for distance of 15 miles from track of guide without contact, then rejoined Raiding Force.

At 0900 did not make contact with the two DD's as planned. 0930 changed course 90 deg. to stbd; 1000 again changed course 90 deg. to stbd. O.T.C. apparently believed he was ahead and to westward of rendezvous. 1100 reversed course. Note: One of the CO's of the two DD's which were to rendezvous at 0900 afterwards told this observer that the two DD's were at the rendezvous on time (probably were since they had only 40 miles to steam) and that the missing CA was waiting for them. The CA and two DD's then steamed on the course to the next position at the speed of advance stated in the operation order (15K).

At 1230 O.T.C. ordered the destroyer squadron commander (Captain D to the British) to detach two DD's with orders to return to base. This observer was embarked in one of the two DD's ordered to return to base.

At 1315 intercepted radio message from O.T.C. ordering the missing CA and two DD's to rendezvous at 1800, giving the position of the rendezvous. (Note: This was the first break in radio silence.)

---

[9]Enclosure A to JHW's Report serial 1388 of 2 December 1940. "G.B. Operations in connection with aircraft raids on German Shipping and Military Land Objectives in Norway, 11-19 October 1940."

[10]Heavy cruisers.

[11]Aircraft carrier.

[12]Officer in Tactical Command.

ANTISUBMARINE SCREEN - DIAGRAM # 2

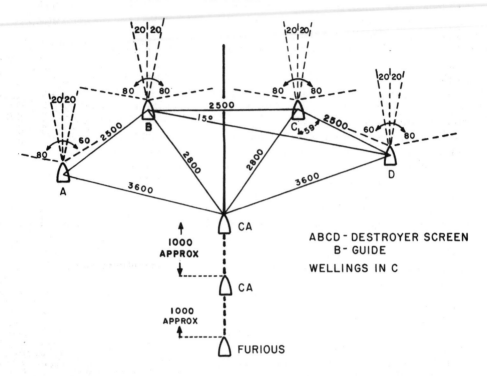

NOTE: Screen designed against long-range torpedo attacks when reliance can be placed on Asdic.[a] Not good
if SS[b] penetrates screen. Most efficient at speeds 15-18-above, according to British.
Angles ahead of each DD indicate Asdic sweep angles. Note the 20 deg. bow overlap.
British have only one Asdic on a DD.

---

[a]Abbreviation for an underwater sound detection device developed by the A[nti] S[ubmarine]
I[nvestigation] D[etection] C[ommittee]; Sonar.

[b]Submarine.

I was later informed by the DD squadron commander that contact was not made until
0900 the following day.

At 1400 the senior officer of the two DD's returning to base sent a radio message to
base giving estimated time of arrival and requesting certain navigation lights to be
turned on during designated periods of the night. (Note: No lights seen.)

At 0730, 14 October, sighted land. (Note: first fix since leaving port—37.5 hours.)

0930 arrived at base, went alongside tanker and fueled to 95% capacity and moored
at buoy. (Note: It is standard procedure to fuel upon arrival in port regardless of time of
day or amount of fuel required for 95% capacity.) . . .

Letter to Mrs. Wellings, 15 October 1940

I am still away on my trip. Everyone has been extremely courteous to me and I believe
I have made a few friends for my company. Of course I am asked all kinds of questions

about everything under the sun. Some, or rather the vast majority, are about my work but everyone always asks two questions which are not in my line. However, my reading of current events and listening to the convention speeches has been a big help.[13] Of course I do not know the answers, neither does anyone else, at this time. I do my best to give them both sides of the story with[out] stating a definite opinion. It really is a lot of fun.

By the way I have two requests from some of my friends. One is for Esquire magazine. Will you please buy a copy for the next few months and send it via the pouch. The other is halfway my own promise to the boys. They have ordered an ice cream freezer,—a 3 qt. hand cranking type. Will you please send some of the mix that comes in packages, enough for about a dozen makings, to me via the pouch. Be sure it has the instructions on how to make the cream. They like it better the way we make it.

My letters are being sent to the Embassy and air mailed from London. This will account for the London postmark. They have special service to London and have very kindly offered to send everything I want by this method.

Last night I saw a "flicker." It was preceded by a buffet supper of *lobster* which was excellent. We all had a very pleasant evening. The movie was titled "Another Thin Man"—William Powell and Myrna Loy. Gosh it was good to hear American voices and watch William Powell playing the smooth detective. Afterwards one of the big boys asked me to his room for *tea* and about five of us discussed our problems until 2400. Yes it was a very pleasant evening . . . .

Personal Diary, 15 October 1940
Tuesday . . . U.W. at 0730 exercises until 1230 . . . .

Report of an Asdic Exercise by a Tribal Class, British Destroyer[14]
1. (a) DATE [15] October 1940.
   (b) AREA Inside Scapa Flow.
   (c) DEPTH OF WATER 18-20 fathoms.
   (d) TEMPERATURE OF WATER 50°F (as indicated by destroyers injection temperature).
   (e) WATER CONDITIONS Excellent. (Flotilla ASDIC expert stated that the other destroyer taking part in this exercise was able to receive good echoes at 6000 yards.)
2. TYPE OF EXERCISE—Listed in ASDIC exercises as a practice designed for primary training of operators and control party.
3. SHIPS TAKING PART IN EXERCISE—1 SS and 2 DD.
4. DESCRIPTION OF EXERCISE. The submarine was required to steer a steady course with speed and depth optional. The submarine towed a small buoy with a flag on it (buoy about the size of an anchor buoy on a BB). The purpose of the buoy was to readily locate the submarine and thereby increase the number of attacks in the time available (0800-1230). Destroyers alternated making attacks. The procedure for each run was as follows: Captain took bearing of buoy and then ordered ASDIC operators to commence searching with limits of search about 40° on each side of bearing of

---

[13]During the 1940 Presidential election campaign, the Republican National Convention met at Philadelphia on 28 June and nominated Wendell L. Willkie. The Democratic National Convention met at Chicago on 15 July and nominated Franklin D. Roosevelt for a third term. Both major parties supported the national defense program, aid to Britain and defense of the Western Hemisphere, but opposed participation in a foreign war. Roosevelt won the election on 5 November.

[14]Report serial 1390 of 30 November 1940.

submarine. (Note: true bearings always used.) Destroyer started approach after ASDIC operators made contact. ASDIC officer on bridge (a reserve sub-lieutenant) informed Captain of courses to steer by means of indicator and when to drop depth charges by means of graphic plotter on bridge. (Note: ASDIC operators (2) located in a small sound proof compartment below the main deck directly under the bridge, i.e., three decks down.)

5. RESULTS OF EXERCISE

(a) As the ship was about to make its first run the transmission key went out of order. Ship unable to locate trouble. A boat was sent to the other destroyer and returned with the flotilla ASDIC expert (a lieutenant). After about an hour and a half the trouble (a burned out resistance) was located and repaired. Two attacks were then made but both were unsuccessful—according to the Captain. On the next attack the graphic plotter jammed just before reaching the firing point which prevented the completion of the attack. Two more attacks were conducted before the ship reached the limit of the training area. These attacks were also unsuccessful in the opinion of the Captain. The submarine was ordered to surface (time 2 hours and 11 minutes after the commencement of the exercise). In surfacing the submarine fouled a dan buoy (the only buoy within about a two mile radius) which caused about a 40 minute delay. About seven more attacks were made but the results were from fair to poor, according to the Captain (observer concurs).

(b) As a final phase of the training period the destroyer and submarine took initial stations about 5-6 miles apart. Destroyer steered a steady course, speed 21 knots. Submarine was informed before submerging of the destroyer's course and speed. The submarine steered an opposite course to the destroyer at any desired speed. Relative bearing of submarine from destroyer zero. The destroyer passed directly over submarine without hearing a single echo.

6. The effectiveness of the British ASDIC should not be judged by this report. The British place great reliance and confidence in the ASDIC which, one must presume, is based on results obtained. The purpose of this report is to show by factual reporting of a primary ASDIC exercise that the British ASDIC is not immune from mechanical failures, that it does require well trained operators plus a closely coordinated control party. In addition this report indicates that even when the ASDIC and operators plus control party are functioning smoothly the results obtained are at times as negative as the search conducted by the man mentioned in a recent Fleet Training report who, having lost his wallet in the Battery, was searching for it in Times Square because the light was better.

7. MISCELLANEOUS NOTES ON EXERCISE.

(a) Before the exercise the Captain stated that he was pleased to have an opportunity to show the observer an actual demonstration of the ASDIC. After the exercise he stated "Just one of those days when everything goes wrong."

(b) The British ASDIC is subject to wake interference. On several occasions the ASDIC operators reported contacts which were the wake of the other destroyer taking part in the exercise. This point was confirmed by the ASDIC expert who stated that it took considerable training on the part of the operators before they could differentiate between a wake and a real contact, particularly the wake of a ship turning.

(c) The submarine which took part in the exercise was an "H" class boat built in the U.S. during the last war. In conversation with the Captain of the submarine (a lieutenant) he stated that the boat must have been well built to still be able to operate. He was well pleased with his command saying that he was able to dive, fire torpedoes, and surface and that was all anyone could ask of a submarine.

(d) Prior to the commencement of the exercise the submarine cruised at periscope depth at low and at high speeds with one and then with two periscopes exposed about 3 feet. All the destroyer lookouts were on the bridge to observe the periscope(s).

(e) When the submarine was submerged the destroyer exploded below the surface 8 ounce charges of TNT[15] contained in a watertight clyindrical case in order to communicate with the submarine. The signals were as follows: one explosion—indicate your position, two explosions—dive deep and remain until further notice, three explosions—surface. The observer was informed that the submarine can hear these explosions at a distance of about 3 miles. Prior to surfacing the submarine fired 2 smoke bombs four minutes apart to indicate his course.

(f) The 8 ounce charge of cast TNT is contained in a brass or composition watertight cylindrical case 8¾″ long and 2⅝″ in diameter. On orders from the bridge these cases are towed from the stern, the end of the line has a 5 pound weight to aid in keeping the case below the surface. The firing circuit consisted of a 12 volt battery with a lead attached to the tow line of the cylindrical case. The TNT is exploded by means of a detonator and primer. The 8 ounces of TNT is in the form of a hollow cylindrical spool 2⅞″ long, outside diameter 2½″, inside diameter 1½″. Hollow cylindrical millboard distance pieces 1⅞″ long are inserted above and below the TNT and separated from the latter by felt washers.

Official Diary, 15-19 October 1940

ANTISUBMARINE SCREEN - DIAGRAM #3

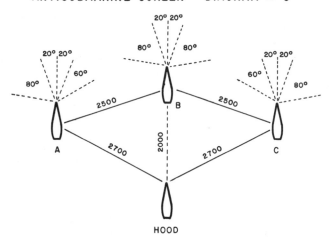

ABC - DESTROYER SCREEN
WELLINGS IN B

NOTE: This screen used when reliance can be placed on ASDIC. [Lines] from DD's indicate ASDIC sweeps. Note 20° bow overlap.

---

[15]An explosive compound, Trinitrotoluene.

ZIGZAG PLAN	TIME	AMT. & DIRECTION TO CHANGE	DEVIATION FROM BASE COURSE
	0	0	0
	6	22.5 R	22.5 R
	15	22.5 L	0
	21	22.5 L	22.5 L
	30	22.5 R	0
	36	22.5 L	22.5 L
	45	22.5 R	0
	51	22.5 R	22.5 R
	60	22.5 L	0

NOTE: The first course of the zigzag is always that course corresponding to zero time regardless of what time during the hour the signal to commence zigzagging is executed.

15 October . . . . Upon completion of exercise fueled as near to capacity as possible and immediately joined two other DD's in harbor, proceeded through swept channel and gates of boom defense in column, distance 600 yards., speed 25K.

Upon clearing gates in boom defense, formed an A/S[16] screen on HOOD, as indicated. Speed 18K, formation zigzagging.

Outside the entrance of the base the formation passed a battle raft (very similar to ours) being towed on an approx. parallel course at a speed of about 8K, range about 11000 yds. The HOOD opened fire at this target alternating with A and B turrets. Each salvo consisted of *one gun*. Time of flight by stop watch, 16-17 seconds. Splashes appeared fairly close to target but no direct hits were observed. Smoke and fire at muzzle of gun appeared much heavier than our 16″ guns. A total of about 20 rounds were fired. Formation cont. its course and speed as though no firing had occurred.

Just prior to darkness the HOOD informed the DD's that it was enroute to act as a Covering Force for the Raiding Force. This supposedly was the first information the DD's had of the intentions of the B.C.[17] (Note—The HOOD was not mentioned in the original operation orders.) Positions which the HOOD intended to pass through were given to the DD's. Just before dark speed increased to 20K. Formation cont. to zigzag all night. Course not changed after dark. Sky overcast, visibility about 2.5 mi. (Note—2400 this date, 15 October, was zero time for Raiding Force to conduct aircraft attacks. Distance between Covering Force and Raiding Force approx. 800 mi.)

16 October. Steaming as before. Sky overcast, low ceiling, visibility 5 mi. At 0600 decreased speed to 16K and changed zigzag plan to as follows:

TIME	AMT. & DIRECTION TO CHANGE	DEVIATION FROM BASE COURSE
0	0	0
5	30 L	30 L
15	30 R	0
20	30 R	30 R
30	30 L	0

---

[16]Antisubmarine.

[17]Battle Cruiser.

TIME	AMT. & DIRECTION TO CHANGE	DEVIATION FROM BASE COURSE
35	30 R	30 R
45	30 L	0
50	30 L	30 L
	30 R	0

NOTE: The first course to be steered is always that course corresponding to zero time, regardless of what time during the hour the signal to commence zigzagging is executed.

At 1830 visibility reduced to about 1 mi. Screen closed the HOOD without signal but maintained their relative bearings. Stopped zigzagging and reduced speed to 13K. The DD squadron commander cautioned the DD's not to lose sight contact. ASDIC used on several occasions to check bearing and distance of squadron commander. At 2200 visibility increased to about 2 miles. The DD's increased distance from the HOOD.

17 October. Steaming as before. At 0200 visibility decreased to about 800 yds. DD's formed column astern of HOOD, distance 300 yds. Fog buoy or searchlight not used. The HOOD had a very strong light at stern (looked like a cargo light). The DD's used their regular fog light which is mounted on the rail at the after end of after deck house.

At 0800 visibility increased to 1 mi., with DD's forming screen on HOOD at reduced distances. Commander B.C. one[18] in HOOD estimated that contact might be made with Raiding Force at any time and if contact were not made by 1300 that he intended to reverse course. All ships practiced firing a few rounds from each Pom-pom and .5" M/G.[19]

1300—did not make contact with Raiding Force, course reversed (Lat. 69 deg. N.) and destroyers ordered to take station astern of HOOD. Visibility reduced to 400 yds. One DD had considerable difficulty in forming column but, with aid of the HOOD's whistle, plus all searchlights from the other two DD's, regained station. Speed increased to 15K. The HOOD stopped fog whistle after the DD's were formed astern. Fog buoys not used. All ships used their regular fog light near the stern and, in addition, searchlights were used at intervals when visibility was about 50-100 yds.

At 1600 changed course and increased speed to 17K. Informed by Comdr. B.C. one in HOOD that at 1600 Raiding Force was 70 mi., bearing 65 deg. T from our 1600 reference position and that the O.T.C. of the Raiding Force was informed of our 1600 reference position, course and speed. Therefore, radio silence must have been broken by both Raiding and Covering Forces. Intercepted radio message from the Admiralty stating that one British plane had landed in Lapland early previous morning and was interned. Plane probable one from carrier with Raiding Force.

18 October. Steaming as before. Heavy fog all night. DD's in column astern of HOOD. At 0700 fog lifted sufficiently to permit visibility of about 3 mi. DD's took station in screen at reduced distances. 0730 fog closed in again. DD's took station in column. 1230 visibility increased to one mile. DD's took station in screen at reduced distances. 1330 received message from HOOD that Phase 2 was cancelled and that the HOOD and 3 DD's would return to port. Two of the 3 DD's which left port previous day had been ordered to escort tanker back to base, the other DD was to reinforce Raiding

[18]Commander Battle Cruiser Squadron One. VADM Sir William Jock Whitworth KCB,CB,DSO (1884-1973). Later, Second Sea Lord, 1941-44; Admiral 1943; C-in-C, Rosyth, 1944. Retired 1946.

[19]Machinegun.

Force screen. 1430 weather conditions improving, visibility about 5 mi., commenced zigzagging.

19 October. Steaming as before. Informed by HOOD that arrangements had been made for the HOOD to conduct one A/A practice and one broadside practice prior to entering port. A/A later cancelled, due to low ceiling. Broadside practice conducted just outside base.

Note: HOOD now has 14-4" A/A guns for broadside battery; 3 twins on each side plus 1 center line twin.

Speed of HOOD during practice, 20K. DD's continued to act as A/S screen. Target a battle raft about 2/3 size of ours. Target course about parallel to course of HOOD. Target speed about 5K. Port broadside firing range about 7000 to 8000 yds. Salvo interval, 7-9 seconds; number of salvos, 10. All but two salvos at least 500 yds. over and to right of target. Two salvos were in line about 200 yds. short. Starboard broadside range 5000-6000 yds. Salvo interval, 6-9 seconds; number of salvos, 10. First salvo landed about 800 yds. short. Target was not crossed until the seventh salvo, which was off in deflection.

Note: The observer was on the starboard bow of the HOOD, distance about 4000 yds., an excellent position to observe the starboard broadside firing.

At 1230, 19 October, the HOOD and 3 DD's returned to base. The 3 DD's again formed column, distance 600 yds., and proceeded at 25K through the gates in the boom defense and the swept channel. As usual, the DD's immediately went alongside a tanker for fuel.

Personal Diary, 20 October 1940

Sun[day] . . . Entered Floating dock to repair leaks in oil tanks.

Letter to Mrs. Wellings, 20 October 1940

. . . Everything is peaceful and quiet today except for the weather which is overcast as usual. However one must expect a little bad weather particularly in this country which is noted for bad weather.

I am still in the best of health—thank God. As I have said before in my letters, I haven't had even a slight cold since my arrival in England. As I promised before I left home, I have endeavored to take good care of myself and will continue to do so. After all one's health is important. Besides I want to arrive home in the pink of condition. I have had to watch my eating because I find that the English eat much more than we do, and in addition more often.

I find their habits quite interesting. It is remarkable how they differ from ours when after all we have many things in common. For example, they have fish (herring) for breakfast. They eat their oranges at the end of breakfast. They use jams, marmalade and other preserves in much larger quantities than we do. Their cup of coffee contains almost 50% of *hot* milk—they call it white coffee. Their afternoon tea really is a small meal. Tea in general is used like we consume coffee, etc. etc. Oh yes, they use their forks in the left hand, knife in right hand as a pusher for the fork. The knife is always in use. Of course they eat with the fork in the left hand. I could go on and on. I really have a lot of fun observing the little peculiarities—so we think—in their eating and mannerisms in general. Personally I will always prefer our way of doing things.

How is the presidential election coming along. I miss reading the American papers and listening to the radio speeches. By now the campaign must be swinging into its final stages. I have no idea what has been said or promised by either candidate . . . .

I don't suppose Willkie has been able to force the president into campaigning. Viewing the situation from this end I believe it is good strategy on his part. With the international situation as it is I believe it will be particularly difficult to defeat the president. By all means send me the papers the day after election so that I can see how the various parts of the country votes. Also the issue of Time magazine the week after the election. You see I want to keep up on our affairs because I have to discuss and am asked many questions on how we run our government and what we think and why.

Personal Diary, 21-23 October 1940
Mon. 21 In Floating dock (letter from Dolly!!)
Tues. 22 " , Stayed at Rear Admiral at Scapa's[20] Home
Wed. 23 " , Dinner again with Rear Admiral at Scapa. The show at Lyness.

Letter to Mrs. Wellings, 25[23] October 1940
I am still away on my original trip. Really I am almost enjoying myself, that is, I am as happy as is possible without you and our little angel. We have a little hard work but there are moments of relaxation.

Yesterday morning I went on an inspection trip in a fine automobile around the surrounding countryside. It was extremely interesting to see this part of the country. Afterwards I made a few detailed inspections in our area and then went to the big Boss' house for dinner and to spend the night. The RA,[21] his two aides and myself had a very interesting evening discussing America and its many differences in the manner of living when compared to England. One of the aides went to the Harvard Business School and the RA was in Washington for three years.

As you know the English like to keep their houses very cold. They think we are crazy the way we have central heating which makes the house too warm. When I was shown my room by the house boy, the room was quite cold with the windows opened. The fireplace was already to light. I looked longingly at the fireplace and the boy understood because he returned in a moment and lighted the fire. In about two hours the room was very comfortable. By the time I went to bed (2330) the red glow from the ashes (they use coal) was extremely restful to the eyes and gave the room that touch of hospitality which makes one feel happy. Darling if you were only with me!!!!!!

After a fine breakfast this morning I was driven back to work. I will again be a dinner guest at the same house at the same place. Afterwards we will attend a smoker at the auditorium. The show is called "Mixed Grill" as every different branch will contribute to the performance. I am anticipating a few good laughs.

Two nights ago at 2345 I was endeavoring to get Lowell Thomas on his 0645 broadcast. While searching the short wave band I heard an American dance orchestra just starting to play "I'll Never Smile Again." It made funny feelings run up and down my spinal column and I immediately thought of our trip to the farm on that excessively hot day when I was on leave, Remember? . . . .

Personal Diary, 24 October 1940
Thurs . . . .Emergency undocking due to Mendip[22] and went alongside Maidstone.[23]

---

[20]Patrick Macnamara (1886-1957). Rear Admiral Scapa. Naval Attaché to United States, 1931. Later K.B.E., 1946.

[21]Rear Admiral.

[22]H.M.S. Mendip. Hunt-class, Type I, Escort Destroyer. Pennant Number L. 60. 907 tons. Later Chinese (Nationalist). Lin Fu (1948); Egyptian, Mohammed-Ali-El-Kebir, (1950); Ibrahim-el Awal (1951).

[23]Submarine depot ship, H.M.S. Maidstone. Pennant Number F. 44. Built 1937.

Report of Explosion on board H.M.S. Mendip (Hunt Class DD)[24]

TYPE OF SHIP:—Hunt class (DD) destroyer, commissioned about 3 October 1940 and sent to Scapa Flow for working up.

TIME:—24 October 1940, at 1135.

PLACE:—Training area inside Scapa Flow.

CIRCUMSTANCES:—Ship engaged in ASDIC training exercise with submerged submarine.

DAMAGE:—Stern blown off.

CASUALTIES:—5 killed, 6 seriously wounded, 3 with minor injuries.

CAUSE:—Unknown at this time. Board of Inquiry convened to determine cause.

TIME TO EFFECT REPAIRS:—About 2 months in the opinion of the man in charge of repairs at the Floating Dock.

GENERAL:—The possibility of explosion being caused by a mine is discounted since the stern tube struts were not damaged, shafting apparently not badly out of line, propellers and rudder not damaged and ship was able to steam at a slow speed after explosion. There was no aircraft warning at the time, the visibility was good (for a change). No aircraft were seen nor heard. This leads one to believe that there is a possibility that the explosion was due to some internal cause. Depth charges are stored on the main deck aft with pistols supposedly in the safe position. Depth charges are also stored just below the main deck aft without pistols. There is also a detonator locker aft below the main deck separated by another compartment from the depth charges.

Small 8 ounce charges of TNT are fitted into brass cases and exploded below the surface when it is desired to communicate with the submarine below the surface during Asdic exercises.

The ESKIMO was in the floating dock to repair leaks in oil tanks when the explosion occurred. Bolts and nuts were immediately substituted for missing rivets, the bottom left half painted, stern tube fairwaters not replaced as the ship was floated in order to dock the MENDIP. As the MENDIP entered the dock a thwartship bulkhead carried away aft flooding a large compartment. The dock master said afterwards that due to the sudden settling by the stern plus about a 5° list that he was lucky to save the ship.

About a week after the explosion this observer talked with the captain of the MENDIP who said that there was no doubt in his mind that the explosion was caused by one of the 8 ounce charges of TNT exploding one of the depth charges.

It is of interest to note that the MENDIP had only been commissioned three weeks with, of course, the majority of the crew composed of recent enlistments and the petty officers advanced to higher ratings due to the shortage of experienced men. It is another example which indicates that while in war time our standards of efficiency should be higher than in peace time actually the ships are much less efficient in war time, due to the rapid expansion of the Navy.

The MENDIP was in the floating drydock from 24 October to 11 November at which time it was towed south for repairs.

Personal Diary, 25-27 October 1940

Fri. 25—Alongside Maidstone until 1600—fueled back to mooring at 1900. Dinner on Hood.

Sat. 26—AA until 1800—then zed 1 berth in Flow.

---

[24]Report serial 1391 of 30 November 1940.

Sun. 27—Return to mooring at 0900—AA rest of day—Dinner with R.A. of DD's.[25]

Naval Message Received 26 October 1940
From: R.A.D.
To: Dido · Curacoa · Quorn · Maidstone
        Eskimo · Lt. Comdr. Wellings
        R.P.C. Dinner tomorrow Sunday 1945 monkey jacket and bow tie.

Letter to Mrs. Wellings, 27 October 1940
. . . my only worry at this moment is to borrow a wing collar and a bow tie to wear at a special dinner to which I have been invited this evening. I left mine in London. Now I find that my friends wear this combination with their regular clothes in lieu of dress clothes at special dinners—some of them wear this combination each evening. However, the RPC (Request pleasure of your company) stated this as uniform. My friends are fiends for using initials. My reply for example was WMP stating the time, place and uniform. (WMP being "with much pleasure")

Personal Diary, 28 October-1 November 1940
Mon. 28—U.W. at 1000—screening *Hood, Repulse & Furious*—in search of a raider or merchantman reported. Dashed northward and patrolled between Faroes and Iceland. No luck—Quite rough.
Tues. 29-Thurs. 31—Same as Monday. Returned to Scapa at 1400 on Thursday. Fueled and then to buoy at 1630 (3 letters from Dolly—Happy.)
Friday 1 Nov.—Alongside *Greenwich*[26] for repairs to shell plating caused by storm.

Letter to Mrs. Wellings, 1-2 November 1940
Sorry sweet I was unable to continue this letter yesterday. I had to go out for dinner with my boss and we did not return until 2430 the latest I have been out for a long time. It was at "Bugs" Eller's place[27]—you remember my classmate who was on duty at the N.A.[28] . . .
I could go on and on about current events but of course I would not be using proper decorum at this time. I have had many interesting discussions since my trip started. I really should have taken a course in constitutional law because I have had to explain our system of government at least a dozen times. It is also interesting to get the viewpoint of the British on our country, its business and government methods. Believe me one has to be diplomatic. Well Darling I have raved on and on. This will be the only letter I have written this week due to the circumstances. The time is now 1000 on the second. I want to get this letter off before I start on a very short trip after noon today. In about 10 minutes I expect Lt. Comdr. Hartman[29] to call and spend the day with me. He left the states about the same time I did but up to now I have not had a chance to see him.

[25]RADM R.H.C. Hallifax.

[26]H.M.S. *Greenwich*, Destroyer depot ship at Scapa Flow, 1939-41. Pennant number F. 10. Built 1915.

[27]In late 1940 LCDR E.M. Eller, USN, was an observer in H.M.S. *Norfolk* and H.M.S. *Hood*.

[28]U.S. Naval Academy, Annapolis.

[29]Kenneth Pendleton Hartman (1902-1966). U.S. Naval Academy 1923; Naval War College, 1949; Assistant Naval Attaché, London; Later Captain.

Personal Diary, 2-3 November 1940

Saturday . . . Underway at 0730—Screened Furious—then worked with South-ampton against high speed targets—Southampton fired. Hartman aboard. Returned to buoy at 2330.

Sunday . . . At anchor *all day*—inspected by RAD at 1100. Sailing in p.m.—Dinner on *Southampton* at night.

Letter to Mrs. Wellings, 2[3] November 1940

Lt Comdr. Hartman came over to see me yesterday at 1015 and stayed until 2330 last night. He is in the class of '23 . . . . We had a grand time talking things over in general and comparing notes (verbal). He is a fine officer in every way. I had not seen him for at least seven years up to yesterday. He has picked up the English accent and manners very quickly. I do hope I am not doing too much of the same thing because unless one is very clever the accent and mannerisms do not seem natural and therefore I believe it is better not to attempt to imitate the English too much . . . .

Tell Anne that Daddy will bring home a red and yellow boat for his little girl. Also a Scotch outfit including the skirt if I can find one in Edinburgh. I intend to stop there on my return to London and hope to have a full day to look around. In addition to seeing the city I want to arrange my train schedule so that I will arrive in London during daylight. If I came straight through I would arrive at night which is quite inconvenient in more ways than one. I will look over the famous Scotch town and see what it looks like. I am really fortunate to have such an opportunity to return as I please with no fixed schedule and all expenses paid by good old Uncle Sam.

Uncle Sam incidentally is one grand man. One does not appreciate it until he sees the way conditions are in England. I don't mean that conditions are bad but we have so much more comfort and opportunities than the people here. In other words, the more one sees of the rest of the world the more one appreciates the good old U.S.A. . . .

Personal Diary, 4 November 1940

Underway with *Furious* in a.m. then worked with *Southampton* rest of day until 2330 at night. Quite interesting to watch the firings. Mail from Dolly and home—quite happy.

Report on Night Encounter Exercise and throw off firing by British Cruiser Southampton *and Destroyer* Eskimo[30]

. . .

2. This observer was in the destroyer which acted as target ship for these firings and was impressed with the informality with which the practices were arranged and the expeditious manner with which they were carried out.

3. The afternoon of the day before the firings ESKIMO was assigned as target ship. That evening the Captain and the observer dined aboard the SOUTHAMPTON.[31] Following dinner the gunnery officer explained and gave us copies of the procedures. The Captain of the destroyer expressed a desire to fire a throw off practice with the SOUTHAMPTON as target and the following morning called on his squadron commander and received permission to fire the same practices with the C.A. acting as target. The DD was limited to 18 rounds for the throw off practice and 18 starshell for the night encounter practice. (DD's have a quarterly allowance of target ammunition.)

---

[30]Report serial 1383 of 1 December 1940.

[31]The gunnery exercises reported on here took place on 2 and 4 November. This is the dinner on 1 November.

4. COMMENT ON CA'S THROW OFF FIRING:

a) The procedure was carried out. The DD changed course several times during the practice; some of these course changes were 30-40 deg.

b) The DD raked[32] the fall of shot and acted as spotter for the C.A. in range since the result of each salvo was immediately sent via radio to the firing ship. It is doubted, however, if these spots arrived on time, due to the usual trouble with communications. The "T" of the rake was mounted on and parallel to one of the guns of "B" mounting. The gun was offset 6 deg. from the director. The director trained on the firing ship with B gun following the director in train.

c) Salvo interval, 8-12 seconds.

d) It is understood that the larger ships have a 6 deg. offset prism in special binoculars which places the splashes on the target, but that very few spotters get good results using these binoculars.

e) Accurate analysis of such firings is not practicable but this form of practice is desirable when target services are not available. There were no transfers of observers, no observers at any guns or fire control stations.

f) From the best information available the SOUTHAMPTON opened up about 1500 yds. short, crossed the target on the seventh salvo and straddled with about four or five salvos.

5. "ESKIMO" THROW OFF FIRING:

a) Same procedure as SOUTHAMPTON except that 3 two-gun salvos were fired from A, B and Y mount in succession.

b) First salvo fired at best gun range but with deflection of 2 R. added to the range keeper deflection. The second salvo was fired at the same range but with a deflection of 2 L. applied to the range keeper deflection (Std. practice). The spots indicated that second salvo straddled from then on few, if any, hits were obtained, due to errors in applying the spots. Salvo interval 10-15 seconds.

c) Casualties—1 gun of A mount miss-fired but gun fired on next salvo.

6. "SOUTHAMPTON" NIGHT ENCOUNTER PRACTICE:

a) Procedure carried out.

b) On each run one searchlight was turned on and immediately followed by a salvo of 2 starshell, with same deflection. As many as 8 starshell were burning at the same time, all within a very small deflection spread. Starshell burned for about an average time of 40 seconds. Several duds were noticed. The difference in the rate of descent between various starshell was particularly noticeable.

c) The SOUTHAMPTON's searchlight remained pointed at the ESKIMO's bridge during all the firing. It was impossible to see the direction in which the SOUTHAMPTON was heading during this period. All that could be seen was the searchlight which, of course, gave an excellent point of aim. On the last run the starshell burst directly overhead the destroyer. The bridge personnel donned their tin hats. Several flares fell very close aboard.

d) . . . when the destroyer was on the disengaged side and the firing ship used its searchlight, the firing ship was silhouetted quite plainly, sufficient to give a good point of aim to permit ranging, but not sufficiently illuminated to permit accurate spotting for shellfire. When the firing ship used starshell the silhouette was even better, but it is necessary for the destroyer to be in line with the firing ship and the starshell.

When the DD was on the engaged side the ship was plainly visible with an excellent point of aim, accurate ranging and spotting possible. The SOUTHAMPTON

---

[32]A "rake" is a mechanical-optical device used by an observer to assist him in estimating the distance by which gunfire misses a surface target.

was much easier to see when the short fuse setting was used. It is understood that the special short fuse settings were 3000 yds. and the regular short fuse settings were 5000 yds.

7. "ESKIMO" NIGHT ENCOUNTER PRACTICE:

A search spread of 8 deg. was employed by firing 4 one-gun salvos from the 4" H.A.[33] A/A gun; each salvo spread 2 deg. None of these salvos was over the target although searchlight was turned on target before starshell were fired. It is believed that this was due to miscalculation in the deflection. Second run was better than first run, particularly in regard to searchlight control.

8. DESTROYER METHOD OF COMPUTING DEFLECTION FOR STAR-SHELL—the following method is used:

a) *Parallax*—1 deg. towards the bow for every 5K of own speed across the line of fire.

b) *Change of Bearing*—Enemy's relative speed across line of fire in knots divided by the range in thousand of yards, the result applied in deg. in direction of enemy's relative speed.

c) *Windage*—1 deg. to windward for every unit of Beaufort scale of true wind across line of fire.

d) Add (a), (b) and (c) algebraically.

Note: Foregoing obtained from Destroyer Gunnery Manual.

No attempt is made to set the fuse settings of the starshell immediately before firing as it is not considered practical. Two groups of starshell are at the gun. One group has the fuses set for 5000 yds., the other for 7000 yds. The starshell control officer designates the group to be used; 2000' is considered the best height at which the starshell should burst.

9. The TRIBAL Class destroyers have one 24" searchlight to illuminate gunnery targets. This searchlight is remotely controlled from searchlight directors on the bridge (one on each side). *The arc is struck and shutters opened by remote control from each side of the bridge.*

10. SOUTHAMPTON'S TARGET PRACTICE DESIGNED FOR USE AGAINST E-BOATS:

Towing ship: Destroyer ESKIMO.

Target: A small double metal float designed for use in mine-sweeping; regular target not specified. Any type of float which can be towed at 24K is used. All that is desired is a point of aim. Destroyer steamed at 24K on a steady course; 600 yd. *wire* tow line (float would not surface with 1000 yd. tow line; manila line not available). SOUTHAMPTON *steamed on an opposite course, speed 24K, range abeam 2000 yds.*

RUN 1—Broadside of A/A guns; shells fused to burst at range of target; 5 salvos fired.

RUN 2—Same as Run 1 except the two forward 6" turrets were fired.

RUN 3—Two forward 6" turrets, broadside of A/A guns (about 5 salvos from each) and all close-range weapons. All the above guns opened fire simultaneously.

11. The above firings were very interesting to watch from the destroyer, particularly the third run. The bursts from the turrets and A/A guns were about 30 yds. above the water and about from 100 short to 100 over. They considered these bursts too high. The SOUTHAMPTON opened fire each run when the target was about 20 deg. forward of the beam. The same type of practice was scheduled for after dark but after

---

[33]High Altitude.

two runs of illuminating the target with searchlights and starshell the SOUTHAMPTON decided that it was too difficult to see the target and the practice was postponed unitl a later date when a better point of aim target will be used.

Personal Diary, 5 November 1940

Tuesday . . . Scheduled exercises with *Furious* cancelled. AA until 1700 when underway for zed one berth in Flow. At 2200 underway to search for *Admiral Von Scheer* which has just been reported as attacking a convoy in North Atlantic. Acted on screen for *Hood, Repulse,* and two CLs[34] + 5 other DDs.

Naval Messages Received on board H.M.S. ESKIMO 5 November 1940[35]

1. From: Rear Admiral Scapa
   To: All ships (by visual)
         52.45N-32.13W RANGITIKI (merchant ship 16,698 gross T) gunned by GRAF SPEE Class
         T.O.O.[36] 1955 - T.O.R.[37] 2003.

2. From: C-in-C[38] Home Fleet (in NELSON at Scapa—arrived today)
   To: REPULSE and HOOD (visual)
         Raise steam with all dispatch (HOOD and REPULSE at Scapa)
         T.O.O. 2013 - T.O.R. 2015.

3. From: C-in-C Home Fleet
   To: Home Fleet Company (visual)
         HOOD, REPULSE, NAIAD, BONAVENTURE, PHOEBE and six TRIBAL Class DD's raise steam with all dispatch.
         T.O.O. 2020 - T.O.R. 2025.

4. From: Armed merchant cruiser—JERVIS BAY (500 KC)[39]—14164 gross tons
   To: Any British Man of War
         1 B C 328 - 12 - 208 Y Z U R 15[40]
         One battleship bearing 328, dist. 12 miles, course 208 from position indicated
         Note: JERVIS BAY is an armed merchant cruiser escorting Halifax convoy HX84.
         T.O.O. *1706* - T.O.R. 2031
         Note: Time of origin is zone time. The corresponding Zone—1 time (British daylight) is 2006. Sunset in Long. of JERVIS BAY 1631 with about 1 hour of twilight.

---

[34]Light cruisers.

[35]Enclosure A to JHW's Report serial 1330 of 26 November 1940.

[36]Time of Origination.

[37]Time of Receipt.

[38]Commander in Chief.

[39]Radio frequency, 500 kilocycles.

[40]Encoded signal translated on the following line.

5. From: Rear Admiral Destroyers Home Fleet
   To: D4 and D6[41]
   Raise steam for full speed with dispatch
   T.O.O. 2016 - T.O.R. 2042.

6. During above dispatches ESKIMO, a TRIBAL Class DD, was anchored in Z1 berth (ready berth) just inside of Novi Skeery boom in Scapa Flow.

7. From: Admiralty
   To: H.M.S. FOLKESTONE (ocean escort for a convoy of 14 ships in a position about 100 miles SE from HX84)
   Enemy raider GRAF SPEE Class attacking HX84 in position 52-45N; 32-13W—steer to southward.
   T.O.R. 2019.
   Note: Above dispatch cancelled by Admiralty at 2132.

8. From: CORNISH CITY (a merchant ship) 4952 gross tons
   To: Broadcast on 500 KC
   RRRR 52-50N; 32-15W—Shelled—T.O.R. 2005.

9. From: SAVAC (a merchant ship of 6,700 gross T)
   To: Portishead Radio
   Raider apparently GRAF SPEE Class is attacking ships one by one leisurely about (portions of dispatch missed, message uncompleted as indicated by an operator's signal)—T.O.R. 2140.

10. From: Rear Admiral Destroyers (at Scapa)
    To: Fourth Flotilla of DD's at Scapa
    Be ready to slip at 2020.
    T.O.O. 2155 - T.O.R. 2204.

11. From: BEAVERFORD (merchant ship of 10,042 gross T)
    To: Broadcast on 500 KC
    Shelled 52-26N; 32-34W.—T.O.O. 1945 - T.O.R. 2254.

12. From: Admiralty
    To: All ships
    Pocket battleship VON SCHEER operating in No. Atlantic. Last known position at 2003 (Zone-1), 5 Nov. Lat. 52-50—Long. 32-15.
    T.O.R. 2030.

13. From: C-in-C Home Fleet
    To: AUSTRALIA (in the Clyde)
    Raise steam and rendezvous as ordered by Comdr. Battle Cruiser Squadron One (in HOOD).

14. From: Admiralty
    To: H.M.S. LEWIS, LINCOLN, LUDLOW (Info. C-in-C Home Fleet,

---

[41]Destroyer Flotilla Four and Six.

C-in-C West Indies)
Close convoy HX84 in position 52-57N; 32-23W., rescue survivors and attack BB by night if opportunity occurs.

Official Diary, 5-6 November 1940
[5 Nov.] At 2230 ESKIMO under way from ready berth inside Nevi Skeery boom gate and layed to. 2300 ordered to pass through Nevi Skeery and Hoxa gates and rendezvous outside gates with other DD's which passed through the Switha gate. Hoxa gate jammed, returned to inside the Flow. 2330 Hoxa gate cleared, joined other DD's. 2400 HOOD, REPULSE, PHOEBE (CL), BONAVENTURE (CL), NAIAD (CL), cleared Hoxa gate and slowed to 9K to stream paravanes.

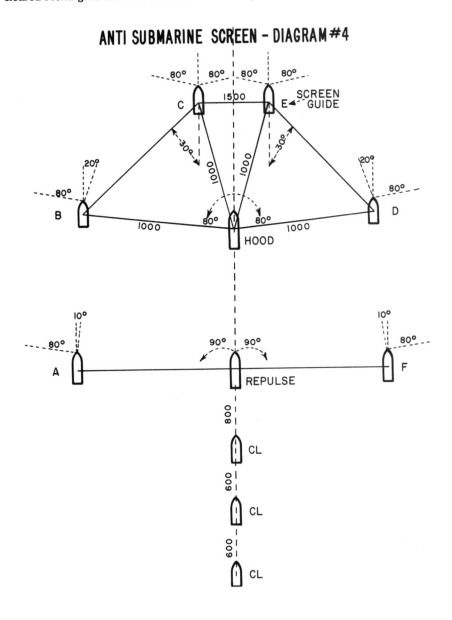

ANTI SUBMARINE SCREEN - DIAGRAM #4

At 0030, 6 Nov. formed A/S screen on HOOD, REPULSE and three cruisers as indicated. Speed 17K. Note: sea calm, night clear.

Dotted lines ahead of DD's indicate ASDIC sweeps. No bow overlap. Observer in Destroyer "D." [See Diagram #4]

At 0100 cleared entrance to Pentland Firth (passed line between Dunett Head and Torness)[42]. 0115 C.C.[43] to 273 and formed screen as indicated below:

ANTISUBMARINE SCREEN — DIAGRAM #5

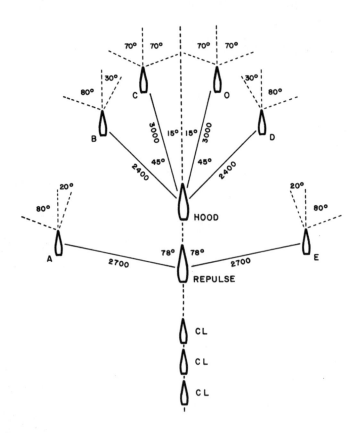

Naval Messages Received, 6 November 1940

From: Comdr. B.C.S.1
To: Ships present (Bat Cru Force)
        It is my intention to pass through 58-40N, 07-30W, then through 55-00N, 13-00W and then down the 13-00 meridian to Lat. 50-00, after which cover the approaches to Brest and Eire. This force will be addressed as Battle Cruiser Force. Air escort expected from dawn on sixth. The battleships

---

[42]Dunnet Head to the South and Tor Ness on the island of Hoy, Orkney Islands.

[43]Changed course.

(NELSON AND RODNEY) will operate between the Faroes and Iceland.
T.O.R. 0236.

Note: This is the only operation order received from the O.T.C.

From: C-in-C Home Fleet
To: NELSON, RODNEY, SOUTHAMPTON, plus six DD's (all at Scapa)
Be ready to sail at 0600, 6 Nov.

From: AUSTRALIA
To: Comdr. B.C.S.1—Info. C-in-C Home Fleet
Have turbine trouble, probably broken blading. Must defer sailing and
examine. Will make further report later.
T.O.O. 0606—T.O.R. 0722.

Note: The FURIOUS is also at Scapa with a machinery derangement which
limits her speed to 23K, also a rudder casualty of some kind. C-in-C Home
Fleet early yesterday recommended docking FURIOUS for three days.
Believe FURIOUS would be of great help in conducting search.

Official Diary, 6 November 1940

0629-CC to 243. 0830 commenced zigzagging as follows: increased speed to 18K;
wind increasing; storm forecasted:

TIME	AMT. and DIRECTION to CHANGE	DEVIATION from BASE COURSE
60	22.5 L	0
51	22.5 R	22.5 R
45	22.5 R	0
36	22.5 L	22.5 L
30	22.5 R	0
21	22.5 L	22.5 L
15	22.5 L	0
6	22.5 R	22.5 R
0	0	0

Naval Messages Received, 6 November 1940

From: Admiralty
To: Comdr. B.C.S.1
HX84 consisted of 38 ships, 8½ convoy; escort JERVIS BAY. Another
convoy of 14 ships, 6.5K escorted by FOLKESTONE in Lat. 51-40, Long.
31-30, steering toward 53-30N; 30-25W.

From: Admiralty
To: Six former U.S. DD's
Steer Tory Island (?) and spread to twice the radius of visibility. If BB
located, shadow by day and attack by night.
T.O.O. 2319—T.O.R. 0120.

Official Diary, 6-11 November 1940, continued

At 1000 the two HUDSON aircraft were relieved by one Sunderland. At 1051
ceased zigzagging. 1100 REPULSE, BONAVENTURE, plus three DD's left
formation and steered a course of approx. 270. HOOD, PHOEBE, NAIAD, plus
remaining three DD's changed course to 210 deg.; DD's formed screen as follows:

ANTISUBMARINE SCREEN - DIAGRAM # 6

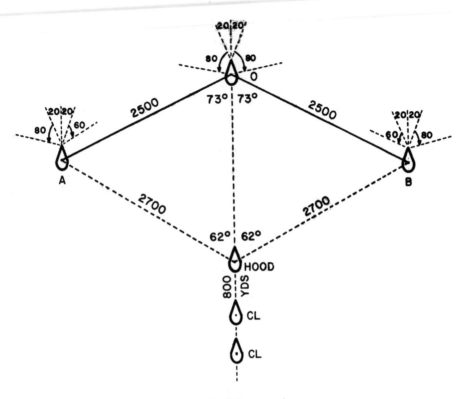

1105 Commenced zigzagging, using the following plan:

TIME	AMT. and DIRECTION to CHANGE	DEVIATION from BASE COURSE
0	0	0
5	30 L	30 L
15	30 R	0
20	30 R	30 R
30	30 L	0
35	30 R	30 R
45	30 L	0
50	30 L	30 L
60	30 R	0

At 12K distance made good—91%.

Intercepted a dispatch which stated that the RENOWN and three DD's left Gibraltar at 0500 today.

Conditions of Readiness—LOOKOUTS—Upon getting under way set what corresponds to our condition of readiness for action No. 2. A half-hour before dawn until about a half-hour after daylight the ship was at action stations (our condition No. 1). From one-half hour after daylight until one-half hour before dark the ship was at cruising stations (our condition No. 3); one of the three 4.7″ mounts was manned. The 2-pdr.[44] pom pom was manned. The 4″ twin high angle AA and the two 4-bbl.-.5″ M/G's[45] were not manned. One man was at the gun director and one in the plotting room. The rangefinder was not manned. Lookouts consisted of one enlisted man on each side of the bridge looking through 8x41 binoculars mounted on a stand above the enemy bearing indicator. These men were both the AA and surface lookouts. The lookouts stand watches in pairs, relieving each other every 5 minutes. Each pair of lookouts is relieved at the end of each hour. No other lookouts used. Note: The above is standard procedure on DD's, according to the information given to the observer. The ship again resumed action stations from about one-half hour before dark to one-half hour after dark and then set cruising stations for the night. Cont. zigzagging all night (good visibility).

At 2210 message from Admiralty stated that D/F on 8400 KC bearings indicated VON SCHEER was about 150 mi. northwest of position in which convoy attacked. Bearings were taken by two stations in England difference between bearings only 20 deg. Admiralty also stated that while bearings were not too reliable, indications are that the VON SCHEER is headed northward. A message was also received which ordered the RODNEY (which was with NELSON patrolling between Faroes and Iceland) to rendezvous and to escort to England an eastbound convoy.

7 *November*—Sea and wind moderated during the night, Speed 17K, formation zigzagging. At 0201 ceased zigzagging. 0230 changed course to 180 deg., 0350 sighted convoy, ceased zigzagging and altered course 60 deg. to starboard to avoid convoy (was informed by Admiralty that convoy would be sighted); 0430 commenced zigzagging, using the same plan. Action stations at 0800, sunrise at 0850, secured from action stations at 0900 and assumed cruising stations (condition 3). Excellent weather conditions, sea very calm.

Note: This is the first time on this or previous trips that celestial navigation has been practicable.

Note: This is a change from his plan to run down the thirteenth meridian to Lat. 50. At 1045 sighted one German aircraft. Rear cruiser fired a few salvos but aircraft was not within range. The DD went to action stations and about one-half hour later set condition 2. (The plane had disappeared after about 10 minutes. It was reported as a Focke Wulfe Condor Transport plane.)

Note: Distance from Brest, nearest German territory, 450 miles. No aircraft have arrived to act as A/S screen. Dispatches indicate German planes active on convoys. One reported 2 bombs, no hits; another 4 bombs, no hits and still another 12 bombs, no hits. At 1215 received a message from Admiralty stating that our position was reported by a German plane at 1140. At 1245 received a message stating that a convoy 40 miles south of our position was being bombed. Admiralty is sending fighters to protect these convoys.

Note: The remarkably clear weather is undoubtedly responsible for the unusual air activity. DD division commander informed DD's that if an S/M[46] or surface ship were sighted all ships were to immediately set watch on their very limited range radio (10 miles claimed) and also set watch on a frequency to be used for gunnery control. Three Hudson aircraft were due to arrive at 1600 to act as A/S patrol and to prevent German

---

[44]Pounder.

[45]Four barrelled, half-inch caliber machinegun.

[46]Submarine.

aircraft from trailing. Hudsons did not appear. O.T.C. stated in a visual message that he intended to change course without signal at 2030 to 140 deg. with one cruiser bearing 360 deg. T and the other 180 deg. T from HOOD, distance 20 miles. Cruisers to take station just before dark. O.T.C. also stated that if the VON SCHEER were sighted the O.T.C. considered that flank marking by a DD would be very helpful, particularly if the VON SCHEER fought a retiring action. At 2030 changed course to 140 deg. Sky became cloudy in afternoon, wind and sea now moderate. Cont. to zigzag all night; visibility good; moon obscured by clouds.

NOTES ON TODAY'S OPERATIONS: Weather conditions ideal for ship-based planes up to about 1700, but no planes used. HOOD does not carry any planes. The same is true of the NAIAD and PHOEBE. No shore-based British aircraft were used for A/S patrol. One German reconnaissance plane was sighted and subsequently reported our position. Thirty minutes after the report was made the Admiralty informed the O.T.C. that the German plane reported our position. Perhaps the plane used a self-evident code which the Admiralty D/F. This would give the Admiralty the necessary information. It is believed that aircraft are essential for an operation of this kind. Same zigzag plan used since leaving Scapa Flow on the fifth. In late afternoon O.T.C. informed Admiralty of his plan to change course to 140 at 2030, to 235 deg. at 0800 on the eighth, to 360 deg. at 2000 on the eighth. Speed 17.5K

8 November—Steaming as before, course 140, speed 17.5K, zigzagging. The two cruisers bearing 360 deg. and 180 deg.T from HOOD. The three DD's in an A/S screen ahead of HOOD. Ship in readiness for action corresponding to our condition 2. During the night Admiralty informed O.T.C. that it was advisable to stay out of reconnaissance area of German aircraft based in Bay of Biscay ports, which Admiralty considered to be 20 deg. W. Admiralty also requested O.T.C. to remain between Lat's 45 and 50 deg. as long as practicable, consistent with refueling of DD's, in order to cover two convoys in this area. Position, course, speed of convoys given. Admiralty also informed REPULSE that while her primary mission was to attack raider, the area in which the convoy was attacked should be searched for survivors by at least one ship. (With REPULSE are one CL and three DD's.) Admiralty also shifted position of ships on northern patrol off Iceland (armed merchantmen) in order to give them more protection.

In accordance with signal last night from O.T.C., DD's have boiler power ready for full speed. At 0800, 8 Nov., changed course to 235 deg. T. Wind and sea moderate from direction of 220 deg. T. Sky overcast. Action stations from 0745 to 0845 (just before until just after daylight). 1030 wind and sea increasing, light rain, visibility about 4 miles. Sighted large merchantman of about 25,000T, three funnels; changed course; O.T.C. communicated with merchantman and apparently was satisfied with identity as formation resumed original course. Ship pounding into head sea, bridge continually being covered with spray; reduced from 17½ to 16K. Orders received from DD division comdr. to house the Asdic dome. Asdic now inoperative. Changed zigzag plan from a 30 deg. change of course to a 22½ deg. change of course. This is the first time the zigzag course has been changed since leaving port—new plan as follows:

TIME	AMT. and DIRECTION to CHANGE	DEVIATION FROM BASE COURSE
60	22.5 L	0
51	22.5 R	22.5 R
45	22.5 R	0
36	22.5 L	22.5 L
30	22.5 R	0
21	22.5 L	22.5 L
15	22.5 L	0
6	22.5 R	22.5 R
0	0	0

Wind and sea moderated slightly; visibility about 6 mi. Resumed using Asdic. Action stations as usual about one-half hour before until one-half hour after dark, then resumed defense stations (condition 2). Weather clearing, bright clear moonlight night. Wind now about 18K. At 2000 changed course to 340 deg., speed 17K, zigzagging same plan as during the day. The two cruisers closed the HOOD at 1700, at 1800 left to take position 10 miles from HOOD, one bearing 000T, the other 180 deg. T. DD's still have boiler power ready for full speed.

General situation as of 1300 today as described by Admiralty dispatch, plus a dispatch from C-in-C Home Fleet. From C-in-C Home Fleet: Present indications raider still to westward. Northern patrol ships (armed merchant cruisers plus trawlers) steer NE by night, SW by day.

From Admiralty: Location of ships as of 1300 today—
NELSON, one CA, plus six DD, between Iceland and Faroes
REPULSE, one CL, plus three DD in Lat. 52-45 N, Long. 32-15 W.
Note: (This is approx. position where convoy was attacked.)
RENOWN in Lat. 40-00 N. Long. 20-30 W (escorting a convoy)
RODNEY in Lat. 56-30 N, Long. 28-30 W, proceeding towards 45-20 N, 52-00 W (Apparently to escort an Eastbound convoy from the Halifax area), which position places RODNEY about 250 mi. bearing 030 from position convoy was attacked.
HOOD, one CL, plus three DD between 45-50 N and W of Long. 20
ARGUS (small CV) and DESPATCH (old CL converted to an AA cruiser), plus three DD, in Lat. 53-00 N, Long. 17-00 W.
The 8″ cruiser AUSTRALIA sailed from the Clyde at 1749 today.
Note: (She has been delayed since start of search by turbine trouble.) She will pass through a series of positions to arrive at 48 N, 20 W at 1300 on the tenth (Nov.) and is to cover the convoy which RENOWN escorted north.
The ARGUS and DESPATCH will be in 45 N, 19-13 W at 1300 on the eleventh, at which time RENOWN and DESPATCH are to return to Gibraltar; ARGUS apparently to return north with three DD's and convoy, later to be joined by AUSTRALIA.
Admiralty concurred with intention of the O.T.C. in HOOD to leave Lat. 47-30 N, 17-00 W at 2100 on the eighth and return to Scapa.

November 9—steaming as before on course 340 deg. T, speed 17K, zigzagging (using same plan as yesterday), three DD's forming A/S screen for HOOD. One CL bearing 000T from HOOD, the other CL bearing 180 deg. from HOOD. Distance of both CL's 10 mi. Wind hauled from SW to W, sky clear, moonlight night, excellent visibility, sea moderate. Action stations from one-half hour before to one-half hour after daylight, then resumed defense positions (condition 2). For the second day celestial navigation practical. 0930 passed the ARGUS (old CV) and DESPATCH (AA cruiser) headed S. 1030 changed course to 020T, apparently headed for Scapa if O.T.C. carries out his intentions. Distance from Scapa about 800 mi. Position at time course was changed—Lat. 51-10 N, Long. 18-30 W. At 1100 received report that EMPRESS OF JAPAN was being bombed about 200 mi. to the northward. Her position was approx. 480 mi. from Brest, the nearest German base.

Wind increased to 37K at 1730, sea moderate, ship commenced to roll about 20 deg. to stbd. Wind about one point on stbd. bow. Ship also pounded about once every 5 min.; slowed to 15K and at 1830 slowed to 13K. Decrease in speed due to ship pounding badly about once every 3 min. Incidentally, nearly every wave was breaking high over HOOD's forecastle. 1900 changed course to 038 deg.

Did not receive any information on the location of the other ships engaged in the search except C-in-C Home Fleet who is in the NELSON patrolling between Iceland and the Faroes requested that a Sunderland search from the Faroes to Iceland tomorrow at daylight. Sunderland to base at Iceland and search the Denmark Straits insofar as practicable. Also, two Hudsons to search from the Faroes towards Iceland all day, searching as far as practicable.

Note: This is the first message received which indicates an air search. It also indicates that no planes are regularly based at Iceland.

November 10—steaming as before on course 038, speed 13K, force of wind about 30K, sea moderate to rough, sky partly cloudy, visibility unlimited, DD rolling badly, formation zigzagging. Above weather conditions remained about the same all day. At 1730 ceased zigzagging due to ship pounding heavily on the port leg of the zigzag. Sea increased slightly during afternoon. Action stations from one-half hour before until one-half hour after sunset. Cruising stations (our condition 3) was then set.

Note: Both officers and men were very tired after 3½ days of watch and watch.

No further information in regard to the search except that REPULSE, which is due to arrive at Scapa tomorrow morning will relieve the NELSON on patrol between the Faroes and Iceland. The BONAVENTURE (CL) plus one DD searched the area for survivors where the convoy was attacked. Admiralty requested BONAVENTURE to make a complete report. The DIDO (CL) is due to relieve the SOUTHAMPTON on patrol in the Denmark Straits. C-in-C Home Fleet asked DIDO if the repairs to her shell rooms were complete and if she were ready to fight in this area.

Note: DIDO's shells came adrift in a storm last week, causing the turrets to jam, which necessitated the DIDO putting in to the Faroes for shelter and repairs.

11 *November*—wind and sea moderated during the night, allowing speed to be gradually increased to 21K at 0600. Resumed zigzagging, using same plan as before. On arriving outside the boom defense at Scapa, speed was reduced to 9K while the HOOD recovered paravanes—time to recover same 8 min. At 1410 the three DD's in column, distance 600, preceded the HOOD, PHOEBE and NAIAD through the swept channel to the fleet anchorage. Speed of DD's 25K. The DD's immediately went alongside a tanker for fuel. (Fuel required 385T—fuel on board before fueling 135T.) Fueling completed at 1800, at which time the DD's shoved off and moored to their buoys.

General Comments on Operations, 5-11 November 1940

DAMAGE TO DESTROYER[47]—One vertical angle iron used as a support for forecastle breakwater pulled away from the dock, causing a hole about 3″ x 4″ in the dock. Considerable water entered this hole to the mess compartment below until the hole was plugged and shored. (Note—last week the corresponding angle iron on the starboard side carried away during another storm, doing similar damage.) One of the two doors in the forecastle breakwater carried away. Four metal spray shields located between the middle and lower life lines on the forecastle carried away and went overboard. Several stanchions for the life lines on the forecastle were bent as much as 20 deg. from the vertical.

Note: The odor below decks was very similar but much worse than our old east coast destroyers after a week at sea.

SUMMARY[48]—A study of . . . [the operation] indicates that as soon as the attack occurred the Admiralty took steps to prevent the raider from returning to Germany between the Faroes and Iceland and between Iceland and Greenland. The raider's entrance to the French Atlantic ports was also covered. In addition, extra escorts were dispatched to the convoys at sea in the general area of the attack. HALIFAX and BERMUDA convoys which were about to sail were ordered to remain in port until the situation was clarified.

The following are considered to be the main points . . . . In addition, the observer has expressed certain opinions which should be weighed accordingly.

a) The sending of these reports by five ships in the same convoy, plus many individual reports of attacks by S/M's and aircraft (which this observer witnessed while en route to England in a similar convoy), is sufficient reason to permit radio operators of merchant ships to have the ship's position available at all times for an emergency without a cutout switch on the navigation bridge. This type of report not only may bring assistance but will allow other ships in the same area to be re-routed to avoid danger. This, of course, requires trustworthy radio operators on merchant ships.

b) The quick destruction of the JERVIS BAY, although "triumphant in defeat," illustrates that armed merchantmen are not suitable ships for ocean escort. They are of no value against S/M attack; in fact, the convoy actually protects the armed merchantman from being attacked by S/M's, which is also true of cruisers acting as ocean escorts. They present a very large target, have relatively low speed (15-18K) plus poor maneuvering qualities, and about the same armament as a modern destroyer. The observer discussed the employment of armed merchantmen with the Admiralty, after passage in a similar convoy. The answer was that under present conditions other types of ships were not available and the risk of losing a convoy had to be taken.

c) Four hours were required before the first heavy units left the fleet base at Scapa Flow. The battle cruisers were apparently on four hours' sailing notice. This illustrates the necessity for a compromise between short sailing notice and upkeep of engineering equipment; also the advisability of "ready" ships in the cruiser and heavier types.

d) Five (5) heavy ships (HOOD, REPULSE, NELSON, RODNEY and RENOWN) acted as separate task groups in widely-separated areas. Three (3) destroyers were assigned to each task group for screening. In addition, three (3) of the task groups contained one or more cruisers. The above distribution of forces into small task groups is

---

[47]Enclosure A to Report serial 1330 of 26 November 1940.

[48]Report serial 1330 of 26 November 1940.

the rule and not the exception in the British Home Fleet. Very often one to four DD's will be ordered as a separate task unit. This distribution of forces emphasizes the fact that (with the possible exception of the Mediterranean area) this is a "captains' war" and the importance of proper training along these lines. One DD captain told this observer that in his opinion the most important difference between peacetime training and operating in war was that now he had to think for himself. Usually there is no division commander to follow and operation orders with their elaborate communication annexes are never seen. After six weeks of operations with DD's, plus listening to the many stories told by the various DD captains, this observer concurs fully with the necessity of adequate training along the above lines and believes that it is one of the most important lessons of this war.

e) It is evident . . . that in addition to providing additional protection to the convoys in the general area of the attack steps were taken immediately to prevent the raider from returning to Germany or to France. C-in-C Home Fleet apparently thought that the raider was heading northward after the attack on the convoy. As a matter of interest, two weeks after the attack an Admiralty dispatch stated that indications pointed to the raider's being in the vicinity of the Azores and order RENOWN and ARK ROYAL to proceed to this area from Gibraltar.

f) The approx. distance between the Faroes and Iceland is 240 mi. and between Iceland and Greenland, 180 mi. After five days in the general area between Iceland and the Faroes with only five hours of visibility over about 10 mi., this observer believes that it is a very difficult task to prevent enemy ships from passing through this area. In addition, the long hours of darkness must be considered. The ice is beginning to narrow the navigable distance between Greenland and Iceland; in mid-winter the navigable distance is reduced to between 20 and 40 mi.

The lack of aircraft search apparently is very evident . . . . The only aircraft believed employed were two Hudsons and one Sunderland, requested by C-in-C Home Fleet to search between the Faroes and Iceland and between Iceland and Greenland. Apparently no British aircraft are stationed in Iceland. It also is questionable whether any high frequency D.F. stations are located in Iceland. As a matter of interest, the FURIOUS is the only aircraft carrier operating with the Home Fleet (at least, insofar as is known to the observer). Ten (10) hours before the attack, C-in-C Home Fleet reported the FURIOUS unable to operate, due to an engineering and a rudder casualty.

The following comments pertain only to the operations of the HOOD, NAIAD, PHOEBE and three (3) TRIBAL Class destroyers. The observer was embarked in one of the latter ships:

a) The HOOD streamed paravanes upon leaving Scapa Flow and cont. to use them until the return to port six days later.

b) The lack of operations orders should be noted.

c) Neither the HOOD nor the cruisers carried ship-based aircraft. The weather was definitely suitable for ship-based aircraft for one day and perhaps suitable on another day. Ship based aircraft would have been very useful. As a result of this and other operations, it is the opinion of this observer that greater emphasis should be placed on the ability of ship-based seaplanes to land and to be taken on board during fairly rough weather.

d) It is of interest to note that only two zigzag plans were used during the days at sea (a 6-day period), with the same plan being used on at least two successive days. The two plans employed are the only zigzag plans the observer has seen to date in any operation. A total of 33 zigzag plans are provided for use under various conditions.

e) The various screening diagrams indicate the confidence the British place in their Asdic. The observer has not had an opportunity to observe an actual contact by the

Asdic but is inclined to believe that the British place too much confidence in the ability of the Asdic to detect and to prevent S/M attack.

f) After about four consecutive days of watch and watch with Condition 1 just before dawn and darkness both officers and men were very tired and their effectiveness reduced considerably. The bad weather conditions undoubtedly had something to do with the ineffectiveness of personnel.

g) The damage sustained by the DD's was relatively small. However, successive operations of this nature without an opportunity for upkeep is beginning to have its effect on the DD's. This is particularly true with DD's which have been in commission about three or more years. The housing of the Asdic dome in rough weather should also be noted. Upon arrival in port it was learned that the bottom of the Asdic dome was cracked. This required the DD to be placed in the floating drydock to renew the Asdic dome.

h) The appearance of German aircraft operating in the Atlantic 450 mi. from their nearest base also is of interest, as is the Admiralty dispatch which advised the O.T.C., to remain outside the German aircraft reconnaissance area, the extreme limit of which was stated to be 20 deg. W. long.

i) The lack of shore-based aircraft to act as A/S patrol should be noted. As a result of this and similar experiences it is the opinion of this observer that plans should be prepared and exercises carried out so that in time of war the NAVY will be ready to provide medium and long-range shore-based aircraft to act as A/S patrol for convoys operating within at least 500 mi. of the coasts, as well as for combatant ships operating within this area. These planes, supplemented by fighters, should be available at focal points of trade routes where enemy air or surface attacks may be expected. The Coastal Command, a branch of the R.A.F. provides these planes for the British. This observer believes that this type of work rightfully belongs to the Navy because it requires efficient coordination with naval surface units every day of the year.

j) A total of 184 coded dispatches consisting of 10,548 groups were deciphered during the 6-day operation. Of this number, 88 dispatches with 5,862 groups were deciphered by officers; 96 dispatches with 4,686 were deciphered by the radio operators. The full time services of one officer are required for deciphering. In this connection, the observer was informed that the British are training a group of enlisted men whose only duty will be deciphering messages. Three (3) of these men are to be assigned to each destroyer.

Personal Diary, 6-11 November 1940

Wed. 6 November - Monday, 11 November. Underway in search of *Admiral Von Scheer*—Steamed down west coasts of Scotland and Ireland about 150 miles offshore then patrolled about 300 to 400 miles off French Atlantic ports covering these ports in order to prevent the *Admiral Von Scheer* from getting in. Ships in company *HOOD, PHOEBE, NAIAD* and 3 TRIBAL DD's. I was as usual in *ESKIMO* (one of the Tribals). Weather very rough for three days. Upon arrival at Scapa went along *MAIDSTONE* (repair ship) to repair minor casualties due to weather.

Letter to Mrs. Wellings, 11 November 1940

Well here I am back in the branch office feeling well and happy, hale and hearty . . . .

The election is over and I suppose as usual many people are disappointed and many more happy. The people made their choice and now we all have to pull together because without doubt the next four years will be very difficult ones for our country and our people. All we have to do is to not let our emotions run away with our common sense.

We should not let the scare of war result in losing our democratic form of government. I am still convinced of my arguments that I set forth before I left home. I honestly believe in what Mr. Kennedy said; namely all aid possible to Britain. If we went to war at the present time our aid would diminish which would be disastrous . . . .

Today is Armistice day, but one would never think so over here. Let us hope and pray that by this time next year God will see fit to have the world at peace so that Armistice day may be given the real homage it is due . . . .

Personal Diary, 12-17 November 1940

Tuesday 12 November—At Scapa. Captain had to be transferred to hospital due to stomach ulcers. Doubt if he will return.

Wednesday 13 November—Entered floating drydock to install new ASDIC dome the bottom of which was cracked during last operation.

Thurs.-Saturday, 14-16 November—in Floating dock. New captain reported today.[49] He was on leave in London and was *supposed* to be married next Monday— Dinner Saturday night with Rear Admiral Hallifax.

Sunday-17 November—At anchor Scapa. Packed and ready to return to London. Really hate to say goodbye to the officers who are grand shipmates. However, it will be good to get back to a real comfortable bed with all night in. Not to mention better food and clean table and bed linen. Had a grand farewell dinner plus movies—"Broadway Melody 1940." Transferred gear and slept aboard the *Maidstone.*

J.H. Wellings (far right) with Officers of H.M.S. *ESKIMO*: Cooke, Galitzine, Gynn, Mason, Ritchie, Russell, Wilkinson

[Photo: JHW Collection]

---

[49]Edward Gerard LeGeyt.

Report on the Officers of H.M.S. ESKIMO[50]

1. The below information on personnel on a TRIBAL Class (1850T) Br. DD is based on observations covering a period of six weeks on one of this Class.

2. Total number of officers and men on board, 220. Officers total 12:

Commander, R.N.	Age 39
1 Engineer Lt. Comdr.	" 32
2 Lieutenants, R.N.	" 26, 24
1 Lieutenant, R.N.V.R.	Age 24
1 Sub-" R.N.	" 20
2 Sub-" (one Royal Canadian Volunteer Reserve, one R.N.V.R.[51])	
	Age 21, 23
1 Midshipman	" 19
1 Lieutenant Doctor	" 36
1 Warrant Gunner	" 28
1 " Torpedo Gunner	" 33

3. [Comdr. St. John Aldrich Micklethwaite] The CO, 39 years old has been a commander since 1935, has had nothing but CO duty since 1930. His present ship is his seventh command; he commissioned the ship in 1938. In conversation with observer the CO stated that he was afraid he may lose his command because he was getting along in years. Awarded the D.S.O. on two occasions—one for convoy work, the other at the second battle of Narvik. Two days before observer left the DD the captain went to hospital with stomach ulcers. His relief was a lieut. comdr., age 35.

4. [Lieut. John Valentine Wilkinson] The executive officer was a lieut., age 26. In addition to being executive officer, he was also first lieut. and gunnery officer. He was not the navigator. The navigator's duties were performed by the sub-lieut. R.N. The executive officer's battle station was at the after ship and gunnery control station located on the searchlight platform just forward of the after deckhouse. The captain stated that he did not want his "No. 1" to be with him on the bridge during action, wanting someone with experience to be able to fight the ship if bridge personnel were killed or injured.

5. [Lieut. Richard Duncan Ritchie] The other lieut. R.N. was gunnery control officer and for all practical purposes was gunnery officer when at battle stations. He acted as spotter for both AA and surface fire. This officer also was in charge of the forward half of the ship for divisional duties and until relieved by the R.N.V.R. lieut., handled all confidential publications and confidential mail.

6. [Sub-Lieut. David Lloyd Binnington] The sub-lieut. R.N. (age 20) was navigator. The captain said this was the sub-lieut.'s first cruise in his present rank and that he (the captain) would teach him the practical side of navigation and, if necessary, do his own navigating. The navigator does not have a quartermaster to correct charts. This rate, with its corresponding duties, does not exist in the British Navy. The number of man hours required to keep even charts of the British Isles up to date is considerable, due, of course, to the ever-changing minefields, buoys, wrecks, etc.

7. [Lieut. Edward Peregrine Stuart Russell] The R.N.V.R. lieut. handled confidential mail and confidential publications. In addition, he stood OOD at sea (a very good watch stander). The Royal Canadian Volunteer Reserve (R.C.V.R.) sub-lieut. [Arthur Dexter Gynn] and the R.N.V.R. sub-lieut. [Nicholas V. Galitzine] (a Russian

---

[50]Report of 4 December 1940.

[51]Royal Naval Volunteer Reserve.

prince) were under instruction, as was the midshipman [John Hallam Murray]. They stood SOOD[52] watches at sea, decoded messages *while on watch* and performed the odd jobs which did not require experience and of which there are many during wartime.

8. [Edward George Mason] The warrant gunner, age 28, was theoretically the flotilla (8 ships) fire control gunner. Actually, his ship duties came first and in his spare time he visited the other ships of the flotilla when in port. His action station was in the after gunnery control station; at night he was the starshell officer. He also stood SOOD watches at sea.

9. [Lancelot Orry Stollery] The warrant torpedo gunner (age 33) was the electrical officer (including fire control). In the British Navy torpedomen perform the duties of our electricians and fire control men. His battle station was at the torpedo tubes. Just prior to observer's visit to the ship the torpedo gunner's battle station was torpedo control officer on the bridge. However, after firing a torpedo during practice with a war head instead of the exercise head, the captain thought the torpedo gunner had better shift to the tubes during battle. Fortunately, the torpedo missed the target ship, exploded on the beach. The torpedo gunner also stood OOD[53] watches at sea and, in observer's opinion, was the best watch stander on board. (Reason: A qualified top watch stander for 7 years in addition to being a good seaman.)

10. At sea the captain was on the bridge during all maneuvers, including large changes in course. At other times he remained in his emergency cabin, a deck below the bridge, reading light literature and sleeping. He told observer that he found out that he could not remain on the bridge all day and all night and be mentally and physically alert when an emergency arose.

11. In the conditions of readiness for action (corresponding to our conditions 2 and 3) there was a junior officer of the watch at all times. This observer believes that in time of war the junior officer of watch on destroyers should keep station, allowing the OOD to supervise all persons on watch. The British ships zigzag night and day when visibility is about one mile or better. If the OOD keeps the ship on station he has no time to keep a good lookout for SS's and planes, plus supervision of other persons on watch. While it is true that special lookouts are on watch, this observer (after six weeks of operations on a DD) is convinced that the OOD is still his own best lookout. Where the junior officers will be obtained is not known. Perhaps chief gunner's mates, chief quartermasters, chief boatswain's mates and chief torpedomen could be trained for this duty.

12. The ship carried a doctor [George Horace Tancred Williams, M.R.C.S., L.C.R.P.] who is a lieut. R.N.V.R. All DD's carry doctors. They not only help morale but, with the chief pharmacist mate, two experienced men are available for duty in battle, one forward and one aft. If one is killed or injured the other may still be available to "carry on."

13. Sixty-five percent (65%) of the enlisted men and 67% of the officers were new to the ship on 1 September 1940, upon completion of the refit required by damage sustained at Narvik. The ship was first commissioned the latter part of 1938. Only forty enlisted men and four officers remain of the original commissioning personnel. About 90% of the new enlisted men who reported on board 1 September 1940 were recruits. The large turnover in personnel was due to expansion of the British Navy. Such large changes in personnel naturally reduce the fighting efficiency of the ships, particularly when so many of the new men are recruits.

---

[52]Sub. or Junior Officer of the Deck.

[53]Officer of the Deck.

14. The officers rely on the petty officers much more than do the officers in our Navy. For example, the signalmen not only read but interpret the signals. They always tell the OOD the meaning of the signal and not the signal itself. They also know the tactical publications very thoroughly. The officers were not concerned with such matters, except the captain who knew the meaning of all the signals. Other petty officers perform their duties in the same manner as the signalmen. There is no officer assigned to the plotting room during action. With the exception of the engineer officer [Engineer Lieut. Godfrey Arthur Cooke] and the two gunners, the officers (in observer's opinion) did not have even a working knowledge of the equipment with which they worked. They did not seem interested in such matters. This no doubt is due to the great reliance placed on their petty officers.

CHAPTER FOUR

THE EMBASSY, H.M.S. *HOOD* AND H.M.S. *CURACOA*
18 November 1940 - 31 January 1941

Personal Diary, 18 November 1940
Monday . . . Left Scapa Flow at 1430 arrived at Thurso at 1620. Capt. Newcomb also returned in same boat (One legged Capt. who is Naval Officer in charge at Thurso). He took complete charge of me until train time at 2000. Visited new aviation field at Thurso, dinner with Capt. Newcomb, who also came down to see me off.—He had arranged for me to have a whole compartment to myself, no sleeping cars on train. He also supplied me with a blanket.

Letter to Mrs. Wellings, 18 November 1940
Well sweet here I am on my way back to the main office . . . .
I am on a night train to Edinburgh. The time is 2200. I have a whole compartment to myself—as there are no sleepers on this train. The entire compartment is through the courtesy of the copyright owners. Of course it is a first class compartment. My small trunk is at one end of the aisle, with my brown and black suitcases on top of it. The three seats across from me have my cap, coat and brown handbag plus my overcoat nesting quietly and nicely folded. On my side, I am in one corner with a blanket draped over my knees, and my white bathrobe over a sweater. I really am quite comfortable, although the heat has not percolated through the train as yet. Oh yes, your cute black alarm clock is in the corner, with the alarm set to 0445 as the train is due at the junction where I change for Edinburgh at that time. In the rack over my head is my gas mask, helmet and capbox. My slippers are resting snugly but comfortably on my feet. Now what do you think of that for a scene????? I will admit I have considerable luggage but there was nothing else I could [do] to reduce the gear. The writing is in pencil as my pen would probably be all over the paper as the train rounds the corners. Yes sweet it is quite a sight to remember and add to my collection of experiences.
When I finish this letter I will turn in as I am with my overcoat as a standby should the weather get cold. I only wish you were here with me . . . .
The train has a fairly large number of service boys enroute to their various stations or perhaps on leave. The Salvation Army has the use of a dining car where the boys can get tea and sandwiches. I was just in for a cup of tea myself. On my way I passed through two bagg[age] cars. The boys were sitting on the baggage singing away having a [grand] train time. Believe it or not a banjo, guitar and violin was providing the music. The boys can certainly amuse themselves. Incidentally none of them were under the influence of liquor. They really are well behaved.
My host at dinner tonight gave me all the information on Edinburgh. Where to stay, what to see and even *phoned* to have a friend of his arrange to take me shopping. Such service I have never seen before. Darling I am afraid your little boy will be ruined . . . .

70

Personal Diary, 19 November 1940
Tuesday . . . Arrived Perth at 0530 changed trains and arrived Edinburgh at 0830.
Took a room at New British Hotel on Princes Street—Grand to have a real hot bath in a
clean bathroom. Met a Miss Cotton, age about 60-65 who took me shopping. Meeting
arranged by Capt. Newcomb last night via phone. Bought Anne a kilt outfit plus
sweater. Also had lunch and visited Edinburgh castle. After tea at hotel said goodbye to
Miss Cotton—then slipped into a store and bought a little Scotch bag for Anne which
Miss Cotton would not approve to be worn with kilt outfit. Met 4 officers from *Punjabi*
including Comdr. Lean the skipper . . . .

Letter to Mrs. Wellings[1]
. . . While I was about to enter the dining room for dinner I met four boys who were
exceedingly nice to me the preceding few weeks. I felt obliged to take them to a real
dinner as previously I was their [guest]. We had a grand time and I only wish you could
have seen us dashing from the hotel in a taxi to the station with 10 minutes to train time.
When we arrived one boy dashed down to hold the train while the rest of us ran to the
baggage room for all my gear. (I previously checked my gear at the station during
daylight.) Of course I just made the train. As the train was pulling out one of the boys
presented me with a quart of Champagne.[2] The time was 1015 p.m. I was glad to be
able to give them a party—which will be on the special account.[3]

Personal Diary, 20 November 1940
Arrived London at 1100—noticed the increase in damage around embassy area
after being away for over six weeks. Was glad to return—send all my laundry for a *real*
cleaning which was badly needed after six weeks away with practically no laundry
facilities. Staff at office had trebled since I left. However, I managed to find a room at
New Pipers our old "estate" thanks to Bill. It was grand to be out in the country and see
the gang again. Two letters from Dolly—the first mail in 2 weeks. Was glad to receive
them!!!

Letter to Mrs. Wellings, 21 November 1940
Well here I am back in dear old London town . . . . Apparently it is the same old
London as the air raid warning is sounding at this moment. It is later than it used to be as
it is not 1005 p.m. However there is a half a gale blowing outside, plus rain which should
mean very little air activity all night . . . .
London looked the same as ever, although of course there was more evidence of
bombing after being away for six weeks. However business as usual was the slogan.
People were going about their work in the usual manner as though it were peacetime.
Honestly I was surprised that there was not more damage. The boys say that the nightly
raids have not been on such a large scale recently. I asked my taxi driver how the
bombing was progressing. He said "Oh yes they come over every night but Jerry can't
scare us—we can and will take it."

[1]Excerpt from letter 21 November 1940.

[2]"I remember as though it were yesterday, how embarrassed I was . . . and right in front [of] me, on the
platform of my sleeping car, watching the entire proceedings—was Rear Admiral Hallifax, Commander
Destroyers Home Fleet, who was enroute to London!" JHW MS. *Reminiscences*, p. 63.

[3]The cost of the dinner for 7 persons was £5 6/-.

All the boys were glad to see me . . . . I spent the rest of the day (4 hours) getting my accounts squared away, sending lots of laundry to be cleaned—Incidentally my large supply of collars were just adequate. Of course I told a few yarns which should be tall stories by the time I arrive home.[4]

At 4:44 we shoved off for the country. We now have the three houses in this area but I was fortunate to be able to find a room in our old estate. I had a grand sleep last night and a holiday today as it is "Franksgiving" . . . . Incidentally, we had a fine 25 lb. turkey today. It reminded me of home except that the turkey was not prepared like the one my sweetie supervised . . . . I have worked on reports most of the day, with a few games of ping-pong thrown in between times . . . .

Personal Diary, 21-28 November 1940

From my last entry to 26 November remained in country, Virginia Waters (New Pipers) writing reports of observations while in destroyer Eskimo. 26 and 27 November went to Embassy with other officers, leaving country at about 0845, arriving Embassy about 0945, leaving Embassy about 1630 and arriving at New Pipers at 1730. During these days I checked up on my baggage, filed one or two reports and purchased food for my thanksgiving dinner to be given on 28 November.

28 November:—Drove to Portsmouth to inspect and watch the Anti-Aircraft Gunnery School in action. Used official car—Buick '38, master 7 passenger sedan—with chauffeur. Members of party—Capt. Kirk, Comdr. Hitchcock, Lt. Comdr. Ammon and myself. A very pleasant one and a half hours drive each way. The English countryside was very quiet and beautiful. Lunch at [H.M.S.] Vernon,[5] air raid right after lunch. The condensate from the exhaust of the planes looked like tad poles in the sky. Raiders driven off—No bombs dropped. Also inspected torpedo station. Met Franny Forest, Waters,[6] and Gay.[7] Franny very happy to show Captain Kirk around. Said he felt like a school boy taking his daddy to school at the end of the year. Arrived back at New Pipers at 1830. Everyone surprised at the turkey dinner. Needless to say it was very much appreciated by all hands—we all ate too much.

Letter to Mrs. Wellings, 29 November 1940

. . . Just had time out. It is 0020, the boys called me out to the dining room where

---

[4]"All the Embassy Officers, particularly Captain Kirk, Commander Hitchcock, Lieutenant Commander Ammon and Lieutenant Forest, were very eager to hear my stories about Scapa Flow and the Royal Navy Operations. They thought the words of the destroyer song, to the tune of "Is It True What They Say About Dixie," were very clever and amusing . . . .

Is it true—what they say—about Sca-pa?
Does the sun—never shine—at any time?
Do the cold and dreary breezes—blow into the Flow?
Are the rough and ready Tribals—always on the go?
Is it true what they say about slipping
Day and night—Morning · Noon · And evening · too?
Do they scream—Do they shout—Run in circles all about?
If they do—Oh, Please—Send us—South!!"

JHW, MS. Reminiscences, pp. 31, 64

[5]The wardroom of this shore establishment in Portsmouth.

[6]Odale Dabney Waters, Jr. (1910-   ). U.S. Naval Academy, 1928. Lieutenant, Assistant Naval Attaché, London, 1940-41. Later Rear Admiral, 1960; Oceanographer of the Navy, 1967-69.

[7]Probably Lt. (jg.) Donald Gay, Jr., permanently assigned at this time as an instructor at the Naval Air Station, Pensacola, Florida.

they had the turkey on the table going to town. Six of us surely made the poor old bird look sick. The group was lead by Capt. Cockran (a naval constructor) who is one of the finest men I have ever seen. The cold turkey sandwiches were followed by pumpkin pie and now they are out in the kitchen making coffee. I would love to see Capt Kirk return right now. He is out on an official party. He would love to join in on the party.

Incidentally *my* thanksgiving dinner last night went off perfectly. When the gang sat down to dinner Capt. Kirk almost fainted when the no. 1 girl brought in a huge turkey (24 lbs.). It was done to perfection. I had bought nuts, mints, fresh pumpkin-mince *etc*. It was a complete surprise to everyone. I really got a huge kick out of the whole show. Incidentally we sat down to dinner at 2000 which was 1400 your time. I thought of you eating your thanksgiving dinner at the same time. I really fel[t] very lonesome for a few minutes until I caught myself because it really was my party. However I do hope and really know you had a grand dinner . . . .

Capt. Kirk just came in and is now "polishing" off the turkey. Capt. Cockran has just brought in the coffee so I am now all set. Really the gang do try to make the best of living around London when one can't get out at night . . . .

Personal Diary, 29 November-4 December 1940

Remained in country—New Pipers, Virginia Waters—to complete reports. On Saturday 30 November listened to Army-Navy game broadcast from U.S. Game started 1930 London time (zone-1) Navy won 14-0. Capt Cockran, Lt. Comdr Huffman, Gay and myself listened to game. Letter from Dolly and mother. Mails very slow. On Sunday 1 December—walked to Englefield Green for mass—½ hours walk.

4 December—Drove to Embassy with Captain. He finally read my reports last night—Began assembling reports. Glad to have them almost finished. Called at D.N.I. and asked about duty on a staff.[8] Stanford[9] somewhat surprised as he had just received a letter from Capt. Kirk asking for me to go to a B.C.[10]—Saw Captain at night who said he would write another letter requesting me to go on a staff. Worked on reports at night plus ping-pong with Captain, Bill & Savvy Forest.

Letter to Mrs. Wellings, 4 December 1940

Capt. Kirk is flying home on Saturday (two days from now).[11] He promised to take personal mail for us so this should be a real chance to get some service.

Capt. Kirk is going home on temporary duty for about a month in order to give the boys back home the straight dope. I wish I could go with him. However he has been here for 18 months so I guess he rates going home. Personally I will be surprised if he returns.

---

[8]"One day in early December I inquired at the Admiralty about my friend and former shipmate, Lieutenant Commander John N. Opie III, who at that time was an observer with the British Fleet in the Mediterranean. The Admiralty officer replied that indeed they had heard of him. He said that they didn't mind his being critical of the way the British conducted some of their operations—but they did wish he would stop using "that old State Department code" in sending his reports to the Navy Department from Alexandria. The British had broken that code long ago and they felt certain that the Germans had likewise broken it. And they did not want the Germans to read Opie's reports!

Our American Embassy officers were very interested, and amused, to hear this story about Jack Opie who was actually a most efficient and very outspoken officer." *JHW MS. Reminiscences*, p. 65.

[9]Arthur Caerlyon Stanford, Commander; Staff, Naval Intelligence Division.

[10]Battle cruiser.

[11]Kirk's departure was later delayed to 14 December.

I believe he will get himself a good job as captain of a big ship. This is only a guess on my part so please do not mention it.

Well darling it looks as though I will not be home for Christmas . . . even if I received orders tomorrow I would have difficulty getting back on time. Very few ships of any size are sailing to the States between now and Xmas. In addition the plane service is very unreliable as to time, in addition reserving a place on the plane is next to impossible . . . .

We are really very fortunate. We have our health, our home, enough money, and above all we have each other. This Xmas there will be millions of people who had at least one of the above requisites last Xmas but who will perhaps have none this year. It will be a sad Xmas for all Europe and my heart is full of sadness for each and everyone of them regardless of nationality, creed or race. I only hope that at this time next year God, in all his mercy, will see fit to have the world at peace . . . .

Personal Diary, 5-8 December 1940

5 December—Drove to Embassy with Captain—continued work on reports—quite a task to get them squared away. Comdr. Sylvester[12] arrived from States—office now has 31 officers. Bought Xmas cards (6) and sent same. Card had a picture of a young mother with her little girl praying in church—title was "faith."

6 December—Drove to Embassy with Capt. Kirk—about 1030 Capt. Kirk called me to his office and said he had bad news for me. He then told me Mother had died and gave me a cable from Dolly . . . .

7 December—Stayed at New Pipers, had the duty . . . . Was very glad when the officers returned at 1600. At night went to Slim Hitchcock's house with Capt. Kirk, Capt. Cockran, and Bill Ammon. Stayed about 2 hours . . . . At 1600, MacDonald called from office and said I would be leaving Tuesday on another trip—very glad to get away.

8 December—Went to 0900 mass at Englefield Green . . . . Took a bus to the Wheatsheaf and met Capt Cockran, Lt. Royal[13] and Miss Ziegler—one of the secretaries at the office. We all went for a long walk through Windsor Forest eventually ending at the "Old House Inn" in Windsor for lunch. Estimated we covered 10-11 miles in three hours. The Inn was once the home of Sir Christopher Wren who remodeled St. Pauls Cathedral and one of Englands famous architects . . . .

Letter to Mrs. Wellings, 8 December 1940

. . . The day was really beautiful—clear sky cool-to-crisp day. The trees, some with leaves were grand. In addition the deer, antelopes, sheep, goats, cows, etc were really something to see. The last part of the walk was from the "Copper Horse Statue"[14] (King George the III the fellow we drove out of Boston or rather his troops) to Windsor Castle. The walk is known as long walk and is exactly three miles of perfectly straight road.

---

[12]Evander Wallace Sylvester (1899-1960). U.S. Naval Academy, 1920. Assistant Naval Attaché, London. Later Rear Admiral; Assistant Chief, Bureau of Ships, 1950-54; Director, Mariners Museum, 1955-1960.

[13]William Freeman Royall (1904-   ). U.S. Naval Academy, 1927; Assistant Naval Attaché, London. Later Rear Admiral; retired 1957.

[14]The Statue by Westmacott on Snow Hill.

About 20 yards on both sides of the road are two rows of beautiful old elm trees.[15] It is supposedly a very famous walk and rightfully so.

We had lunch in the "Old Castle House" in Windsor which is a very old hostilery right on the banks of the Thames. Across the river is the famous English school of Eaton.[16] A number of the boys were having lunch with their proud mothers and fathers. The younger boys (about 12 years old) wore striped trousers, short jackets and of course the famous Eaton (buster brown) collar. The older boys (age about 15) wore tails complete—including the top hat as do the younger boys. It really was very interesting . . . .

Personal Diary, 8 December 1940

. . . After lunch we walked over the bridge crossing the Thames in order to get a good view of Windsor Castle, then took a bus to Englefield Green and then walked to New Pipers—about 2 miles. Tea was welcomed for we were quite tired. Took a good hot bath and an hours nap. At night wrote to Dolly—played a few games of Ping-Pong and then to bed. The walk was a great relief for me—Capt. Cockran, Royall and Miss Ziegler knew all the various kinds of trees, shrubs, animals, etc.—I tried to forget my troubles. Capt. Kirk in bed with a sore throat—London appeared to have had an unusually active night of enemy bombers.

Letter to Captain Willis A. Lee, c. 8 December 1940 [Draft]

Perhaps you have been wondering what I have been doing since I left Washington. In order that you may have some idea of my work and incidentally, my opinions (for what they are worth), I am taking the liberty of writing this letter. I know you will treat it as confidential as I do not wish to have anyone think that I am submitting unofficial reports. Of course you may show this letter to Admiral Leary. I feel as though Fleet Training has just as much interest as the material bureaus in what is going on over here. Practically everything that I will say will be substantiated by official reports but some remarks will be personal opinion formed on the general situation.

My convoy reports have been received by now so I will not comment further on this subject except to say that the submarines are continuing to operate further west with night surface attacks on convoys. The German planes are operating as far west as 20° west, particularly west and northwest from the French Atlantic ports. This will require better A.A. escort for the convoys in this area. At present on a clear day the planes give the merchant ships h— in this area. As for ocean escorts what happened to the *Jervis Bay*[17] is what I predicted in the convoy report. Don't waste money and equipment by installing elaborate gunnery equipment on merchantmen. They are satisfactory only to fight off submarines if the submarine comes to the surface or fight other armed merchantmen, capturing unarmed merchantmen, and for patrol where negative information is expected. Incidentally the convoys which pass through Pentland Firth down the east coast to Roseyth are being subjected to attacks by torpedo planes at night . . . .

---

[15]The elms were planted by King Charles II. They were replaced after 1945 by horse chestnut and plane trees.

[16]Eton College founded by King Henry VI in 1440.

[17]The armed merchant cruiser *Jervis Bay* was the only escort for the 37 ships of the homeward bound, Halifax convoy HX84. Attacked by the German pocket-battleship *Scheer* on 5 November 1940, *Jervis Bay* made a gallant, but self-sacrificing defense which saved all but five ships of the convoy.

I believe we will have to permit our radio operators on merchantmen to have the ship's position on hand at all times without a cut out switch on the bridge. This of course means having reliable radio operators. The ship's position and the type of attack is very valuable in plotting the attacking ship's position and rerouting convoys and ships sailing independently. For example, right now the British are waiting for some ship to report being attacked by the *Admiral Scheer* in order to find some point from which to start the search again. The few moments between sighting the enemy and receiving orders not to use the radio may be the difference in getting out the report. (Ship sunk and crew abandoned if order is violated.)

When the *Admiral Scheer* attacked convoy HX84 the British sent the *Hood*, *Repulse, Nelson, Rodney* and *Renown* out as independent task units. Each screened by three DD's and some of them had one or two CA's or CL's along also. Of course this is in addition to several CA's and DD's acting independently. The importance of training C.O.'s[18] and the DD's in this type of independent duty cannot be over emphasized. In the Home Fleet it is a C.O.'s war. Incidentally out of 5 days in the general area of Iceland there were only about 5 hours in which the visibility was as much as 5 miles. I can now see how the German ships get through.

Destroyers are always on the go. BB's[19], BC's or CV's[20] do not dare to leave port without 3 or 4 DD's as a screen. These many independent operations add to the work of the DD's which are showing definite signs of the lack of proper upkeep. Operating in the North Atlantic around Iceland and the Orkneys at this time of the year is like operating off Cape Hatteras in the winter. The destroyers take a terrific beating. Our operations in the Pacific may lead us to false conclusions if we ever have to operate in force in the North Atlantic. I am convinced that our destroyers should be big, rugged, able to operate effectively in fairly rough weather, plus a good cruising radius. I know this sounds like a young cruiser but that is what they have to be. I was in an 1850 standard ton boat (tribal class) which had a hard time "taking it." The only times we were in port for over a day were to repair damage—Forecastle and oil tanks leaked, bulkheads wrinkled, side plating pushed in, boats broken up, Asdic dome cracked, etc. If we ever get into a war like this destroyers, with dual purpose guns, will be worth their weight in gold. We will need all we can build, borrow or steal. Incidentally the tribal class DD's have replaced one twin 4.7, 40° elevation, with a twin 4", 80° elevation mount. How about our 1850's?

I have just written a dispatch at Captain Kirk's request which covers the high lights of my observations. Since this dispatch covers most of the main points I will not repeat them here although I have already covered some of them.

As for their signal book and Visual Manual, the latter corresponds to our G.T.[21], I do not recommend swapping ours for theirs. I honestly believe ours is much better. My reports will cover the important information on the Visual Manual and will forward later the data on the Signal Book. Incidentally my reports should all be in the same pouch as this letter. They will be voluminous but I hope of value to the people interested.

As we all know but seldom put into effect, some matters which appear most important in peacetime seem very inconsequential in wartime. I wish you could see how the destroyers operate. In regards to cleanliness I perhaps can better describe it by telling a

---

[18]Commanding Officers.

[19]Battleships.

[20]Aircraft carriers.

[21]General Tactical Instructions.

story. The captain of "my" destroyer said he would like to meet a Spanish naval officer. When I asked why he said that during the recent civil war in Spain he used to see the Spanish destroyers which operated off Gibraltar. They were the dirtiest looking ships he had ever seen and he did not understand how any captain would allow a ship to get so filthy. Now he knows and would like to apologize for what he said about the Spanish ships. The guns are definitely dirty with rust very common, particularly on the close range weapons. I doubt if we would permit them to fire. The gunnery officer of the destroyer said they would not do so in peacetime. This all adds up to the fact that the material also has to be rugged—in addition to the personnel.

The close range weapons have no remote control nor director to date. I have met two skippers who claim to have shot down planes with pom-poms. I am convinced that any hits were due only to the volume of fire. At a conference with Admiral Bailey's committee before I left town I asked for a breakdown by types of guns of the total number of planes brought down by naval A.A. fire. I hope you have received it.

Apparently the British are reluctant to let anyone observe the workings of their staffs. Captain Kirk has done his best but the British say C. in C. Home Fleet has no accommodations. I hope the new C. in C.[22] finds a hammock at least. I honestly do not see any further necessity of my being in a ship without a staff in so far as observing operations and tactics from a general viewpoint. It is extremely difficult to see the complete picture unless one knows everything that is going on. Incidentally there must be considerable operational planning at the Admiralty and at C. in C. Western Approaches. I hope to crash these gates before I return—if possible.

As far as observers are concerned I believe the more we send the more and better information we will get. I believe I will be a much better naval officer for having had this experience. I consider operational experience just as valuable, if not more so, than the technical information our experts are getting. After all it is the line officer who has to use the technical equipment and fight the ships. We should be able to know and say what we want from experience in actual warfare. To be specific may I suggest that we should send as many as possible of our outstanding and rugged senior commanders and relatively junior captains to observe operations and tactics and rotate them after about three months. I know the objection will be that they are too senior for accommodations and the C.O.'s of the ships they may have to "ride" but after all they will be our future flag officers and in addition perhaps be operation officers on our staffs if we get into this war. The majority of these officers should go to the Mediterranean because, as you know, that is where most of the naval actions are taking place. In addition I think we could use a good all around material ordnance man to advantage particularly one who has also had a lot of practical gunnery experience. In the latter statement I believe everyone at the embassy including Eller is in agreement. Captain Kirk strongly concurs with my remarks on observers. He has written several letters saying practically the same thing.

I could continue on and on but perhaps it is better if I sign off. However before I close may I suggest that you ask Comdr. Mills (EDO)[23] who has just returned to call on you. I believe you can get considerable information from officers who have been here, particularly officers like Comdr. Mills.

Please give my best regards to Admiral Leary and all the officers in Fleet Training.

---

[22]Adm. Sir J.C. Tovey relieved Adm. Sir C. Forbes as Commander in Chief, Home Fleet, on 2 December 1940.

[23]Engineering Duty Officer.

Personal Diary, 9-10 December 1940

9 December—Went to town on the train—two changes plus a taxi due to last night's raid—Capt. Kirk stayed at New Pipers. I took in about half my gear for going away tomorrow. Upon arrival in office almost 1030 sent a cable to Dad. Mother's funeral at 0900 Boston time. Wish I could be present to say goodbye. Had my hair cut, bought 18 wing collars, 2 dress ties—lunch at 32 Grosvenor Street with MacDonald and Huffman. Bought railroad tickets, about to leave for home at 1630 when Comdr. Hitchcock asked me to go to Admiralty to learn why I could not be assigned to a staff. Guess I finally forced any answer. Stanford as usual very diplomatic and *tried* to explain. Took a cab to Clapin [Clapham] Junction, there train to Virginia Waters—and walked to New Pipers—no cab—suitcase very heavy when I arrived at top of hill.

At night signed a few of my last reports, packed for leaving tomorrow. When I arrived at New Pipers, Admiral Ghormely was calling on Capt. Kirk. At Capt. Kirk's request I told them about my call at the Admiralty.

10 December—Left late—0950 with Capt. Kirk. He very kindly took all my gear in the official car. Drove to London by a new way in order to see the scenery. He was in grand spirits, stopped at Hampden Hall[24] to look at old castle—finally arrived in town at 1130. Capt. Kirk stopped at Harrods,[25] for a haircut. Tims drove me to Admiralty to receive a letter for the captain of *Hood*—then back to office—got everything cleared up, wished all hands a Merry Christmas and then Tims drove me to station for 1300 train.

The R.T.O. had reserved a compartment for me. However Joe Broadhurst—Admiralty courier I met on my way back to London—had adjacent compartment—so we both shared his compartment which permitted mine to be used by four young sublieutenants. Had a fairly good lunch—train making fairly good time. Broadhurst as usual had a number of good yarns—should have as he has been travelling all over the world for over 30 years. Due to arrive at Thurso at 1000 tomorrow.

Letter to Mrs. Wellings[26]

Your little boy is away again on a visit. The train ride was quite interesting although I was a little restless at the end. The English and Scottish countrysides are as pretty as ever except of course the leaves have all fallen from the trees. However the farm lands and fields, criss crossed with small streams and the farm houses are really wonderful to see at anytime. Perhaps part of my enthusiasm is due to the fact that they are so quiet and peaceful. From all appearances one would never think that the country was at war . . . .

Personal Diary, 11 December 1940

11 December—Slept very well. Arrived at Thurso at 1130—lunch at Royal Hotel, called Capt. Newcombe (RN) on phone and paid my respects then left for 1300 boat—*St. Ninian* for Scapa Flow—Capt. Newcombe at dock to see me off. Capt. of *St. Ninian* turned over his cabin to me—had tea with him on bridge—shaved and got

---

[24]Hampton Court Palace, begun in 1514 by Cardinal Wolsey, was a favorite royal residence from about 1529 to 1760.

[25]Harrods, the department store, in Knightsbridge.

[26]13 December 1940.

already to report for duty. 1530 arrived on *Dunloose Castle*[27] (Repair ship), Exec.[28] as usual very pleasant with lots of stories. *Hood*'s boat called alongside and at 1645 I reported on board *Hood*—my new home for the next few weeks—perhaps until about 15 February. Comdr. Cross[29]—the exec. met me at the gangway and showed me my room. Called on Capt. Dennie[30] the C.O. before dinner—Wardroom officers very kind and unusually pleasant. They seem like a fine group of men. A marine private assigned to me as my servant—(all mess boys are marines). Service—wonderful—my cabin is the admiral's guest cabin 17' x 9'—*bed*; good desk, heater, desk lamp, rug, two chests of drawers, large locker for hanging clothes, large porthole, room on main deck— Believe it will prove to be very comfortable—*No* hot and cold running water however— Servant supplies same—of course there is a wash basin.

12 December—At anchor—First Lieut. (Lt. Comdr. J.L. Machin)[31] assigned as my liaison officer. He took me on a tour of the ship—It certainly is a large ship—42,000 tons or more. The largest man of war in the world.[32] Called on Vice Admiral W.J. Whitworth before dinner. Seemed very friendly type of man. Now all settled in room. Service *is* excellent—Food much better than on destroyer. Mess well regulated. Breakfast 0730-0900, lunch 1200-1300, dinner 2000. Drinks before lunch and dinner. No special seats at table—except for Mess President and vice president— Different officers preside for a week at a time. Quite a good idea. At dinner tonight Exec. off. took the chair—He toasted the President of the U.S.—I answered with a toast to King George the Sixth.

13 December—Underway 0930—1530—Fired AA guns. Ship screened by 3 DDs including *Eskimo*. Seemed odd to be in *Hood* and not in *Eskimo*. Bad weather prevented surface target practice. Unable to pick up buoy upon return to port due to rough weather.

Contract between the Ward Room Officers, H.M.S. "HOOD" and Chief Petty Officer Steward W.E. Atkins, Messman.

1. Officers will pay 2/- per day for each day on which they are victualled, or £3 per month, except that :-

(a) At home ports officers who live on shore as a permanent arrangement and who notify the messman accordingly shall pay:

Breakfast and Lunch Members . . . . 1/- per day
Lunch Members . . . . Nil.
Dinner only . . . . 1/- per day

(Such officers when on board for all meals, to pay the usual charge of 2/-)

(b) Officers who are absent from the ship for 24 hours or more and who give

---

[27]*Dunluce Castle*. 8114 tons. Built 1904. Base ship Pennant number 2. Requisitioned 1939, scrapped 1945.

[28]Leslie Richard Romer, Commander.

[29]William Kenneth Ramsden Cross.

[30]Irvine Gordon Glennie (1892-   ). Later Rear Admiral Destroyers, 1941-42; Home Fleet Destroyers, 1943-44; Vice Admiral, 1944; Commander in Chief, America and West Indies, 1945-46; KCB, 1945.

[31]John Lee Machin.

[32]She was surpassed in size by World War II construction, mostly notably by the Japanese battleship *Yamato*.

H.M.S. *HOOD*, 1939

Launched 1918, completed 1920, Clydesbank. 856' length overall, 106' beam, 32½' draft. 45,200 tons displacement at full load. Speed 32 knots. Complement 1,716 men. For a large part of the *Dreadnought* era, *HOOD* was the largest warship in the world.

[Photo: Imperial War Museum A 111]

the messman at least one day's notice of their intentions to be absent, shall not pay messing for any whole days of absence.

2. All victualling allowance will be paid to the messman.

3. All monies due to the messman to be paid not later than the 5th of the month following.

4. The messman is to close his bills and deliver them as required by the Mess Secretary.

5. The messman will provide meals as follows:-

BREAKFAST. Fruit, Cereals, Porridge, Fish (another hot dish) such as Eggs, Kidneys, Mushrooms, and Bacon, etc. Cold meats, marmalade (three kinds including Oxford). Honey, jams, rolls, toast, butter, tea, coffee, and fresh milk (when procurable).

LUNCH. Soup, fish, one hot dish, cold meats (at least seven), salads in season, potatoes, second vegetable, sweet butter, cheese (at least 5 including prime Stilton), biscuits, pickles and sauces, coffee.

TEA. Tea, cakes, bread, butter, jams, honey, marmalade.

DINNER. Hors d'oeuvres, soup, fish, entree or one joint, two vegetables, sweet or savoury, fruit (one piece), coffee.

SUPPER. Soup, fish (two kinds), cold meats (at least ten including game or poultry), salads, potatoes, sweets, cheeses, coffee.

GUEST NIGHT. Hors d'oeuvres, grape fruit, soup, fish, poultry or game, sweet, savoury, gruit, coffee, etc.

6. Poultry or game will be served at twice a week and food to be of the best quality.

7. Morning tea will be provided without charge.

8. Guests, or any officers not victualled, shall pay 4/- per day.

CHARGES FOR INDIVIDUAL MEALS FOR GUESTS:-

BREAKFAST 1/-
LUNCH 1/6
TEA .... /6
DINNER 2/-
GUEST NIGHT 2/6

9. Complaints and suggestions will be dealt with by the Mess Committee and are not to be made by officers direct to the Messman.

10. The messman is to exercise a close supervision over the cooking and serving of meals, also the work of his staff, any lack of co-operation is to be reported to the Mess Committee.

11. The mess to pay for all cleaning gear, table decorations and washing required by the mess.

12. Mess Committee to arrange times for all meals.

13. No meals are to be served in cabins except with permission of the Mess President (sick officers and private parties excepted).

14. The Fair Extra Book written up to date is to be placed in the Ward Room for inspection after divisions on Sundays.

15. The prices of extras to be agreed upon mutually by the Mess Committee and the messman.

16. The messman will endeavor to carry out all private commissions for officers to his utmost ability, but these are not to interfere with his catering duties. Advances of cash to any individual officers are not to exceed £2 a month.

17. This contract may be terminated on either side with notice in writing with one month in home waters and three months abroad.

MESS COMMITTEE.   MESSMAN.
W.W. Davis, Com.   W.E. Atkins
F.B. Lloyd, Comdr.
L.E.S.H. Le Bailly, Lieut. (E)

Letter to Mrs. Wellings, 13 December 1940

. . . My present office is much better than my last one, in so far as comfort and conveniences are concerned. The food is better with more variety. Music at dinner does add [aid] ones digestion. Really sweet I will be spoiled when I return. I warn you that I will expect all kinds of service—of course, that does not mean I will get it . . . .

Personal Diary, 14-17 December 1940

14 December—Underway at 0930 in order to pick up buoy. Went on bridge. It took about 4 hours to moor to buoy. Wind very strong—about 40 knots.

15 December—At anchor—wrote to Bill and Capt Kirk, walked for about 1½ hours on deck. Still difficult to take my mind off Mother's death. Will make a determined effort to carry on as she would have wanted me to. At Dinner wore my No. 1 uniform with a wing collar and a bow tie—movies in Wardroom after dinner—*The Doctor Takes a Wife*—Loretta Young—quite amusing. Capt and Admiral in for movies.

16 December—At anchor—rained all morning—the navigator took me on a Cooks Tour of his Department—name Lt. Comdr. S.J.P. Warrand.[33]—Quite an interesting tour. Two hour nap in p.m. called on C. in C. H.F. Admiral Tovey at 1700. Very pleasant call.[34] Then called on *ESKIMO. ESKIMO* was like coming home. Stayed for a buffet supper and movies—left at 0100—they certainly are a grand crowd. Received pictures taken when I was on board.

17 December—At anchor—up at 0750—walked for ½ hour on deck, then inspected X turret (marines) from top to bottom quite a workout (2½ hours). Walked for ½ hour after lunch, read some gunnery pamphlets, 1½ hour nap. At 1600 my servant brought me coffee (my Nescafé)—then worked on diary plus reading gunnery data. Wrote to my sweetheart. Hope I will soon get mail from her.

Letter to Mrs. Wellings, 17 December 1940

. . . Well sweet I am all settled in my new office and am being treated like the King himself. Such service!! Oh how I wish you were here to share it with me. The food is also excellent so I guess I will have to watch my weight. I weigh 169 lbs now which is two pounds less than my heavy weight when I left home and two pounds more than my Washington weight.

The food is much better than at the main office. Grapefruit every morning so far—, cereal or rolled oats, ham or bacon and eggs, toast, marmalade or butter (or both) and coffee. How is that for a breakfast???

I have given up afternoon tea as I don't want to gain on this job which is much easier than my last one. At four my servant brings me a cup of boiling water, sugar and milk. Then he goes to *your* coffee and makes me a fine cup of coffee. The last two afternoons he has had to call me from my afternoon siesta to give me my coffee. (Incidentally please send me over two of the large cans of coffee you gave me when I left my sweetheart.)

---

[33]Selwyn John Power Warrand.

[34]John Croynn Tovey (1885-1971). Commander in Chief, Home Fleet, embarked in H.M.S. *Nelson*; Later Commander in Chief, the Nore, 1943-46; Admiral of the Fleet, 1943. Created first Baron Tovey of Langton Matravers, 1946.

I try to get a half hours walk in the morning and the same after lunch because I want to keep in good condition. I do stay up at night until about 2300 or 2400. I find that it is a good time to tell and hear stories.[35] Last night I visited my old pals and they gave me a party . . . . Incidentally I gave them your recipes and they all wish to thank you. I bought them an ice cream freezer while in London town so they can experiment as soon as it arrives.

Oh yes—my servant calls me at 0800, brushes my clothes, shines my shoes and lays out the rest of my clothes. Right this moment my *bed* is turned down, pajamas laid out evenly, slippers under the bed. I take my bath before dinner in order not to go out afterwards and possibly catch cold—(yes, the tub is drawn—or rather the water is drawn and just at the correct temperature). I will have to pay more attention to these things when I get home. *Our servants* have had things too easy. *Ahem* . . . .

Personal Diary, 18-19 December 1940

18 December—At anchor until 0830—then underway for gunnery practice—Intermittent rain squalls—finally fired HA and LA. At 1630 joined other ships—*Nelson, Repulse*, 4 cruisers & 10 destroyers underway all night. Night cruiser search exercise.

19 December—Underway. Practiced repulsing aircraft attacks from about 1100-1300, Tracking exercises by cruisers in afternoon and at night.

Letter to Mrs. Wellings, 19 December 1940

. . . I feel fine and am in good health. Incidentally I have yet to have my first cold (knock wood). I have my supply of A.P.C.'s[36] ready at all times but so far I have only used one as a preventative. I have however used my entire original supply. I am called Dr. Wellings at our country estate. I administered my pills to the cook, her little boy, Bill Ammon, Franny Forest, Capt. Cockran, Comdr. Mills, and the two secretarys. Now however our doctor has received a supply from Washington so I have taken in my shingle and renewed my own supply.

Today is a big day. I finally shifted to my woolen underwear purchased upon my arrival in dear old England. I bought them on the advice of the boys in the office. So far I have not used them, but today I thought it better to break them out as winter is officially only two days away. Everyone else wears them. Consequently I thought it better to take no chances. Of course I will have to continue now with them until the weather gets warmer.

Everything is quiet and peaceful around these parts. Really it is like being on a vacation. I make every effort to get my daily exercise and plenty of fresh air. All night in every night is a treat. I will have to come back to earth when I start to work again. I do manage to do considerable reading and talking which helps to pass the time away. Of course we may at any moment get a few customers and perhaps work overtime . . . .

---

[35]For example: "Winston Churchill . . . had completed a visit to the *Hood*—pride of the Royal Navy—just a few days before my arrival . . . . During his visit in the *Hood*, Mr. Churchill was having a Scotch and Soda in the wardroom before dinner. A young officer queried, 'Mr. Prime Minister, do you really believe all those inspirational remarks you tell the people on B.B.C.?' In his usual oratorical manner, Mr. Churchill quickly replied, 'Young man,—I have told many a lie for my country in the past—and I shall continue to do so in the future! . . . . Does that answer your question?—I think I'll have a refill on my Scotch and Soda!'" *JHW MS. Reminiscences*, pp. 72-73.

[36]Acetyl salicylic phenacitin and caffeine compound.

Personal Diary, 20-25 December 1940

20 December—Arrived Scapa Flow at 1000—moored to regular buoy. Mess night at dinner—toasted the King.

21 December—at anchor at Scapa all day. Daily routine—up at 0800—nap in p.m. Up to 2330 talking in Hood's wardroom.

22 December—At anchor—visited Comdr. Philipps[37] in *Maidstone*. Toured *Hood's* plotting room after lunch, then visited HMS *Lincoln*—our old destroyer *Twiggs*.[38] Quite interesting to hear their remarks how they liked the ship. Stayed two hours—back to *Hood*, bath, no. 1 suit, wing collar, bow tie and then to dinner with Admiral W.J. Whitworth in *Hood*. Very fine dinner followed by movies—Pinocchio in Wardroom, returned to Admiral's cabin for nightcap and then to bed—time 2330.

23 December—Left *Hood* at 0810 and went aboard battleship *King George V* to observe gunnery firings—*K.G. V* is a new battleship "working up" at Scapa. Underway at 0900 and returned at 2150. Inspected Y Turret, & all living quarters, watched AA practice firing. Churchill spoke on radio at 2100—subject—Italians—why they entered the war—very good.[39] Back aboard *Hood* at 2200. In Wardroom telling boys about my visit—to bed at 2400.

24 December—At anchor until 1630—then underway with *Edinburgh* and 4 destroyers to patrol off *Iceland* during Christmas holidays. Very fine weather— Christmas Eve—and here I am a long ways from home—Quite disappointed—thought continually about Dolly and Anne, and home. Wish Mother could have had another Xmas with us. Watched the clock and pictured Dolly putting Anne to bed—turned in at 0005—wrote to Dolly.

25 December—Christmas Day—on patrol off Iceland—what a way to spend Xmas. Oh well, if I cannot be with my two little girls I don't mind being here—It is all for the flag??? Grand weather for a change in these parts. Lat. 64N Long. 2E at noon . . . .

Letter to Mrs. Wellings, Christmas Day 1940

. . . I have had a very pleasant day so far. Everyone has been so kind to me. However I am sorry at not being able to go to church on Christmas day in order to thank God in his home for his many benefits and blessings. However I have thanked him in "the silence of my lonely room" which I know is perfectly satisfactory under the present conditions.

The big, big boss and the big boss have written me notes which I appreciate very much and will be added to my collection. As there was no opportunity to purchase small presents I sent them one of our Embassy Christmas cards and a carton of Chesterfields. Believe me they appreciated the thought. Chesterfields just cannot be bought these days, except through the Embassy. Even in peacetime they are about 60 cents a package—it was the thought behind the gift which made the big hit.

The dining room is all decorated with colored paper and looks similar to our dining rooms at this time of the year, although there was no Christmas tree to set off the decorations.

The dinner was really grand—just finished, and after this letter I will promptly take a

---

[37]Arthur Trestain Phillipps, Paymaster Commander.

[38]*Town*-class destroyer, Pennant number G. 19, 1211 tons displacement. *Lincoln* was U.S.S. *Yarnell* (DD-143), built 1918 and transferred to U.K. 23 October 1940, loaned to the Royal Norwegian Navy, 1942, transferred to U.S.S.R. and renamed *Druzhny*, 1944. Returned to U.K. and broken up, 1952.

[39]"To the People of Italy." Text published in W.S. Churchill, *Blood Sweat and Tears* (New York: Putnam, 1941), pp. 439-443.

nap. We had soup, fish, turkey and stuffing, potatoes, brussel sprouts, mince pie, cheese, crackers, nuts and coffee. The only thing lacking was cranberry sauce. It really was very well prepared and I must say I was surprised at having such a fine Christmas dinner under our present conditions. Of course as I said before the food here is really exceptionally good, much better than on my last visit and even better than I received at our country estate in London. I have had to watch my eating in order not to gain weight . . . .

Letter from Admiral Whitworth, 25 December 1940
HMS HOOD
Xmas Day, 1940

I much appreciate the card and handsome present which you have sent me for Xmas.

May I take this opportunity of saying how much we are sensible of the sympathy and practical help which your Country is giving us, to rid the world of an evil, which I trust may never return.

With the help of our good friends across the sea, I hope that we shall have completed our business before another Xmas comes upon us. If my hopes are realized, you will spend next Xmas under happier circumstances and will perhaps recall with satisfaction that you spent Xmas Day 1940 in H.M.S. Hood.

Personal Diary, 26-31 December 1940

26 December—Underway—on Patrol—Report that a raider was breaking through about 50 miles off southeast coast of Iceland, course N.E.—Headed south by no luck by dark—incidentally sunrise at 1150, Sunset 1428. About 2 hours of twilight.

27 December—Underway—on patrol—No sign of raider—weather getting rough. Temperature 33°F, Wind about 30, sea picking up. Reached Lat. 66N—O.W. and headed south at 1700—nap in p.m.—worked on reports, dinner—discussion on British vs. U.S. promotion, Pay corps and what have you—Quite interesting. Turned in at 2330. Hood *squeaks* to beat the band when weather gets rough. However very comfortable—

28 December—Under[way] on patrol still heading south. Weather improved during the night. Sky still overcast temperature now 40—usual daily routine—on bridge 1000—1200—1500-1630—sunset 1530—Headed for Scapa at 1700 expect to arrive at 0900.

29 December—Arrived at Scapa at 1100—fueled immediately. Nap and walk in p.m. wrote to Dolly and Dad. Played poker at night in execs. cabin, present Exec.,[40] First Lieut.,[41] Chief Eng.,[42] Ass. Chief Eng.,[43] Staff gunnery officer.[44] Won 5 schillings—my first poker game in years.

30 December—At Scapa—Turned cold during night—Surrounding hills covered with light snow. Temperature 37, snow made me sort of homesick. A good 2 mile walk on quarterdeck (quarterdeck is *100 yards* long). Nap in p.m. then at 1530 left in drifter for Lyness (20 min. boatride) to see Will Fife, the Scotch comedian give a performance

---

[40]Cdr. W.K.R. Cross.

[41]Lcdr. J.L. Machin.

[42]Robert Terence Grogan, Commander (E).

[43]John Gordon Morrison Erskine, Lcdr. (E).

[44]Robert Alexander Currie (1905-   ). Lcdr.; Later Rear Admiral, 1954; Chief of Staff to Chairman, British Joint Service Mission, Washington, D.C., 1954-57.

for the ratings in the recreation hall. Quite good. Stopped at officers club for a beer while waiting for the boat. Return trip made in a snow storm, drifter had to stop about 3 times due to lack of visibility. Arrived on board at 1900. Shifted, shaved and dinner—wore a wing collar and bow tie as usual for dinner in port. Captain & Admiral in Wardroom for a drink before dinner. After dinner talked with exec. about ways of decreasing convoy losses—quite interesting—To bed at 2330.

31 December—Last day of 1940—up at usual time 0745—breakfast, a good 1½ mile walk on quarterdeck, more snow last night—Hills are really very pretty—wish I were home. On bridge watching ship shift berths—Not a very good job—cut mooring buoy. Watched the crew get their ration of rum—quite a ritual. Called on the Warrant Officers—had a gin(s) (2). Lunch, read, nap—First Lieut. in for a cup of coffee at 1730. Dressed for dinner—at 1830 called on the midshipmen in the gunroom and the Warrant Officers before dinner. Had a very fine turkey dinner.

After dinner remained in wardroom—talked with Warrand, the navigator, and Owens.[45] Just before midnight the officers returned from the C.P.O. party. Browne[46] (Lt. Paymaster) rigged up ships bell in Anteroom of wardroom. At 2400 bell was struck 16 times, an old custom. Captain, Admiral, his staff, exec. and practically all officers returned to Wardroom. We all drank a toast to 1941—Peace and Victory. One of the midshipmen from the gunroom came in with a bagpipe and played Scotch tunes. Everyone started to dance the various Scotch dances from the Admiral down to the lowest midshipman. The Wardroom tables were cleared away and a regular party was in full swing. It was a very unusual sight to see the Admiral, Captain, staff, Wardroom, gunroom, and Warrant officers dancing. Included in the party but not dancing was the Chief Master - at arm and Sergeant Major of the marines. Such a comradship one would never suspect from the English who are supposed to be so conservative. I was impressed very much. Such spirit is one of the British best assets. This spirit will go far to bring about victory in the end. At 0145 I left the party in full swing and turned in but not before thanking God for his many blessings in 1940 and saying goodnight to my two sweethearts.

—Farewell to 1940—all in all not a bad year although I regret to say I will remember this year as the year my mother died and the year in which I was separated from my sweetheart, for five months. With God's will may 1941 bring peace to the world and happiness to us all—Ring in 1941.

Letter to Mrs. Wellings, 1 January 1941

. . . When midnight arrived the dining room was crowded with all the boys. The big boss was among those present. He ordered drinks all around and we drank to 1941 "Victorious and Peace."

All hands admitted that 1940 was a bad year from the viewpoint of the war. However they were all confident that the tide had changed and that 1941 would be a better year. I sincerely hope so because we cannot stand many years like 1940. My personal opinion is that by summer we will know Hitler's latest threat. Whatever it may be I have confidence in the British being able to cope with the situation. By the fall I hope and believe England will be in a much better position than it is today. Of course no-one knows when it will all be over. Time alone can tell. There are so many "ifs and buts" that a true prediction is impossible . . . .

---

[45]Lt. George Edward Mills Owens, Assistant Gunnery Officer.

[46]Robert Harold Percy Browne. Paymaster Lieutenant on Staff of Commander, Battle Cruiser Squadron One.

Last night we had another grand dinner with turkey and all the fixings. We all thoroughly enjoyed it but of course we ate too much. I believe I will have to watch my weight or I will be putting on extra pounds. The food quality here is the best I have seen to date over here—outside the No. 1 restaurant in London . . . .

Personal Diary, 1-3 January 1941

1 January— . . . At anchor at Scapa. The boys were rather tired in the morning. I took a good 1.5 mile walk on quarterdeck—still quite cold. Temp. 36. In p.m. I had a 2 hour nap—wrote some official papers and then wrote to Dolly and Dad. Turned in early at night.

2 January— . . . An anchor routine until 1630 when underway with 4 DD's to cover mine laying operations off the Faeroe Islands.[47] Cleared Pentland Firth at sunset—one of the most beautiful sunsets I have seen for a long time. Weather cold (36°) sea calm, wind light. Speed 19 and zigzagging.

3 January— . . . Underway—made contact with mine laying force—*Edinburgh*[48], 4 Minelayers—ex-merchant ships[49] and 4 DD's. Weather now rough reduced visibility—incident of *Edinburgh* opening fire, *Hood* going to action station and increasing speed to 25 knots. Spent considerable time on bridge.

Letter to Mrs. Wellings, 3 January 1941

. . . While it is only 2230 I must turn in as I have to get up real early tomorrow—for a change. Yes I am still watching my health and I insist on getting at least seven hours sleep plus my afternoon nap of about an hour. I find a nap quite useful. I don't know what I will do when I have to go back to real work all day. I know I am rapidly being spoiled in every way. However I may as well take things easy. I can find enough to do to keep me comfortably busy if I try real hard. My present trip is about a hundred percent easier than my last one. Partly because I know the work a little better so that there isn't so much research. It is a fascinating game from every angle . . . .

Personal Diary, 4 January

. . . Still underway in connection with minelaying operations. Weather very rough. DD's astern and rolling badly, their boats being battered, frames buckling. Completed minelaying operations at 1730 and headed for Scapa. *Hood*'s decks very wet, etc.

Letter to Mrs. Wellings, 4 January 1941[50]

. . . I ate too much at lunch. I will have to start a New Years resolution to cut down on my food. The menu today consisted of soup (pea), a choice of about three main courses in which I took cold roast beef. For vegetables I had boiled potatoes, beets, and squash and for a "sweet" I had a currant roll. Of course a small cup of coffee wound up the meal. Now you know that is too much for a noon day meal.

---

[47]In January more than 2,000 mines were laid in two lines between Iceland and the Faeröe Islands. Mining operations in this area had high priority as a means to restrict the waters through which enemy surface vessels could pass to reach the North Atlantic trade routes.

[48]H.M.S. *Edinburgh*. Southampton class cruiser 613′ length, 63¼′ beam, 17′ beam. Launched 1938. Lost 1942.

[49]Auxiliary minelayers of 1st Minelaying Squadron.

[50]Continuation of 3 January letter.

I have already given up tea in the afternoons, except once in awhile. I have a cup without any cookies, toast or rolls. Some of the boys make a regular meal of afternoon tea . . . .

Personal Diary, 5-9 January 1941

5 January—Arrived off Scapa boom defense at 0930, incident of mine cable being caught in port paravane when paravanes were recovered. Anchored in fleet anchorage at 1100—fueled as usual. Weather warmer (43°) snow disappearing from hills.

Walked in p.m. for about an hour on the quarterdeck. No movies tonight. (Sunday night is the usual night for movies.)

6 January—At anchor, daily routine. Went ashore in p.m. to Flotta to see movies—went with Warrand. Saw "Three Smart Girls" with Deanna Durben. Aboard at night. Wrote to Dolly.

7 January—At anchor. Daily routine. In p.m. went ashore with Warrand for a walk on Flotta. Walked from 1350 to 1610. Quite a good walk. Had tea upon return. Wrote some official papers at night.

8 January—At anchor. Went to Kirkwall[51] in Drifter. Left ship at 0800. Returned 1330. Kirkwall is the one real town in the Orkneys. It is a very old Scotch town. The people are really descendants of the Norwegians who first colonized the islands. The town has a very old Cathedral—very impressive—built 1190 so they say. Bought 21 yds. of Orkney tweed—Hope I did not make a mistake. Aboard at Night.

9 January—At anchor—daily routine. In p.m. went aboard *Repulse*[52] with torpedo officer for a lecture on bomb disposal from the Fleet bomb disposal officer. Very interesting. Remainder of day—usual routine.

Letter to Mrs. Wellings, 9 January 1941

I received your Thanksgiving Day letter . . . the day before yesterday and your grand Christmas presents last night.

I was so happy to receive both your letter and the presents. Thanks loads for the pajamas, neckties, coffee, cigarettes and soap . . . . As a matter of interest, they both reached London on 29 December but were delayed in forwarding to the branch office. Ordinarily the London mail to me takes three days. This isn't bad—for mail over here.

I thought the pajamas were grand . . . . So far I have continued to wear the ones I brought from home. The weather isn't too cold as yet. The lowest temperature has been 33°, generally it is around 40°. If it does not get worse I will not complain . . . . The coffee came at the right time as I am just about to run out of the coffee you so kindly packed for me when I left home. I used my last Chesterfields at Christmas time. We can get them at a reduced price (6 cents) but they must be ordered 3 months ahead of time. Yours will hold me over until I get my next consignment. There is plenty of soap over here as a matter of information but don't think I did not appreciate your thoughtfulness . . . .

Personal Diary, 10-14 January 1941

10 January—At anchor—usual daily routine including walk in a.m. and p.m. on quarterdeck. Late in evening ship made preparations for getting underway.

11 January—Underway at 0010 cleared Pentland Firth at 1300. Ships present—

---

[51]Kirkwall on the island called Mainland.

[52]H.M.S. *Repulse*. Battle cruiser. Built 1916. Lost 10 December 1941 off Malaya with H.M.S. *Prince of Wales*.

Hood, Repulse, Edinburgh, Birmingham, 6 DDs. Stood to the westward and then northwestward at 20 knots. Purpose of operations—to act as covering force for two large convoys. It was suspected from radio transmissions that a German raider was within 100 miles of convoys.

12 January—Underway—changed course for Scapa at 0100—sea calm—Incident on sighting smoke on horizon which turned out to be British DD's. *Hood's* speed, *etc.* At 2330 was off Scapa.

13 January—Underway—changed destroyer screen. Other ships entered Scapa. *Hood* plus new DD screen headed down east coast of Scotland to Roseyth. Arrived at 1600—quite foggy in Firth of Forth. *Hood* to have a much needed overhaul. No liberty as the ship will have ammunition removed beginning at daylight tomorrow. Holiday atmosphere prevailed in Wardroom. Officers and men glad to be back to civilization. First time men will get ashore for a real liberty in 6 months. Admiral had an at home in his quarters at 1800. Very fine party. Had 2 martinis which were quite strong. Dinner in Wardroom afterwards quite lively. I was toasted—made a short speech.

14 January—At anchor—made preparations to leave *Hood.* All arrangements completed for my going to *Curacoa* in about two or three days. Arranged to have *Curacoa* inform Admiralty when I should report. Plan to go to London for a day. Called on Admiral and Captain. Had lunch, said goodbye to all the officers and at 1420 left *Hood* with bag and baggage. I certainly had a grand 5 weeks in *Hood.*

Took a taxi to Edinburgh (about 8 miles—14 shillings). Gave 3 of the *Hood* midshipmen a ride to town. Stopped at Royal British Hotel, inquired about sleeper ticket—looked doubtful, all booked. R.T.O.[53] promised to do his best before train time. Walked along Princes St., (main street) shopped at Forseyths—bought blouse & sporran for Anne. Met Major[54] & Captain[55] of *Hood* marines at Royal British. Went to Caledonian Hotel and met about 15 of the *Hood's* officers. I had five to dinner at the Aperetiff—quite expensive.[56] They all came down to station to see me off. R.T.O. had a sleeper for me on the 2220. Au Revoir Edinburgh.

Time at Sea and Distances Steamed, 11th December 1940-14th January 1941 [57]

18th Dec.-20th Dec.	2 days 2 hours	735 miles
24th Dec.-29th Dec.	4 days 18 hours	1,635 miles
Jan. 2nd-Jan. 5th	2 days 20 hours	825 miles
Jan. 11th-Jan. 13th	2 days 16 hours	1,027 miles
TOTAL	12 days 8 hours	4,222 miles
	A. St. C. Armitage	
	[Midshipman]	

Personal Diary, 15 January 1941

Fine nights sleep on train The British sleeper accommodations are very good (a compartment to each berth). Arrived London 1000. Boys at Embassy surprised to

---

[53]Robert Neville Stopford, Commander; retired 1929, recalled to active service.

[54]Maj. Heaton Lumley, Royal Marines.

[55]Capt. Thomas Desmond Cartwright, Royal Marines.

[56]Cost: £10 9/-

[57]The total sea time of JHW in H.M.S. *Hood.*

see me. Went to Admiralty and explained my arrangements for the *Curacoa*—probably leave tomorrow. Met Count Austin at Admiralty, we walked back to Embassy in a light snow storm. About 1″ of snow in London. Lunch with Count Austin at Selfridges. Worked on reports at office (Defense of fleet at sea). Drove to New Pipers—out in Virginia Waters in Admiral Ghormley's official Buick sedan. The Admiral has left London—will leave England tomorrow for the U.S. Good to see the gang at New Pipers. Comdr. Lee[58], Savvy Forest, Bill Ammon, Comdr. Sylvester, Mrs. Ripman and Miss Ziegler now staying at New Pipers. Capt. Cockran left two days ago with Admiral Ghormley. Savvy Huffman left 10 days ago for home . . . . Played ping-pong after dinner. Wrote to Capt. Lee[59] saying I would be ready to go home about 1 April . . . worked on reports—turned in at 0130.

Letter to Mrs. Wellings, 15 January 1941

. . . London seems to be carry[ing] on as usual despite the bombing and incendiaries. I really expected to see much more damage. As a matter of fact there isn't hardly any difference around the West End where the Embassy is located. I understand other parts of the city have received more damage but on the whole the city is still far from "ruins." As I came from the station today business was proceeding as usual in all the stores. The people are determined to carry on and to my mind this is going to be one of the decisive facts in the war in favor of the British. Of course I have not seen other severely bombed areas, but I understand the people in these places are also determined to carry on to victory. The British spirit is such that one has to take his (or her) hat off to them . . . .

Incidentally yesterday while in Edinburgh I bought a sporran (belt and bag) and a white shirt waist to go along with the outfit for Anne. I did *not* have my shopping guide[60] as I knew she would not listen to me buying these articles. The man in the store however absolutely refused to sel[l] me a jacket, so I guess you will have to make or buy one.

Mails have been and are still slow. I have not received a letter from you for over two weeks. The boys in the office say that quite a few pouches were lost enroute. A number of the boys lost the Christmas gifts enroute to London. Thank the Lord mine got through.

The boys are playing ping-pong right next to me. It is our favorite and only sport, outside of walking. We have matches, tournaments, etc. Right now they are having a terrific discussion over a handicap of one of the boys. Bill Ammon, '23 is the champ. I am learning rapidly and in about a month (if I were here) I think I could give him a close game with a handicap of about two points in the regular 21 . . . .

Personal Diary, 16 January 1941

Went to office with Bill and Mrs. Ripman in Capt. Kirk's official car. Incidentally the latter arrived in Washington on 23 Dec. He traveled by air. Worked on reports—travel accounts—took out $5000 more life insurance (special government insurance). At 1210 Admiralty informed me that I was to leave for Scapa at 1300 train—made it with all my baggage . . . .

---

[58]Paul Frantz Lee (1895-1979). U.S. Naval Academy, 1925; Assistant Naval Attaché, London. Later Rear Admiral.

[59]Willis A. Lee, previously noted.

[60]Miss Cotton.

Letter to Mrs. Wellings, 17 January 1941

. . . I only wish you were with me on this train ride. It really has been an experience. It is a special train with only one first class car and no sleeping compartment. As a result my compartment is occupied by three others besides myself—one in each corner. You remember how the European trains are arranged?

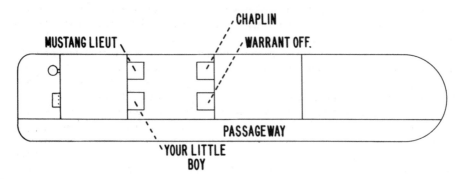

The warrant officer is an old timer, sleeps all the time except when he wakes up for about a half hour every four hours to smoke a foul pipe.

The Chaplain (Church of England) is about 38 (just a boy) and apparently a fine "bloke."

The mustang Lieut. is also an old timer who smokes a pipe incessantly—even when he closes off every 30 minutes for a 15 minute nap.

We left London at 1300 yesterday and were due to arrive at our destination at 1000 today. However we are already one hour late and have about two to three hours more to go. The 22 hour (so far) train ride has been quite an experience. I bought some magazines and papers, the Chaplain did the same, the other two bought sandwiches on the assumption that there would be no diner on the train. Of course you remember each compartment is separate by sliding doors. The train was not exactly warm yesterday so these doors were always closed until the pipe smoke got too thick, then either the Chaplain or myself would suggest opening the door for a few minutes. The other two would grunt or make no reply if they were fast asleep. It has been quite a problem to keep the air fresh.

There was a diner on the train and the Chaplain and I had lunch (2 hrs.) and dinner (4 hrs.). The dining car was quite comfortable and we hated to leave. By going in for the second and last call we could stay as long as we wanted. Last night at 2330 just before we left the diner we had two scotch and sodas to help fight off the germs (our only drinks). Incidentally the British drinks are only 1/3 to 1/2 the size of ours. I followed my drinks with one APC pill to prevent any possible cold—as I don't want to break my healthy record.—

At 0200 today we stopped at a station for almost an hour. I went out on the platform and had a grand walk. The air was cold, frost on the car windows, and about one inch of snow on the ground. The night was clear and the moon was looking down with a friendly smile as though to say "All is clear." I could not help but think that the same moon was looking down on you and smiling in the same friendly way and saying "your little boy is safe, healthy and happy except that he misses you very, very much and asked me to send you all his love" . . . .

I got almost an hours sleep between 0200 and 0400, then I apparently went soundly to sleep for the next thing I knew the conductor was announcing the name of the station[61] saying "All out for identification." I looked at my watch and it was 0815. The Chaplain and I went to the station restaurant and had coffee, toast, marmalade, bacon and two fine eggs. (The diner has been removed.) Believe me it was *almost* as good as our Sunday morning breakfasts . . . .

The identification took a very short time. More cars were added and in a half hour we were underway again.

I, of course have my Shetland blanket with me. I always take it when I ride on the trains. The main reason is that the English like their trains much colder than we do (same for their houses). In addition I don't like drafts in trains.

I must tell you about what I saw at lunch yesterday. A lady sat across the aisle from me with a rosy cheek, gold haired little girl about 2 to 2 and a half years old. The little girl was hungry—not having eaten since 0730 and fussy due to travelling on a train since the same time. The mother had a thermos bottle of milk. The child wanted to drink all of it but the mother just gave her enough to hold her over until lunch was served. I thought she would never get lunch. The poor baby was ravenous and begged for food. I almost went out to the kitchen and got her something to eat. The waiters were terribly slow—they clear off the first setting, set tables, one knife, one fork, plates, napkins for every place, wait for the *patrons* to arrive, serve a drink to everyone that wants it including water, then soup to everyone, then the main course. I was almost mad waiting for all this ritual while the baby was crying for something to eat . . . .

Personal Diary, 17-23 January 1941

17 January— . . . Arrived Thurso at 1500—took a room at the Royal—a hot bath and a 3 hours nap. After dinner called on Capt. Newcombe (R.N.) the Naval Officer in charge at Thurso. Quite a character. He told me about Churchill's visit two days before. With Churchill were Harry Hopkins[62], Admiral Ghormley, Capt. Cockran & Lord Halifax.[63] The latter three left for the U.S. from Scapa.[64] About 3" of snow in Thurso. Back to hotel at 2300 and to bed.

18 January—Friday up at 0840, fine nights sleep—fire built in fireplace for me. Wrote to Dolly after breakfast with Chaplain. Went for a short walk. Capt. Newcombe sent his car for me. We drove out to Castleton airport (6 miles) with one of his Wrens who had to go to Kirkwall for an interview for a commission. She was in plane and about to take off when a snow storm set in—result no Kirkwall—lunch with Capt. Newcombe—held boat until we were finished—then went aboard the boat for Scapa at 1420. Arrived at 1700. Called on Rear Admiral Destroyers[65], then went to the *Curacoa* my new home. Capt Hughes Hallett[66] very fine officer and gentleman. Met all the ships officers, dinner, and to bed at 2230. Room very small, but O.K.—quite cold.

19 January—At anchor at Scapa. Squared away my gear, wrote to Dolly, inspected ship. Rear Admiral Destroyers invited Capt. and myself to dinner on his flagship

---

[61]Inverness.

[62]Harry L. Hopkins (1890-1946). Head, Lend-Lease Program, 1941; Adviser and assistant to President Roosevelt, 1941-45.

[63]Edward Frederick Lindley Wood, Earl of Halifax (1881-1959). Secretary of State for Foreign Affairs, 1938-40; British Ambassador at Washington, D.C. 1941-46.

[64]They sailed in H.M.S. *King George V.* See description in Halifax, *The Fulness of Days* (London: Collins, 1957), pp. 237-38.

[65]Rear Admiral Hallifax.

[66]Cecil Charles Hughes Hallett (1898-   ). Later Vice Admiral, 1952; Admiral, British Joint Services Mission, Washington, D.C., 1952-54; KCB, 1954.

H.M.S. CURACOA

Ceres class cruiser converted for antiaircraft work. Launched 1917 at Pembroke by Harland & Wolff. Length overall 451½′, beam 43½′, draft 14½′, speed 29 knots. Displacement 4190 tons, complement 400 men. Armament:8·4″ AA, 4·2 prev AA, 8··5″M guns. Lost 2 October 1942 when she was rammed and sunk by *Queen Mary*, the Cunard liner she was escorting in the Western approaches. Photo: [Imperial War Museum: A 10645]

followed by movies. Had a very pleasant evening. Glad to see Comdr. Phillips—R.A.D.'s flag secretary again.

20 January—At anchor until 1230 then underway to act as air escort for convoy from Pentland Firth, down east coast of Scotland. Stayed with convoy until 2 hours after sunset—really dark. Idea is to remain until it is too dark for German planes to launch torpedo attacks on convoy. Thought we saw one German shadower in p.m. fired a few salvos to indicate position to our escorting Hudson planes (2). Fighter planes arrived shortly afterwards but, no excitement. Arrived at Scapa at 2330—blinding snow storm as we entered the Flow. On bridge most of time. President Roosevelt made Inaugural address—listened to same.[67]

21 January—At anchor Scapa—terribly bad weather—snow storm and very rough. Aboard all day—inspected gunnery Dept. and read. Had a long talk with Captain in his cabin. A bright man.

22 January—At anchor—Convoy delayed due to storm. Supposed to get underway at 1230 but will not get underway today. Called on American DD with Captain. Seemed natural to be aboard them again. Talked with Captain in his cabin about convoys, etc. Called on Warrant Officers—dinner and to bed at 2230.

23 January—At anchor. My 4th wedding anniversary. Wrote to Dolly. Wish we were together today. Called on *Punjabi* at 1145 with Comdr. Lee (E).[68] Good to see Captain Lean and his officers again. Nap in p.m. Bought a round of drinks to celebrate wedding anniversary. Read a little official work. Discussed convoys with Exec.

Letter to Mrs. Wellings, 23 January 1941

. . . Well darling I feel grand. This branch office is not quite so comfortable as my last. However I will only be here four more days when I will shift to a much more comfortable one.

I must now close—I have [to] put on my bow tie and have dinner with my present boss. He has invited three for dinner besides myself . . . .

Personal Diary, 24-26 January 1941

24 January—At anchor. Daily routine. Dinner in Captain's cabin with Capt. and Capt. M.H. Evelegh[69] of the *Bramble*[70] and Comdr. Boutwood[71] of *Iron Duke*[72]. Very interesting evening.

25 January—At anchor—called at 1130 on Comdr. Boutwood in *Iron Duke* and Capt. Evelegh in *Bramble*. Met Lt. Comdr. Terry[73] of the *Jason*[74] when he called on the

---

[67]Third Inaugural address: "In the face of Great Perils Never Before Encountered Our Purpose is to Protect and to Perpetuate the Integrity of Democracy." Printed in *The Public Papers and Addresses of Franklin D. Roosevelt, 1941* (New York: Random House, 1950), pp. 3-7.

[68]T.S. Lee, Commander, (E) Engineer officer, H.M.S. *Curacoa*.

[69]Markham Henry Evelegh.

[70]H.M.S. *Bramble*, Minesweeper.

[71]John Wilfrid Boutwood.

[72]Pre-World War I battleship demilitarized in 1931 for use as a gunnery training ship. Used as base ship, Home Fleet, 1939-1945.

[73]Reginald Ernest Terry.

[74]H.M.S. *Jason*, Minesweeper.

captain. Had dinner with him on board his ship. His Exec. was Exec. of The *Crowninshield* (Harry Henderson's DD) when she was taken over by the British.[75] He thought Harry an excellent officer.[76]

26 January—Underway at 1030—escorted an WN convoy[77] 16 ships down east coast of Scotland. Headed back for Scapa just after dark (off Peter Head). Anchored at Scapa at 2330. Passed through two or three snow squalls. Temp. 36°.

Letter to Mrs. Wellings, 26 January 1941

. . . Where I am now there has been about 4″ of snow, but it doesn't last very long. The high hills which can be seen all around are covered with snow and are really unusually beautiful. The temperature right now . . . is quite cold compared to the rest of the winter. All in all the winter has been much milder than I expected, for which I am unduly thankful . . . .

I am really and actually my own boss over here. It is really independent duty. I can come and go where I please, and do what I want. In a great many respects it is really a vacation from the high pressured work I had in Wash[ington]. Of course, the *work* is entirely different. Perhaps I am being completely spoiled . . . . However I am doing my best to keep my sense of balance and not really think that I am a special character. I believe I can keep one foot on the ground and return as I was before—and perhaps a little better in many ways. I have learned considerable which I hope I can put into practice when I return. The most important single lesson is patience and not to worry. I hope I can continue to follow these cardinal principles. They are important . . . .

Personal Diary, 27-28 January 1941

27 January—Informed upon anchoring last night at 2330 that we would get underway at 0600 for special duty. Finished fueling at 0300. Underway at 0600 and stood to the westward, passed Cape Wrath and then south through the Minches.[78] Speed 20, paravanes rigged. We have a good idea of the special work. Weather overcast, wind 4, sea medium, ship rolled quite easily . . . .

Letter to Mrs. Wellings, 27 January 1941

. . . I doubt now whether I will return to the main office before the first of March. I will send you a cable when I return. I have decided to stay here and clean up some odds and ends in case I should be ordered home about the end of March. It will save me another trip to these parts, *I hope*. However all in all this present trip has been very enjoyable, with just enough work to keep me interested. It is far better than my first trip in every way. Of course I have made a lot of friends and almost seem like one of the natives. As I have said before in my previous letters—I am getting a liberal education that money cannot buy and I hope I can only remember half of what I have seen and learned. I will be wealthy in experience even if not in money.

---

[75]U.S.S. *Crowninshield* (DD-134) was transferred to the U.K., 9 September 1940 and renamed H.M.S. *Chelsea*, pennant number I. 35.

[76]Harry Havelock Henderson (1904-1976). U.S. Naval Academy, 1925; Later Rear Admiral.

[77]An Atlantic convoy which passed north about the British Isles and joined with the Firth of Forth—Thames coastal convoys.

[78]The Minch or North Minch is a 35-mile wide strait separating the Outer Hebrides Islands of Lewis and Harris from the mainland of Scotland. It is continued by Little Minch, 15-25 miles wide, separating Skye from North Uist and Benbecula.

Now that January is almost over only one more month of winter remains. England is definitely lasting out the winter in much better condition than when it started—much to everyone's surprise—even their own I believe. One has to give them credit. They can take off their coats and go to work with tremendous energy even under adverse conditions once they make up their minds. Their spirit is wonderful. I only hope that our people can do the same—if they are ever called upon to make sacrifices.

Of course everyone is expecting some kind of move by Hitler sometime in the spring. What it will be no one knows. Personally, I doubt if it will be invasion. If it is Hitler will be taking a big gamble because he cannot stand a defeat and my personal opinion is that he will lose in an attempt to invade England . . . .

Personal Diary, 28-31 January 1941

28 January—Underway—Passed through North Channel—Entrance to Irish Sea at 0030, this is the place my convoy was bombed on my passage to England.—Headed south towards Liverpool. Sea last night was a little rough causing us to slow to 15 knots. Captain requested a later rendezvous with *Prince of Wales*—the new Battleship[79] we are to escort north around the North of Scotland and down to Roseyth. Stood south as far as the entrance to Liverpool channel, then turned around. Visibility only about one mile. Supposed to rendezvous with the *Prince of Wales* at 1630—however did not make contact until 1800 due to *P.O.W.* being 1½ hours late plus low visibility. On bridge about 8 hours. Rather interesting to see the convoy and trawlers pass by in reduced visibility. When contacted at 1800 *P.O.W.* was firing test shots from her A.A. guns—visibility ½ mile. I hope we did not hit anyone. On bridge from 2300-2400.

29 January—Underway astern of *Prince of Wales*, heading north. Passed through North Channel at 0100—speed 15, visibility a little better enough to see the navigational lights ashore. Increased speed to 18 knots when cleared of channel. *P.O.W.* escorted by four destroyers, in addition to ourselves (*Curacoa*). (Destroyers were built by the British for Brazilian Navy but taken over by the British just before delivery.)[80] At 0313 one DD left formation to go to the aid of a convoy reported attacked in Lat. 56, Long. 15-56. In late morning weather cleared, sea calm, excellent visibility, passed through Minches—beautiful scenery along Scotch coast. Mountains all covered with snow. At 1545 *Nigeria* (CL) and 3 DD's joined formation from Scapa. Two of three DD's which were already with us returned to Oban to fuel and to leave immediately afterwards to escort an east bound convoy. The other DD is to remain with us and proceed to Roseyth for refit. *Nigeria* tried to make a 180° turn at about 20 knots when joining formation. She turned too late and was inside her tactical diameter. As a result she almost collided with the *Prince of Wales*, the latter ship had to turn away 90° and stop. Air escort by Hudsons all afternoon. Passed through Pentland Firth 2200-2300. Westerly current plus southeast wind made the sea very rough. Ship pounded considerably forced to slow to 8 knots.

30 January—Steaming as before down east coast of Scotland towards Firth of Forth acting as AA escort for *Prince of Wales*. Wind and sea on port beam all morning causing ship to roll considerably. Did not get a good nights sleep. Speed 19 at 0800—did not zigzag. One Hudson and 3 Hurricaines acted as air escort after daylight—the Hudson left at 1100. Arrived at May Island (entrance to Pentland Firth) at 1200. *Prince of Wales, Nigeria*, plus 4 DD's continued on to Roseyth. We (*Curacoa*) turned around and headed for Scapa arriving at 2030. Very dark night on entering the

---

[79]*Prince of Wales* was not completed by her builders, Cammell Laird, until March 1941.

[80]*Hunt*-class (Type IV) escort destroyers of 1,340 tons displacement.

Flow. Had a sherry with Captain after anchoring. Officers in jovial mood in W.R.[81]—
had a singsong. Turned in at 2300.

31 January—At anchor Scapa. Made preparations to transfer to *Birmingham* at
1630. Called on R.A.D. in *Maidstone* at 1100. Arranged to stay in *Maidstone* for one
week after I finish in *Birmingham*. Rec'd a large envelope from Embassy containing
mail from home. First mail in 5 weeks . . . . Called on Warrants before lunch, bought
all officers a drink in W.R. as a farewell drink. The Chief Engineer, Commander Lee (E)
presented me with a cartoon entitled "The Neutral Observer Makes an Observation."
Quite good, I believe. Called on Captain and Exec., said goodbye to other officers and
was underway for the *Birmingham*—a 9000 ton C.L. anchored in the big ship
anchorage.

---

[81]Wardroom.

CHAPTER FIVE

H.M.S. *BIRMINGHAM*: GREENOCK TO CAPE TOWN
31 January-21 March 1941

Personal Diary, 31 January-2 February 1941

31 January . . . Usual procedure in meeting officers in *Birmingham*. They seem to be a happy lot. Called on Captain Madden[1] at 1930, had a gin. He seems to be very pleasant. Comdr's name is St. Quintin[2] also appears to be O.K. No. 1—Lt. Comdr. Daltron[3] will be my liaison officer. Have a very fine room. Tonight was guest night in Wardroom—12 guests quite a party. I stayed up to 0100—despite my good intentions to turn in early.

1 February—At anchor—tour of ship with First Lieut. then inspected mess decks with Comdr. Called on Warrants before lunch. 2.5 hour nap in p.m. Dinner as usual at eight. Returned to room at 2200. Read until 2330 and to bed.

2 February—At anchor. Up at 0730, breakfast at 0810 . . . . Had lunch as guest of Captain of *Rodney* (BB),[4] Rear Admiral MacNamara & Captain of *Nelson* also present. Captain [Chapman][5] is C.O. of *Nelson*. Attended movies "Dodge City" afterwards. Returned to *Birmingham* at 1700. Dined with Capt. Madden of *Birmingham* at 1945 followed by movies—A Saint in London—Quite an entertaining day.

Wines, Spirits, Liqueurs, Ales, Cups
Price List

Port I Ruby per bottle 4/4 per glass 5d
Port II Imperial per bottle 4/- per glass 5d
Sherry I Fino Mi Niña per bottle 5/8 per glass 6d
Sherry II Fino Catalina per bottle 3/11 per glass 4d
Sherry III Adelphi per bottle 3/11 per glass
Madiera per bottle 4/2 per glass 6d

Champagne	Du Roy. Vintage '28 @ 6/8 s.p. 7/-
	Du Montel Pere '32 @ 4/8 s.p. 5/-
Hock	Niersteiner '29 @ 3/-
	Liebfraumilch '34 @ 4/3

---

[1]Alexander Cumming Gordon Madden (1895-1964). Later Admiral; Second Sea Lord, 1950-53; Commander in Chief, Plymouth, 1953-55; KCB, 1951.

[2]Charles Frederick William St. Quintin.

[3]John Hartley Dathan.

[4]Frederick Hew George Dalrymple-Hamilton (1890-1974). Later Admiral, British Joint Services Mission, Washington, D.C., 1948-50; KCB, 1945.

[5]Alex Colin Chapman (1897-1970). Retired 1949.

H.M.S. *BIRMINGHAM*

Southampton-class cruiser. Launched at Devonport 1 September 1936. Length overall 591½'; beam 61¾'; draft 17'; Speed 32 knots; displacement 9100 tons. Armament, 12-6", 8-4" AA, 8-2 pdr. AA, 8-5" guns, 6-21" torpedo tubes, 3 aircraft. Complement 700. Served China 1939. Home Fleet 1940, South Atlantic 1941-42, Eastern Fleet 1942-44, Mediterranean Fleet and refit in U.S.A. 1944, Home Fleet 1945. Scrapped 1960.

[Photo: J.H. Wellings Collection "Presented by The Ship's Company H.M.S. Birmingham, April 1941"]

White Wines	Graves Superior	@ 2/6s.p. 2/8
	Chianti	@ 1/5 s.p. 1/6
Burgundy	Beaune	@3/5 s.p. 3/6
Red Wines	Medoc (Claret)	@ 2/7 s.p. 2/8
	Chianti	@ 2/8 s.p. 3/-
	Pommard	@ 4/6

Cape Wines	White	Sparkling Constantia	@ 5/- s.p. 5/-
		White Constantia	@ 1/10 s.p. 2/-
		Witzenburg	@ 1/10 s.p. 2/-
	Red	Chateau Constantia	@ 1/10 s.p. 2/-
		Vlakenburg	@ 1/10 s.p. 2/-

| Gins | Plymouth Gin | @ 4/2 2d. 3d. & 5d. |
| | London Gin | @ 4/10 2d. 3d. & 5d. |

| Whiskey | Canadian Club | @ 5/8 4d. (1/2) & 7d. |
| | John Haig | @ 5/8 4d. (1/2) & 7d. |

Brandy	Neukow	@ 7/6 5d. & 9d.
	Hennessey+++	@ 7/6 5d. & 9d.
	Cape Brandy	@ 4/2 3d.

| Rum | Lemon Hart's West Indian | @ 4/10 2d. & 5d. |

Liqueurs	F.O.V. Brandy	7d.
	Kummel	3d.
	Benedictine	4d.
	Cherry Brandy	4d.
	Curaçoa	3d.
	Cream de Menthe	3d.
	Drambuie	5d.
	Cointreau	5d.
	Grand Marnier	5d.
	Van der Hiem	3d.

| Cups | Pimms No. I | 4d. |
| | | 4d. |

Sloe Gin

Bitters	Italian Vermouth (Martini Rossi)
	French Vermouth
	Noily Prat
	Calverts
	Votrix

Cocktails (No. 1 Champagne)		5d.
Ales		3d.
	per 1/2 pint	
Hewits		
Bass	per glass	5d.
Castle		
Allsoppo Lager		4d.
Punch 100%		5d.
Planters Punch		4d.

Note from R.A. Smith, Leading Steward, H.M.S. *Birmingham*

You will observe that a small profit is made on these Wines and Spirits. This is to cover cost of loss by accident or rough weather—and selling at under cost price which we have to do quite often to enable members of the mess to get their full whack for the amount of their Wine allowance. I cater for 46 officers and apart from ales, can carry a six months supply in the small space allowed to me for stowage.

Letter to Mrs. Wellings, 2 February 1941

. . . Little did we think in 1938 in Long Beach when you and Betty used to have your coffee sessions that Boot[6] would be in China, me in London and our two sweethearts back with their "mommies" in Massachusetts. Such is Navy life darling. We have our disappointments but it is still a good navy and deep down in our hearts we love it—and so do you and Betty. Although I suppose the pair of you would have sold out your interest for ten cent Mex. (as Betty would say) the first day you two got together . . . .

Personal Diary, 3 February 1941

At anchor—up at 0730, breakfast at 0805. Walked in deck for about ½ hour—seems good to have enough space to get my daily exercise again. Watched morning colors. Watched 6" loading drill and the T.S. rehearsing con[cen]tration firing. Lunch guest of Vice Admiral Holland[7] at 1230 in *Edinburgh*—First Lieut.[8] and C.O.[9] of *Edinburgh* also present. Very pleasant lunch. Used Admirals barge to go to Northern AA. range to watch A.A. practice. Range is on S. Ronaldsay.[10] Returned to ship at 1705, tea and wrote these notes for yesterday and today.

---

[6]Edward Ney Dodson, Jr. (1905-   ). U.S. Naval Academy, Class of 1926. Dodson had been assigned to Destroyer Squadron 29 on the Asiatic Station.

[7]Lancelot Ernest Holland (1887-1941). Later Commander, Battle Cruiser Squadron One. Lost in H.M.S. *Hood*.

[8]Colin Wauchope, Commander.

[9]Charles Maurice Blackman, D.S.O. (1890-   ). Captain, Later promoted to Rear Admiral for war services.

[10]The most southerly island of the Orkney group.

Letter from Vice Admiral W.J. Whitworth, RN, 3 February 1941

Thank you for your letter. I am so glad to hear you enjoyed your time in *Hood*, and found it good value. I quite agree that it is most helpful that you and your brother officers should stay in our ships and thus be able to discuss practical problems, under active service conditions.

I am only sorry that we had not the opportunity of showing you *Hood* in action. Apart from the service aspect of your visit, we all enjoyed having you with us as a shipmate.

Very good luck in the future, and I hope to see you again sometime.

Personal Diary, 4-6 February 1941

4 February—At anchor until 1100—walked on quarterdeck from 0930-1000. Met Captain who asked me to go with him to his cabin. He said the ship would probably leave Scapa tomorrow for Glasgow where it would meet a convoy and act as escort to Freetown in Africa and perhaps the ship would then go to Alexandria for one trip via the Mediterranean. He asked me if I wanted to go and I replied "By all means yes." If the trip does take place it is expected to be gone about 5 to 6 weeks. Such a trip should complete my experiences as an observer. Underway with *Edinburgh*, *Nigeria* and *Mauritious*. Fired a long range throw off practice in p.m. followed by a night encounter exercise with *Edinburgh* after dark. Returned to Scapa at 2230. On the bridge during most of the afternoon and night. A very drafty open bridge. Quite cold—but sea smooth. Also had a tour of Engineering spaces in the late afternoon. At night (until 0130) worked on official reports.

5 February—At anchor. Stars came out during night. Wind very strong, sea rough, intermittent snow squalls. Weather moderated slightly in afternoon. 1527 Underway with *Edinburgh* for Greenock. I wonder when the ship will again be in Scapa. Convoys were "hoved to" west side of Pentland Firth. Weather continued to improve as we passed through the Minches . . . .

6 February—Enroute Greenock, weather clear, sea calm. Arrived Greenock at 1200. Beautiful scenery steaming into the harbor. Over 100 merchant ships anchored off Greenock, some of which quite large. Ashore with Commander St. Quentin at 1445. Went to Bay Hotel to call Embassy. No luck. Went to Bagatelle—Headquarters of F.O.I.C.[11] at Greenock. They succeeded in getting the Embassy on the phone via the Admiralty line. Talked with Bill Ammon and Comdr. Hitchcock. Received permission to make trip in *Birmingham*. They promised to send an officer to meet me at the Bay Hotel tomorrow noon with my white uniforms now at the Embassy. Walked for an hour. Met Comdr., P.M.O.[12] and Torps.[13] at hotel waiting for their respective wives. They were impatient—stood watches outside hotel. Wives finally arrived—one had a 2½ month old baby, another a 4 year old boy. Quite a sight—reminded me of home. Dinner at Bay Hotel with No. 1[14], Guns,[15] Pay[16] and the Marine.[17] 2200 boat back to ship.

---

[11]Flag Officer in Command.

[12]Principal Medical Officer: Surgeon Cdr. G.F. Abercrombie, R.N.V.R.

[13]Francis Doyne Godfrey Bird, Torpedo officer.

[14]J.H. Dathan.

[15]Archibald John Fitzwilliam Milne-Home.

[16]Clement Edward Glenister.

[17]Angus George Sutherland Forrest, Captain, Royal Marines.

Letter to Mrs. Wellings, 7 February 1941

. . . I met three officers who were anxiously waiting for their wives to arrive . . . . After two hours the three wives arrived in one car. They . . . had packed up on ½ hours notice and drove about 60 miles to get here then there was the problem of rooms. The hotels were all filled so they had to go in search of rooms at private houses. Eventually they were dug in and happy. I guess Navy wives are the same the world over. All grand sports who are used to packing up on a moments notice ready to go anywhere. We all agreed that a huge monument should be dedicated to Navy wives . . . .

Wendell Willkie[18] has left England for the U.S. He made a marvelous impression here. He travelled everywhere and saw almost everything. His apparent unlimited energy surprised everyone. I believe the British people were very pleased over his visit. At election time they doubted that if he were elected that he would aid Britain half as much as President Roosevelt. Now they know he is sincere. I believe he will do everything he can to help out the British. It will be interesting to hear his comments on the Lease and Loan bill . . . .[19]

Personal Diary, 7 February 1941

At anchor Greenock. Met Lt. Royal who brought my whites and mail from London and gave me the latest news from the Embassy. Met him at Bay Hotel—Gaurock. He left on the 1700 train for London. Attended convoy departure in Gaurock (N.C.S.O.[20] Greenock) with Captain and Navigator[21] of *Birmingham*. All merchant skippers and Captains of escort ships attended. Believe it will be quite a large convoy with some large ships. Returned to *Birmingham* after conference as I believe I know too much and it is better for me to stay aboard . . . . Had cocktails with Captain and his wife in his cabin . . . .Weather conditions very bad. Convoy sailing postponed 24 hours.

Official Diary, 7 February 1941[22]

The observer attended the departure conference at the Naval Control Service Office at Greenock. Captains of all merchant ships, plus the Admiral commanding the ocean escorts and his staff, the commanding officers of ocean escorts and their navigators, the captain in charge of the local escorts, and the division commanders of the local escort destroyers were present. Convoy to consist of 33 merchant ships, 18 of which are troop transports, remainder material transports. Ocean escort to consist of 2 light cruisers,[23] 1

---

[18]Wendell L. Willkie (1892-1944). Republican candidate for President of the United States. Defeated by Roosevelt in November 1940. Willkie made his visit to London with Roosevelt's blessing, but the trip proved an annoyance to Roosevelt. See Joseph Lash, *Roosevelt and Churchill 1939-1941* (New York: Norton, 1976), pp. 318-19.

[19]The Lend-Lease Bill was drawn up primarily to replenish exhausted British credit for the purchase of war supplies. It was approved 11 March 1941.

[20]Naval Control of Shipping Office.

[21]Alexander Robert Kennedy, Lcdr.

[22]This and subsequent official diary entries from Enclosure D "Diary for Convoy W.S. 6" to Report of Convoy Operations, Clyde to Freetown 9 Feb.-2 March 1941, serial 724 dated 5 May 1941.

[23]H.M.S. *Birmingham* and H.M.S. *Edinburgh*.

A.A. cruiser latest type[24] and 1 armed merchant cruiser.[25] Local escort to consist of 13 destroyers plus aircraft within their cruising range. Convoy speed 10 knots. Maximum speed of 3 ships is 11 knots, remainder have a higher maximum speed. Total gross tonnage 268,066. Gross tonnage of largest ship 19,700, of smallest ship 4,500. Troopships supplied with additional water. First port of call Freetown, Sierra Leonne, in Africa. Convoy to get underway beginning at 2200 today. Formation, single column passing through the boom defense gate, five minutes between ships at gate. Each ship to have a pilot until clear of gate. When clear of gate convoy to form into two columns until clear of North Channel (between Mul of Kintyre). Then form into 5 columns. Outside the North Channel the Liverpool and Milford Haven sections are to join convoy. 20 ships sailing from the Clyde, 8 from Liverpool and 6 from Milford Haven area. At end of conference it was announced that the departure of convoy was delayed 24 hours due to unfavorable weather conditions in the Clyde.

Official Report[26]

Type of Convoy. The convoy was not an ordinary convoy but a special convoy of troop transports and material transports containing troops and essential war materials for the military forces in other theatres of operations. 14 of the ships were troop transports and 15 material transports. 29 ships is not considered a large convoy, however the total gross tonnage of 268,066 tons is a large tonnage for a single convoy. The size of the individual ships (average gross tonnage 9,244) plus the number of specialized personnel (R.A.F. and landing force) and the type of war material carried, clearly indicate that the convoy was a very important one. Official designation of convoy—W[S]6.

Departure Conference. The observer attended the departure conference. The following attended this conference: Captains of all merchant ships in the Clyde due to sail in the convoy, the commodore and vice commodore of the convoy, the two destroyer division commanders, plus the squadron commander of the local escorts, the admiral in charge of the ocean escorts and his staff (admiral and his flagship detached from convoy before convoy sailed), the commanding officers and their navigators of the ocean escorts. Similar conferences were held at Liverpool and Milford Haven for the ships of the convoy sailing from those ports. The local and ocean escort representatives, naturally did not attend the conferences at Liverpool and Milford Haven. The fact that departure conferences were held in three different places for the same convoy indicates the necessity for coordination and accurate dissemination of information. With no attempt at criticism, the departure conference was not conducted with the efficiency and the clarification of doubtful sections of the instructions as was a similar conference attended by the observer in Halifax. The type of sailing orders, envelopes containing orders and time of sailing, secret positions, etc., were the same as submitted in the report of the Halifax convoy, and now on file in O.N.I. The envelopes containing all the information for commanding officers of each merchant ship were collected after the conference and delivered to the commanding officers just prior to sailing. (Sailing time delayed 24 hours due to unfavorable weather.)

---

[24]H.M.S. *Phoebe, Dido*-class cruiser.

[25]H.M.S. *Cathay.* Armed merchant cruiser. Pennant no. F. 05; 15,225 tons, built 1925. Former P&O liner. Commissioned 11 October 1939. Converted to troopship, 1942; Armament: 8-6", 2-3" AA guns.

[26]Paragraph 3 and 4 of Report.

Letter from Captain Irvine Glennie, RN, 8 February 1941

Thank you most warmly for your letter. I was delighted to hear from you and do so much appreciate your kindly thought. I, too, enjoyed your time in "Hood," and am in complete agreement about the value of such contacts.

Whatever minor troubles and difficulties may be in existence, I, personally, have no doubt whatever that the preservation of a clean and decent form of life, based upon freedom, good cheer, compassion, and kindliness, is dependent entirely upon our two countries pulling well together. All good luck.

Personal Diary, 8 February 1941

At anchor—Greenock. Weather moderate. Stayed aboard—No regular shore leave today. Ship on 2 hours notice. At 1600 *Edinburgh* which was to go with us and be O.T.C.[27] received orders to sail immediately to join units of the Home Fleet in a search for a German cruiser. This leaves us OTC and may alter the ships plans about returning home. I may have to modify my plans later on—time will tell . . . . All hands wondering where we are going.

Official Diary, 8 February 1941

Late in the afternoon of 8 February the light cruiser which is the flagship of the Admiral in charge of the ocean escort received orders to sail immediately to take part in a search for a reported enemy unit in the North Atlantic. His correspondence was turned over to the next senior captain (Commanding Officer of the light cruiser in which the observer was embarked). This will leave one light cruiser, 1 A.A. cruiser, and 1 armed merchant cruiser to act as ocean escort, which, to the observer, appears inadequate due to importance of the convoy plus the fact that a number of raiders are believed to be at sea.

Personal Diary, 9 February 1941

At anchor—Greenock—Merchant ships started to sail at 2200 last night . . . . First port of call Freetown, Sierra Leonne—South Africa. 4000 miles by the route we are taking—about 20 days at sea. Started to read all the convoy instructions and details about this special convoy. Quite interesting. Weather today fair. No sea.

Official Diary, 9 February 1941

Underway at 0400 9 February, from Greenock. Delayed arrival in North Channel until daylight in order not to interfere with convoy. Convoy carried out the procedure stated at the departure conference. A total of six hours were required for the convoy to be completely formed up. Information received by radio that two ships did not sail. Two additional ships were also missing. It was discussed whether to send two of the local escort destroyers back to search for the missing ships or to turn the convoy around and wait for them. It was believed that the senior officer of the escort forces would have been informed if the two ships had not sailed. Finally one of the three aircraft acting as A/S escort was requested by flashing light to search for the missing ships. Search conducted—ships not located. One destroyer was detached to proceed to a port in Northern Ireland for fuel. This destroyer had apparently escorted the Milford Haven section and would not have had sufficient fuel to continue with the remaining destroyers.

V/S[28] messages are passed to the leading ships in each column who are in turn

---

[27]Officer in Tactical Command.

[28]Visual signal.

responsible for the ships in their respective columns. The local escort commander detailed two destroyers to act as rescue ships providing these ships were not in contact with the submarine. He also designated two ships of the convoy to act as rescue ships as long as the local escort is present—after which no rescue ships are detailed. Weather—sea calm, wind light, visibility—good, temperature 0800—45°, 2000—49°, ceiling—unlimited.

The convoy is formed into 10 columns, three ships to a column. Speed of convoy 9 knots. Distance between columns 1000 yards, distance between ships in column 600 yards. Station keeping between columns fair, between ships in columns fair to poor. Very few ships showing smoke. Location of ocean escorts: the armed merchant cruiser about 800 yards ahead of middle of convoy. The light cruiser zigzagged on the outboard side of No. 1 column. The A.A. cruiser took station astern of No. 9 column (approximately). (The convoy did not commence zigzagging until 1845—Plan No. 15.) Later in the afternoon the light cruiser steamed in circles outboard of No. 1 column at about 12-14 knots speed.

Personal Diary, 10 February 1941

. . . Now in dangerous submarine area. Sea increasing during the day but moderated at night. Weather warm for this time of year . . . . Spent a large part of the day on the bridge. Slept with clothes on last two nights (also life jacket) just a precaution.

Official Diary, 10 February 1941

. . . Weather—partly cloudy, visibility about 6 miles. Temperature at 0800—46°, at 2000—48°. At daylight the distance between ships in column average about 1200 yards. The distance between columns averaged about 1400 yards. Therefore the ships had opened out during the night. Two ships had straggled during the night, one was about 3 miles astern, the other about 4 miles astern. The light cruiser dropped astern to urge the ships to regain station and to find out if they would be able to rejoin. Unable to get a satisfactory answer from the merchant ships. One regained station shortly afterwards. The other did not regain station until about 1700. A destroyer was detailed to stand by the latter ship as A.A. escort as the German planes in this area prefer to attack stragglers due to the planes (Focke-Wulf Condors) being so vulnerable to damage even by .5 machine guns. Should the light cruiser have left the protection of the destroyer screen to investigate the merchant ship?

Eight ships have kites but only three were flown. At departure conference ships with kites were told to fly them during daylight as they definitely have proved to be a deterrent to attacking planes.

Passed a derelict in the afternoon. Convoy informed by Admiralty that it may be seen. A destroyer investigated, reported no sign of life and that derelict was worth salvaging. This information plus its position was given to one of the planes which forwarded the report upon return to base.

Air escort of three planes acting as A/S escort during daylight hours. Our position given to planes before they left to be given to Admiralty upon return to base. Last night Admiralty said convoy would have air escort during the night. Aircraft not seen nor heard,—bright moonlight night.

At 1700 an aircraft reported attacking an SS with depth charges. "SS surfaced and on fire, estimate two hits, am standing by." The position of the submarine was 70 miles ahead of the convoy on the convoy course. Two destroyers were about to proceed to the reported position when the aircraft made a further report "SS sank astern first on fire, am returning to base." Should not the plane have stayed longer in order to see if any wreckage or men came to the surface in order to verify the destruction?

The A.A. cruiser reported having steam available for 24 knots,—full speed on 1.5 hours notice, and that it had just about enough fuel to reach destination. The light cruiser has speed available for 24 knots and full speed on one half hours notice. Both ships will have to conserve fuel for possible eventualities. The above indicates the necessity for a long cruising radius. To insure as much as possible the safety of the convoys wide detours must be made so that the distance between ports is no indication of the actual miles steamed. To this must be added the delay caused by zigzagging and detours made after dark to evade shadowing submarines. In addition the speed of combatant ships with slow convoys may not be the most economical speed. In addition the combatant ships may use more radical zigzags than the convoy, will probably perform more general maneuvering, which will further reduce the cruising radius. (Checking up on stragglers, investigating smoke, etc.)

During daylight and at night the light cruiser took station astern of the convoy, approximately between columns two and five and used an irregular radical zigzag. The armed merchant cruiser retained its position ahead of, and zigzagged with, the convoy. The A.A. cruiser stated that it "preferred to remain astern of column 10 so that she would not have to zigzag." Reason—conserve fuel. In this position the A.A. cruiser was protected ahead and on the port side by the convoy and on the starboard side by destroyers the nearest of which was 4000 yards away. Taking into consideration the location of the destroyers, the steady course and slow speed (9 knots) of the A.A. cruiser plus the average asdic reliable range, the protection against submarine attack was only fair, in the opinion of the observer.

Last night and tonight the ships were very well darkened. The light cruiser called attention to only one ship for showing a light after dark. The importance of a well darkened convoy cannot be over emphasized.

Communications—Radio silence an absolute necessity. No radio messages sent to date and none will be sent except in an emergency. All communications by flag hoists or flashing lights. Commodore uses flag hoists to order changes of course, speed, etc. The signals for changes of course to be made at night are made during the late afternoon. Provision of course is made to change course at night without previous signals by using light signals. (See CONSIGS). The merchant ship's radio are not manned when the convoy is escorted except during low visibility conditions, if they become separated from the convoy, report enemy contact, and when ordered by Commodore. One of the escort ship guards the commercial distress frequency. All the escort vessels guard the Admiralty broadcast frequency and the broadcast frequency of the Admiral in charge of the area in which the ships are operating—if sufficient operators are available on the small ships. The senior escort ship is directly responsible for all such intercepts and the Senior Officer of the Escort Forces, being responsible for the safety of the convoy, takes the necessary action on messages addressed to the convoy or other escort ships. As a result the senior escort ship sends and receives a large number of flashing light messages particularly during the first few days at sea. For example: the first day at sea 26 messages were handled by the senior escort ship, 17 of which were outgoing; the second day 65 messages of which 32 were outgoing. Multiple addresses were counted as one message. About half the outgoing messages were sent to more than one addressee. 40 messages were decoded today. It is interesting to note that the chief signalman is already complaining about using too many carbons in the 20" searchlight and at the present rate the supply of carbons will soon be exhausted. (Signalling should be reduced considerably during the next few days.) In general too strong a light is used. The O.T.C. has commented several times on this point and has taken the necessary action.

At 2145 starshells were seen about 5 miles ahead of the convoy. The ship went to action stations. For about 25 minuites starshells illuminated the area ahead and on the starboard side of the convoy. Apparently a destroyer in the screen thought it had seen a submarine on the surface and fired starshells in accordance with the present (new) doctrine. Other destroyers illuminated the adjacent areas—also according to doctrine. Depth charges were heard detonating in the area. The present doctrine is to illuminate the area, force the submarine to dive and then conduct an intensive asdic search.

Before dark the sea had moderated sufficiently to permit the light cruiser and A.A. cruiser to recover paravanes—convoy now outside of possible mined areas.

Personal Diary, 11 February 1941
. . . Weather quite rough during day . . . .Storm predicted. On bridge a large part of the day. Feel grand. Very rough in afternoon and evening. Ship rolled 37°. Two ships of convoy straggling behind. Hope for their sake they catch up. Turned in at 2330— Doubt if I will get much sleep due to rolling. Bunk is fore and aft. (On one roll I slid across chart house, breaking glass of barometer with my hand—slight surface cut on hand required a little iodine.)

Official Diary, 11 February 1941
. . . Weather, overcast, visibility 5 miles. Temperature at 0800—44°, at 2000— 47°. At daylight one ship was about 5 miles astern. Ship said that due to being light the propeller was constantly coming out of the water when the ship pitched, as a result she could only make good about 8 knots. One additional ship missing. About 1000 a ship was sighted on the horizon. Investigation proved it to be the missing ship which rejoined convoy in the afternoon. During the morning one ship had a steering casualty and dropped astern, one destroyer stood by, ship rejoined in afternoon. Average distance between columns about 1400 yards, average distance between ships in column about 1200 yards.

Seas quite rough. The light cruiser rolled considerably—maximum roll was 37°. The O.T.C. suggested a change of course. The Commodore replied that if the course were changed to the southward the smaller ships would make no headway, and if course were changed to the westward more damage would result from heavy rolling. The soldiers in the troop transports must be having a terrible time. Convoy making good about 8 knots. One troopship carried away one fresh water tank losing 100 tons of water. The commanding officer informed O.T.C. that unless we made better headway his ship would run out of water. (Note—Tanks were hastily installed just prior to sailing.)

Convoy speed all day was 8 knots, making good 7 knots. Visibility until 1600 was about 4 miles, after which the visibility improved to about 8 miles. One ship had a light showing after dark. Station keeping very poor due primarily to unfavorable weather. One destroyer searched astern for a distance of five miles just before dark. Convoy did not zigzag today. 37 messages handled by flashing light during the day of which 16 were outgoing. About half the outgoing messages had multiple addresses, these were not counted in the number of messages handled. 61 despatches decoded by the coding board today. No air escort today.

Personal Diary, 12 February 1941
Lincoln's birthday! . . . . Slept from about 0300 to 0830 . . . Ship still rolling quite badly on certain legs of the zigzag. On bridge and in chart house a large part of the day. In chart house from 2130 to 2400 discussing situation in general with captain and navigator. Our captain being S.O.P.[29] is in charge of the safety of the convoy and as such orders all changes of course aided and abetted from the Admiralty.

---

[29]Senior Officer Present.

Official Diary, 12 February 1941

. . . Wind suddenly subsided about 0100. Ship continued to roll heavily until about 0400 when the roll became normal. Commenced zigzagging at 0300 using the same plan as before—Plans has not been changed since leaving port. The ship "X" was again about 5 miles astern at daylight and was about 2 miles astern at dark. Ship was ordered not to zigzag in order to try to maintain contact with convoy. One slow ship causes considerable trouble.

Three destroyers were detached at 0930 with orders to return to base. Reason—lack of fuel—it has been 3 days since the convoy cleared the North Channel. Destroyers were ordered to conduct an asdic sweep while returning to base. The ship that reported one fresh water tank carrying away now reports a total of 3 tanks carried away. Total loss of water 250 tons—(Ship reported using 60 tons per day).

At 1147 (zone minus one time) received a rebroadcast from England stating that a convoy was being shelled, several ships sunk or sinking in lat. 37-10 N, Long. 21-20 W. (About 800 miles west of Gibraltar.) Later learned convoy was unescorted, raider was a German cruiser (probably Hipper class). At night German radio claimed 13 ships sunk. No information from Admiralty on number of ships sunk. Nearest British combatant ships ordered to proceed to area to rescue survivors. No combatant ships in immediate vicinity. Original despatch from one of ships being shelled was 1035 G.M.T. (1135 zone minus one). This indicates that 12 minutes after the raider attacked all British ships at sea were informed. The rebroadcasting of such messages with a minimum time delay is important. This convoy approximately 1000 miles from convoy attacked.

Remainder of destroyer screen left convoy at 1910, and conducted an asdic sweep enroute to base. Convoy was just outside active submarine area as indicated from Admiralty positions of approximate location of German submarines. (Observer hopes Admiralty information correct.) The destroyer screen left on orders from Commander in Chief, Western Approaches, which is the usual practice. Convoy cleared North Channel 3.5 days ago. The convoy now has 1 light cruiser, 1 A.A. cruiser and 1 armed merchant cruiser as escort. Before departure one destroyer closed the senior escort ship and received various despatches to be sent at sunrise tomorrow morning at which time the destroyers will be well clear of convoy. Sending the despatches at sunrise makes accurate D/F more difficult. One of the despatches gave convoys position and speed, and stated that the margin of fuel remaining in the A.A. cruiser was small. Today the armed merchant cruiser retained its position ahead of the convoy, the light cruiser astern of column 3-5 using a more radical zigzag then the convoy, the A.A. cruiser remained astern of column 10, and did not zigzag in order to conserve fuel. After the departure of the destroyers the armed merchant cruiser employed radical zigzags, patrolling across the front of the convoy. Course was not changed after dark as Commodore believed due to the very bright moon and large convoy a change of course was not worth while. The Commodore preferred to retain the present course and zigzag all night. As usual the rendezvous for the day after tomorrow was given to the convoy by the Commodore in the late afternoon.

In the early evening O.T.C. received orders to proceed to a position to the northwestward at 0700 tomorrow. This position is about 200 miles from our estimated 0700 position tomorrow. Upon arrival course was to be altered so as to pass through three additional new positions.

The convoy is to be at the three new positions at definite times. A battleship (RODNEY) is proceeding from Scapa Flow at best possible speed to reinforce the escort until the arrival of a battle cruiser (RENOWN) and an aircraft carrier (ARK ROYAL) at the last new position. After passing through the last new position the convoy will continue its original route instructions. Convoy expects to be at the first new position at 1200 the day after tomorrow.

49 messages handled by flashing light today, 25 of which were outgoing. This count does not include the multiple addressees which resulted in transmitting about 15 additional messages. 21 despatches decoded today.

Personal Diary, 13 February 1941

At 0520 action station sounded. I was on the bridge quickly as I had my clothes on. Sighted a merchant ship on almost an opposite course. Challenged, turned on searchlights, guns loaded . . . .

Official Diary, 13 February 1941

. . . At 0530 sighted a suspicious vessel. Sounded action stations. Vessel challenged and made incorrect reply. Searchlights turned on, vessel a merchantman. Vessel gave name by light. Rangefinder range 4250 yards. At this point without orders from the Commanding Officer a salvo of seven 6″ guns was fired. Fortunately they fell astern of the merchantman. Investigation indicated that the firing pointer in the director slipped when the ship rolled and stepped on the foot firing pedal. Upon learning the merchantman's name—a British ship—its secret call was flashed, the reply was correct. The ship stated that it had straggled from a convoy.—Another *good* reason for not straggling. The Captain of the cruiser flashed "Good night and thank you." The observer had considerable difficulty making his way to the bridge due to hammocks of passengers sleeping in passageway . . . .

At daylight the Commodore was requested to change course to the northwest and that an explanation would be given when the light cruiser closed the Commodore's ship. The same ship was again about 5 miles astern at daylight. The A.A. cruiser dropped astern and informed the straggler of the change of course. When course was changed the light cruiser took station between columns 3 and 4 which had opened out to double distance (interval). The light cruiser took this station for protection against submarines and to facilitate signalling with the Commodore who was in the leading ship of column No. 3. The A.A. cruiser took station astern of about column 7 as it believed this position afforded good submarine protection and in addition it would be in a good position to swing out astern in case of eventualities from that direction and in addition it would be in a good position to communicate with stragglers. (Also save fuel.) The armed merchant cruiser remained ahead of the convoy carrying out radical zigzags.

The original plan was to form the convoy into two sections for ease in maneuvering when the local escort had left the convoy and the convoy was outside of the most probable submarine areas. Due to the fact that the convoy was returning into a probable submarine area plus the necessity for considerable maneuvering in this area the O.T.C. and Commodore concurred in retaining the convoy in one section.

Course was changed after dark—sky completely overcast—with the convoy returning to the original course three hours later. One light was showing from one ship after dark. Station keeping only fair. Ships will not close up. The distance between ships in column is supposed to be 600 yards. Actually the distance averages about 1200-1400 yards.

33 messages handled by flashing light today, of which 21 were outgoing. The above count does not include messages with multiple addresses which numbered about 9. 60 despatches decoded today.

At noon today the gunnery organization assumed a watch in three organization. As a result of the difficulty encountered in going to action stations at 0530 two days ago the sleeping arrangements of the crew and officers were changed to decrease the time to assume action stations. All officers whose action stations are in the bridge structure now must sleep in the immediate vicinity. This resulted in two officers being forced to sleep in the wheel house (not used as such as the ship is steered from the lower conning station). The observer had considerable difficulty in reaching the bridge when action stations were sounded at 0530 due to the congestion in the passageways and ladders. Part of this was caused by the 312 passengers. The passengers now stand fast until the crew have manned their stations.

Personal Diary, 13-14 February 1941

. . . Weather clear, a lot colder . . . . Convoy will receive additional escorts. A rendezvous has been designated to meet the reinforcements. German radio claims to have sunk 13 ships of the convoy attacked today. Since convoy was unescorted and since raider was supposed to be a regular German cruiser 13 ships is not too many to lose—although it is a terrific loss in tonnage and supplies. Ship did not roll too badly today. At slow speeds the ship rolls at the least disturbance in the water. Turned in at 2400.

14 February—St. Valentine's day—wonder how my sweetheart is today . . . . Ship riding a little better on this course. On bridge and in chart house a considerable part of the day. Wrote to Dolly—my Valentine.

Letter to Mrs. Wellings, 14 February 1941

. . . I was listening to American broadcasts on short wave last night. I have not heard them for a long time. The reception was fairly good . . . .

From the news on the air the Balkan situation appears to be getting acute and Japan seems to be almost to start another drive further south. The old world seems to be upside down. Japan no doubt is being urged on by Germany. Personally I believe Japan will be using very poor judgment to force us to take action. I just cannot see what she will gain and therefore believe that she will be careful not to quite reach the point where we will be forced to take action.

As for the Balkan countries trouble will start very soon—in my opinion. Perhaps by the time you receive this letter the critical stage will have arrived. Hitler is determined to force all the Balkans under his rule in order that he may take what he wants to enable him to defeat England. It will be interesting to watch the results. No one can predict what he will do or what the outcome will be . . . .

Official Diary, 14 February 1941

. . . Steaming as before towards the first of the three new positions designated by the Admiralty two days ago. One ship had a light showing last night. Ship still rolling badly. Wind decreased but a heavy swell on the starboard beam caused excessive rolling, rolls of 35° are constantly being recorded.

Commodore expects to average 220 miles a day after convoy passes through the second of the three new positions. This apparently based on 10 knots speed plus zigzagging. Passed through the first new position at 1300 and steamed for two hours to the northeast with the hope that the battleship might be sighted. No contact—wheeled convoy around and headed on a southerly course. It took approximately 4 hours to turn the convoy around by wheeling due to the low reserve speed. The same ship was again about 5 miles astern at daylight. It cut corners on all changes of course. However at 1902 she informed O.T.C. that she had stopped to repair minor defects.

One of the ships in the convoy reported receiving messages in a merchant code which it did not have, neither did the Commodore. I do not believe the Admiralty intended them to have it as all communications for the convoy is handled via the escort. In addition the N.C.S.O. at the departure conference stated that the radio was not to be manned except in periods of reduced visibility or separation from the convoy. C.B.04024(40) states ships in convoy would not man the radio except: when ordered by Commodore, periods of reduced visibility, separation of convoy, or to report enemy attack. The armed merchant cruiser reported 79% of fuel remaining as of noon today. Believe its fuel supply will also be low when we arrive in Freetown. At 1530 sighted a British merchant ship—Halifax to British Isles—hope she makes it. Commodore stated that the convoy would have to steam at 8 knots tonight as some of the large ships cannot keep station below 8 knots. This means that the convoy will arrive at the second of the three new positions at about 0200 instead of 0900. The O.T.C. had warned the Commodore that this may happen but the Commodore desired to get the convoy turned around before dark which prevented the convoy from standing as far to the northward as the O.T.C. desired. Expect to do radical zigzags in the morning to decrease speed along the mean line of advance

The Armed Merchant Cruiser was ordered to leave the convoy at 0700 tomorrow and return to the second of the three new positions in order to endeavor to make contact with the battleship ordered as additional escort. If the battleship had averaged 18 knots it would have made contact today just before dark. Apparently the weather had slowed the battleship, or the three destroyers acting as A/S screen, to a maximum distance consistent with fuel required to return. If the convoy had been at the second new position at the time ordered the O.T.C. had decided to send the armed merchant cruiser and the A.A. cruiser 15 miles on the starboard and port beams respectively in order to increase the chances of contact. They were to return to the convoy as soon as they had reached these positions. Ocean escorts retained same stations as yesterday.

Latest intercepts indicate that at least 8 ships were sunk. Survivors are being rescued. 71 were picked up from one raft. One combatant ship stated that survivors had definitely identified the raider from silhouettes as a Hipper class cruiser. Another combatant ship said that survivors had positively identified the raider from silhouettes as the Scharnhorst.

Latest information as to escorts indicate that the battleship should join convoy tomorrow at about 1200. Upon arrival of the battle cruiser and aircraft carrier the day after tomorrow the battleship will leave the convoy and dash northwest to pick up an unescorted Halifax convoy. When the battleship joins the convoy the A.A. cruiser now acting as escort will leave for Gibraltar, fuel and rejoin convoy. After the battle cruiser and aircraft carrier have been with the convoy 4 days they will be relieved by another battleship. The above indicates what will happen when a convoy is not adequately escorted and a raider attacks another convoy in the same general area.

The senior escort ship handled 47 flashing light messages today, of which 26 were outgoing. The number of outgoing despatches does not include multiple addresses as two despatches. There were about 10 despatches to multiple addresses. Despatches decoded today, 40.

Personal Diary, 15 February 1941

Made contact with BB, we have more than enough protection now.

. . . We still have about 3400 miles to go, and averaging about 210 a day this means about 17 more days at sea. I suppose the soldiers on the troop ships were glad to see the BB. They must be having a terrible time in their cramped quarters. I know our 310 passengers do not like it. Ship rolling badly again. I suppose the cruisers were not designed for comfort at slow (or any speeds). Slept a little better last night. First night without being fully dressed.

Official Diary, 15 February 1941

. . . At 0035 commenced zigzagging (about 30 minutes after moonrise). Same zigzag plan as before. Ship still rolling quite badly—uncomfortable. At 0700 the armed merchant cruiser left its station in the convoy and proceeded to the position the convoy was supposed to be in at 0900. Convoy actually passed this point at 0200. The purpose in sending the armed merchant cruiser astern was to rendezvous with the battleship due to pass through the second position at 0900. At 1000 commenced 40° simultaneous turns to reduce the distance made good along the mean line of advance in order not to be ahead of the third new position where the convoy is due at 0900 tomorrow and where the battle cruiser and aircraft carrier should join as escorts.

1230 sighted the armed merchant cruiser and battleship astern. The battleship took station about 1000 yards ahead of the light cruiser. The armed merchant cruiser resumed its former station ahead of the middle of the convoy. The Commanding Officer of the battleship is now the officer in charge of the escort and convoy. The light cruiser passed all the necessary information via flashing light. This required 2.5 hours of signalling. The positions of the various points which the convoy will pass were sent in code. At 1400 the A.A. cruiser left for Gibraltar to fuel and then rejoin the convoy. Additional positions which the convoy will pass on the day and day after the A.A. cruiser expected to rejoin were given the A.A. cruiser prior to departure. It also had orders to report our position course and speed as of 1300 today when she arrived at Gibraltar. The battleship at 1530 said "unable to steer this course am going on a jaunt." Apparently the Commanding Officer does not like wallowing around in the trough of the sea at 8 knots—can't blame him. The new O.T.C. stated that the convoy would not be separated into two sections for the present. At 1610 changed course about 40° and remained on this course for two hours in order to avoid a possible submarine reported about 50 miles ahead by the Admiralty. If it is a submarine he is not operating in the usual submarine area. (Not fair.)

At 1900 on orders from the O.T.C. the light cruiser took station 3 miles ahead of column 10, the battleship the same distance ahead of column 1, the armed merchant cruiser two miles astern of the center of the convoy. The light cruiser is responsible for the starboard half of the convoy, the battleship for the port half. Believe the above stations are satisfactory outside submarine areas. However, due to the reported submarine ahead it is submitted that the light cruiser and battleship should be inside the convoy. At 1900 received information that the battle cruiser and aircraft carrier are delayed by weather and would not join convoy until about 1200 on the 17th—a day and a half late.

In regards to the attack on the SL convoy on 12 February survivors reported (Admiralty dispatch) that 4 ships were not damaged and that these ships picked up many survivors. The Admiralty reported considerable W/T[30] activity south of Brest in the Bay of Biscay last night. At 1200 Admiralty also reported that the German cruiser Hipper returned to Brest at 1100 today. Above information plus the fact that some of the survivors said the raider was a Hipper class cruiser leads one to believe that the raider actually was the Hipper. A ship in general vicinity of where radar attacked convoy had 2 torpedoes pass close aboard. Apparently the Germans or Italians sent submarines to this area.

29 messages were handled by flashing light today. 13 of these messages were outgoing, multiple addressees were not counted as two messages. 38 dispatches decoded today.

---

[30]Radio, i.e., wireless telephone or telegraph.

Personal Diary, 16 February 1941
   . . . This is Sunday I decided to take things more than easy, and therefore took a good 2 hour nap—thanks to the ship not rolling too badly—feel grand hope I will feel as good 15 days from now when we are due to arrive in Freetown. The BB left the convoy at dark. We are again S.O.P.

Official Diary, 16 February 1941
   . . . Commenced zigzagging at 0130—shortly after moonrise. Light cruiser stationed ahead of column 10, the battleship ahead of column 1, the armed merchant cruiser astern and zigzagging independently. At dawn the light cruiser steamed towards the west on orders of the O.T.C. in order to cover the convoy from surprise attack due to increased visibility towards the east. Sea improving but ship still rolling quite badly. The light cruiser asked the battleship about 6 messages which could not be deciphered. The battleship concurred in 4 and sent the translation of the other 2 to the light cruiser. One ship dropped astern for one half hour to make repairs, covered by armed merchant cruiser. At 1900, just before dark the battleship was detached in accordance with Admiralty orders to leave and join a Halifax convoy as ocean escort. The battle cruiser and aircraft carrier are due to join the convoy in the morning. At night the light cruiser zigzagged across the front of the convoy. The armed merchant cruiser did likewise across the rear of the convoy. 21 messages were handled by flashing light, 8 of which were outgoing. 59 messages were decoded today.

Personal Diary, 17 February 1941
   . . . Steaming as before—in a generally southerly direction. Passed through the last SS area (area that has been reported as such during the night 48-50 27-30).[31]

Official Diary, 17 February 1941
   . . . Continued zigzagging all night. The armed merchant cruiser was ordered to take station on port quarter at dawn to facilitate rendezvous with battle cruiser and aircraft carrier. However at dawn the battle cruiser (RENOWN) and aircraft carrier (ARK ROYAL) were in sight on the port quarter. The aircraft carrier looked very large. Both ships presented a beautiful silhouette against the eastern horizon. Weather extremely calm, hardly a ripple on the water. At 0900, about an hour after dawn the aircraft carrier launched 6 aircraft and maintained an A/S patrol during the remainder of daylight. The flag officer in the battle cruiser sent a signal "Good morning, now give me the news." Convoy not split into two sections as planned by Admiralty—The O.T.C. said he preferred the convoy to remain together for better A/S and surface protection. Exchanged greetings with Lieutenant Commander Clark, U.S. Navy, in RENOWN.
   The new O.T.C. ordered the following formation for escorts—During daylight the battle cruiser, light cruiser, and armed merchant cruiser within the convoy (actually just astern of the convoy) and the aircraft carrier acting independently. At night the aircraft carrier took station as the second ship in column five—just astern of the convoy Commodore—the battle cruiser took station within maneuvering distance and outside of column 10. The armed merchant cruiser took the corresponding position outboard of column 1 and the light cruiser zigzagged across the front of the convoy just keeping within visibility distance. Used our R/D/F (type 284)[32] on the carrier got excellent results, at the 7 miles distance of the aircraft carrier. Changed course 30° at 2200 and

---

[31]Latitude 48° 50'N, Longitude 27° 30'W.

[32]Radar.

30° back to the mean course at 2400 *without further signal*. The aircraft carrier sent the light cruiser two signals endeavoring to verify the time the zigzag started (zero time with British is not at the even hour). Changed frequencies guarded by escort—now in the area controlled by Commander in Chief, North Atlantic at Gibraltar. Light cruiser informed battle cruiser that convoy was manning W/T only (1) fog, (2) enemy reports, (3) when separated, (4) when ordered by Commodore. Commodore guarding 500 KC. Started to rain about 1900—very dark night. Sea still very smooth—temperature rising—now 54° (2000).

Personal Diary, 18 February 1941
. . . the best day I have seen for a long while . . . . Oh how peaceful and quiet. Remained on bridge for two hours—1400-1600, walked on quarterdeck for an hour. It seemed good to get some sunshine for a change. Did considerable reading. Discussion in Wardroom after dinner—U.S. enlisted men vs. English enlisted men also promotion in both navies. I know all the answers by now. Wrote to Dolly—I suppose she is worrying about me and here I am well protected and leading a life of leisure.

Letter to Mrs. Wellings, 18 February 1941
. . . Today is one of those days which one dreams about but seldom sees. "What is so rare as a day in June"[33] certainly applies to a day like today. The temperature is 60°, the sky is a deep blue and there is not a single cloud to mar the symmetry of the deep blue dome as the sky reaches down and touches the horizon in a perfect circle. "Painted ships upon a painted ocean"[34] was written for a day like today. Everything is peaceful and quiet with heaven and earth being completely in tune . . . .

Official Diary, 18 February 1941
. . . Temperature at 0800—56°, at 1900—61°.

Commenced zigzagging at 0300—shortly after moonrise. Dawn action stations as usual. Shortly after daylight the light cruiser changed station from within visibility distance ahead of convoy to astern of No. 6 column. The battleship changed station at the same time from outboard of No. 10 column, within visibility range, to No. 2 ship in column 5. The armed merchant cruiser changed from outboard of No. 1 column, within visibility range to astern of column No. 5. The aircraft carrier from No. 2 in column No. 5 to acting independently, operating aircraft as an A/S patrol and scouting. Remained in above stations during daylight. Just prior to dark the night stations were again assumed.

Wind light, sea very calm, no swell. Speed advanced to 11 knots in afternoon and reduced to 10.5 at night. Still using the same zigzag plan—has not been changed during the passage to date. Ceased zigzagging at 2100. Course changed 30° at 2200 and 30° to the mean course at 2400.

In connection with A/S patrol by aircraft, the aircraft do not maintain an inner A/S patrol close to the surface within visibility distance of convoy. 4 aircraft on patrol at a time. 25 seconds between take offs, 30 seconds between landings. Once the aircraft take off they are not seen until they return from patrol. Apparently they are being used

---

[33]James Russell Lowell (1819-1891) "Vision of Sir Launfal" part I, prelude:
"And what is so rare as a day in June?
Then, if ever, come perfect days."

[34]Samuel Taylor Coleridge (1772-1834) "The Ancient Mariner," part ii:
"As idle as a painted ship -
Upon a painted ocean."

exclusively for scouting. Submarine danger in this area not great. Now guarding W/T frequencies in accordance with schedules from Commander in Chief, North Atlantic at Gibraltar.

19 messages handled today, of which 7 were outgoing. 41 despatches decoded.

Personal Diary, 19 February 1941

Another grand day—temperature now 61—on bridge for 2 hrs. in p.m.—followed by playing deck hockey for the *senior* officers vs. the C.P.O.'s. Never played before. I had a marvelous time—and a good workout. Uniform shorts, sneakers, khaki shirt. Read and on bridge until 2430 listened to Lowell Thomas at 2345 made me home sick. Now just south of the Azores.

Official Diary, 19 February 1941

. . . Steaming as before—0530 commenced zigzagging—visibility improved due to moonrise. Dawn action stations as usual. Ceased zigzagging at 2000—dark night. Did not take night stations at dark. O.T.C. decided to retain the day stations for the night. The aircraft carrier took station astern of column No. 5, the light cruiser astern of No. 6, the armed merchant cruiser astern of No. 4, the battle cruiser in station 52 (astern of Commodore). The main battery is completely manned at night. (Men stand 8 hours on and 4 off.) (Additional personnel taken from the 4" H.A.) Speed 11 during daylight— sea smooth—ships can keep station. Sighted one merchant ship at 1235. Investigated by armed merchant cruiser. Result—British.

Handled 16 flashing light messages, 6 of which were outgoing. Decoded 32 despatches today. Temperature during the day 61°-63°.

Personal Diary, 20 February 1941

Getting warmer—fog from 0300 to 0930. Sun came out about noon. Worked on reports. Played deck hockey again—took it easier today—my muscles ached, but feel grand . . . .

Official Diary, 20 February 1941

. . . Steaming as before. 0300 fog set in and did not lift until 0935. Dawn action stations as usual. When fog lifted ships in convoy, plus the battle cruiser were badly out of station. Some ships have dropped from ahead to the rear of the column and one ship went from astern of one column to leader of the adjacent column. No fog whistles heard (left to discretion of Commodore—when sounded column leaders only sound whistle blowing the morse equivalent of their column number).

Sea still very calm, temperature 63°. At 1213 commenced zigzagging and increased speed to 11 knots from 10.5. At 2109 ceased zigzagging, decreased speed to 10.5. At 2222 the aircraft carrier signalled to the light cruiser that a man was lost overboard and that the lighted life buoy was dropped 11 minutes *late* (2 miles—speed 10.5). Search was conducted by light cruiser—unable to locate man. Searchlights *not* used to search area but were used to insure man was not on buoy. Abandoned search at 2415.

Escorts did not take their night cruising stations at dark but remained in day stations except that the light cruiser took station astern of column 10 and the armed merchant cruiser astern of column 1, the aircraft carrier astern of column 5. All turret guns completely manned during darkness. Crews stand 8 hours on and 4 off. This requires additional gun crews which are taken from the 4" H.A. guns. (A total of 18—6" gun crews are trained for the 12—6" guns.)

The aircraft carrier conducted A/S and reconnaissance patrols from *shortly* after daylight to dark. A total of 4 aircraft in the air at one time for these operations. Planes to take off at dawn but wait until about an hour later. In the afternoon the aircraft carrier operated Fulmars to make dummy dive bombing runs on the convoy and escorts.

22 messages handled by flashing light today, of which 6 were outgoing—volume of traffic reduced. 41 dispatches were decoded today.

Personal Diary, 21 February 1941

. . . Another grand day—sun shining—not a ripple on the water. Temperature now 65. Starting to think about whites. On bridge in a.m. . . . Discussed gun crews with gunnery officer.

Official Diary, 21 February 1941

. . . Steaming as before. At 0340 rejoined convoy after unsuccessful search for man overboard from the aircraft carrier. Smoke from convoy enabled convoy to be seen 12 *miles* away. There was not much wind so that smoke rose almost vertically. Dawn action stations as usual. 0700 commenced zigzagging same plan as before. Speed 10.5. At 1020 sighted the MALAYA[35], the battleship which is to relieve the battle cruiser and aircraft carrier. 1027 increased speed to 11 knots. 1115 the battle cruiser and aircraft carrier left the convoy. The MALAYA is now O.T.C. Stations for escorts now as follows: day—the MALAYA astern of Commodore's ship in 5th column, station No. 52, light cruiser astern of column 6, the armed merchant cruiser astern column 4. At night the battleship retains her station, the armed merchant cruiser astern column 1, the light cruiser astern column 10, at dawn and low visibility the light cruiser moves out to starboard of the convoy, the armed merchant cruiser to port, and the battleship may go ahead of convoy. All three keep within visibility distance. The aircraft carrier this morning launched 9 aircraft, 3 for inner A/S patrol and 6 for reconnaissance. At 2055 ceased zigzagging, speed 10.5. At 2130 took night station astern column 10. Weather excellent—temperature now 70°.

43 flashing light messages handled today, 23 of these were outgoing. Number of messages decoded 41.

Personal Diary, 22 February 1941

Washingtons birthday . . . on bridge in a.m. Played deck hockey for the *veterans*. In trying to stop quickly I struck my heel of the right foot violently on deck causing an ankle bruise—had a decided limp—no pain. Had ankle strapped . . . . Hobbled to bridge . . . hoping to see some excitement . . . .

Letter to Mrs. Wellings, 22 February 1941

. . . Today I had my first casualty of the war. I should claim a wound chevron for gallantry in action. What happened? I turned my ankle playing deck hockey and now have a decided limp. Xrays taken indicate that no bones were broken and I am assured that I will be back in fighting trim in two or three days.

While sitting around taking things easy I decided to read *Capt. Hornblower, Royal Navy* . . . . It is really a grand story about the old British Navy and of course Capt. Hornblower in particular. Parts of it are very funny and the entire book is extremely interesting. The author is C.S. Forester. The book is really three stories in one book— "The Happy Return," "A Ship of the Line" and "Flying Colors."[36] While on the subject

---

[35]H.M.S. *Malaya. Queen Elizabeth*-class battleship. Launched 1915. Assigned to Force "H."

[36]Of the ten Hornblower volumes, these three were the only ones published before the war, in 1937 **and** 1938. The remaining volumes were published between 1945 and 1962.

of books I read one a few weeks ago called *"I Lost My English Accent"* and published by G.P. Putnam & Sons. The author is the New York correspondent for the *London Daily Mail.* [37] The book is really an answer to *Malice Toward None.* [38] I strongly recommend this book. Maybe it is because I am getting to appreciate the British point of view that I laughed so much while reading the book . . . .

Did I tell you that Capt. Kirk is now Director of Naval Intelligence? This means a new attaché. I have no idea as to whom the *lucky man* will be. However it should not affect me in any way because I am more or less my own boss as far as the office is concerned. It will be a good job for someone. I do hope they appoint a real live wire who has lots of common sense.

Official Diary, 22 February 1941

. . . Steaming as before. Weather good, practically no sea, temperature 71°, speed 10.5. At 0815 took station on right flank of convoy—dawn station. Dawn action stations as usual. 0900 commenced zigzagging, speed 11. Resumed station astern of column 10 an hour after daylight. 1845 the armed merchant cruiser reported smoke on horizon on port side of convoy. The light cruiser left convoy to investigate. Steamed at 20 knots for a distance of 16 miles. Nothing sighted, resumed station astern column 10 at 2145. Convoy not zigzagging upon return. During the night three ships had a light showing. The light cruisers plane was to be ready at 5 minutes notice at dawn. While getting plane ready it swung around on the catapult and the fuselage struck an open hatch—result—a hole about 6″ in the fuselage. Hole patched and ready for operations at noon. Plane was not used. Should it have not been used when investigating the smoke described above?

31 flashing light messages handled today, 16 of which were outgoing. Number of despatches decoded 35.

Personal Diary, 23 February 1941

. . . Sunday. Foot swelled a little. Have a decided limp. Remained in W.R. all morning reading . . . Took it easy all day. In shorts in latter part of afternoon, on deck watching the officers getting their exercise. Had a good sun bath. Marvelous weather. Played a new type of dice game with No. 1,[39] Senior Assistant Eng.[40] and the paymaster.[41] Quite a lot of fun. No money involved . . . Foot feeling better. Should be in port 2 weeks from today.

Official Diary, 23 February 1941

. . . Steaming as before, wind and sea calm, temperature 71°. 0600 the armed merchant cruiser steamed ahead of convoy in order to assist the A.A. cruiser in rendezvousing with the convoy at 1000. The A.A. cruiser had left the convoy and proceeded to Gibraltar to fuel and return to convoy. 0800 the light cruiser moved out to the starboard wing of the convoy remaining within visibility distance—purpose to avoid a surprise action on convoy at dawn. Went to dawn action stations as usual. 0930

---

[37]Cevil V.R. Thompson.

[38]Mrs. Honoré McCue Willsie Morrow, *With Malice Toward None* (New York: Grosset, 1938).

[39]J.H. Dathan.

[40]Engineer Lieutenant Milne.

[41]C.E. Glenister.

resumed station astern of column 10. 1025 increased speed to 11 knots and commenced zigzagging. 1127 the armed merchant cruiser and the A.A. cruiser were sighted ahead of convoy. They closed and took station within the convoy in accordance with the O.T.C.'s new stations for escorts:—Battleship third ship in 5th column (Commodore's column) day and night. At dawn the battleship may take position just ahead of convoy. The armed merchant cruiser astern of column 5 day and night. The light cruiser astern of column 3 during daylight and astern column 1 at night. The A.A. cruiser astern column 6 in daylight and astern column 10 at night. During moonlight, dawn and low day visibility the light cruiser and A.A. cruiser move out to their respective flanks remaining within visibility distance. At 1800 speed 9 knots (speed not to be regulated to arrive off Freetown at 0800 on 2 March in accordance with radio orders). At 1810 one ship fell out of formation due to breakdown—rejoined just before dark. 2115 ceased zigzagging. At 2200 changed course 30° for two hours and then resumed original course. Radio intercepts indicated that a light cruiser sighted a pocket battleship about 100 miles due north of madagascar. Wonder what will be the result? Message also stated that she planned to trail by day and attack at night. (Note: Learned afterwards the pocket battleship escaped during night. Pocket battleship had a R.D/F[42]—GLASGOW did not.)

25 flashing light messages handled today, of which 10 were outgoing. 18 dispatches decoded this date.

Personal Diary, 24 February 1941

. . . Another good day, foot feeling better. Remained in room all morning getting my whites & white shorts ready. Uniform today is optional between blues and white shorts. I will have to set my own uniform of shorts as we do not have any regular uniform. It is grand being your own boss and able to set your own uniform. The whole trip is quite an experience. The P.M.O. took another look at my foot—getting better, but bruise is now beginning to show (black & blue) . . . .

Official Diary, 24 February 1941

. . . Steaming as before, speed 9, sea calm, wind light. Dawn action stations as usual. 0849 increased speed to 18 knots and made a sweep about 7 miles on the port flank of the convoy to prevent surprise at daylight. 0915 retained position on port flank of convoy due to reduced visibility—3 miles. This reduced visibility is due to sand blowing from Africa, across the Cape Verde Islands (we are about 70 miles west of these islands). Sand noticeable in ventilation blowers. 1000 commenced zigzagging, speed 10, same plan as before. 2100 took station astern of column 1. 2105 ceased zigzagging, speed 9 knots. Changed course 30° 2110 and back to original course at 0100.

4 flagship light messages handled today, 2 were outgoing. 10 dispatches were decoded.

Personal Diary, 25 February 1941

Sea calm, wind light, temperature delightful 72° at 0800, 76° at 2000. Lazy weather. Everything proceeding perfectly. Dust in air prevented good visibility . . . . Apparently it "funnels" between two mountain ranges and blows in direction of Cape Verde Islands[43] . . . . Ankle feeling much better. Can now walk normally but cannot

---

[42]Radar.

[43]"Along the coast of Mauritania, a wind from the north-east or east often comes from deep in the interior and arrives hot, dry and dusty. This wind is called a harmattan. It becomes increasingly frequent south of

play deck hockey for a few days—will probably be too hot then. Did considerable reading—finished *Captain Hornblower* plus some professional reading—flew off our aircraft for the first time today . . . . Uniform now whites—shorts, open sleeveless shirt, socks and white shoes. I use my shoulder marks attached to shirt—same as British.[44]

J.H. WELLINGS ON BOARD H.M.S. *BIRMINGHAM* WEARING HIS WHITES
[Photos: JHW Collection]

Official Diary, 25 February 1941

. . . Steaming as before, speed 9, sea calm, wind light. Dawn action stations as usual. 0800 took station on port flank of convoy and then made a sweep away from port flank perpendicular to mean line of advance for a distance of 5 miles to avoid surprise action at daylight, and to search for 2 destroyers due to arrive as local escorts. The armed merchant cruiser took station 5 miles on starboard beam for same reason. Convoy commenced zigzagging at 0830, speed 10. Ceased zigzagging at 1015 and changed course to get on mean line of advance so as not to miss destroyers in reduced visibility due to sand in the air. (See yesterdays report.) Resumed base course at 1219 and commenced zigzagging. At 1219 the light cruiser sighted the two destroyers. The converted yacht "SURPRISE"[45] joined the convoy just before dark. The local escorts

---

about 20°N. It blows as far south as Conakry [Guinea] in winter. Along the Mauritania coast the *harmattan* occurs most often from November through February." *Sailing Directions (Planning Guide) for the North Atlantic Ocean* (H.O. 140), Washington: U.S. Govt. Print. Off., 1976, p. 172.

[44]A tropical uniform of this description was first permitted in the U.S. Navy by the uniform regulations approved on 31 May 1941.

[45]Armed, antisubmarine yacht, *Surprise*, built 1896, 1322 tons Thames measurement, lost 28 February 1942.

took stations as follows:—Converted yacht 45° on bow of column No. 10, one destroyer 45° on bow of column No. 1, the other destroyer ahead of the center of the convoy, distance about 2,000 yards. At 2200 changed course 30° and at 0000 returned to the original course (regular change of course for after dark). Handled 21 flashing light messages today, 12 were outgoing. 17 dispatches were decoded.

Personal Diary, 26 February 1941

. . . Dashed to horizon twice . . . once we overhauled a ship—British OK—the last time we must have been looking at a mirage. On bridge most of day. Sun is quite warm. Getting a tan—but taking it easy. Lengthy discussion in Wardroom . . . .

Official Diary, 26 February 1941

. . . Steaming as before, sea calm, wind light, temperature at 0800—74°, at 2000—76°. Dust which reduced visibility past two days to about 4 miles is still present. Visibility however is increased to 6 miles. 0345 advanced ships clocks ½ hour. For internal use ship keeping G.M.T.[46] Convoy official time is B.S.T.[47] (Zone minus one). Dawn action stations as usual. At dawn shifted station from astern column No. 1 to port beam of convoy. Then made usual morning sweep out to the flank for a distance of about 7 miles, then returned to convoy—reason prevent surprise attack. 0952 speed changed to 9 knots, course changed to 114°, now headed for Freetown. Due to arrive at 0800 Sunday, 2 March. At 1025 left convoy to search for MILFORD[48]—an escort vessel. Convoy is about 40 miles from mean line of advance which is reason for going out to mean line of advance. Speed 28 knots. Sighted one ship—formerly Danish now British—which signalled that she needed a doctor. Circled ship at high speed. Ordered her to steer a course for convoy. Later informed that medical assistance given and ship continued on its way, 1222 returned to convoy and took station on port beam, and commenced zigzagging. Catapulted aircraft to conduct search. Aircraft in air 1.5 hours—visibility and ceiling too low for effective scouting—no luck. Recover of aircraft—fair to poor, no net used. This is the first time the observer has seen ship based aircraft operated. At 2030 left convoy to search for smoke—speed 28—darkness prevented ship from searching beyond 10 miles. Returned just before dark. Took station astern of column No. 1 with the armed merchant cruiser astern of the light cruiser. The armed merchant cruiser is due to leave convoy at 0300 tomorrow to arrive at rendezvous where 2 more destroyers are supposed to join as local escorts. The converted yacht broke down during the night and dropped astern. Our R.D/F was D/F[49] by the armed merchant cruiser at a distance of 1 mile—further tests to be conducted.

34 messages handled by flashing light today, 15 of these were outgoing. 13 dispatches were decoded.

Letter to Mrs. Wellings, 27 February 1941

. . . Everything is progressing marvelously on my new assignment. The weather is just perfect although it may get a little too warm in a few days. Up to now one could not

---

[46]Greenwich mean time.

[47]British summer time.

[48]H.M.S. *Milford*, *Bridgewater*-class sloop. Pennant number L. 51.

[49]The bearing of transmissions from *Birmingham*'s radar was determined by a direction finder on board *Cathay*.

ask for better conditions . . . . I am wearing shorts and a sleeveless open neck shirt all day—except at dinner I wear long white trousers. It is a very cool "rig" and a very sensible one. I also have a sun helmet which I hope to have an opportunity to wear very soon . . . .

After the war I will have to get foreign duty in these parts so that we can enjoy life together in England and surrounding countries plus a visit or two south. Do you suppose I will ever [be] fortunate enough to get assignment to such duty?

. . . I am able to get the American news on the short wave radio every night now. It is so much fun to listen to Lowell Thomas and other commentators. I never realized how much I like them until I was unable to listen to them whenever I desired. The American news seems to be more alarming than the British news. Of course it is always more dramatic. We like excitement. The Japanese question seems to be getting acute. I cannot understand what is behind it all, except Germany urging on Japan, to start trouble in order to divert our aid to Britain. I am sure Japan must know this. I still can not see why she wants to pick a fight with us. She has everything to lose and nothing to gain. I also hope we are making plans to insure that aid to Britain is not diverted. We can blockade Japan easily, particularly she will feel the loss of our exports . . . .

Personal Diary, 27 February 1941

. . . No more dust—Sea clear as crystal and very calm, Sun quite warm. Worked all morning on my *news* broadcast for tonight. I gave it at 2100 calling it the special NBC news broadcast. A Canadian officer read the advertisement for Pepsodent[50] & Sahlhepatica[51]—Went over very good. Of course the broadcast was on the ships circuit only.[52]

Official Diary, 27 February 1941

. . . Steaming as before. Wind light, sea calm, temperature at 0800—75°, at 2000—77°. At 0104 the armed merchant cruiser's HF D/F[53] heard our R.D/F. Usual action stations at dawn followed by sweep to port flank of convoy—stationed astern column 1 last night. 0830 convoy commenced zigzagging same plan as before. The converted yacht of first World War vintage had a casualty and dropped astern at 0840. 0925 sighted two more destroyers joining as local escort. At 1500 the sloop MILFORD also joined as local escort. 1800 conducted trials on our R.D/F to see how far CATHAY could D/F. Went out 8.5 miles—easy detection, but bearing only within 20°. At 2015 dashed out to horizon, investigated smoke—British ship—warned her to keep clear of convoy. 2100 took station astern column No. 1. Changed course 30° at 2200 and back again at 2400.

Handled 47 flashing light messages today, 28 of them were outgoing. Decoded 15 dispatches.

Personal Diary, 28 February 1941

. . . Weather getting warm—76° at 0800, 77° at 2000 . . . . Worked on answers

---

[50]A toothpaste.

[51]Sal Hepatica, a laxative.

[52]Internal announcement system.

[53]High Frequency Direction Finder.

to questions to be asked tonight at 2030 by Chaplain[54] on ship's radio—interview broadcast—it was O.K.—excellent said the officers. Wonder if they were just polite. Long discussion in Wardroom afterwards on importance of No. 1 officers in key positions. To bed at 2330 but read *Josephine*[55] until 0030 . . . .

Official Diary, 28 February 1941

. . . Steaming as before. Weather same as yesterday. 0645 usual procedure going from astern column 1 to port flank of convoy and searching to port of convoy at dawn. Usual action stations at dawn. 0900 S.O.S. from a merchantman being attacked by a submarine 50 miles from Freetown. 0900 commenced zigzagging, same plan as before. After daylight took station astern column 3. At 1418 catapulted aircraft to search for two destroyers due to join as A/S escort—located 40 miles away. 1600-1700 exercised pom-poms and U.P.[56] 1730 recovered aircraft—good recovery. 1800 the battleship and two destroyers left convoy with orders to proceed to Freetown to fuel and sail to escort another convoy. We took station astern column 5. Ceased zigzagging at 2047. Two ships had lights showing—notified—discussion regarding time (B.S.T., G.M.T., zone plus one), error in interpreting by battleship has caused all the trouble about being late at rendezvous(s). Took station astern of column No. 1 after dark. Aircraft due to be catapulted at dawn.

Handled 55 flashing light messages today, 30 of which were outgoing. Decoded 11 dispatches.

Personal Diary, 1 March 1941

. . . This is to be our last day at sea before entering Freetown. At 0033 was on bridge with captain after a long discussion on escorts in his cabin. Suddenly heard shouts of a man in the water about 50 yds. off the port bow. Stopped ship and rescued him. He had jumped from the third ship ahead of us in column—attempted suicide—man quite slightly delirious but will recover. Time to recover—30 minutes . . . .

Official Diary, 1 March 1941

. . . Weather same as yesterday. 0033 heard cries of a man in water on port bow—stopped and recovered him—time to do so 27 minutes. Man had fallen from 3 ships ahead—man O.K.—lucky. 0140 rejoined convoy. 0700 dawn action stations followed by usual procedure of searching to port flank of convoy. 0828 catapulted aircraft to search as follows: 50 mile course 060, 75 mile course 150, 65 mile course 240, 59 mile course 003. Convoy course 114, speed 9. 0930 took station astern of convoy. 1140 raised steam for full speed—plane overdue has fuel for 3.5 hours. 1145 plane requested D/F bearing said it was shifting from 274 to 8845 kc. Ship D/F plane. Ship headed in wrong direction due to gyro[57] not being cut in at the D/F. Turned around and headed in correct direction after steaming 5 miles about 140° from right course. Now using relative bearings on D/F. At 1258 PHOEBE (A.A. cruiser) heard S.O.S. from aircraft on 8830 kc. This meant that he was landing according to the officers in the light cruiser. Ship was able to D/F plane but not to read messages from plane. Why?

---

[54]Rev. George Reindorp.

[55]Possibly the book by K. Coyle.

[56]A type of antiaircraft rocket projector.

[57]Gyrocompass.

Bearings constant. PHOEBE and light cruiser conducted search to 76 miles ahead on bearing—no luck. PHOEBE searched area to left and light cruiser to right—on return to convoy. Returned just before dark. Commander in Chief, South Atlantic notified, air search being conducted. One destroyer to search on reciprocal bearing tomorrow morning. Aviators have food for 3 days, sea is calm, weather clear. I hope they are located (2 aviators, one mechanic). Streamed paravanes at 1900 (just inside 100 fathom curve) . .

Convoy zigzagged as usual during daylight, same plan as before. Convoy changed course 30° at 2200 and back to original course at 2400.

Handled 80 flashing light messages today, 49 of which were outgoing. Decoded 11 messages. Temperature at 0800—76°, at 2000—79°.

Personal Diary, 2 March 1941

. . . Ship very short of fuel—plans to enter Freetown tomorrow morning as planned, fuel and immediately return to resume search . . . . Very warm at night below decks— Wardroom rather gloomy over missing plane which contained two R.N.V.R. Sub Lieut.[58] plus one enlisted man.

Official Diary, 2 March 1941

. . . Sky a little overcast, sea calm, wind light. 0645 dawn action stations plus searching to port of convoy. Made preparations for entering port in accordance with order of entry prescribed by Commander in Chief, South Atlantic,—0800 took station ahead of convoy. Convoy formed in single line, fast ships increased speed—Vice Commodore section slowed. 1027 anchored in Freetown, Sierra Leone. Convoy entered after the light cruiser, armed merchant cruiser and A.A. cruiser. Three hours for convoy to enter port. The destroyers patrolled outside searched channel while convoy was entering port. A boom defence with one gate vessel was located at the inner end of the swept channel.

Personal Diary, 2-7 March 1941

. . . Anchored at Freetown, Sierra Leone, 21 days after leaving Greenock, Scotland. Actual miles steamed 5197. Native canoes thronged around ship. Negro boys diving for coins, etc. Typical tropical scene. Freetown doesn't look like an exciting place. It is used as an assembly port for convoys and a port of call between England and Cape Town. Took Dayton Clark's mail over to a DD which sails at 1400 for Gibraltar. Tanker came alongside immediately and fueled us. At 1700 we were underway again with a plane borrowed from the Naval plane tender ashore on board. Set course to again commence search in the morning at daylight.

3 March . . . Plane off at daylight back at 1000 for fuel and off again. Plane flew 7 hours. Ship steamed at 30 knots all day. Plane not seen. Will continue search in morning. Rather unusual for plane to lose contact under ideal conditions unless he had a casualty . . . .

4 March—Still underway conducting search for missing plane. A long high swell prevented the plane from taking off at daylight (pilot inexperienced—Captain did not wish to take chance of losing plane on recovery). At 0945 plane catapulted and will conduct search enroute to Freetown—100 miles away. Ship continued search but unable to locate plane. Returned to Freetown at 1700. An escort plus one DD is also assisting in search. Ship had to return to transfer the 312 passengers and to clean boilers

---

[58]Peter Joseph Warrington; Edward James Trerise.

before continuing with convoy . . . . Slept on deck in a cot at night. Very excellent sleeping under the quarterdeck awning, cool breeze, etc.

5 March—Freetown—Visited American ship in harbor. Gave captain letters to mail in New York . . . went ashore and called on American Consul—cashed check for 60.00. Bought one pair stockings. Total time ashore one hour. Returned to ship just in time to attend latter part of cocktail party for a few of the merchant ship captains. At 1330 a native sailboat hove too off the gangway and in it was our three aviators. They came aboard amidst great cheering on the part of the crew. Champagne all around. They were in fair to good physical condition. Their landing, mistake in navigation, sailing the plane using parachutes, abandoning the plane, paddling the rubber life boat over night, picked up by native fisherman who did not want to take them ashore due to it being French territory and their sailing two days to Freetown make a grand story . . . .

6 March—Slept on deck last night—grand sleeping.—Worked from 0610 to 0750 on reports—Saw captain about ships further movements—believe I will stay on board. Worked on reports again in morning. At 1600 went ashore with Commander—Landed at King Tom Pier. Met Flag Lt. to C. in C. S.A.[59]—used Admiral's car to drive to Hillside Station Club—900 ft. up in the hills—about 5 miles from pier. Nice cool breeze—good scenery, typical tropical club—tennis, billiards and a bar. Met PMO at club—had a lemon squash (soft drink). Called on No. 1's Sister Mrs. Jeffrey Lanthorn who lives about 5 minutes walk from club. She is married to the Attorney General . . . very congenial—her husband is a much older-sedate individual. Took cab from club to landing (Gov.) back aboard on 1900 boat. A number of guests (male) for dinner. To bed in my cot on quarterdeck at 2300.

Letter to Mrs. Wellings [60]

. . . drove up to a club in the hills and spent a grand lazy few hours, just looking at the scenery and enjoying a nice cool breeze. It really was a beautiful sight. Later on we (my boss and I) called on some people he knew who lived near the club. The house was a typical tropical bungalow, built on stilts above the ground, with large windows everywhere, grass rugs and above all delightfully cool. The house was well staffed with colored servants who served us with a refreshing "whiskey soda with ice" for my special benefit. They do not use ice in their drinks. We were back in town in time for dinner and as usual I slept outdoors where a nice cool breeze soon lulled me fast asleep.

Official Diary, 7 March 1941 [61]

. . . Same general information as at departure conference at Greenock. Convoy [sailing to the Middle East via Cape Town, South Africa] will be composed of the same ships that were in convoy from Greenock plus the 4 ships which failed to sail from Greenock and which were escorted by a light cruiser to Freetown. Total number of ships in convoy, 33, of which 18 will be troopships. Total gross tonnage of convoy, 305,171. Average gross tonnage, 8,971. Gross tonnage of largest ship, 19,700, of smallest ship, 4,500. First ship to pass gate in boom defence at 1130 tomorrow. Ships to pass gate at 4 minute intervals. Convoy to form into two sections of five columns each, one astern of the other until clear of swept channel when convoy will be formed in one section of 10

---

[59]Geoffrey Martin Bennett (1909-   ). Later Captain; a well-known naval historian and a novelist writing under the pseudonym "Sea-Lion."

[60]Excerpt from letter of 10-11 March 1941.

[61]This and subsequent entries from Enclosure A to Report: convoy operations of convoy W.S.6 from Freetown Sierra Leone to Cape Town, 8-21 March 1941, dated 5 May 1941.

columns. Order of ships in sailing arranged to facilitate forming up. Slow section to sail first in following order 101, 102,103, 91, 92, 93, 81, 82, 83, 71, 72,73, etc.

Commodore discussed station keeping, smoke, lights, zigzagging, speed and signals which he said could be and should be improved, based on the performance from Greenock to Freetown. Channel to be swept just prior to convoy sailing. Air escort to be provided from 1200-1800 the first day. Local escort to consist of two destroyers, one sloop, and two corvettes. Ocean escort 1 light cruiser, 1 A.A. cruiser and 1 armed merchant cruiser until 11 March when 1 heavy cruiser will join and the armed merchant cruiser will leave.

Personal Diary, 7 March 1941

. . . Weather apparently always the same—clear—warm—a good breeze. Attended departure conference on *Edinburgh Castle*[62] at 1000 with Captain and Navigator. Decided to definitely stay aboard due to fact that *Maritius*[63] not sailing until latter part next week, a new ship—etc. Also we are due to return to Freetown at high speed. Back aboard at 1300, shifted into a fresh suit of shorts then ashore to have lunch [with] the Admiral—C. in C., S.A.[64] We drove to his house—near Hillside station. A very large and comfortable tropical house. It really is the Governor's summer house—Gov.[65] has been on leave for 6 months and he turned it over to Admiral. Very pleasant lunch. Back to town at 1545—walked around town (15 min.) bought a pair of leather sandals. Nothing else to buy—a little perfume was on sale in an Indian shop but I was afraid it was watered. Back aboard at 1645. At 1930 called on Commodore Martin in the *Landgibby Castle*.[66] Gave him Hartman's & Opie's mail to deliver at Alexandria as we are due to return from Cape Town. Very pleasant chat on convoys—back aboard at 1900—guest night—fine dinner—a large number of guests—to bed at 1130. Read a new copy of *Life* (Feb. 9) before turning in on deck.

Letter to Mrs. Wellings[67]

. . . I attended a luncheon which lasted from one to four. It was given in a huge house up among the hills, in a setting that one reads about in tropical stories. I thoroughly enjoyed myself. I guess I was born lazy with more than a desire for comfort.

Letter to Mrs. Wellings, 8 March 1941

. . . I must admit that the sunshine is a wonderful asset after a winter around England. The past few days I have seen more sunshine than I have in the past four or five months.

I really feel wonderful. Of course I take things easy in the middle of the day—no[t] very difficult for me, in order to stay out of the hottest of the sun's rays . . . . The sleeping outdoors is perhaps the best part of my present location. The cool evening breeze is perfect for sleeping and makes one feel like a million dollars in the morning. For example, the time is now *0700* and I have completed a half written letter . . . . I am up

---

[62]Base ship at Freetown. Built 1910. Scuttled at Freetown, 1945.

[63]*Fiji*-class cruiser, *Mauritius*.

[64]Vadm. Sir Robert Henry Taunton Raikes.

[65]Sir Douglas Jardine, K.C.M.G., O.B.E.; Governor of Sierra Leone, 1937-41.

[66]*Llangibby Castle*, launched 1929. Union Castle Mail Steamship Co., Ltd. passenger liner, built 1929, 11,951 tons.

[67]Excerpt from letter of 10-11 March 1941.

at 0615 and have breakfast at 0730. Generally I do some reading or make some notes during this period when it is very cool. After breakfast I turn to again and by 1030 I have completed almost a tropical days work. There is a cool breeze all day but the sun does get hot so that one has to take things easy. The people here know and practice the best way to live in these climates . . . .

Personal Diary, 8 March 1941

. . . At 0900 went ashore and gave Neilson[68] (Amer. Consular Agent) 4 letters to mail . . . . They will leave on next American steamer (3 days). Glad to get them off because Dolly must be worried . . . .

Official Diary, 8 March 1941

First ship passed through gate at 1130, last ship of first section 31 minutes late in passing gate. Second section however made up 10 minutes so that entire convoy (33 ships) was 21 minutes late in passing gate. The armed merchant cruiser sailed immediately after the last ship of the convoy. The light cruiser and A.A. cruiser sailed at 1610, streamed paravanes when cleared of harbor and joined convoy just before dark. Paravanes recovered just before joining convoy. Convoy formed into 10 columns, 1,000 yards between columns, 600 yards between ships in columns. Convoy speed 10 knots and zigzagging. Local escorts stationed as follows. The sloop—one mile ahead of the center of the convoy zigzagging across front of convoy; one destroyer 80° on starboard bow of leading ship of column 10, distance 2,500 yards; one destroyer 80° on port bow of leading ship of column 1, distance 2,500 yards; one corvette 10° abaft the beam of the rear ship of column 10, distance 4,000 yards; one corvette 10° abaft the beam of the rear ship of column 1, distance 4,000 yards. Ocean escorts stationed as follows: Day—light cruiser prolonged column 3, A.A. cruiser prolonged column 7, armed merchant cruiser astern of center; Night—light cruiser astern column 1, A.A. cruiser astern column 10, armed merchant cruiser astern center. At dawn light cruiser make a sweep outboard from the port flank of the convoy, A.A. cruiser to sweep outboard from the starboard flank of the convoy.

At 1600 (GMT) the MALAYA escorting a north-bound Sierra Leone convoy reported sighting a large vessel, giving bearing and distance. Ten minutes later the aircraft from the MALAYA reported that the two battle cruisers were sighted. This report was confirmed by the MALAYA which stated that it was retiring on the convoy. Last message from the battleship stated that the two battle cruisers (SCHARNHORST and GNEISNEAU) were on course 240, speed 20. The 1600 position of the two battle cruisers was 22°-00′ N, 20°-00′ W, about 900 miles from our convoy. The 1600 contact report was rebroadcasted from Gibraltar which Freetown in turn rebroadcasted. The first message was received by the light cruiser at 1717 (GMT), one hour and seventeen minutes after the initial contact report. The captain of the light cruiser (senior escort commander) anxiously awaited further reports but none were received. Apparently the two battle cruisers did not desire to attack by day or night because they did not wish to be damaged even though they should be more than a match for the battleship and should have been able to sink a large number of the convoy. As usual ships were rushed to the aid of the convoy.

The captain of the light cruiser began to figure how long it would take the two battle cruisers to overhaul his convoy. At 24 knots they could arrive at 0000, 12 March, at 22 knots, 1200, 12 March, and at 20 knots, 2400, 12 March. The captain again

---

[68]Christian K. Nielson. An employee of a steamship company who also served as the U.S. Consular Agent in Freetown.

commented on the lack of adequate escort for this convoy. Only one light cruiser and one armed merchant cruiser are available at Freetown, one 8″ heavy cruiser is due to arrive from the south to reinforce the ocean escort. Perhaps the Admiralty will send heavy ships that are now enroute to the Sierra Leone convoy to this convoy if all goes well.

Weather clear today, sea calm, temperature at 0800—78°, at 1200—84°, at 2000—78°. Handled 14 messages by flashing light today (since leaving port), 10 of these were outgoing. Decoded 35 messages today.

Personal Diary, 9 March 1941

. . . everything running smoothly. No further information on German ships. Worked on report for trip to Freetown. rather warm below decks . . . .

Official Diary, 9 March 1941

. . . Convoy zigzagged all night. Made sweep at dawn to port of convoy to a distance of about 7 miles, speed increased to 18 knots and zigzagging. Usual dawn action stations. Assumed day stations upon completion of sweep (prolonged column 3). One ship smoked badly for about 4 hours last night. Smoke could easily have been seen for 10 miles. At 1410 the A.A. cruiser stated that two men had sighted a large land plane. No officers or regular lookouts sighted this plane. No plane supposed to be around this area. Captain of light cruiser tried to determine whether captain of A.A. cruiser believed plane was seen. Finally the A.A. cruiser captain said "No." It may have been a commercial plane off its own course or a very large Vichy patrol plane. The captain of the A.A. cruiser sent to the captain of the light cruiser an appreciation of our present situation in regards to the movements of the two battle cruisers. This appreciation was very interesting. In general the A.A. cruiser captain believed that our convoy was the objective. As a result of this appreciation plus no instructions regarding strengthening our escort, the captain of the light cruiser gave one of the destroyers a ciphered message with orders to sweep astern of convoy at dusk and then to proceed to Freetown, sending the message by radio when just outside Freetown. The destroyer was to enter Freetown and not rejoin the convoy. Captain asked about desirability of splitting the convoy, the personnel ships going ahead at best speed (12 knots) escorted by the light cruiser and A.A. cruiser, the material ships making a wide detour to the eastward escorted by the armed merchant cruiser.

Due to moonlight night convoy did not change course after dark, but zigzagged all night. Ocean escorts assumed regular night stations (light cruiser astern column 1). Due to departure of one destroyer there is no local escort on port quarter of column No. 1.

Handled 72 flashing light messages today, 45 of which were outgoing. Decoded 25 messages. Wind light, sea calm, excellent visibility. Temperature at 0800—80°, at 1200—85°, at 2000—86°. Distance run from Freetown to noon today—249 miles.

Personal Diary, 10 March 1941

. . . Worked on report. Slept below terribly sticky.

Official Diary, 10 March 1941

. . . Convoy ceased zigzagging at 0405 (moonset). Made regular sweep outboard of port flank of convoy to a distance of about 7 miles at dawn. Usual dawn action stations. At 0700 before returning to convoy speed increased to 22 knots, ports opened, wind scoops in—the idea was to blow fresh air through the ship after being battened down all night. Humidity high—observers stateroom 95° at 2330 (slept on deck). 1445 one of the troop transports left the convoy and proceeded on an easterly course in accordance with prearranged plans—destination—Takoradi.[69] Convoy only making good 9 knots in order not to overrun rendezvous with heavy cruiser due tomorrow at 1400. Captain of light cruiser does not like this low speed.

At 1900 three local escorts (sloop and two corvettes) left the convoy. Captain of light cruiser decided to retain the one remaining destroyer until tomorrow in order to send any messages back to Freetown. (He did this on his own initiative—orders were for all local escorts to leave at dusk tonight.) At 1900 the Commodore's ship reported a casualty to one of its two diesels. Maximum speed on one engine 11 knots.

At 1730 received answer from Commander in Chief, South Atlantic at Freetown to our ciphered message. (Incidentally this ciphered message was sent to Admiralty for information.) Answer said not to split convoy, proceed at highest sustained speed without fear of breakdown and that heavy cruiser would be advised to expect convoy beyond rendezvous on mean line of advance. Convoy speed increased to 11 knots. Apparently we will not get any additional escorts. Sighted one merchant ship at 1730, investigated—British. Ship is keeping a plot on all merchant ships in area between Freetown and Cape. Information for this plot is received daily from Commander in Chief, South Atlantic. For example today 21 ships are north-bound, 6 south-bound, 3 east-west bound within normal trade route Freetown—Cape Town. The one remaining destroyer zigzagged across front of convoy when other escorts left convoy.

Handled 47 flashing light messages today, 26 of which were outgoing. Decoded 28 messages today. Weather overcase with occasional showers, sea calm, good visibility. Temperature at 0800—81°, at 1200—87°, at 2000—82°. Distance run noon yesterday to noon today—338 miles.

Official Diary, 11 March 1941

. . . Convoy speed 11 knots and zigzagging until moonset at 0420. Made usual search to port flank of convoy (7 miles) at dawn. Dawn action stations as usual. 0830 commenced zigzagging using same plan as before. Plan has not been changed since leaving Freetown. (Same plan as was used all the way from Greenock to Freetown—21 days.) 1108—Commodore's ship broke down and forced to leave formation. Commodore reported that ship would be stopped for ½ hour, that maximum speed for next 5 days would be 10 knots and when weather became cooler the ship may be able to do 11 knots—ship is diesel drive. Under present conditions with raiders in this area this situation is not good. After one hour Commodore decided to shift his flag to another ship—via the one remaining destroyer with us, and to send his old ship back to Freetown escorted by the destroyer. Freetown is a good 2.5 days run at 10 knots, no facilities except one converted repair ship; ship has about 2,000 troops on board. Retaining the destroyer until today was a fortunate decision. The A.A. cruiser was stationed 5 miles on starboard beam of convoy and the armed merchant cruiser at visibility distance to starboard of the A.A. cruiser—reason to assist the heavy cruiser in rendezvous due about noon.

At 1205 sighted heavy cruiser on opposite course. Heavy cruiser passed through the columns, made a 180° turn, hoisted the flag to indicate that he was senior officer of the escort, catapulted a plane, sent the light cruiser a message saying to take station 7 miles ahead of the center of the convoy, the A.A. cruiser was ordered to take station 7 miles on the port quarter of the convoy and the armed merchant cruiser ordered to proceed independently to Cape Town in accordance with previous orders. The whole performance was very efficient, perhaps a little too efficient as the heavy cruiser did not

---

[69]Gold Coast, now Ghana.

wait for the light cruiser to turn over many important signals and general information. The light cruiser had all this information compiled and started to send same when ordered to take its station.

The new O.T.C. ordered the following dispositions for the ocean escorts: No. 1 *Day*—Light cruiser 7 miles ahead center of convoy, A.A. cruiser 7 miles on port quarter of convoy, heavy cruiser 7 miles starboard beam convoy; No. 2 *Day*—Light cruiser 7 miles on port bow of column No. 1, Heavy cruiser 7 miles on starboard bow of column No. 10, A.A. cruiser 5 miles astern of convoy. At sunset the light cruiser and A.A. cruiser are to open out on their lines of bearing to 15 miles returning to their night stations by one hour after sunset. No. 3 *Night*—Light cruiser 2 miles on port bow of center of convoy, A.A. cruiser 2 miles on starboard bow of center of convoy, Heavy cruiser 2 miles astern of convoy. Disposition No. 1 to be used when danger of attack by the 2 battle cruisers, or 2 battle cruisers plus one pocket battleship; No. 2 to be used when liable to attack by one pocket battleship, one pocket battleship and one armed merchant cruiser, or one armed merchant cruiser.

The O.T.C. sent an appreciation of our present situation in regards to raiders and what he proposed to do if two battle cruisers were met, or two battle cruisers and one pocket battleship, or one pocket battleship, or one pocket battleship and one armed merchant cruiser. He requested comments from the captain of the light cruiser . . . .

1900 assumed night station (Disposition No. 3), 2 miles on port bow of center of convoy . . . .

Handled 50 flashing light messages today, of which 24 were outgoing. Decoded 9 messages today. Weather—clear—intermittent showers, very high humidity. Temperature at 0800—85°, at 1200—83°, at 2000—81°. Temperature of sea water at equator 86°. Distance run noon yesterday to noon today 341 miles.

Letter to Mrs. Wellings, 11 March 1941
. . . The time is now 1925. I have just finished my afternoon sunbath plus a *little* light exercise consisting mostly of a modified tennis where one uses grommets and throws them over the net. It is good fun and not too strenuous. I am gradually acquiring a marvelous coat of tan which will be the envy of all the boys in the main office when I return.

In another half hour dinner will be served after which we all listen to the news, take a little walk in the open air—nice cool breeze and then another day will be ended—except tonight I must read and make a few notes.

The food is really unusually good for war time. I cannot complain in any manner. We are having mostly cold food during the hot days. The salads are really delicious. In general the English do not eat salads as often as we do, so that these cold salads are a real treat for me. We have plenty of butter, although we make sure not to waste any, very fine marmalade, good ham and bacon, etc. Really I have all I want to eat and in many cases I eat too much. So therefore my little girl do not think that I am being starved . . . .

Personal Diary, 11 March 1941
. . . King Neptunes heralds came aboard with due ceremony at 1900 and said to be prepared to meet the King, Queen and their court at 0945 tomorrow in order to get permission to enter their domain & to initiate all land lubbers who have not previously crossed the line. Ship actually crossed the equator at 2145. Long 5°-15W.

"CROSSING THE LINE"
H.M.S. "Birmingham," March 11, 1941

NIGHT BEFORE CEREMONY.

Pipe:	"Clear Lower Deck. Hands to cross Equator."

Masth'd Lookout: "Line Ahead, Sir."

Captain: "Stop Both." *(The ship is stopped. Herald and Trumpeters with Bears Mermaid in attendance appear on the Forecastle. Coloured beams from 20″ S/Ls.[70] Spray from hoses.)*

Fanfare by Trumpeters.

Herald: "Ship Ahoy. What ship is this?"

Captain: "His Britannic Majesty's Ship, *Birmingham*, and who are you?"

Herald: "I am the Herald of His Watery Majesty, King Neptune Emperor of All the Seas."

Captain: "Welcome, Herald, Pray advance, I have sighted the Dominion of your Royal Master and have stopped my ship until I receive permission to clear the line and proceed.

Herald: "My Royal Master down below has been expecting you, Sir.

And sends His Royal Greeting to you and to your crew, Sir.

He instructs me to instruct you that he gives you his permission,

To proceed until tomorrow on your Southward expedition."

Captain: "Our very humble greetings to His Majesty, your Master
We know we cannot enter his domain without disaster
Until we pay him homage, so we beg to be allowed
To receive him in the morning with his Court—we'll have a crowd
To receive initiation in the very solemn rite
Of crossing the Equator on this happy Tuesday night."

Herald: "I bring a parcel from his liege
Which now I give to you,
Containing Neptune's summonses
For many of your crew.
Our policemen don't like shirkers.
Our bears are fierce and strong.

---

[70]Searchlights.

Our barbers don't like whiskers
Or hair that grows too long."

Bears: "Shave him and Bash him
Duck him and Splash him
Torture and Smash him
But don't let him go."

Herald: "I thought I'd give you warning,
    I'll take your message down below,
Farewell until the morning."

Captain: "Farewell until the morning." *(Fanfare by Trumpeters.)*
    (Off 20" S/Ls.)

Captain: "Clear the Line."

Masth'd Lookout: "Line cleared, Sir."

Captain: "Half speed ahead, both."

NEXT
MORNING: *(NEPTUNE and COURT assemble in the waist.* Route for
procession:—Aft the stbd. side and forward the port side. Up on
to the Hangar Deck by brow abreast the 2nd Whaler. *Order of
procession:*—Herald and Trumpeters, Judge and Judge's
Clerk, Police, Bears, Doctors, Barbers. NEPTUNE and
AMPHITRITE, Mermaid.)

. . . *on arrival of Herald and Trumpeter [at Hangar Deck] there is a Fanfare.)*

Herald: "His Majesty's Court Approaches.

(*He announces each in turn.)*

"His Majesty's Judge and Judge's Clerk.
(*They take position on Dais.)*

"His Majesty's Police." *(Arrange themselves round arena.)*

"His Majesty's Bears." *(Muster on left of the Guard.)*

"His Majesty's Doctors." *(Muster on the Platform.)*

"His Majesty's Barbers." *(Muster on the Platform.)*

(FANFARE by Trumpeters.)

"His Majesty King Neptune and Queen Amphitrite."

*(Neptune and Queen Amphitrite
are met by the Captain in middle of
the Dais.)*

Captain: "I have much pleasure, Honoured Sirs, to welcome you on board.
Together with your Royal Spouse and all your humid horde
And now I pray your Majesty, Inspect your guard of honour
And bring the Queen, for every marine wants to feast his eyes
upon her.

(NEPTUNE, AMPHITRITE and CAPTAIN inspect Royal Marines.)

DURING INSPECTION:—

NEPTUNE: "Come here, my dear, don't linger near that scupper.
You needn't frown, for when we get down, you can have a bootneck's supper.

(To the Captain.)

"Pray pardon this domestic scene,
But the Queen is very partial to a Royal Marine."

AT END OF INSPECTION:—

NEPTUNE: *(To Captain of Marines.)*

"I'm always impressed by the elegant pose
Assumed, when in doubt, by His Majesty's Jogs.
Congrats, Mr. Marsh, on a splendid collection.
Their motto, I know is Per Mare Perfection.
I'm especially pleased by the splendid peruque
Of this elderly, dignified Royal   Jerock."

(After inspection of Guard CAPTAIN, NEPTUNE and AMPHITRITE take up position in Dais.)

NEPTUNE: "I'm delighted to welcome the Birmingham
For I've heard many stories concerning 'em
   How they've boasted that they
   Crossed four times in one day
Without giving me chance of confirming 'em.

(To the Captain:)

"Captain, Sir, when last we met, Methinks you looked more chubby,
Weren't you in *Inflexible*—a blue-eyed, blushing subby?

CAPTAIN: "Yes, the very first time I crossed the Line
   We were bound for the Falklands' shore
We'd a call to pay on Admiral Spee
   With his *Scharnhorst* and *Gneisenau*.

We presented a bill for Coronel—
　The result I don't think you've forgotten.
For both of these ships we sent down as tips
　And you've still got them both on the bottom.

"And now to your seas we've brought salts and O/R's
　Who have never been South before.
I hope you'll accept them for sacrifice
　In accordance with ancient tradition
And allow us to enter your Southerly Sea
　With a blessing on this commission.

"But before you proceed, there is someone you need.
　To see that no novice goes light.
There'll be many who'll sigh, "Let the sleeping dog lie"
　But his bark is much worse than his bite.
He has eyes, it is said, in the back of his head
　For loafers or the least speck of rust.
He's crossing the line for the twentieth time
　And is willing to twist and go bust.

(Introduces FIRST LIEUTENANT as NEPTUNE's A.D.C.)

NEPTUNE:　　"The appointment is good.
　　　　　　　I am right, am I not.
　　　　　　We first met in the HOOD
　　　　　　　At this very same spot.

　　　　　　(To the Captain)

　　　　　　"I must thank you indeed for the courteous way in which I have
　　　　　　　　been received,
　　　　　　The joy of my court when they saw your approach should be
　　　　　　　　seen to be really believed.
　　　　　　My Barbers below have been itching to go from the very first
　　　　　　　　moment they heard,
　　　　　　That of all the ships in the Royal Navee, the *Birmingham* had
　　　　　　　　most beard.
　　　　　　I have brought all my Doctors, Policemen and Bears, to apply
　　　　　　　　the traditional rites
　　　　　　And I'm sure we shall have an enjoyable day and some very
　　　　　　　　unusual sights.
　　　　　　But first, Captain Madden, my Court it will gladden and joy to
　　　　　　　　the company bring
　　　　　　As, for nights without number, you've broken our slumber
　　　　　　And there's no means of stopping your ASDIC evesdropping,
　　　　　　　　We appoint you THE GREAT PING KING."

NEPTUNE:　　(To U.S. Naval Officer, Lt/Cdr. WELLING:)

　　　　　　"Welcome, Mr. Welling, let me say how glad I am,
　　　　　　To initiate a delegate from my old friend, UNCLE SAM.

This ship is proud to have you (Tho' if it must take lodgers,
Between you and I, they wonder why they weren't sent Ginger
Rogers.)
The last time we met, I will never forget, 'twas a most
remarkable feat,
For you crossed the line at the very same time as the whole
American Fleet.
Now, as you've seen how they keep my sea clean from that Nazi
landlubber lot,
I think you'll agree, tho' your Navy's T.T.[71] that there's much to
be said for a tot.
So now, my dear Wellings, for the tale you'll be telling; back
home in the Land of the Free.
'Tis right, I suggest, to adorn your chest with the HANDS
ACROSS THE SEA."

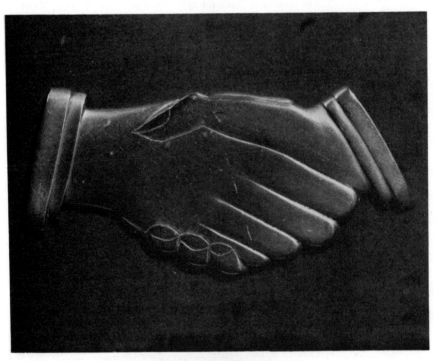

HANDS ACROSS THE SEA
Clasped hands of steel engraved on back
"Lieut. Comdr. J.H. Wellings, USN., 12.3.41 Equator"
[actual size]

---

[71]Teetotal.

NEPTUNE: (To PAYMASTER/COMMANDER GLENISTER.)

"Greetings, Pay Commander, this really is a pleasure
To meet the man who sends tin can to swell my ocean treasure.
Tho see your mighty torso, does not the least surprise us
For I and the Queen have frequently seen your morning exercises,
I'm told there's none can touch you at tearing off a sonata
And the only man on board who can eat herrings in tomato.
But in spite of your sins in opening tins with the lust of a
                              Jack the Ripper,
Kneel, I request you, that I may invest you, with the BADGE of
                   TAINTED KIPPER.

NEPTUNE: (To Master Gunner, Mr. CLEARY.[72])

"Welcome, Mr. Cleary, King of Master Gunners,
You've seen half a hundred winters, though they might have all
                              been summers.
I'm very glad to see you here, for we've had many dealings.
Just one little matter—I don't want to hurt your feelings—
Do you remember, last November, when you sent me down a diver,
That he only paid me half-a-crown and borrowed another fiver?
When this war is over and you return from sea
I expect you'll spin them many a yarn, with your grandchild on your knee;
And maybe you'll go further to impress the little crawler
And boast how once you went and sank a great big German trawler.
So now, my elf friend, on both knees bend, and I'm sure my Bears
                              won't skimp it,
With considerable glee, I confer the degree of the ANCIENT CRUSTED
                   LIMPET.

NEPTUNE: (To Midshipman STUART.[73])

"Here stands the Senior Kiddy, whose fame has crossed the Atlantic,
Where news of his wonderful tropical growth has driven my Mermaids frantic.
I'm really glad to meet you, Sir, and see what I've heard from the birds
That they're tough, mighty tough on the Birmingham, where even the middies
                              have beards.
As you stride up and down, with a terrible frown, you can see three
                              badgers quaking:
"Keep out of the way," you can hear them say, "It's an Admiral in the
                              making."
So now, my dear Stuart, it's high time that you ought to take your place
                              among us,
So with this in view, I confer on you, the BADGE of the DEEP-SEA FUNGUS."

---

[72]Commissioned Gunner James Sidney Cleary.

[73]Geoffrey Claude Edwards Stuart.

NEPTUNE: (To Ldg/Stoker CRAWSHAW.)

"Now here's our dear old Tanky, Leading-Stoker Crawshaw,
Who's been on every ocean and in the pubs on every foreshore,
He says it was in 'thirteen that we did first receive him,
But I do not think that anyone is likely to believe him.
He's stuck to that tall story and maintained expression inn'cent
Ever since they lost his papers at the battle of St. Vincent.
He's got a wicked sense of humour, only found among the old
For it's he who makes you scald yourself from every tap marked "COLD";
And it's he who keeps on drinking all the "icers" in the ship,
For years the acknowledged master of the steady, lukewarm drip.
But in spite of all his failings, he's a decent sort of chap,
So I pin on him the ORDER of the LEAKING WATER TAP.

NEPTUNE: (To Boy STEPHENSON and Marine/Bugler HUSBAND.)

"And, lastly, two Boys, 'their Mothers' joys,' despair of Leading Seamen,
Who joined up as tots, just out of their cots, but soon grew into he-men.
I'm very glad to greet you both and hope to see you more.

(TO BOY STEPHENSON)

Tho' I must say, for a sailor, you look very much paler, since my Bears
                         have smelt your gore,
It is down in my books that your good looks, suitable dues shall be paid.
So if you can afford her, I give you the ORDER of LULU the GOLDEN
                         MERMAID.

(TO Marine/Bugler HUSBAND)

"As you spoil our ease with ear-splitting "G's" and frighten the poor ship's cat,
I wind up the day, in the time-honoured way, with the BADGE of the OLD TIN
                         HAT."

CAPTAIN:

"I am honored, O King, by the Badge of the Ping, and am subject always to you,
So please make use of my ship as you wish and instruct your watery crew,
To supply enough pills to cure all the ills of my marine novices, so that they may
Conduct themselves as your servants should, in a decent seamanly way.
I earnestly hope that the razor and soap of the Barber will raze many hairs,
So Policemen, go to it, and see they go through it, and then heave them unto the
                         Bears.

NEPTUNE:

"Old Shellbacks and Scribe, and the rest of your tribe,
Are you ready to act as you ought?
Is everything ready?

CHORUS:

"Ready, Aye, ready."

NEPTUNE:

"Then OPEN KING NEPTUNE'S COURT.

(The two Warrants are then produced by A.D.C.)

NEPTUNE:

"And now, so that my Bears may have their fun
Bring me Warrant No. 1.
Policemen! Do not at your duty falter.
Fetch me here my first defaulter."

(A.D.C. hands warrant to Judge or Judge's Clerk who reads:—)

JUDGE'S CLERK:

"Whereas it has been represented to me that
NAME:—Charles Frederick St. Quintin. RATING:—The Bloke.
CONDUCT:—Filthy. CHARACTER:—None. LEAVE:—Plenty.
Did,
Endeavor to evade paying his dues to His Wet Majesty, King Neptune, and
to sneak over the line by disguising himself as a bearded lady.

(2) Did fail to give a make and mend during the first two months of 1941.

(3) Did cause to be confined contrary to Habeas Corpus the gun turret
crews of A.B.X. and Y turrets for unreasonable periods during the present voyage;

(4) Did belay or cause to be belayed fourteen pipes in one day, thereby
causing confusion and dismay among His Majesty's loyal servants;

(5) Did cause the starboard watch to "out" P.V.'s ten times running.

(6) Did cause the port watch to "out" P.V.'s ten times running;

(7) Did endeavor to capture satellites of His Majesty's Court, to wit
Mermaids, in order to compel to paint ship whilst in harbour.

JUDGE: "I do hereby adjudge him, the aforesaid, to be shaved with black
soup, given sundry pills for his inner comfort and to be
immersed four times with North End up and four times with his
South End up.

"Before awarding the foregoing punishment, I did in the
presence of the accuser and the accused, investigate the matter,
and having heard the evidence of the said Mermaids, three

Bears and One Sea Slug in support of the charge; the accused not being allowed to offer any defence; I do hereby adjudge him to be punished as afore stated.

"Given under my hand on the Equator, on the twelfth day of March, Nineteen Hundred and Forty One."

NEPTUNE: (After execution of Sentence No. 1.)

"It gives great pleasure, as it ought
To see an old offender caught.
Now Policemen, I look to you
To bring Defaulter Home."

(The CHAPLAIN is forcibly arrested by Policemen and brought to Platform. A.D.C. hands Warrant No. 2 to JUDGE'S CLERK.)

JUDGE'S CLERK: "Warrant No. 2."

"Whereas it has been represented to me that
NAME: George Reindrop.   RATING: Sky-pilot.
CONDUCT: Unpredictable.   CHARACTER: Loose.   LEAVE: Stopped.
      Did,
Display unseemingly mirth in the presence of his Wet Majesty, King Neptune;

(2) Did make improper advances, to wit winking, at one of his Majesty's subjects, to wit a Mermaid (black) whilst bathing at Lumley Beach;

(3) Did scandalise said subject by later frolicking improperly clad on said beach;

(4) Did talk too much on many occasions;

(5) Did appear improperly clad in church, to wit wearing shorts underneath his surplice.

JUDGE: "I do hereby adjudge him, the aforesaid, to be thrown to my Bears, to be dosed with three pills and a tonic, to receive a close shave and to be ducked once with his chancel end uppermost and once nave downwards.

"Given under my hand on the Equator on the twelfth day of March, Nineteen Hundred and Forty One."

(The Sentence is executed.)

NEPTUNE:	"And now, with chief offenders caught,
	Deal with the others as you ought,
	After the Novices! In with the first!
	Bears and Barbers, do your worst!

(General ceremony then proceeds.)

End.

Official Diary, 12 March 1941

. . . Steaming as before. Convoy speed 11 knots and zigzagging. Light cruiser stationed 2 miles on port bow of leading ship of column 5. Dawn action stations as usual, during which assumed daylight stations. Light cruiser 7 miles ahead of center of convoy, Heavy cruiser 7 miles on starboard beam, A.A. cruiser 7 miles on port quarter of convoy. All ocean escorts zigzagging. At 0615 the Heavy cruiser launched one aircraft to search to the westward—returned at 0915. Unable to see recovery of this aircraft. The O.T.C. changed the A.A. cruisers station in disposition No. 1 to 4 miles on port quarter of convoy, and in disposition No. 2 to 4 miles astern of convoy. (Originally the distances were 7 and 2 miles respectively.) At 1030 the Heavy cruiser left station to investigate smoke to the westward—returned at 1130.

At 0945 King Neptune with her Royal Highness the Queen, plus their court came aboard and conducted the usual crossing the line ceremony. The observer and captain were presented special emblems for being "shellbacks." However, this did not prevent the observer from being summoned and thrown in the tank later on in the day. Ceremony carried out as in peacetime, excellent for morale.

The Heavy cruiser informed the Light cruiser and A.A. cruiser to install two red and two white horizontal lights aft to show 30° forward of the stern on each side. Purpose of lights is to warn Commodore by flashing when it is considered that the convoy should make an emergency turn to port (red lights) or to starboard (white lights) to avoid danger. Ships ahead of convoy have full permission of the O.T.C. to use these lights at their discretion.

During the afternoon the light cruiser had several long messages to send to the O.T.C. in the heavy cruiser concerning the details of the convoy—which the heavy cruiser did not have time to receive yesterday. The light cruiser requested permission to close the heavy cruiser to send these messages as the light cruiser desired to conserve the limited number of carbons for the 20″ searchlights. When closed it required 2.5 hours to send these messages. Two signalmen used semaphore and one aldis lamp was used continually. After sending all messages to the O.T.C. the light cruiser was ordered to take disposition No. 2. Apparently O.T.C. believes there is no longer danger from attack by the two battle cruisers, or the battle cruisers plus a pocket battleship. At sunset increased distance to 15 miles from convoy then took station one hour after sunset 2 miles on port bow of center of convoy.

The O.T.C. proposed the following gunnery exercises while in company with the convoy:

(1) Range and inclination exercise daily.

(2) Splash target for point of aim for sub calibre practice and close range weapons.

(3) Full calibre throw off firings.

(2) and (3) to be conducted next week if air reconnaissance indicates no enemy.

The heavy cruiser said one of its planes had a damaged main plane and requested the light cruisers spare. After exchange of signals it was decided to send plane to light cruiser and to be used by light cruiser until arrival Cape Town. The heavy weather cruiser apparently has two planes (unusual as ships now are allowed only one plane due to shortage of Walrus planes.) This is in accordance with Admiralty letter. Heavy cruiser said it only had *one* observer. The light cruiser's own plane was lost the day before this convoy arrived in Freetown, pilot, observer and gunner saved.

In order to save the A.A. cruisers fuel the heavy cruiser and light cruiser will investigate all ships sighted. The heavy cruiser's plane will assist when possible.

At sunset opened out to 15 miles ahead of convoy and assumed night station 2 miles on port bow of leading ship of center of convoy at one hour after sunset.

The convoy ceased zigzagging at daylight today. Orders were to zigzag until 800 miles from Freetown. Convoy was more than 800 miles from Freetown at daylight. Convoys daily run should now increase as the zigzag plan used reduced the distance made good by 15%.

Handled 42 flashing light messages today, 18 of which were outgoing. Decoded 18 messages today. Temperature at 0800—80°, at 1200—84°, at 2000—82°. Sea calm, wind light, excellent visibility. Distance run noon yesterday to noon today 327 miles.

Personal Diary, 13 March 1941
. . . Slept on deck last night. Rained out at 0200 but 10 minutes later was back & to sleep. Up as usual at dawn action station—0610 . . . .

Official Diary, 13 March 1941
. . . Steaming as before. Convoy speed 11 knots. Convoy not zigzagging. Ocean escorts in night cruising disposition No. 3. Usual dawn action stations with light cruiser increasing distance from convoy to take cruising disposition No. 3, 7 miles on port bow of column No. 1. During both day and night the ocean escorts zigzag at about 2 knots above convoy speed in order to patrol their station. 0700 the heavy cruiser catapulted one aircraft for reconnaissance to the westward. Plane returned at 1015. At 0915 took station for range and inclination exercise (1600 yards on port bow of heavy cruiser, the A.A. cruiser is 16,000 yards on port quarter of heavy cruiser).

1015-1100 conducted range and inclination exercise. The first 10 minutes all ships steered a steady course and ranges were exchanged in order to get accurate fix. During the remainder of the exercise each ship used a different standard zigzag plan with the times on each leg reduced one half. The plotting room, range finders, directors and inclinometers (instrument to measure inclination (target angle)) were manned, the rate officer with the aid of the inclinometer operator estimate the inclination and speed. The problem was worked out in the plotting room and afterwards checked when the ships informed each other of the zigzag planned used. This is one of the favorite exercises conducted by the British whenever the opportunity permits.

At 1545 closed the heavy cruiser which lowered one aircraft to the water. The aircraft taxied to the light cruiser and was taken aboard—not flown due to a damaged lower wing which will be repaired on light cruiser. The light cruiser will use this plane until arrival at Cape Town. The heavy cruiser still has one aircraft. Armament of heavy cruiser as observed when the two ships were close aboard—8-8" guns in 4 two gun turrets; 2 twin 4" H.A./L.A. mounts on each side; 1-8 barreled pom-pom on each side, outboard No. 1 funnel; 1-4 barreled .5 machine gun on each side outboard of the bridge.

At 0129 this morning, convoy changed course 20° to the eastward in order to pass through a new position. After passing through this position course will be altered to pass through original positions to the southward. This change of course ordered by

Commander in Chief, South Atlantic, has the effect of translating the convoy to the east of the original route a maximum distance of 240 miles before again slowing converging to the original route. This detour to the eastward was one of the suggestions made by the captain of the light cruiser to Commander in Chief, South Atlantic when the destroyer returned to Freetown with the Captain's suggestions and concern over the safety of the convoy after the two battle cruisers were sighted by MALAYA on 8 March.

At dusk took night cruising disposition No. 3, light cruiser 2 miles on starboard bow of center of convoy. The O.T.C. during the afternoon ordered the A.A. cruiser and light cruiser to exchange stations in this disposition, hence the light cruiser now on the starboard bow. This change undoubtedly was made to place the light cruiser to the westward (convoy course 124) which is the most likely direction of an attack on the convoy.

Spotting waves (frequencies) were assigned to the aircraft by the O.T.C. (4570, 4950 kc's), fire-control frequency 136' kc, flank marking to be sent by visual and by fire-control frequency.

Handled 30 flashing light messages today, of which 14 were outgoing. Decoded 16 messages. Sea calm, wind light, unlimited visibility, beautiful moonlight night. Temperature at 0800—80°, at 1200—81°, at 2000—80°. Distance run today 333.2 miles, fuel remaining 1246 tons.

Personal Diary, 13-14 March 1941

13 March . . . At night I go [to the] bridge about 2100 & remain until 2330-2400. Too hot below decks. Gave a talk to one of the divisions on the U.S.N. Had a grand talk with captain on bridge until 2400. A beautiful moonlight night, with a calm smooth sea, and a cool breeze. Oh how I wish my Dolly were here.

14 March—Another warm day although not so humid. Temperature gradually decreasing but sun hot. My legs got a little too much sunburnt yesterday, but doubt if they will peel. Marvelous sleeping on deck last night. On bridge a large part of the morning and afternoon . . . . Lazy weather—am trying to take things easy. Up each morning at six for dawn action [stations], this is the most dangerous time of the day. Doing a little easy reading, but have not accomplished much the past few days—Too hot.

Official Diary, 14 March 1941

. . . Dawn action stations as usual during which the light cruiser moved ahead and across front of convoy to take station in cruising disposition No. 2 (7 miles on port bow of leading ship in column No. 1). At 0600 the heavy cruiser launched its aircraft for reconnaissance, returned at 0900. Light cruiser zigzagging on its station, speed 12.75. During morning the heavy cruiser and light cruiser conducted another range and inclination (target angle) exercise, after which they resumed their regular stations. In afternoon the escorts and convoy practiced meeting a pocket battleship, all contact reports and maneuvering signals by visual. The heavy cruiser reported the mythical pocket battleship bearing on the starboard bow of the convoy, distance 17 miles. The convoy made one 40° turn together and was about to make another when the exercise ended. In the opinion of the captain and navigator the convoy turned in the wrong direction. The light cruiser was attempting to close the heavy cruiser when the exercise was completed. As a result of the length of time required to concentrate the heavy cruiser and light cruiser from their stations in such an event the captain of the light cruiser suggested changing the day dispositions to the following: A.A. cruiser 8-10 miles ahead of the center of the convoy, the heavy cruiser and light cruiser astern of the convoy, either prolonging two of the interior columns or stationed 2 miles astern. He believed that this disposition would give the best combination of early information from ahead (to allow the convoy more time to scatter) plus early concentration of the light cruiser and heavy cruiser in order that they may attack the pocket battleship in force as far away from the convoy as possible. The general situation in regards to the simulated attack was as follows: Convoy course 128°, front of convoy about 5 miles (10 columns 1,000 yards between columns). Heavy cruiser 7 miles on starboard bow of leading ship of column No. 10, light cruiser 7 miles on port bow leading ship of column No. 1, pocket battleship sighted bearing 167° T., from heavy cruiser, distance 17 miles, course 025, speed 18, heavy cruiser increased speed to 20 knots (maximum allowed for exercise) and changed course to 120°.

Assumed night station at dusk—2 miles on port bow of center of convoy. Heavy cruiser and light cruiser to fire a throw off practice tomorrow using the A.A. cruiser as a target. Copies of orders and procedures will be included as enclosures to indicate simplicity in arranging these practices. The aircraft received from the heavy cruiser will be repaired by 17 March, at which time the heavy cruiser's plane will maintain reconnaissance patrol from 0600-0900 and from 1500-1800, the light cruiser's plane will patrol from 1100-1400. The following day the heavy cruiser and light cruiser will reverse patrols. During daylight aircraft not on patrol to be on 10 minutes notice. The O.T.C. ordered all ships to have speed ready for 25 knots on short notice, and full speed on one hour's notice. Up until now the light cruiser had steam for 25 knots ready at all times and full power at ½ hours notice. All boilers are cut in and ready for full speed about ½ hour before dawn action stations.

Sea calm, sky overcast, good visibility. Temperature at 0800—79°, at 1200—80°, at 2000—78°. Distance run noon yesterday to noon today 340.9 miles. Handled 19 flashing light messages today, 11 of these were outgoing. Decoded 11 messages. Fuel oil remaining 1153 tons.

Personal Diary, 15 March 1941

Practically the same as yesterday, although I did not sleep topside for fear of being rained out . . . .

Official Diary, 15 March 1941

. . . Steaming as before. Convoy speed 11, convoy not zigzagging, ocean escorts in night disposition No. 2. A.A. cruiser 2 miles on port bow of leading ship of column 5, light cruiser 2 miles on starboard bow of leading ship column 5, heavy cruiser 2 miles astern of center of convoy. Ocean escorts zigzagging. At 0230 changed course 28° to the southward, convoy having passed through the new position ordered by Commander in Chief, South Atlantic. The convoy is now displaced 240 miles to the east of its original track, from now on convoy will slowly converge towards its original track. Purpose of displacing convoy was to avoid possible raiders in this area. (2 battle cruisers are in the Atlantic perhaps near this area. 1 pocket battleship also may be in this area.) At 0345 set clocks ahead ½ hour. Ship now keeping zone -1.5. Official convoy time is G.C.T. At 0353 increased speed and changed course to take day station (7 miles on port bow of leading ship of column 1) at dawn. Usual dawn action stations. No aircraft reconnaissance due to moderate swell. Conducted range and inclination exercise instead of throwoff firing due to decrease in visibility plus lack of air reconnaissance. As part of range and inclination exercise the heavy cruiser and light cruiser exchanged ranges on a steady course for 10 minutes, then both ships carried out a different standard zigzag plan using half the time intervals. The object is to have the plot figure out the plan used and to check the changes of course and times with the standard plan used by the other ship (this plan is signalled at the end of the practice). The officers on the bridge and in the bridge plot try to guess the plan—all books allowed. It really was very interesting and a good test for the rate officer (estimates enemy speed and target angle) and the plotting room personnel.

In the afternoon the heavy cruiser and light cruiser conducted a range taking exercise to check their rangefinders against the R.D/F in the BIRMINGHAM (type 284). Incidentally in the morning range and inclination exercise the heavy cruiser was reading 900 yards high on the light cruiser (light cruiser using second string operators). In the afternoon the heavy cruiser and light cruiser were within 300 yards of each other but both of them were 1000-1500 yards low on the R.D/F, which is supposed to be very accurate. The light cruiser used 4 rangefinders exchanging operators, infinity test given rangefinders last night using stars, found O.K. Could the R.D/F be wrong? The expert on board says "No" but he is making a complete check-up.

The light cruiser received an answer to its recommendation for changes in cruising disposition by day as a result of the rehearsal run in sighting a pocket battleship.

Handled 31 flashing light messages today, 16 of which were outgoing. Decoded 8 messages. Temperature at 0800—77°, at 1200—77°, at 2000—75°, fuel remaining 1073 tons, distance run last 24 hours (noon to noon) 337.1 miles. Weather cloudy in morning with a moderate swell, cleared in afternoon, swell moderated but no flying.

Personal Diary, 16 March 1941

. . . Sunday—Dawn action stations as usual. This was the engineers day at church services (Church of England). I promised the Chief Eng.[74] that I would attend & did. Front row seat, church held in starboard hangar, The Chaplain prayed for the health of the King & President. President spoke over radio on Lease & Lend bill[75] very strong speech, at least the part that the British rebroadcast . . . . Definitely getting cooler . . . sleeping below nights now, legs did not peel but were very sore for a few days . . . .

Official Diary, 16 March 1941

. . . Steaming as before. Convoy speed 11, convoy not zigzagging, ocean escorts zigzagging in night disposition No. 2 (same disposition as last night). At 0325 altered course and increased speed to 15 knots to be in day disposition at dawn (light cruiser 7 miles on port bow of leading ship in column 1). Usual dawn action stations. Conducted a R.D/F test in the morning. R.D/F still high on the rangefinders about 1000 yards. At 1750 increased speed and increased distance to 15 miles from leading ship of column No. 1. Note: This is usual procedure at sunset, the sweep must be completed and the light cruiser in disposition 2 miles on starboard bow of leading ship of column No. 5 by one hour after sunset.

At 1821 the MALAYA sighted a submarine on the surface in Lat. 11°-40' N, Long. 20°-12' W. MALAYA proceeding north from Freetown to reinforce ocean escort for convoy S.L. 68, having turned S.L. 67 over to Force H.

Cloudy all day, visibility good, sea—moderate swell, nor aircraft operations. Temperature at 0800—71°, at 1200—75°, at 2000—76°, distance run from noon

---

[74]Leopold Edward Rebbeck. Engineer Commander.

[75]Probably excerpts from Roosevelt's address at the Annual Dinner of White House Correspondent's Association, 15 March 1941: "The Light of Democracy must be kept burning," printed in Public Papers and Addresses of Franklin D. Roosevelt, 1941 (New York: Random House, 1950), pp. 60-69.

yesterday to noon today 388.3. Note: This distance run is computed from rpm's which includes zigzags, changing stations, etc. It is not the distance made good along the line of advance. Fuel oil remaining 986 tons. The A.A. cruiser has 50% of fuel remaining, uses 5% per day. Handled 16 flashing light messages today, 8 of which were outgoing. Decoded 25 messages today. There are always about 4 ships of the convoy smoking sufficiently to allow the convoy to be sighted by its smoke.

Personal Diary, 17 March 1941

. . . *St. Patrick's day.* Intermittent clouds, cooler, slight swell . . . . *Nap* in p.m. and then worked on reports. Walked the equivalent of 3 miles on quarterdeck today. At night introduced "La-de Da" the destroyer match box game in the Wardroom after dinner.

Official Diary, 17 March 1941

. . . Convoy speed 10.5, convoy not zigzagging. Escorts in night disposition No. 3 until dawn then assumed disposition No. 2 (light cruiser 7 miles on port bow leading ship column 1, heavy cruiser 7 miles on starboard bow leading ship column 10, A.A. cruiser 4 miles astern of convoy). Usual dawn action stations. Weather conditions unsuitable for flying. In the morning the heavy cruiser and the light cruiser fired individual throw off practices using the A.A. cruiser as a target to represent a pocket battleship. The heavy cruiser fired 36 eight inch single gun salvos total time 25 minutes, the light cruiser fired 30 six inch single gun salvos in 16 minutes. The throw off was 6° to the right (ahead) of the A.A. cruiser which changed course and speed at will to prevent straddling. Light cruiser speed 18, A.A. cruiser speed 15-20 . . . .

At sunset searched ahead 8 miles on the line of bearing from the leading ship in column No. 1 and then assumed night station 2 miles on starboard bow of leading ship of column 5 by one hour after sunset.

Weather— . . . temperature at 0800—69°, at 1200—70°, at 2000—69°. Distance run by light cruiser noon to noon 301 miles. Oil remaining 925 tons, oil used last 24 hours 61 tons. Handled 24 flashing light messages today, 8 of these were outgoing. Decoded or deciphered 9 messages today.

Personal Diary, 18 March 1941

. . . Still cloudy but sun was out a large portion of the time. On bridge all morning . . . . Another range and inclination exercise in morning—Again I guessed the zigzag plan, although this time it was quite difficult . . . . Played "lie and cheat" in Wardroom after dinner for an hour. To bed at 2245.

Official Diary, 18 March 1941

. . . Convoy speed 10.5, convoy not zigzagging. Escorts in night disposition No. 3 until dawn and then assumed disposition No. 2. Usual dawn action stations with all boilers ready for full power. Weather unsuitable for flying, moderate sea with white caps. At 0915 conducted range and inclination exercise with the A.A. cruiser. The heavy cruiser also took part in this exercise. The light cruiser again guessed the zigzag plan used. At 1000 towed a splash target for the heavy cruisers firing. The heavy cruiser steamed on parallel course and at the same speed as light cruiser, distance about 2500 yards. Fired sub-calibre from 8", also regular 4" and pom-poms. Light cruiser fired U.P. to demonstrate its firing to the heavy cruiser. Sighted a merchant ship at 1105 and another at 1715. Investigated—2 British ships. Ships were expected from plot being kept on merchant ships in area, they also made the correct reply when their secret calls were made. At 1500 conducted searchlight exercise with heavy cruiser . . . . At 1800 searched ahead of convoy to a total distance of 15 miles at sunset then assumed regular night station 2 miles on starboard bow of leading ship in column No. 5 by one hour after sunset.

Aviation observer placed on sicklist—only observer on board. Can the additional pilot assume the observers duties?—No. The recent over reading of the R.D/F has been corrected. The local oscillations used as a base in measuring the distance was not quite up to the designed frequency of 162 kc. An additional capacity was inserted to give 162 kc. Wonder if this error is common.

Handled 52 flashing light messages today, 26 of these were outgoing. Decoded 21 messages today. Temperature at 0800—68°, at 1200—68°, at 2000—66°. Sky overcast most of the day. Fuel on hand 842 tons.

Personal Diary, 19 March 1941

. . . Up as usual at dawn action stations—0600—the action stations generally last an hour. Then back to room, a bath, shave, and to breakfast at 0745. On bridge from 0830 until 1100—worked on range & inclination exercise. Before lunch did a little paper work. Walked on quarterdeck for ½ hour after lunch then interviewed an enlisted man who is going to become an officer. Quite interesting experience. He is a graduate from Cambridge, was at one time a conscious objector, believes the English officer is more interested in his position than in his work. Read *Uneasy Oceans*[76] during part of the evening, then more work on reports.

Official Diary, 19 March 1941

. . . Convoy speed 10.5 knots, convoy not zigzagging. Escorts in night disposition No. 3 until dawn then assumed day disposition No. 2. Usual dawn action stations with all boilers ready for full power. Weather unsuitable for flying, moderate sea with white caps. A range and inclination exercise was conducted between the light cruiser and A.A. cruiser. A scheduled firing at a splash target by the A.A. cruiser was cancelled due to the sea being too rough to tow a splash target. The heavy cruiser and light cruiser conducted a searchlight exercise in the afternoon—for accuracy in pointing a searchlight exactly on the bridge of the enemy. In the late afternoon the light cruiser closed the heavy cruiser and received a long flashing light message stating the supplies the heavy cruiser desired at its next port of call. Message to be sent by light cruiser upon arrival in port,—about 3 days prior to heavy cruisers arrival. The O.T.C. in the heavy cruiser broke radio silence and sent a despatch to the Naval Officer in Charge at Cape Town requesting permission to detach 5 of the large troopships tomorrow and have them proceed to Cape Town escorted by the light cruiser. Reason—water supply running short. These ships are scheduled to stop at Cape Town for water and then proceed to Durban for fuel. Ten additional ships are scheduled to stop at Cape Town for fuel and water, the remainder to call at Durban—about 1000 miles up the east coast of Africa from Cape of Good Hope. The slowest of the five ships referred to above can make 13 knots so that by detaching them early they can receive additional water in time to rejoin the Durban section of the convoy off the Cape of Good Hope. This will facilitate escorts. The dispatch also stated that the light cruiser had a serious refrigerator defect which would require the unloading of 12,000 lbs. of meat. A leak has developed in the CO_2 system.[77] All the CO_2 has been expended, the temperature of the cold room is now 40° instead of 10. It is feared that all the meat will spoil.

---

[76]Kenneth Edwards, *Uneasy Oceans* (London: Routledge, 1939).

[77]Carbon dioxide refrigerating system.

Investigated two merchant ships in afternoon—both British. Handled 40 flashing light messages, 19 of which were outgoing. Decoded 18 messages. Temperature at 0800—65°, at 1200—64°, at 2000—67°. Fuel remaining 750 tons.

Personal Diary, 20 March 1941

. . . 5 ships of convoy went ahead at 13 knots. They are to be escorted to Cape Town by *the* CL (my ship) . . . . We are going to Cape Town & not Simondstown[78] (20 miles away) due to a refrigerator defect . . . . Due in Cape Town tomorrow afternoon at 1700. Wonder what it will be like. We fired a 6" throw off practice this morning. I witnessed firing from inside "Y" turret which fired twelve—6" 3gun salvos. Rather interesting. *Phoebe* also fired . . . . Worked on reports at night plus listening to Captain's radio talk and our own "Information Please"—Wardroom vs Petty Officers. Turned in at 2230—busy day tomorrow.

Official Diary, 20-21 March 1941

March 20 . . . Convoy speed 10.5, convoy not zigzagging. Escorts in night disposition No. 3 until dawn then day disposition No. 2. Usual dawn action stations with all boilers ready for full power. At daylight the A.A. cruiser took station near the light cruiser to conduct R.D/F ranging runs in preparation for firing a throw off practice of 5.25 using the R.D/F for ranges and bearings.

A message was received approving the request to send 5 ships in ahead of the remainder of the convoy escorted by light cruiser. These ships increased speed and formed in two columns 1,000 yards between columns, distance between ships in column 600 yards, speed 13. Remainder of convoy was rearranged so that the Cape Town ships were all together to facilitate their detachment at 0800, 22 March. (Supposed to arrive Cape Town at 1100 same date.) Weather conditions too rough to return heavy cruiser's plane. Plane will fly overland to Durban and join heavy cruiser.

The A.A. cruiser conducted its throw off practice—range 8,000 yards, R.D/F used for ranges and bearings, 12° throw off ahead, two firing runs, 6 single gun salvos to a run. First two salvos of run 1 landed about half way to the target, remainder of firing looked fair. Later the commanding officer of the A.A. cruiser said that his firing was very erratic and not satisfactory.

The light cruiser fired a throw off practice using its R.D/F for ranges and bearings . . . .

Upon completion of the above firings the A.A cruiser returned to the main section of the convoy. The light cruiser took station 5 miles ahead of the five ships and zigzagged. At night the light cruiser took station 2 miles ahead of the 5 ships and zigzagged. Speed 12.5.

Handled 43 flashing light messages, 20 of which were outgoing. Decoded 31 messages today. Temperature at 0800—64°, at 2000—63°. Fuel oil remaining 680 tons.

MALAYA was torpedoed while escorting convoy S.L. 69 at 2355 G.C.T. in Lat. 20°-03' N, Long. 23°-55' W. She should have been inside the convoy at night if she followed the same procedure as when with this convoy before arrival at Freetown.[79]

March 21—Steaming as before escorting 5 ships to Cape Town, due to arrive at 1600 today. Speed 12.5. At dawn increased distance to 5 miles ahead of 5 ships. Usual

---

[78]Simonstown, British Naval Base and dockyard.

[79]*Malaya* was not sunk.

dawn action stations. At 0700 sighted a merchant ship—investigated, result British. Shortly after investigating this ship and before regaining station a steering gear casualty caused the ship to stop for 3 hours. The following is quoted from the official report on this casualty. "The jamming of the rudder in the full starboard position was caused by a screwed pin dropping out of position and preventing the hunting gear control from shutting off the pump when the required rudder was obtained. The screwed pin became unscrewed due to the previous shearing off of the locking split pin." Type of steering gear—telemotor system. Steering gear should be carefully watched in wartime due to higher ship speeds which causes more vibration in steering gear room plus continual use of zigzags which naturally causes more wear and tear on the steering gear.

Rejoined the 5 ships at 1230. At 1400 sighted Table Mountain at Cape Town. At 1600 arrived at Cape Town but due to location of docks—in a basin, plus lack of pilots and tugs the light cruiser was not moored alongside until 2000. The merchant ships moored first in order that they could commence taking fresh water as soon as possible. They sailed at 0800 the next day and joined the Durban section of the convoy outside Cape Town. The same morning 10 ships from the main section of the convoy entered Cape Town. They remained 3 days and were escorted to Durban by the A.A. cruiser which entered Simons Town (Royal dockyard 55 miles from Cape Town) for fuel and supplies.

Temperature on arrival Cape Town 63°. Handled 34 flashing light messages today, of which 20 were outgoing (majority of these were transmitted in Cape Town harbor). Decoded 30 messages.

Personal Diary, 21 March 1941

. . . Beautiful sight approaching Cape Town—Table mountain can be seen at least 40 miles away. Cape Town is built at bottom & on the foothills of Table mountain. Cloud effect on mountain plus white buildings with red roofs very impressive. Dinner at 2100 & remained aboard. A number of the officers dashed ashore but I thought it better to remain on board. Turned in at 2300. Will have to wear civilian clothes ashore.

CHAPTER SIX

H.M.S. *BIRMINGHAM*: CAPE TOWN TO SCAPA FLOW

22 March-23 April 1941

Personal Diary, 22-23 March 1941

22 March—At Cape Town—0930 Drove with Captain & Comdr. to Simons-town . . . very beautiful drive. Simonstown under British control—not South African. Visited *Phoebe* alongside *Shropshire*, *Dorsetshire* and *Cathay*[1] also at dockyard. Returned at 1300—called at American consuls office—he was out but saw a Comdr. Sears (ret)[2] who has just been appointed (arrived 3 weeks ago) as naval attaché. Had lunch with him and Major Ennis[3] of the Army who is enroute to Egypt with convoy (tank expert). After lunch arranged for my party tonight at Del Monico's. Grand party, stag . . . We had everything from "soup to nuts." Afterwards went to Bohemian Club where a dance was in progress. Most of our officers present. Capt. & Comdr. had a grand time. Back to ship at 0515 . . . .

23 March—Sunday—up at 1040—Late church—called on Commodore Fitz-Maurice of our convoy on board his ship in afternoon. Aboard at night . . . .

Letter to Mrs. Wellings, 23 March 1941

Your little boy is in Cape Town, located about 30 miles north of the Cape of Good Hope, the extreme southern point in Africa.

I arrived two days ago and will leave tomorrow for England . . . .

Cape Town is a very attractive city of about 300,000 located at the foot of the famous Table Mountain, which rises almost from the shore to a height of about 4000 ft.[4]

The approach from the sea is really a remarkable sight. Table Mountain was visible 50 miles away. As we entered the harbor the white houses with red tile roofs running from the shore to the hills on the slopes of the mountain appeared like a picture book story.

Yesterday the captain and I drove down to Simonstown, about 20-25 miles to the southward to call on the senior naval officer. An official car and chauffeur were placed at

---

[1]Cruisers H.M.S. *Shropshire*, H.M.S. *Dorsetshire* and H.M.S. *Phoebe* with armed merchant cruiser H.M.S. *Cathay*.

[2]Arthur Wesley Sears (1881-1962). U.S. Naval Academy, 1905; Naval War College, 1923. Later Captain.

[3]Riley Finley Ennis (1897-1963). A U.S. military observer in London and Cairo in 1941; Later, Major General.

[4]Letter to Mrs. Wellings, 26 March 1941: "The people are very hospitable, so much so that if one were to accept all the invitations there would be no time for work, particularly if the visit were relatively short."

our disposal so that we had a generous view and tour of the countryside. The scenery all around this part of the world is very interesting.

We returned at 1300 after which I called on the American minister. He was out but a retired Comdr. has recently been assigned as Naval Attaché. We had a grand lunch together . . . . He must have retired years ago as he appeared to be at least 58 years old.

After lunch I made arrangements for *my* dinner party at *the* best club in town. It was one of the very few opportunities I have had to repay the many kindnesses and favours, so I put on a No. 1 party. It was stag, of course. The captain, Comdr., gunnery, navigator, and torpedo officers, First Lieut., Doctor Paymaster and his two and a half striper assistant, the Engineer and his assistant plus *yours* truly made up the party.[5] If I do say so it was a tremendous success. The English reserve was completely broken down after a few of my martinis (prepared to *our* formula). Wines, champagne, liquers, etc. were included in the best dinner the house had. The steaks were delicious (filet mignon) and the roast turkey was cooked to the Queen's taste. I could rave on and on about it. Really I was just a little bit proud of the way the whole party progressed. I hate to tell you the cost (97.50) but it will be included in my expense account. A real chance to spend some of it—I only wish you were here to see the party and the smooth way everything went off.

This morning I must admit I was not exactly 100% efficient. I had to call on a commodore and talk shop at 1100. In the afternoon I took a good nap and worked on a few reports . . . .

P.S. Please do not advertise where I am—or was.

Personal Diary, 24-28 March 1941

24 March—Cape Town—Ashore at 0900. Cashed check at bank. Bought odds and ends plus perfume for Dolly & doll for Anne—sent doll to Anne. Called on American Consul & American minister . . . . Saw Comdr. Sears again then back to ship at 1130. Ship sailed at 1300 for Freetown—speed 23—sailing alone—quite a contrast.

25 March—Underway enroute Freetown. Quite cool at 23 knots, due in Freetown on 29. Wrote reports, took things fairly easy. Read part of *Uneasy Oceans* . . . .

26 March— . . . Raider (warship) attacked a merchant ship about 500 miles west of Freetown. As a result we received orders to overtake a special merchant ship sailing independently to Freetown at 16 knots, & escort ship to Freetown. Sighted ship at 1800. slowed from 30 to 16 knots. Will not arrive in Freetown now until Tuesday a.m. unless another ship relieves us of escorting the merchant ship. Worked on reports—attended movie "The Mikado" in technicolor—quite good . . . .

27 March—Enroute to Freetown escorting merchant ship (Christiaan Hugens).[6] Up for dawn action stations as usual. Spent all morning on gunnery. Read part of official report on Battle of Spartavinto . . . . [7] Broadcasted on ship's radio "Sports in America." On bridge about 2 hours at night. Turned in on deck at 2330.

---

[5]Capt. A. Madden, Cdr. C.F.W. St. Quintin, Lcdr. A.J.F. Milne-Home, Lcdr. A.R. Kennedy, Lcdr. D.G.F. Bird, Lcdr. J.H. Dathan, Surgeon Cdr. G.F. Abercrombie, Paymaster Cdr. C.E. Glenister, Paymaster Lcdr. Henry, RNVR, Cdr. (E) L.E. Rebbeck, Lt. (E) Milne.

[6]*Christiaan Hugens.* Launched 1927; 16,287 tons. Dutch ship owned by N.V. Stoomv., Maats., Nederland.

[7]Battle of Spartivento. On 9 November 1941, Force K, a light cruiser and two destroyers, attacked a convoy of seven merchant ships with a close escort of six Italian destroyers, and an Italian support force of two heavy cruisers and four destroyers. In a brief action, all the merchant ships and one Italian destroyer were

28 March . . . Holiday for crew—"Fun & Frolic" from 0900 to 1200—very good for morale—Nap in p.m. Worked on reports. Getting quite warm. Taking things easy—Slept on deck.

Letter to Mrs. Wellings, 29 March 1941

I have a little time this morning (0830) before the intense heat arrives . . . . By ten a.m. my cabin is too hot to remain in it for over five minutes at a time. By midnight it is again cool enough to be bearable. However I sleep topside under the tropical sky dotted with stars and the cool breeze lulls me off to sleep very quickly. Every so often—about one night in three I am awakened by a tropical shower. I "pick up my bed and walk." In about ten or fifteen minutes the stars are again shinning in all their tropical brilliancy and once more I am off to sleep. At about 0600 to 0630 daylight awakens me and another day begins.

Each day is "the same" as the preceding one except on Sunday there is a change in the routine, including church. I am pleasantly surprised at the large voluntary attendance at church. Part of it is due to a young chaplain who is a reserve officer and an excellent man for his type of work. He is constantly thinking of various ways of entertaining the crew. The ship's loud speakers are constantly used for various talks, contests, experiences, etc. He has even convinced and persuaded me to appear at the "Mike" on three different occasions.[8]

My tan is getting darker each day. If I were to return home tomorrow I doubt if you would recognize your husband. One shade darker and I will be eligible to vote in the African elections.

Incidentally, I am feeling very, very well, thank God. I have not had one day's illness since I came over here. I do try to watch my health . . . . In this hot weather I usually endeavor to take a nap in the afternoons or read some book professional or otherwise, preferably the latter. I really will have forgotten how to settle down to our high pressure Navy when I return home. I doubt if I ever will—or at least I hope not. I have had many moments to reflect on the past and have decided that one's health comes first in any walk of life, and in the Navy in particular. One does not go far if his health is not next to perfect—particularly in wartime. I also believe that I have learned not to worry. I only hope I will be able to continue to do so when I again start the U.S. Navy routine . . . .

Personal Diary, 29-31 March 1941

29 March—Enroute to Freetown—very hot due to cross equator tomorrow a.m. Worked on reports in a.m.—nap in p.m. . . . A little quite reading, slept on deck.

---

sunk. The British force was unscathed. J.H.W. read the report in *Home Fleet's Technical Orders* of 5 February 1941.

8"I broadcasted over the ship's loud speaker system about once each week. This system had outlets in all the enlisted men's living compartments, plus the wardroom, the warrant officers mess room and the midshipmen's bunk room. I used the Walter Winchell radio introduction . . . 'Good evening, Mr. and Mrs. America and all the ships at sea. Let's go to Press!' 'Flash! Winston Churchill made the following announcement over BBC today (BBC being 'British Broadcasting Co.') British aircraft production increased 10% last month despite the increased bombings by the Germans.' I would be careful, of course, in the above instance to paraphrase a BBC release by Churchill as received in our radio room. Perhaps the second news item would be: 'Flash! President Roosevelt made the following announcements concerning the War in Europe today' (Again I would quote a Presidential press release). I also conducted several 'Information Please' broadcasts which answered questions submitted to me by the officers and enlisted men.

Captain Madden was most interested in these broadcasts because he believed the programs improved morale by adding something that was a little different from our regular routine." JHW *MS. Reminiscences*, p. 127.

30 March . . . Dawn action stations as usual. We have not sighted a ship since leaving Cape Town—speed 16—Sunday—worked on reports in a.m. & p.m. would like to finish reports to date by time we arrive at Freetown so that I will be free for next operations.

31 March—Practically everything same as yesterday. Except at 1130 Sighted a British armed merchant cruiser with its "friends."

Letter to Mrs. Wellings, 1 April 1941

Today is April "Fools Day." I suppose the joke is on me as I thought when I started this tour that I would be back in England by the first of April. However one must expect orders to be changed, particularly in war time. I do expect to return to England sometime in the near future . . . .

There is not much news since my last letter. Life in the tropics is very much the same day in and day out. The weather is a little cooler than it was around the equator, chiefly because we got a little breeze plus afternoon showers which tend to decrease the heat during the middle of the day.

I was surprised to learn on the radio that the President had ordered all Axis and Danish ships in American ports to be seized.[9] Apparently he had information of sabotage and did not want the ships to be disabled in our ports. Personally I think it was a good idea.

I have lost touch with the political and international situation as viewed from our country. I must try again to listen to Lowell Thomas and his news broadcast. I will have to take a few days off in London to read the latest information. No doubt events behind the scenes are happening very fast these days. I believe the diplomatic situation all over the world is more acute now than ever before. I base my opinion on the belief that Hitler will have to make a decisive move very soon. Where this move will take place and what it will be is perhaps anyone's guess but I believe it will take place. When it does Italy, France, or Japan may be involved, perhaps all three. If Hitler is to win I believe he will have to win this year. This means he must take a big step very soon. The Japs may be lead into active participation by Hitler. This would create a difficult situation in the Dutch East Indies and the far east British possessions, also for British ships in the Pacific and Indian Ocean. I doubt if we would become involved at the beginning but I can see where we may be involved in such a situation. The Japs, I hope, have more sense than to provoke a war with us. They have everything to lose and nothing to gain.

Hitler of course will probably enter Jugo-Slavia and Greece. There is a limit to how far he will permit Italy to be weakened. Turkey's attitude will be very important in such a crisis. I doubt if she will fight unless her territory is invaded. However recent events in the Mediterranean may cause her to change her mind. The whole situation is critical and subsequent events will be very interesting . . . .

Personal Diary, 1 April 1941

1 April—Arrived off Freetown at 0630. Anchored at 0745. Had lunch with No. 1 (Lt. Comdr. J.H. Dathan) ashore at brother-in-law's home. The latter is the Attorney General for Sierra Leone. Also present was the Secretary of the Treasury for Sierra

---

[9]On 30 March, the U.S. Coast Guard seized and took into "protective custody" 27 Italian, 2 German and 35 Danish vessels in U.S. ports. The purpose of this action was to make these vessels available to the British for lend-lease shipments. The Axis governments protested that, in international law, the United States was not a belligerent nation and the vessels could not be seized. The United States argued that the deliberate sabotage on board 25 Italian ships was a felony under U.S. law.

Leone.[10] On way to lunch (up in hills—"Hill Station") brought mail including letter to Dolly written this morning—to American Consul—Mr. Nielson. He will send mail home on an American steamer. Had a fine lunch—all hands took a 2 hr. nap afterwards. Back to ship at 1900. Officers had a big dinner party on *quarterdeck* . . . .

Letter to Mrs. Wellings [11]
. . . the Captain and officers had a dinner party in my honor, partly in return for my party to the heads of department at Cape Town and partly because it was the last chance to have dinner in port before we sailed for England where I expect to leave on arrival.

The dinner was under the awnings on the quarterdeck. Cocktails before dinner with the usual wines, etc. during dinner. The Marine ship's band provided the music. Just picture the above setting beneath a tropical cloudless sky with electric lanterns providing the lighting and you have the idea.

All the officers on board plus the warrant officers and midshipmen were present. It really was a fine party which I appreciated very much. Toasts to the President and the King were made (I am getting used to the procedure now, with or without a band to play the National Anthem). Speeches were made by the President of the Mess, the Captain and yours truly. The party lasted until 2345 and before we finished everyone had made a speech and a fine sing song was in order. In addition to appreciating the dinner in my honor it was good for the officers to let their "hair down" after a long trip from Cape Town and an even longer trip to England starting the next day . . . .

Personal Diary, 2 April 1941
. . . quiet morning, cocktails at lunch in honor of Sub lieutenant White[12] becoming a Lieut. Underway at 1600 . . . . We will pass inside Cape Verde Is. and about 50 miles off the coast at Dakar. Wonder if we will see any French activity???

Official Diary [13], 2 April 1941
BIRMINGHAM (CL) escorting *Christiaan Huygens*, a 15,700 ton Dutch merchantman carrying 1200 naval personnel to England, arrived at Freetown yesterday morning from Cape Town., Original orders called for fueling and provisioning, and sailing immediately thereafter to overtake and escort convoy No. S.L. 70 which sailed from Freetown 30 March, for England. However due to a leak in the stern tube glands of the *Christiaan Huygens*, the two ships did not sail until 1600 2 April.

The captain of the light cruiser will be senior officer of the escort and as such will be in charge of the convoy as well as the escort. At present the escort consists of one armed merchant cruiser and two corvettes as A/S screen. Corvettes due to leave convoy at dusk 4 April. The commanding officer of the light cruiser received all the information of the convoy from the Naval Control Service Officer prior to sailing. Prior to sailing the light cruiser received 300' of 3.5 fueling hose. Present plans are for light cruiser to fuel at sea from a tanker on 11 April.

Paravanes were streamed outside the boom defence and were not recovered until late the following afternoon when outside the 100 fathom curve.

---

[10]C.J. Hodgens, M.C., Treasurer of Sierra Leone.

[11]Excerpts from letter of 11 April 1941.

[12]Peter White.

[13]Enclosure A to Report dated 6 May 1941: "Convoy Operations of Convoy S.L. 70 from Freetown to Clyde, 2 April-22 April 1941."

Speed of advance 16 knots, both ships zigzagging. (Plan No. 2—not the usual No. 10 or 15.) The light cruiser took station 1.5 miles on the beam of the *Christiaan Huygens* until dusk when the distance was reduced to .75 miles and the zigzag plan changed to No. 11. All signals to *Christiaan Huygens* to be in G.M.T.—Still confusion about what time to use. Zigzag No. 2 is 35° course changes every 7.5 and 10 minutes. No. 11 is 20 and 30° course changes every 10 minutes. The *Christiaan Huygens* had its attention called to a light showing after dark. Rendezvous given for day after tomorrow to *Christiaan Huygens* in case it will be necessary to scatter.

Personal Diary, 3 April 1941
. . . worked on reports in a.m. & p.m. except for 2.0 hours in afternoon when Captain and I went to the movies—"For the Love of Mike"—Fair. Also worked at night.

Official Diary, 3 April 1941
. . . Steaming as before escorting *Christiaan Huygens* and enroute to join convoy No. S.L. 70 as ocean escort. Speed of advance 16 knots. The light cruiser stationed .75 miles on port beam of the *Christiaan Huygens* until dawn with both ships zigzagging. At dawn increased distance to 1.5 miles and changed zigzag plan. Dawn action stations as usual on the light cruiser.

Two turrets manned during daylight, three at night.—Watch in three.

One 4" H.A./L.A. mount on each side manned during daylight. At night one mount manner on each side ready to fire starshells.—Only one mount crew on watch.—Watch in three. All control parties in watch in three except A.A. control stations not manned. Pom-pom and .5 machine guns not manned. Lookouts in a watch in three. H.A. lookouts acting as additional submarine and surface lookouts.

At dusk closed in to .75 miles and changed zigzag plan to No. 11 (20 and 30° course changes every 10 minutes).

Weather clear, sea smooth, temperature 0800—71°, 1200—75°, 2000—72°. Decoded 30 messages today.

Radio reports indicate that two ships (one an escort vessel) of convoy S.C. 26 (Sydney, N.S.) were sunk during the night in the start of the Western Approaches. Three other dispatches concerning the "rounding up" and protection of remainder of convoy.

Personal Diary, 4 April 1941
. . . Passed Dakar at 0640, Sighted nothing. Worked on reports & had a long talk with Captain in p.m., worked at night for awhile & then began to wonder if my orders to go home might be waiting for me. I am ready to go. I miss my two girls—Dolly & Anne.

Official Diary, 4 April 1941
Underway with *Christiaan Huygens* as before. Speed 16. Zigzagging, the *Christiaan Huygens* stationed .75 miles on the starboard beam of the light cruiser. Dawn action stations—Distance increased to 1.5 miles, zigzagged changed to No. 11 (35° course changes). At 0015 commenced sweeping with 284 type R.D./F every 30-45 minutes. No contacts. 0345 shifted clocks back ½ hour. Ship now keeping G.M.T.

The route is such that the two ships passed within 60 miles of Dakar just before dawn this morning. After dawn action stations all 4" H.A./L.A. plus pom-poms and .5 machine guns were kept manned in order to be prepared for any possible attacks from Vichy planes.—No aircraft seen.

At 1527 port engine of the *Christiaan Huygens* broke down. 3.0 hours required to make repairs during which time the *Christiaan Huygens* made 8 knots on starboard engine and the light cruiser carried out radical zigzags.

At dusk took station on starboard bow of the *Christiaan Huygens*, distance .75 miles and changed to zigzag No. 2 for the night.

Commander in Chief, South Atlantic, in a dispatch states that a "U"-boat is within 300 miles of Freetown and has ordered one of the corvettes with S.L. 70 to return immediately without fueling at Bathurst (Gambia) if possible.—The two corvettes were due to leave S.L.70 today at dusk. Radio dispatches indicate another ship sunk in Western Approaches today.

Weather clear, sea smooth, temperature 0800—68°, 1200—68°, 2000—67°.

Personal Diary, 5 April 1941

. . . Turned in at 0020 & read. At 0100 my stomach went suddenly out of order. Just made the head—diarrhea and vomiting. Same again at 0330. Finally to sleep at 0415. Stayed in the bunk until 1800. No breakfast only lemonade until noon, then toast & scrambled eggs. Light dinner. Feel a little better but not quite perfect.—Wish Dolly were here to take care of me.

Official Diary, 5 April 1941

. . . Underway as before with *Christiaan Huygens*. Speed 16.5. Zigzagging, the light cruiser is stationed .75 miles on starboard bow of the *Christiaan Huygens*. At 0255 commenced sweeping with R.D/F every 30-45 minutes.—No contact. Sweep started at this time due to moonset. Dawn action stations as usual, after which the light cruiser opened out to 5 miles on starboard bow of the *Christiaan Huygens* and changed to the day zigzag plan.

At 1549 sighted the convoy No. S.L. 70, consisting of 29 ships arranged in 9 columns. Distance between columns supposed to be 600 yards and between ships in column 400 yards. Commodore of convoy on sighting and exchanging recognition signals with light cruiser opened out the distance between columns 6 and 7 to 1200 yards. At 1745 the light cruiser and *Christiaan Huygens* took station between these columns. The light cruiser about 200-300 yards astern of the line between the leading ships of columns 6 and 7. The *Christiaan Huygens* 500 yards astern of the light cruiser. To increase the submarine protection for the *Christiaan Huygens* the Commodore shifted stations of one ship to astern of the *Christiaan Huygens*. Convoy not zigzagging, speed of convoy 7.75 knots. The armed merchant cruiser was zigzagging across the front of the convoy about 1.5 miles ahead of the leading ships in the columns. One merchant ship was zigzagging outboard of the starboard flank column and one outboard of the port flank column. These ships were making about 11 knots, patrolling along the flanks as they zigzagged.—Not a bad idea.

Convoy time is zone plus one. When approaching convoy the absence of smoke and rubbish in the water was very noticeable, also the station keeping appeared to be very good. Commanding Officer of the light cruiser congratulated the Commodore on these points—It is unusual.

The armed merchant cruiser carries 7-6" guns, 2-3" H.A. Cruising range at 15 knots—8600 miles, maximum speed 16. Name BULOLO.[14] Maximum range of guns 14,000 yards. Carries 8 depth charges. Armed merchant cruiser stated that she would fly a large blue flag when investigating strangers. The commanding officer of the light cruiser sent a long policy signal to the commanding officer of the armed merchant cruiser and the Commodore of the convoy . . . . Convoy will not scatter except on orders from the Commodore, which will not be given until 1 to 3 emergency turns have been made.

---

[14]H.M.S. *Bulolo*. Built 1938, 6267 gross tons. Commissioned 1940. Pennant No. F. 82. Converted to Landing Ships Headquarters, 1942. Returned to owners 1946.

At dusk the distance between columns was increased to 1000 yards, after which "evasive steering" diagram No. 10 was carried out until daylight. This is in accordance with the new Admiralty policy of using evasive steering at night instead of zigzagging for convoy speeds under 11 knots. Diagram No. 10 was as follows—each *leg* is *one hour* long, distance made good 88°.

Time in *hours*	Amount to Change	Direction to change
0	20°	Port
1	20°	Port
2	30°	Starboard
3	30°	Port
4	30°	Starboard
5	20°	Starboard
6	30°	Starboard
7	30°	Port
8	30°	Starboard
9	20°	Port
10	20°	Port

The Commodore informed the light cruiser that a light was showing after dark. Decoded 34 messages today. Weather clear, sea calm. Temperature 0800—60°, 1200—66°, 2000—66°.

One merchant ship sunk off Freetown today. Estimated Admiralty "U"-boat positions indicate that 11 German and 1 Italian submarines are operating in the Atlantic.

Personal Diary, 6 April 1941

. . . Palm Sunday—Feel much better—up for dawn action stations . . . . Beautiful day—wind light sea calm—Went to movies at 1630 in Stbd. hangar.—"Alexanders RagTime Band"—Alice Faye—when I saw it before I was with Dolly—Wish we could see it together again. Germany invaded Jugo Slavia & Greece today—the spring drive is on. Wonder where it will end. Feel normal—I make a poor patient . . . Turned in at 2330 . . . .

Letter to Mrs. Wellings [15]

. . . I went to church services on board. The starboard hangar (stowage of aircraft) was all decorated for Palm Sunday . . . the service was Church of England and very interesting. When the Chaplain requested prayer for the health and protection and guidance of the King and the President, it made me feel that it was for my benefit (For being present). It really did touch me in an odd way as I was the Pres. representative . . . .

Official Diary, 6 April 1941

Underway as before acting as ocean escort for convoy S.L. 70 bound for England. One armed merchant cruiser also acting as ocean escort. No A/S screen except the two merchant ships zigzagging, one outside each flank column. Neither the armed merchant cruiser nor the light cruiser has asdics. Convoy speed 7.75. Evasive steering until dawn. R.D/F sweeps every 30-45 minutes after moonset—when visibility decreased. Dawn action stations as usual. After dawn action stations the light cruiser and the *Christiaan*

---

[15]Excerpt from letter of 11 April 1941.

Huygens changed their stations from between columns 6 and 7 to between columns 5 and 6 (more A/S protection from convoy). A merchant ship was also placed astern of the *Christiaan Huygens* to afford greater submarine protection. The *Christiaan Huygens* is by far the largest ship in the convoy—15,700 tons. In addition it has on board 1200 navy personnel returning from duty in the Near East.

During daylight—2 turrets are manned, at night three turrets are manned. During daylight 1 4″ H.A./L.A. mount on each side is manned. Same at night except guns ready to fire starshells. No pom-poms or .5 machine guns manned. Danger from air attack very unlikely, only possible by ship based aircraft.

Convoy consists of 29 ships. Total gross tonnage 171,300. Average gross tonnage 5,907. Gross tonnage largest ship 15,700, smallest ship 1,800.

The armed merchant cruiser investigated one merchant ship in the afternoon—Greek, Class Y, had navicert.[16] Shortly after dark commenced evasive steering—same plan as last night. At dusk one tanker left the convoy and proceeded to Gibraltar. Before dark the light cruiser informed the *Christiaan Huygens* astern that an increase in revolutions by the light cruiser would be indicated by "A" flag a decrease by "Y" flag—just an aid in station keeping. The light cruiser is repeating all flag hoists and light signals made by the Commodore in order to assist the convoy. After dark the light cruiser called two ships attention to lights showing. Height top of light cruiser's foremast 133′, mainmast 94′. Height of top of foremast of *Christiaan Huygens* 160′. One ship has a seaman (age 16) sick, diagnosis yellow fever. Light cruiser's doctor prescribing for patient. Light cruiser received report giving destination of 10 ships in convoy. Report passed on to Commodore (light cruiser guarding this frequency).

The Commodore in a message to the Commanding Officer of the light cruiser stated that this was his 21st convoy and that he has not lost a ship. Reply—"Congratulations—we are all touching wood."

Admiralty estimated "U"-boat positions indicate 12 German, 1 Italian plus others unknown operating in Atlantic. Also that best information is that 5 submarines are about to pass through the straits of Gibraltar—outbound.—Wonder why so many submarines are operating. More than usual. Does it indicate important operations about to take place.

The two German battle cruisers—SCHARNHORST and GNEISNEAU are still at Brest. Indications are that they are about to leave. The British have several strong task groups strategically located waiting for them. Will they come out? If they do the resulting operations will be interesting to watch—via the dispatches. Wonder what would happen if they both made contact with this convoy????

Weather excellent—sea very calm—"Painted ships upon a painted ocean." Decoded 43 dispatches today. Temperature 0800—65°, 1200—69°, 2000—68°.

Letter to Mrs. Wellings, 6 April 1941

. . . the letters I send or rather write on my way north will be sent via pouch upon arrival. I am sending them pouch because I want to be a little more free in what I say in order to give you a real letter for a change—now that it is known that observers are with the British Fleet . . . .

---

[16]Navicerts were part of the British system to control contraband. Ships sailing from a neutral port bound for a European port or certain Atlantic islands and neutral ports in North Africa were required to obtain certificates of non-enemy origin for all items in their cargoes. Any ship not fully certified was liable to be seized as a prize.

Personal Diary, 7 April 1941

. . . Another wonderful day—our convoy looks like a painted ship on a painted ocean. Not a ripple on the water. Worked on gunnery in a.m.—A good sun bath & nap in p.m. (rice & curry for lunch.)

Official Diary, 7 April 1941

. . . Steaming as before escorting S.L. 70 bound for British Isles. One armed merchant cruiser also acting as ocean escort. Dawn action stations as usual. Ceased evasive steering after daylight. Convoy steers a steady course during daylight. The armed merchant cruiser zigzags across front of convoy, distance about 2 miles. One *merchant* ship zigzags outboard (about 2000 yards) of starboard flank column, another zigzags outboard of the port flank column. Speed 7.75.

The convoy as a whole is very good about not making smoke. However over 50% of the time the convoy could easily be sighted by its smoke. The Commodore stated "Some of the replies about smoke are quite pathetic. I am sure the poor old dears are doing their best. Freetown coal was awful."

The Commodore stated that the light cruiser was of great assistance in repeating signals. He also stated "of my 4 signalmen, 3 have never been to sea before. An 8 weeks conscript course at Skegness is all their knowledge. My leading hand is excellent and he was new to the sea in March 1940."

At 1500 the light cruiser sent a motor boat with the Junior doctor to the ship having the sick patient. Weather very calm, patient better. Sending the motor boat was as much a gesture as it was to inquire about the sick man. The Commanding Officer of the light cruiser has always been a great admirer of the British Merchant Navy—so they tell me. Prior to sending the motor boat the engineers checked everything from A to "Zed." The engine(s) performed excellently but the crane broke down just as the motor boat was about to be hoisted aboard. Delay 15 minutes.

At 1600—Set clocks back ½ hour. After dark again commenced evasive steering—same plan as before.

Admiralty's estimate of "U"-boats in Atlantic—German 15, Italian 3. Weather excellent, sea calm. Temperature 0800—67°, 1200—67°, 2000—66°.

Personal Diary, 8 April 1941

. . . Weather still grand. Same routine—up for dawn action stations 0630 now. worked on reports—everything routine.

Official Diary, 8 April 1941

. . . Steaming as before. Speed 7.75, used evasive steering plan No. 10, instead of zigzagging until daylight—No zigzag nor evasive zigzag plan during daylight. Sweeps with R.D/F every 30-45 minutes beginning at 0200 and ending at daylight. Usual dawn action stations. Distance between columns changed from 1000 to 600 yards after daylight—usual practice. At 0830 changed the line of bearing of leading ships in columns preparatory to changing course at 0845. New course 355, former course was 295. At 0800 speed increased to the maximum sustained convoy speed—8 knots, 1000 practiced in streaming fog buoys. At dawn each morning the armed merchant cruiser takes station on the western bow of the convoy—to prevent surprise action on convoy. The light cruiser remains inside the convoy to conserve fuel. The light cruiser was to leave the convoy tomorrow at dusk and proceed to a rendezvous with a tanker for fueling—then rejoin convoy on 11 April. (Rendezvous about 170 miles from track of convoy.) However orders received today cancelling the fueling due to no other ship being available to relieve the light cruiser as ocean escort. At 1250 and at 1720 smoke sighted. Armed merchant cruiser investigated both contacts with light cruiser moving out of convoy and taking station between armed merchant cruiser and convoy. One ship Portuguese—Fayal to Freetown—O.K., other ship British. At 2020 armed merchant cruiser two miles ahead of convoy—sighted a steamer with lights. Armed merchant cruiser proceeded ahead with the light cruiser again placing itself between armed merchant cruiser and convoy. Ship refused to stop until armed merchant cruiser fired a few rounds of machine gun bullets (with tracers) ahead of ship. Ship proved to be the French Vichy ship *Fort of France* (4800 tons) from Martinique to Casablanca. Light cruiser closed the armed merchant cruiser and ordered the armed merchant cruiser to send the ship to Gibraltar with an armed guard for examination. This is in accordance with orders. The *Fort of France* broadcasted on 500 kcs, stating that she was being attacked by a British ship, and gave her position. Commanding Officer of light cruiser quite peeved at this . . . .

Report on Convoy S.L. 70[17]

(f) . . . The following dispatches are of interest in connection with this incident.

From: BIRMINGHAM   To: Commodore
The lighted ship we met last night was S.S. *Fort de France*. BULOLO could not make her comply with his orders and eventually fired a burst of machine gun fire wide of him. Ship then made W/T signal giving his position followed by the words "Attaque Brittainique." I then told BULOLO to board him, send him to Gib. if necessary and cancel the "attack" signal on ships set. This was done and ship is now on her way to Gib. under armed guard. BULOLO asked if he could break W/T silence to inform F.O.C.N.A.[18] and C.in.C.S.A.[19] but I do not think this would be wise. (0708)

Reply:—Your 0708. Many thanks. If I may say so I think the action you both took was entirely correct. (0730)
Light.   P.L.   TOR.. 0735   9/4/41

From: BULOLO   To: BIRMINGHAM
It is learned Vichy ships have orders to report being attacked as soon as they suspect they are about to be stopped by British-man-o-war. Request instructions as to breaking W/T silence to make following. To F.O.C.N.A. (R) C.in.C.S.A. from BULOLO. Expected time of arrival at Gib of Vichy s.s. *Fort de France* a.m. 13th. April in charge of armed guard. Ends. The cancellation of attack message had to be made by Telegraphist of boarding party. (0641)

Reply:—Your 0641. Thank you. These Vichy ships are very tiresome. We must maintain W/T silence. Request you will signal brief account of boarding, including attitude of Captain and crew. For how long were you endeavoring to make her comply with your orders. (0707)
Light.   P/L   TOR. 0727.   9/4/41

---

[17]Paragraphs 9 (f) and (g) of JHW's report dated 6 May 1941.

[18]Flag officer commanding North Atlantic.

[19]Commander in Chief, South Atlantic.

From: BULOLO   To: BIRMINGHAM
Your 0707. She steamed for about ten minutes after receiving order to stop but after two wide bursts of machine gun obeyed all orders promptly. Captain and Mate young, well educated good class, attitude resigned, not likely to cause trouble, stated sister ship captured this vicinity last month. Crew 37 French 1 Chinaman not likely to cause trouble, 13 French passengers including 2 women and 2 children. Considerable number of private fire arms were collected and placed in custody. No enemy nationals discovered. Proceeding 14 knots. Cargo bananas, sugar and rum. Armed guard 1 Lieutenant R.N.R. 1 Acting Sub.Lieut. R.N.R. 1 P.O. and 6 men. Routed North of Madeira. (0851)

Light.   P/L   TOR...1000   9/4/41.

From: BIRMINGHAM   To: Commodore (R) BULOLO
The Vichy ships signal although it did not report convoy must at least have drawn attention to the position we passed through about 2230 last night. In view of this and of known S/M activity on latitude of 34° 45' N. between 23° 21' and 21° 00' W. do you think it a good idea to diverge to the Westward for a bit and pass through position 34° 45' N. 30° 42' W. thence to position G. I do not think this should delay us appreciably in reaching rendezvous but if you think it might, I am not in favour of doing it. (Note: Greatest displacement from original mean line of advance was 65 miles at the latitude indicated above.) (Discussion with C.O. of Birmingham concerning this divergence was quite interesting.)   (0951)

Reply:—Your 0951. I think it would be well worth while to make the alteration and will do so. (1030)

Light.   P/L.   TOR..1035.   9/4/41.

   (g) A dispatch received 4/14/41 is also of interest in regards to French ships. This dispatch stated that Masters of French ships have orders to scuttle their ships if intercepted but Masters to date have been reluctant to do so. They attempt to obtain a promise that the ship will not be detained after examination. If this promise is not given they will not assist in working or navigating the ship. British ships were warned not to give this promise because except in Asiatic waters it is the present policy to detain or seize all French ships.

Official Diary, 8 April 1941

   . . . At 1301 the Panamanian ship HPWB (name unknown) sent to the American ship *Colaradin*—"Can you hear me," frequency 640 meters, signal strength 7. At 1308 the American ship WAR (name unknown) to the American ship *Colaradin* "Please change frequency to 640 meters," signal strength 7, frequency 640 meters.

   British reconaissance indicates the two battle cruisers are still at Brest. British ships are still waiting on patrol for them to come out.

   0558 today British ship *Eskdene* torpedoed in Lat. 24°-43' N, Long. 23°-21' W (150 miles south of the Eastern end Azores). We will pass within 200 miles of this position in 3 days.

   Weather still good. Slight swell and cloudy sky in afternoon. Clear at night. Temperature 0800—67°, 1200—68°, 2000—68°. Decoded 62 messages today.

Personal Diary, 9 April 1941

   . . . apparently no submarines intercepted the merchant ships report, at least no subs, in this area as all is well—7 knots is a *slow speed* to be travelling . . . .

Official Diary, 9 April 1941
. . . Evasive steering plan No. 10. Columns 1000 yards apart. The light cruiser between columns 5 and 6 about 100 yards astern of the line between the leading ships of columns 5 and 6 (usual station). The armed merchant cruiser patrolling across front of convoy distance about 2 miles. R.D/F sweeps every 30-45 minutes from moonset until daylight. Usual dawn action stations. Evasive steering Plan No. 2 at 0900. This is a two hour plan. Leaders of columns execute the turns together, others in succession. (Division head of column movement.) The instructions say that evasive steering is designed for use during daylight but may be employed at night at Commodore's discretion.

Evasive steering plan No. 2 is as follows.
Suitable for visibility of 12 miles or greater.
From mean line of advance at zero.
Numbers refer to positions in the diagram and not times.

Each leg two hours

At	Alter course	To
0	20°	Port
1	20°	Port
2	40°	Starboard
3	40°	Starboard
4	20°	Port
5	20°	Port

Changed distance between columns from 1000 to 600 yards during daylight. Did *not* increase to 1000 yards at night. At 1700 changed from No. 2 to No. 10 evasive steering plan. In late afternoon Commander in Chief, North Atlantic reported a ship torpedoed about 300 miles due east of convoy. (Lat. 31°-13' N, Long. 23°-14' W.) Convoy still very good about station keeping and lack of smoke. Best the observer has ever seen in any convoy.

The following message and reply are of interest.

From: Commodore   To: BIRMINGHAM
What is your opinion please about using merchant ships as an A/S screen, innocent as they are of depth charges, etc. This is the first time I have tried it and I am not quite sure that it is fair on them. (0915) 9/4/41.

From: BIRMINGHAM   To: Commodore
Your 0915. As long as the ship can maintain a really good zigzag, I do not think it is unfair on them and they certainly form a physical deterrent to any submarines ahead of convoy. May I suggest that they should keep well on the bow of the convoy between 1 and 2 miles. (1015) 9/4/41 . . . .

Weather today—overcast in A.M., partly cloudy in P.M., sea smooth with slight swell. Temperature 0800—66°, 1200—66°, 2000—67°. *Note*: Plane operations from ship based aircraft would have been possible every day—so far, Unfortunately the light cruiser lost its only aircraft outside Freetown 6 weeks ago. Decoded 89 messages today—getting north where the traffic load increases.

Letter to Mrs. Wellings, 9 April 1941
    . . . From the professional side I . . . think it is time for me to return. I have all the major points fairly well "taped," as the British say. From now on what I learn will be more from experience of seeing the same thing over and over again. Therefore what I learn will be all out of proportion to the time spent. I am definitely of the opinion now that it would be much better to send some one else around the same tour. We would have two officers educated, in addition to confirming my opinion or otherwise . . . .

Official Diary, 10 April 1941
    . . . —Steaming as before. Same procedure at dawn as yesterday. At 0900 changed from evasive steering plan No. 10 (2 hour plan) to No. 2 (a 1 hour plan), changed back to No. 10 at 2100. The Commanding Officer ordered all 4 boilers connected and therefore ready for maximum speed. Normally the procedure has been to have 24 knots (2 boilers) ready at all times, power for full speed ½ hour before dawn action stations and at ½ hour notice at other times. Reason for full power being ready tonight is to be ready if a submarine attacks convoy—due to being lead into position by any trailing submarine.
    The following dispatches regarding distance between columns is of interest. The procedure has been to have 1000 yards between columns at night and 600 yards during daylight.

To: Commodore   From: BIRMINGHAM
As the station keeping of the convoy is so good do you think that on very light nights there would be an advantage in leaving the columns 3 cables apart. (1857)

To:BIRMINGHAM   From: Commodore
Your 1857. Decidedly yes. I will not open them out tonight. (1905) 10/4/41.

    The observer believes the above recommendations are open to question and had a long discussion on this subject with the Commanding Officer of the light cruiser. In addition evasive steering decreases the protection afforded the light cruiser and the large merchant ship astern of the light cruiser. (Special personnel ship carrying 1200 navy personnel.) The chief advantage of evasive steering is that it prevents to some extent the concentration of one or more submarines ahead of the convoy based on a contact report by another submarine.
    Usual rendezvous for 1200 the day after tomorrow—given—bearing and distance from one of the secret positions. The light cruiser called attention of convoy that some ship was tuning its W/T. The *Fort de France*, the Vichy ship sent to Gibraltar with armed guard two days ago is routed directly through a position where a ship was torpedoed yesterday. Will she get by? Patient on one of the merchant ships getting better. The doctor of the light cruiser is still in attendance via the signal searchlight. BULOLO will float its mail for United Kingdom via watertight container before she departs. The British Merchant Navy Code has been compromised. All ships now have recoding tables for use with this code. However positions in Lat. and Long. are not given as such. Position is now always reported as a bearing and distance from a secret position, said secret position being known by the Admiralty. The Captain of the light cruiser conducted various drills or exercises yesterday and today. Extra turret crews of "B" and "Y" turrets changed stations, train through maximum limits of train and elevation, extinguish incendiary bomb on top of "B" turret, fires in various places at the same time, man injured by electric shock on bridge, etc. "Anything to get the men away from continual watch standing which causes mental laziness." Weather today overcast

until noon—then clear—Entering Horse latitudes. Temperature 0800—67°, 1200—65°, 2000—64°.

Letter to Mrs. Wellings, 11 April 1941

. . . We have had ideal weather for the past month and today is one of the best so far. Sea calm, sky clear, with a light breeze which is just strong enough to make ripples on the water.

We are still wearing whites and I must say they are very comfortable. When I say whites I mean white shorts. The British call it "tropical rig." . . . In the evening for dinner we wear either a regular white uniform, long trousers and jacket or long trousers with the short sleeve white shirt plus a black silk about 4" wide, around the waist. If the weather is cool, they sometimes wear blue trousers, black shoes, the silk and the white shirt.—The English insist on changing for dinner . . . . I bought five of their shirts and shorts plus the stockings and two of their canvas white shoes . . . . I also bought a white tropical helmet. When I went ashore at Freetown or Cape Town I just took off my shoulder marks and substituted the helmet for my uniform cap . . . .

Official Diary, 11 April 1941

. . . Same routine maneuvers as yesterday. No. 10 evasive steering diagram during darkness, No. 2 during daylight. Station keeping still better than average. Ships are smoking more than they did the first part of the passage. Perhaps that "Freetown coal is awful." Two merchant ships sighted—via smoke during the day. Investigated—British. Latest reconnaissance indicates the two German battle cruisers are still at Brest, 11 German and 6 Italian submarines definitely known to be on patrol in Atlantic, dispatch said more Germans than those indicated in dispatch were in the Western Approaches.

The two merchant ships that zigzag on the bow of the wing columns during daylight, resume their station within the convoy at night. BULOLO (AMC)[20] makes a sweep astern just before dusk each night. In regards to yesterdays discussion concerning distance between columns, the captain of the light cruiser sent a message to the Commodore saying that after due reflection he thought the columns should be 1000 yards apart at night. The Commodores reply stated that due to bright moonlight nights (full moon tonight) he believed the distance should be 600 yards between columns in order to get better A/S protection. The Commanding Officer of the light cruiser then decided to agree with the Commodore. See dispatches under station keeping of the basic report of this convoy operations. Very interesting. Observer still believes columns should be 1000 yards apart at night.

Commodore hurt his back and in bed. Captain of his flagship is acting as Commodore—aided and abetted by the Commodore. The Commanding Officer of the light cruiser informed the *Christiaan Huygens*—the 15,700 ton ship carrying 1200 navy personnel—that in case of submarine attack on convoy she should increase speed to a maximum (16 knots) and carry out wide zigzags ahead of the convoy.

Weather—sky partly cloudy, sea calm with slight swell. Temperature 0800—62°, 1200—67°, 2000—62°. Decoded 47 messages today.

Personal Diary, 11-12 April 1941

11 April . . . Commodore of convoy slipped in his bathroom and injured back. In bed—the C.O. of the merchant ship is acting as commodore . . . .

12 April—Same as yesterday—Routine will be monotonous by the time we arrive in port. Had a grand sun bath in p.m.—followed by a nap.

---

[20]Armed Merchant Cruiser.

Official Diary, 12 April 1941
   . . . Steaming as before, speed 7 knots. Same routine maneuvers as yesterday. Evasive steering diagram No. 10 during darkness (1 hour legs), No. 2 during daylight (1 hour legs). One merchant ship on the bow of each flank column during daylight zigzagging independently, speed 10-11. Armed merchant cruiser patrolling across front of convoy with a sweep astern at dusk. Light cruiser stationed between columns 5 and 6 about 100 yards abaft the line of bearing between the leading ships of columns 5 and 6. Distance between columns 600 yards and between ships in column 600 yards. Dawn action stations as usual.
   Two ships were sighted during the day. Investigated by armed merchant cruiser— result British. In the morning the armed merchant ship took station ahead of the light cruiser and transferred mail to light cruiser via a line and watertight container. The mail was the ships companys' personal mail to be posted in England. Armed merchant cruiser not returning to England. Two ships had lights showing last night. In order to provide better A/S protection the *Christiaan Huygens* shifted station to astern of the Commodore's ship. *Christiaan Huygens'* station number now 52. *Christiaan Huygens* was astern of the light cruiser. Ship which was in station 52 took station astern of the light cruiser.
   The two German battle cruisers are still at Brest according to latest reconnaissance reports. Commander in Chief, North Atlantic reported that at 1300 one French heavy cruiser, one light cruiser and two destroyers were in Lat. 35°-52′ N, Long. 09°-17′ W, course 300°. Position is in Atlantic, outside Gibraltar. Where are they going and why? Suppose they intercept the *Fort de France*—the French merchant ship enroute Gibraltar under armed guard. Latest Admiralty reports indicate 12 German and 6 Italian submarines operating in Atlantic. They are increasing. Weather partly cloudy in A.M. Clear in P.M., slight swell. Temperature 0800—62°, 1200—64°, 2000—63°. Decoded 38 messages today.
   Following dispatches in regards to distance between columns are of interest. Personally it is believed that it makes no difference as ships open out at night so that in reality the distance between columns is 1000 yards (5 cables).

To: Commodore   From: BIRMINGHAM
My 1857/10. On reflection I think it better to have columns 5 repetition 5 cables apart at night.
(re Columns 3 cables apart during clear nights.)   1715

To: BIRMINGHAM   From: Commodore
Your 1715. As regards 5 cables, I feel that a convoy so drastically spread may well be attacked by a submarine which penetrates the convoy, on the other hand a submarine which attacks convoy from either flank has a poor chance of browning the whole convoy with a salvo of torpedoes. With a full moon a convoy may be almost said to be cruising in broad daylight so that three cables in that case is perhaps a sensible disposition, I will of course open as you suggest.   (1820)

From: B'ham..My 1715 and your 1820. We have had a magnificent argument on this subject lasting all day, it is still going on and I will signal results shortly.   (1900)

From: B'ham..Your 1820. Your casting vote has won the day. Please keep three cables distance. It certainly affords better A/S protection to centre ships.   (1908)
Light   P/L   TOD..1915   11/4/41

Personal Diary, 13 April 1941

. . . Easter Sunday—First bad day—At dawn actions it was raining—cold and dreary. Even God is disatisfied with the world so that he permits Easter Sunday to be our first bad day . . . . Attended church—Church of England service. Art—picture exhibition in hangar in p.m.—quite good

Official Diary, 13 April 1941

Steaming as before. Same routine maneuvers as before. *Easter Sunday*—Convoy passed between Flores and Fayal of the Azores islands at 0530.

First morning of passage that weather could be called unfavorable. At dawn action stations, heavy rain, with following wind and sea. Rather cold and disagreeable. Stopped raining at 1000 visibility only about 2 miles. The two merchant ships on flanks of convoy returned inside convoy. The armed merchant cruiser took station just ahead of convoy, distance about 1000 yards. Distance between columns increased to 1000 yards. In P.M. the visibility improved to about 5 miles. Evasive steering diagram No. 10 was not started until 0000 due to visibility conditions. Temperature 0800—62°, 1200—65°, 2000—62°. Decoded 51 messages today.

Sighted two merchant ships today. Investigated by armed merchant cruiser—result British. When the ocean escort is inside the convoy between two columns, the column leaders adjacent to the light cruiser should be instructed not to keep station on the light cruiser as the light cruiser drops back in order to secure better A/S protection during evasive steering. Speed reduced to 6.5 knots. We only have to average 5.6 knots to reach rendezvous on time. The *Christiaan Huygens* cannot steam below 6.5 knots—even then it is only using one engine.

Information report, grade 02 from Brest indicates GNEISNEAU hit aft by 2 bombs. Report being verified. (Brest is being bombed daily in an attempt to damage the two battle cruisers.) The ocean boarding vessel Mardale[21] has been ordered to join convoy on Friday. It is enroute Gibraltar to England and is joining convoy to secure A/S protection. At 0625 the *Rajputana*, an armed merchant ship was torpedoed in the Denmark Straits (was on duty as part of Northern Patrol). Five destroyers rushed to scene. At 1541 two destroyers arrived, picked up 277, 41 still unaccounted for, 2 known to be dead. At 2326 *Ville de Liege* torpedoed Lat. 59°-40′ N, Long. 29°-50′ W.

Personal Diary, 14 April 1941

Weather improved a little but still cold (61°)—shifted to blues yesterday—will be lost without my white shorts. Walked on quarterdeck for hour in p.m.—followed by 2 hours on bridge, Nap and lots of reading rest of day. Duplicated *Southampton's*[22] bombing at damage control practice—quite interesting. In Lat. of Boston at 1200—wish I were there.

Official Diary, 14 April 1941

Steaming as before. Routine and maneuvers in general same as yesterday. 0442—a bright flare-up appeared on one of the merchant ships for about 20 seconds. Inquiry after daylight resulted in following reply—"Sorry—native fireman—galley caught fire." At 0245 set clocks ahead one hour. Ship now keeping zone minus ½ time. Official

---

[21] H.M.S. *Marsdale*, built 1940, acquired by Royal Navy 1940; returned to owner 1945.

[22] A cruiser of the same class, H.M.S. *Southampton* was attacked in the Mediterranean by German dive bombers. She caught fire and had to be sunk on 11 January 1941.

convoy time is still zone plus one—ship now has on bridge a board with 4 clocks painted on it, above these clocks are convoy time,—G.M.T.,—Local Time,—Ship time. The hands of the G.M.T. are on 12, the others adjusted accordingly. The British do not like to use zone descriptions to identify the various times. 1300 speed reduced to 6.5 knots.

At 1845 the ship zigzagging on the port bow of the left flank column reported a periscope between it and the leading ship of column No. 2—course of periscope 225°. At 1852 the convoy made a 40° simultaneous turn to starboard and at 1916 returned to the original course. Upon questioning, the reporting ship said 4 or 5 men in different parts of the ship saw the periscope which was visible for 4 or 5 seconds. Also the periscope appeared "as twin wavelets about one foot high with short feathers." The following two dispatches are interesting.

To: Commodore   From: BIRMINGHAM
We must assume this to be a submarine but we observed black fish and sharks from the ship this afternoon.   (1935)

Reply: We think it might have been a bird. (1940)

To: BIRMINGHAM   From: Commodore
How about 5 cables tonight (1000 yards distance between columns)   (1903)

Reply: Your 1903 I think yes.   (1905)

At 2100 commenced periodic sweeps with R.D/F every 30 minutes. The light cruiser guarded the German submarine frequency. No report was made from this area. No ships sunk—Commenced evasive steering plan No. 10 at 2000 instead of at midnight.

In regards to Commodore's injury—he fell in bathroom. Examination by Captain of merchant ship indicated "Pain drawing breath. Tender spot 4.5" east northeast from tip of hip bone and 2.5" from back bone on left side. Trust medical officer will understand nautical directions." Diagnosis—by Medical Officer of light cruiser—broken rib.

Admiralty states indications of new periodical submarine activities—17 German and 6 Italians now in Atlantic. Plot indicates they are working area in threes'.

Had a damage control problem this morning trying to duplicate the fires as occurred in SOUTHAMPTON's bombing. Very interesting problem. The ship learned considerable. Believe ship has a lot to learn regarding damage control.

A corvette at 0100 reported making "8 deliberate depth charge attacks on a firm submarine attack—am remaining in vicinity, diverted escort and other ships—have 5 depth charges left." Location off Gibraltar. Another corvette ordered to assist, both ships to remain in area until *dusk* today.

Commander in Chief, North Atlantic reports 3 French submarines will pass through Gibraltar westbound on 15 April, escorted by a mine laying ship.

Weather clear—wind changed from south to northwest at 1400—slight sea from same direction. Temperature 0800—59°, 1200—57°, 2000—57°.

Personal Diary, 15 April 1941
. . . Same general routine—No walk however—due to rain all day—visibility only about 2 miles—Good from viewpoint of SS.[23] Gunnery turned in with a cold. Captain has one also. Perhaps it is the change from the warm climate. Feel fine as usual. Rain in p.m., action stations all night due to reduced visibility. Quite cold . . . .

---

[23]Submarines.

Official Diary, 15 April 1941

. . . Steaming as before. Routine and maneuvers in general same as yesterday. Distance between columns changed from 1000 to 600 yards during daylight. Speed 6 knots at 0800. Convoy is about 120 miles ahead of schedule. Really difficult to slow below 6 knots. Will have to lose some of this distance tomorrow if not we will arrive in the edge of an area where submarines are reported patrolling the day after tomorrow. This is a dangerous area to "kill time."

Weather at dawn and remainder of day unfavorable. Following wind and sea plus rain. Visibility 2-4 miles. Difficult for ships to keep station. At 1350 the merchant ship abeam of the light cruiser suddenly swung to port. Only the prompt action of the light cruiser avoided a collision. Very close. Ceased evasive steering at 1412. The two merchant ships zigzagging on the bows of the two flank columns returned to their stations inside the convoy. The armed merchant cruiser ceased zigzagging and took station about 1000 yards ahead of convoy. The *Christiaan Huygens* was unable to keep station and was ordered to perform wide zigzags about 4 miles astern of the convoy. Two ships lost steerage way. Station keeping naturally poor. About dark visibility increased to about 5 miles. The *Christiaan Huygens* remained astern all night. Distance between columns increased to 1000 yards. (In reality the distance was at least 1000 yards all day.) The armed merchant cruiser took station ahead of column 3, the light cruiser remained inside the convoy between columns 5 and 6. Periodic sweeps with R.D/F every 20 minutes during the night.

At 2030 the light cruiser went to night action stations and remained in this condition until after dawn action stations. The reason was reduced visibility. The turret crews slept in their turrets. The 4″ H.A./L.A. crews stood watch as follows: 1 mount crew actually on watch with starshells ready to be fired on either side; 2 crews slept in the starboard hangar, about 40 yards from their mounts, 1 crew in the officer's galley compartment about 10 yards from the H.A./L.A. mounts. L.A. control parties stood watch and watch—complete crews—additional men taken from the H.A. control which were not manned. Pom-poms and .5 machine guns were not manned. All engineers off watch were assigned to the three repair parties or to the four fire parties and slept in the part of the ship where these stations are located. Engineers actually stand a watch in three in their own department. O.O.W.[24], Principle Control Officer, and lookouts continued to stand watch in three.

Reconnaissance of Brest today indicated both SCHARNHORST and GNEISENAU still in Brest. No conformation as yet that GNEISENAU was hit aft by a bomb. Admiralty informed Force H (RENOWN and ARK ROYAL) that a Focke Wolf aircraft was operating in its vicinity and gave present position of aircraft as Lat. 38 N, Long. 12 W. A merchantman at 2100 reported being attacked by a raider in Lat. 37°-09′ N, Long. 18°-43′ W. An hour later another merchantman reported being followed by a suspicious vessel in Lat. 28°-25′ N, Long. 16°-53′ W. Eighteen German submarines and 5 Italian submarines reported by Admiralty today as being on patrol in Atlantic. As usual majority are in the Western Approaches. Commander in Chief, Western Approaches movement report today indicated 12 convoys in Western Approaches. Number of escorts for these convoys as follows:—9, 14, 3 plus one submarine, 4, 2, 9, 2, 8, 10, 3, 4, and 5. Apparently there is rough weather in Western Approaches as several dispatches indicated escorts for various convoys would be late at rendezvous.

Temperature 0800—57°, 1200—54°, 2000—55°. Decoded 17 despatches today. (Now decoding all Area B dispatches) (Western Approaches).

---

[24]Officer of the watch.

Personal Diary, 16 April 1941

. . . Slept as usual in First Lieut. cabin—Better bunk, further from end of ship. No vibration due to propellers . . . . We will have to lose part of the 120 miles we are ahead of schedule in order not to delay in the probable submarine area. Worked on reports in a.m. In afternoon read more publications, two hours on reports, a nap and on bridge. In chart house after dinner . . . turned in at 2300.

Official Diary, 16 April 1941

. . . Same general routine as yesterday. Sea and wind moderated. 600 yards between columns during daylight and dark. In A.M. stations of merchant ships were changed to facilitate dispersing convoy upon arrival United Kingdom. The assignment of stations was based on the destination of the ships. Convoy is still ahead of schedule. Mean line of advance is 22° but from 0800 until 2200 mean course was changed to 062° with the convoy using evasive steering diagram No. 2 from this course. At 2200 course was altered to 22° and an hour later to 330°. Actually made good 110 miles today. We will have to do the same tomorrow to avoid detours in dangerous submarine areas. *Christiaan Huygens* rejoined formation at daylight. With a slight head sea and a speed of 6.5 knots she was able to maintain station. One ship in convoy has its degaussing gear out of commission. The light cruiser is endeavoring to recommend the correct repairs, but so far not successful.

Admiralty reports 19 German and 5 Italian submarines in Atlantic. One ship of S.L. 69, the Sierra Leone convoy ahead of us, reported as being bombed in Lat. 55°-14' N, Long. 12°-51' W. Yesterdays diary commented on the number of convoys and local escorts in the Western Approaches. Both figures are large as is the number of "U"-boats operating in the area. Two convoys had their routes changed today by emergency signals from Commander in Chief, Western Approaches. Admiralty reported last night that three submarines had made W/T sighting reports and warned the convoys, particularly mentioning one convoy in each case. SCHARNHORST and GNEISENAU are still at Brest.

Station keeping yesterday and today was definitely worse than previously. It indicates the difference a moderate sea and beam wind makes on station keeping. At dawn this morning the average distance between ships was about 1000-1200 yards. One ship of convoy (1800 tons smallest ship) reports that 6.5 knots is its maximum speed under todays conditions.—(The ship is listed as a 7.75 ship.)

Letter to Mrs. Wellings, 16 April 1941

. . . Everything is progressing as per schedule although the slow speed is getting monotonous, particularly when the ship is able to do four or five times the speed we are now making. Of course we have to keep a watchful eye on our large brood of chickens, some of which are not able to walk very fast. It is a rather fascinating job however and makes one realize what command of the ocean really means. Also one realizes that the ocean is a big big expanse of water which at times and under certain conditions a ship(s) is like a fly speck on a desert. When I return to London I will have completed this type of duty. I must say I have learned a whole lot and could write a much better book on the subject now than I did a year ago this time.[25] In a few days we will turn over our chickens to a number of small cocky roosters who will guard them carefully until they arrive in port. We will in turn increase to a very high speed which practically insures complete protection and our remaining time at sea will be very short. We have not received orders

---

[25]A reference to JHW's work in his previous assignment with the Office of Fleet Training, Washington, D.C. During that time he revised the manual for the U.S. Navy's convoy and tactical instructions.

as to where we will go. However the initial plan called for our returning to the U.K. And now with our present location plus fuel remaining there is no other place for us to go.

The sea has subsided but our warm tropical days are over. The temperature this noon was 60 which is cold for me. I am getting my notes and reports squared away so that I will not wish that I had paid more attention to this or that when it comes time to make a complete report. This plus the fact that the next few days (after tomorrow) we will arrive in possible interesting areas may cause me to omit writing . . . .

Well now lets see, I haven't talked of finances. I am getting along very well. The money I receive is more than ample. As a matter of fact I have about $500.00 on the books. I get $150.00 a month for entertainment allowance and cannot spend over half of it due to my type of duty.—Never getting ashore where there is any place to spend it. This is the reason why I gave such an expensive party in Cape Town. In addition, I have received $6.00 a day for the first two trips which has really been a God send. Whether they will give it to me this time I don't know—due to the fact that I have been away so long . . . .

Personal Diary, 17 April 1941
. . . Weather a little better this morning . . . . This 7 knots speed is getting monotonous. However it will be over on the 20th when we are due to pick up local escort and then we should increase speed to England.

Official Diary, 17 April 1941
. . . Same general routine and maneuvers as yesterday. The light cruiser secured from action stations, which were manned all night, after dawn action stations. During daylight three turrets and two 4″ H.A./L.A. mounts manned. Pom-pom and .5 machine guns not manned. See 15 April for stations manned at night. Weather improved today. Again steered 40° to starboard of the mean line of advance and conducted evasive steering from this course—Plan No. 2. From 1700 until dark made a series of 40° changes of course by wheeling to starboard. At dark changed course to the left of mean line of advance until midnight, then returned to mean course. Object of all this maneuvering was to lose distance made good in order not to arrive at rendezvous ahead of time. At noon convoy only had to average 5.5 knots to arrive at rendezvous on time. Rendezvous with local escorts scheduled for 0800, 20 April. Distance between columns 600 yards by day and increased to 1000 yards at night for additional safety in maneuvering.

One ship broke down in the morning. Able to rejoin convoy 4 hours later. Admiralty informed a convoy that a submarine had just made a first sighting report.—This shows importance of studying enemy reports. Visual reconnaissance indicates the two German battle cruisers are still at Brest. Admiralty reports 23 German submarines in Atlantic, 16 of which are in Western Approaches. Eight Italian submarines are in Atlantic, 4 of which are in Western Approaches. Eleven convoys are being escorted by local escorts in the Western Approaches today. The number of local escorts for these convoys are as follows: 13, 4, 15, 3, 6, 3, 12, 12, 6, 4, 7.

Temperature at 0800—55°, 1200—52°, 2000—54°. Decoded 58 messages today. The following dispatches are quoted for information:

To: BULOLO (R) Commodore　　　　　　From: BIRMINGHAM
　　　Christiaan Huygens
(1) As from A.M. tomorrow—Friday, BRIMINGHAM and BULOLO will by day in good visibility both cruise at best available speed independently in the vicinity of the

convoy taking maximum A/S precautions. Present stations will be maintained in low visibility by day.

(2) By night BIRMINGHAM and BULOLO will cruise 5-10 miles on port and starboard bow of convoy respectively.

(3) If a submarine report is received (First sighting report) tonight, Thursday, BIRMINGHAM will move out to station referred to in para. 2.

(4) My 1711/11 to *Christiaan Huygens*. In the event of submarine attack *Christiaan Huygens* is to cruise ahead of convoy. (1854)

Note: The 1711/11 message instructed *Christiaan Huygens* to steam ahead of convoy and zigzag at high speed (16 knots) . . . .

To: BIRMINGHAM   From: *Christiaan Huygens*
Your 1854. Para. 4, consider extremely difficult and hardly possible and full of risks. Cannot re-adhere to your 1711/11.   (2000)

Reply: Your 2000 Yes, this is intended but I would like you to do it ahead repetition ahead. Is this clear Please.   (2030)

Reply: Your 2030 clear.   (2110)

Personal Diary, 18 April 1941
. . . Weather suddenly became worse at 0300. Ship rolled badly at such low speed . . . . unable to do any paper work. Gradually approaching the submarine area—have been in a probable area for past two days.—

Official Diary, 18 April 1941
. . . Speed 6, evasive steering diagram No. 4. Usual dawn action stations after which fire and repair parties secured. Turrets and fire and repair parties at action stations all night. Other personnel slept near gun stations. At 0030 one ship's funnel caught fire causing a very bright light for 20 minutes. At 0300 wind and sea increased. At 0700 seas moderate, wind 35 knots. BIRMINGHAM unable to remain inside convoy due to steering and zigzagged outside convoy 2-5 miles until 1630. At 1725 again unable to remain in convoy and again zigzagged outside returning at 2000. Station keeping naturally very poor. However all ships were within visual signalling distance. From 1700-1900 wind increased to 45 knots, seas rough but astern. At dawn this morning one ship was 3 miles ahead of convoy. Ship said she lost convoy during rain squall,—6 knots is a very poor speed for station keeping with a following sea when some ships cannot reduce below this speed. Ceased evasive steering at 0600. One ship reported "convoy too slow unable to steer." Another reported it had only 5 days provisions remaining and requested permission to proceed alone.—Not granted. Ships continued at 1000 yards between columns but in afternoon and at dark distances between columns varied from 1500-3000 yards, same for between ships.

Evasive Steering Diagram No. 4
Two hour legs—Good for visibility above 12 miles, also at night. 85% of distance run made good.

ENCLOSURE (A)
From Mean Line of Advance

At	Change Course	To
0	40°	Port
1	20°	Starboard

At	Change Course	To
2	40°	Starboard
3	40°	Port
4	40°	Starboard
5	20°	Starboard
6	40°	Port

Ship now on Mean Line of Advance.

Received message that 2 destroyers are to meet *Christiaan Huygens* at 0800, 20 April, and escort ship to United Kingdom. At 0957 a sloop which is part of local escort for a homeward bound Gibraltar convoy reported "one flying boat—4 bombs near miss on----(name of merchant ship), Lat. 55° N, Long. 11°-46′ W." Tug being sent to meet convoy. Later a German flying boat made a forced landing on south coast of England. Crew captured—Admiralty said plane damaged from A.A. fire.

Course of an outbound convoy altered to avoid "U"-boats, new course will take convoy 40 miles southwest of us. In afternoon our course altered with new positions to avoid "U"-boats. Two hours later change in course cancelled. One hour later a message ordered us to proceed to our next scheduled position where we are due to arrive at daylight and then alter course for a new position and a new rendezvous with local escort at 0800 20 April.—order, counter order, disorder. At 1800 weather conditions such that convoy unable to make headway towards position where we are supposed to arrive in the morning.—A course was set for the following position. If weather moderates convoy will endeavor to return to mean line of advance.

The ocean boarding vessel which was supposed to rendezvous with convoy today did not appear. She knows our route instructions and will probably join up later.—Reason for joining up—to secure A/S protection when we meet local escort.

Reports indicate 20 German submarines in Atlantic, 15 of which are in Western Approaches, 8 Italian submarines in Atlantic, 4 of which are in Western Approaches.

All British dispatches from ships at sea conclude with a weather report. Believe this is a good idea.

Temperature 0800—54°, 1200—48°, 2000—51°. The BIRMINGHAM rolled considerably all day. Decoded 57 messages today.

In the diary for 17 April, dispatches were quoted in regards to the location of the two ocean escorts and the *Christiaan Huygens* while the convoy is in probable submarine waters. The following dispatches pertain to this same subject.

To: *Christiaan Huygens*   From: BIRMINGHAM
My 1711/11 and my 1854/17 para 4. I am afraid this was not very clear. What I meant was that in the event of S/M attack your position for zigzagging at high speed would be ahead of convoy. *Birmingham* and *Bulolo* occupying the port and starboard bow positions respectively. Are you quite happy about this now please. (1620) 18/4/41.

To: BIRMINGHAM   From: *Christiaan Huygens*
Your 1620, is clear and satisfying V.M.T. (very much thanks) (1710) 18/4/41.

To: BIRMINGHAM   From: BULOLO
Do you intend that BULOLO should remain near the convoy or act in accordance with our 1854/17.   (1710)

Reply: Your 1015. I think that for the present you had better zigzag with frequent alterations somewhere near convoy. I am going to work around convoy gradually. (1035)

To: Commodore (R) BULOLO   From: BIRMINGHAM
I intend to proceed on a four hours cruise in vicinity of convoy commencing shortly. Have you anything to communicate before I go please. (0956)

Reply: Your 0956. No thank you. We should have left Freetown at least 24 hours later than we did.   (1010)   18/4/41.

Personal Diary, 19 April 1941

. . . Weather still rough but sea and wind a little better at night. Hope we are not ahead of our rendezvous tomorrow morning. In submarine area but not the worst area according to Admiralty reports. No sleep to speak of last night.

Official Diary, 19-20 April 1941

. . . Speed 6.5. No evasive steering due to rough weather. Wind and sea astern making steering very difficult. Columns supposed to be 1000 yards apart but in reality at daylight they were about 2000-3000 yards apart with the ships in column about the same distance apart. Considering the sea and wind conditions (wind 40 knots) plus the types of ships the formation is believed to be good. At least all the ships are with us. At 0427 the BIRMINGHAM decided to leave station inside the convoy and zigzag independently ahead of convoy. Very difficult to keep BIRMINGHAM on a steady course. Usual dawn action stations. All close range A.A. weapons manned during daylight plus all 4" H.A./L.A. mounts in addition to the turrets. All turrets were completely manned all last night. At 1000 changed course 40° to the northward to arrive on our mean line of advance. Reached this line at 1400 and changed back to original course. Sea moderated slightly.—Wind 25-30 knots.

At 1440 sighted the ocean boarding vessel *Marsdale* which was due to join yesterday. Commanding Officer of *Marsdale* said he was unable to join yesterday due to weather plus lack of fuel. He only has fuel left for a speed of 7 knots. *Marsdale* carries one 6" mounted on a platform in the bow, one 3" on the stern, close range weapons and two torpedoes. Tonnage 3000. This ship has been on patrol in Bay of Biscay.

BIRMINGHAM returned inside convoy at 1650 and remained inside during the night.

Rendezvous with local escorts is 0800 tomorrow. BIRMINGHAM received orders from Admiralty to proceed to Scapa Flow upon arrival of local escorts.

Admiralty reports 21 German submarines in Atlantic, 14 of which are in Western Approaches. 8 Italian submarines are in Atlantic, 5 of which are in Western Approaches.

Temperature 0800—45°, 1200—48°, 2000—47°.

20 April—Steaming as before. Wind increased to 51 knots at 0330. The BIRMINGHAM changed station to outside the convoy at 0415 due to difficulty in station keeping. The *Christiaan Huygens* zigzagged outside and astern of the convoy all night due also to difficulty in station keeping. At daylight convoy still together but distances between ships in column and between columns about 1500-3000 yards. At least they were all present which is unusual after a storm. Shortly after daylight wind and sea moderated slightly. BIRMINGHAM located *Christiaan Huygens* 10 miles astern of convoy. The following visual messages are quoted for information.

To: BIRMINGHAM   From: *Christiaan Huygens*
Have both engines running with not less than 65 revs. Am zigzagging at speed 9½ knots. If port engine is stopped she probably cannot be started again. Am very restricted in movements. In order not to get more damage on deck by running sea.   (0545).

Reply: Your 0545. As I do not think your escort will arrive for 9 hours can you zigzag in rear of convoy. Your destination is now finally settled as Liverpool.   (0603)

To: BIRMINGHAM   From: Commodore
I think *Christiaan Huygens* should rejoin and take station astern of you. (1015)

Reply: Your 1015. Agree and I have already negotiated with him on this point but he says if he stops one of his engines he probably will not be able to get it going again and he is very nervous about his maneuvering. I ordered WINCHELSEA to stay with him until other escorts join. (1019) 20/4/41.

Note: *Christiaan Huygens* has diesel engines. Her superstructure is very high. Her
      Commanding Officer wanted nothing to do with the convoy in rough weather.

At 0710 sighted one of the two destroyers assigned to escort *Christiaan Huygens* to the Clyde. This destroyer attempted to screen the *Christiaan Huygens* as she zigzagged astern and close to the convoy but without much success due to the rough weather and speed of the *Christiaan Huygens*.

The Commanding Officer of the BIRMINGHAM decided to leave the convoy upon arrival of the destroyer as the convoy was not in probable raider area and the Commanding Officer did not want to endanger his ship any more than necessary. However the destroyer requested that the BIRMINGHAM remain as long as possible to provide A.A. protection. Convoy now is very probable area for air attacks. As a result the BIRMINGHAM remained with the convoy taking up her regular station between columns 5 and 6. Sea moderated considerably by noon. Wind dropped to 18 knots.

The convoys rendezvous with the local escorts was 0800 today. The convoy was 20 miles ahead of rendezvous at 0800. At 1410 sighted one two-engined flying boat— *Consolidated*, Catalina type. One of these aircraft was reported to have made a forced landing this morning about 100 miles to the west of us. The following visual messages were exchanged between the BIRMINGHAM and the aircraft. As soon as the aircraft received our position it left immediately. Apparently he was lost. (distance from N. Ireland—400 miles).[26]

To: BIRMINGHAM   From: Aircraft
What is number of convoy.

   Reply:— S.L. 70.

From: BIRMINGHAM—Are you staying with us.

Reply: —No. Request position.

---

[26]Comment in Personal Diary, 20 April: "The British had better learn how to navigate these long range aircraft."

At 1600 B.S.T. 52°-15′ N. 17°-38′ W. Course 040 speed 6½. If time please look a few miles astern for destroyer HARVESTER (H PT 19) and tell her where convoy is. (TOD....1630)

To: BIRMINGHAM   From: WINCHELSEA
How about telling aircraft to search astern for Harvester. (1618)

Reply: Have done. (1620) Light. P/L TOD..1627 20/4/41.

At 1430 the WINCHELSEA after receiving permission from the Commanding Officer of the BIRMINGHAM sent a coded message to the HARVESTER, information to the BEAGLE (Senior Officer of local escort)[27] on its limited range radio (30 miles?) since these ships had not joined—all ships proceeding to this convoy after leaving outboard convoys.

At 1715 sighted 4 corvettes and 15 minutes later 4 destroyers came over the horizon. Upon their arrival the Commanding Officer of the BIRMINGHAM made certain the local escort commander had all the information on the convoy including the route instructions and dividing the convoy into 2 portions—fast 19 ships—10 knots, slow 8 ships—7 knots. Incidentally the local escort commander is the youngest commander in the British Navy—Age 32. One of the above destroyers was the HARVESTER—which was the missing destroyer of the *Christiaan Huygens* escort. The HARVESTER and the WINCHELSEA left the convoy and proceeded with the *Christiaan Huygens* on their assigned route—speed 16 knots. We were all glad to see the *Christiaan Huygens* leave, escorted by 2 destroyers. She is a large, fast ship with 1200 experienced navy ratings aboard from the Mediterranean.—Quite a responsibility to the Commanding Officer of the BIRMINGHAM.

Two of the local escort destroyers were ex-American destroyers. The observer was a little homesick to see them. They looked a little strange with their razzle-dazzel camouflage, the stacks shortened about 4′, and only a pigstick for a mainmast.

When all information had been exchanged everything was clear except splitting the convoy into two sections. The following dispatches show the necessity for clear and concise orders to "all hands." In this case the local escort did finally split the convoy—Perhaps he eventually located his orders.

To: BEAGLE   From: BIRMINGHAM
Commodores orders read as follows. The convoy will be met by two local escorts and will then be split in Fast and Slow portions. One local escort going with each. Cruising orders arranged to facilitate this. Fastest portion consisting of ships of 9½ knots and above. The Oban portion should be detached in position 55°-45′ N, 8°-30′ W, ends. is this clear please.   (2040).

Reply: This is quite clear except that I understand only *C.H.* was in the fast portion and she is leaving now escorted by *Harvester* and *Winchelsea*. (2040)

From: *B'ham*... Presume you will get Commodore to split convoy tomorrow morning when other escort arrives.   (2055)

Reply: I have no information about another escort arriving except two trawlers and I shall not split unless the other escort does arrive. (2100) 20/4/41.

---

[27]Richard Taylor White, D.S.O. (1908-   ). Later Captain; D.S.O. with two bars.

This morning at 0108—The *Empire Endurance* was torpedoed in Lat. 53°-05' N, Long. 23°-14' W.—Routed independently. In the late afternoon an aircraft located 4 lifeboats with survivors. A destroyer is proceeding to rescue them.

No aircraft reconnaissance of Brest today.

The intelligence report which stated that the *Bismarck* plus 2 cruisers were passing through the Skaw[28] course 300 on 18 April was reported by the Admiralty to be in error. They left on the 14th of April.—(All the ships at Scapa sailed on the 18th to endeavor to intercept them.) 14 German and 5 Italian "U"-boats in the Western Approaches today. 6 German and 3 Italian in Atlantic but not in Western Approaches.

At 2105 the BIRMINGHAM left its position inside the convoy and at 25 knots steamed back and forth once across the front of the convoy with the International signal flying to the masthead "Good Bye and a safe voyage." The BIRMINGHAM then headed for Scapa Flow routing *itself* to avoid reported submarine areas. A half hour later one *rescue* ship and two trawlers were sighted. They are part of the local escort for the convoy. The convoys bearing and distance was given to them. At 2359 a dispatch was sent to the Admiralty giving the BIRMINGHAM's position, course, speed and expected time of arrival at Scapa. Also the convoys 2000 position, course and speed and that the local escorts had joined . . . .

The following is quoted for information:

To: BIRMINGHAM   From: Commodore

We are all most grateful to you for your patience, courtesy and care. When do you leave. (1040)

Reply: Your 1040. Many thanks for your most kind signal. I am genuinely sorry that fuel makes it necessary that we should leave you about 1700 G.M.T. today. I hope we may meet again on another voyage. Your convoy if I may say so has been splendid and I have much appreciated your acceptance of my comparative inexperience. I hope you are now fully recovered and wish you every further success with your convoys. P.S. We all think that GUNDA deserves a "Special mention." (1135)

Personal Diary, 20-23 April 1941

20 April— . . . The local escort will now lead the ships past the submarines—I hope—At 25 knots we headed for Scapa Flow. Farewell broadcast on radio. Crew gave me a ships picture[29] . . . framed and engraved plate. Made me very happy.

21 April— . . . All by ourselves . . . quite a thrill to be off on our own after 18 days of 6-7 knots. Party for the three middies on board who passed their sublieutenants exam . . . . Trying to get all my papers in order—Quite a job to catch up on loose ends. Captain broadcasted tonights program. Paid me all kinds of compliments—Made me blush.

22 April—Arrived at Scapa at 0700. A beautiful morning—clear sky—pond like sea. Terribly busy trying to get ready to leave ship tomorrow. As usual I am rushing at the last minute. Sent a note to Captain Newcombe at Thurso to arrange for a sleeper out of Edinburgh for me on Thursday. Plan to leave Scapa tomorrow. Dinner with Captain & Comdr. followed by movies and concert by captain afterwards in Wardroom—until 0100.

---

[28]The Skagerrak. *Bismarck* left Gotenhafen on 19 May and passed through the Skagerrak on 20 May.

[29]See photo at beginning of Chapter 5.

23 April—My birthday 38 today—wish I were home with Dolly to celebrate today. Oh well Sherman was right.[30] Called on "Captain of the Fleet" in the *K.G.5*[31] to tell him about my movements. He showed me a dispatch from the Embassy dated 21 March ordering me to return to London and then proceed to Liverpool in connection with Atlantic convoys. He seemed to be excited & called the Admiralty by phone (direct wire) & told them about my return. He also said I should talk to the Embassy. Unable to get call through so I returned to ship as I was having a birthday cocktail party before lunch and leaving to catch the boat to Thurso at 1345. Before I left *Birmingham* the call to Embassy got through. Captain of the Fleet sent me a message saying for me to return at once & that I would go to Liverpool for convoy work.—Quite disappointed—thought my orders for home would be waiting for me. Hope it is not a permanent job—Maybe they sent someone else up to Liverpool to handle it when they could not get me on 21 March (was actually at Cape Town) and that I will only go there to get the organization—I want to go to Boston—not Liverpool—Will be anxious to get to London to get all the news.

Cocktail party very fine (2 drinks for me). Paid all my bills and said "au revoir." Captain, Comdr-& all wardroom officers on board were at the gangway to see me off. Master At Arms bade me farewell on behalf of the crew. They certainly were kind to me. Saw Comdr. Rowe on *Dunluce Castle* and then went aboard *Morialto* for trip to Thurso—Captain turned over his cabin to me. 2 hour trip. Sidebottom[32] (Lt. RNVR) waiting for me at Thurso with car for baggage—What service—Captain Newcombe arranged a compartment for me & a Comdr. Harrison R.N.—Fine man—Captain Newcombe came to train to see me off. Interesting discussion with Harrison on DD's before turning in—we each had one side—my shetland blanket came in handy—at 2300—to sleep—what a day—the *Birmingham* will long be remembered—12 happy weeks.

Report on Gunnery, H.M.S. Birmingham[33]

. . . Overall gunnery efficiency fair to poor. The captain and gunnery officer of the BIRMINGHAM also concur in the above statement. The gun crews are fairly well trained, particularly so when one considers the large number of new personnel plus the fact that all turret crews are trained to fire the 4" A.A. guns and vice versa. The British are now training recruits in close range fire and in long range A.A. fire before they are being assigned to a ship. The various control personnel, particularly the officers, are not well trained due chiefly to the inexperience of the officers. Since our practices indicate that the control parties "make or break" a practice it is the considered opinion of the observer that the general gunnery efficiency must be considered fair to poor.

Since the expansion of our navy will undoubtedly result in a shortage of experienced gunnery personnel it is strongly recommended that steps be immediately taken to train leading petty officers and reserve officers in the fundamentals of fire control.

---

[30]"War is Hell."

[31]William Rupert Patterson (1893-1954). Commanding Officer, H.M.S. *King George V*. Later K.C.B., 1947; Admiral, 1949. Retired 1950.

[32]Derek Chappe Sidebotham.

[33]Paragraph 10(b) and (c) of JHW's Report dated 10 May 1941: "Gunnery Installation H.M.S. *Birmingham*—6"—9100 ton cruiser."

Report on Engineering, H.M.S. Birmingham[34]

... *Operations.* Operated with Home Fleet at Scapa Flow for 8 days. During this period the ship was underway five days, standard speed 20 knots. When at anchor at Scapa Flow the ship was at 4 hours steaming notice. The BIRMINGHAM then proceeded to Greenock at 25 knots, remained at Greenock two days at 4 hours steaming notice and then sailed as ocean escort for a convoy to Cape Town, via Freetown and return. The ship arrived at Scapa Flow 71 days later. During this period of 71 days the ship was underway on 67 days and actually underway 65 full 24 hour days. Upon arrival at Scapa Flow ship was placed on two hours steaming notice. While engaged in this convoy duty speed for 24 knots was available at all times with full speed available on one-half hours notice. When stationed inside the convoy the ship steamed at convoy speeds of 7-11 knots. When stationed outside the convoy the ship steamed at 16-18 knots, zigzagging independently.

Boilers. The idle boilers were actually cut in on the main steam line for about one and a half hours each morning at dawn action stations, on several occasions when investigating merchant ships when speeds of 28-30 knots were used, and on several nights when action with raiders or submarines was most probable. At other times the steam pressure was boosted periodically to working pressure—350 lbs. The steam from idle boilers was not used for auxiliary purposes. Water sides of boilers are supposed to be cleaned every 750 hours and fire sides a minimum of once a quarter. Actually they are cleaned with the water sides. Due to operating conditions two boilers were cleaned in Freetown with 1430 and 1370 boiler hours respectively and two were cleaned at Cape Town with 1270 and 1240 hours respectively. The water sides of these boilers were relatively clean. Boiler tubes were "punched" by hand. The ship does not have flexible cable and brushes run from a portable electric motor. No trouble was experienced with the automatic feed regulators. The brick work, while not in good condition, was considered satsifactory and was not renewed. The boiler floors were warped and trouble was experienced with the cone brickwork in the boiler fronts caused by carbon from the burners. Plastic boiler fronts are not used. When all four boilers were cut in on the line due to a sudden large increase in speed the main feed pump discharge fluctuated about 100 lbs. for about the first half hour. No breakdowns of any nature occurred during the 11 weeks period. The make up feed was large averaging between 55-60 tons per day. The make up feed did not increase with the speed. The chief engineer was very dissatisfied with the large make up feed and conducted several tests and inspections without success. Fresh water consumption averaged 13 gallons per man per day. It did not increase to any extent in the tropics as the increase in water used by the enlisted men was offset by the officers taking showers instead of "tubs." The 312 passengers on board however increased the fresh water consumption.

Main Engines. No trouble experienced. There is no standard acceleration or deceleration table. All bells are answered as quickly as possible. When a stop bell is received steam is admitted to the astern turbine to actually stop the propellers (this was also standard practice in the HOOD and the Tribal class destroyer ESKIMO). Leaks from the gland steam very noticeable. Engineer stated gland packing badly in need of renewal. Cruising turbine used up to 24 knots.

Auxiliaries. No trouble experienced except with steering engine and refrigeration plant. The rudder jammed in the full starboard position by reason of a screwed pin dropping out of position and preventing the hunting gear control of the telemotor system from shutting off the pump when the required rudder was obtained. The screwed

[34]Paragraph 2-5 of JHW's Report dated 5 May 1941: "Engineering Operation, Personnel and Equipment, H.M.S. *Birmingham.*"

pin backed off due to the previous shearing off of the locking split pin. The BIRMINGHAM vibrated so badly at speeds of 20 knots and above that the observer was unable to sleep in his cabin which was over the starboard after screw. This excessive vibration plus continual zigzagging places a considerable strain on the steering gear equipment.

The refrigerator plant developed leaks which could not be located. All the CO_2 was used in an effort to save the meats, etc. However all meats, etc., had to be surveyed upon arrival at Cape Town, 3 days after serious leaks developed. Leaks were located and a new supply of CO_2 received in Cape Town after which there was no further trouble . . . .

Report on Operations and Tactics[35]

. . . Convoys with local escorts seldom attacked by submarine in daytime. At night submarine approach from bow or quarter on surface with conning tower awash usually fire at ranges one to two thousand yards and retire on surface in same direction from which they approached. Only one definite case of submarine approaching from directly astern and torpedoeing rear ships of center columns. Local escorts fire starshells on side of convoy in which ship torpedoed or submarine sighted. If side unknown all sides illuminated. Object is to sight submarine, force it to dive and then conduct intensive asdic search and attack. Admiralty recommend evasive steering instead of zigzagging for ships under 11 knots. In evasive steering course changed every hour to two hours from 20 dash 40 degrees. In submarine area best station large ocean escorts is center of convoy by day and night unless fuel permits zigzagging at high speed ahead of convoy at night. Fuel consumption of ocean escorts very high for distance made good each day. British now starting to fuel cruisers at sea.

When ships investigate merchantmen possibility of submarine operating with merchant ship is assumed, also possibility of merchant ships being disguised raiders. As soon as boat is lowered for boarding, ship should steam away as quickly as possible. Boat should not be recovered in same area.

Radio operators on American Merchant Ships chatter too much. System of recognition signals between U.S. combatant and merchant ships essential.

Due inexperienced personnel caused by rapid expansion target practices and other exercises most important. British handicapped by lack of proper target services.

Reliability of engineering equipment most important due to little if any time available for upkeep. Example on recent trip underway 65 full 24 hour days out of 71 days, upon return ship placed on two hours steaming notice.

R.D/F type 285[36] installed primarily for surface gunnery not giving results expected. Competent repair personnel and good operators essential on board ship. British severely handicapped by lack of same. Strongly recommend training technical personnel and operators now. One officer with R.D/F technical and repair ability will be required on each cruiser and heavier ship.

Not desirable to man one half close range AA weapons, all or none.

Shelters for exposed gun crews most desirable. At night all gun crews, fire and repair parties should sleep at or near their action stations. Flexibility in conditions of readiness for action important. Armament manned should be based on existing situation, not on the book. Turret crews should be able to man AA guns and vice verse. This is important

---

[35]Paragraphs 2-15 of JHW's Report dated 29 April 1941: "Operations and Tactics."

[36]A type of radar.

on long operations when passing through various areas where different types of attacks are most probable.

U.P. 7″ mounting believed by British officers in Home Fleet to be of little if any value.

By using one inch primer to ignite cordite in six inch guns British do not use black powder at end of powder bags. Flashless propellent for starshells great help in preventing disclosure before ship opens fire.

Asdic efficiency mainly dependent on ability of operators. Asdic teachers excellent for training operators and officers. In general large number of depth charges required for successful submarine attack.

On 21 April at least 14 German submarines and 5 Italian submarines operating in Western Approaches according to Admiralty dispatches. Submarines located on two lines, one at 30° W., other at 20° W. 3 to 5 "U"-boats assigned to same general area.

Imperative for all naval aircraft to be able to communicate with surface ships by flashing light signals.

Strongly recommend more operation officers in British Fleet.

CHAPTER SEVEN

LONDON AGAIN
24 April-20 May 1941

Personal Diary, 24-25 April 1941

24 April—Dollys Birthday—Arrived Edinburgh at 0900—usual worry about baggage and sleeper accommodations—all set in Ed. Called Comdr. St. Quintins wife & told her I had letters from her husband—Lt. Comdr. Bird, Abercrombie and from Capt. Madden—Letters cannot be mailed. Suggested they all come to Edinburgh—they are staying in some town 5-10 miles outside Edin.—collect the letters & have dinner with me. Asked if I were not afraid of 4 wives—she accepted immediately for all hands— they want to get the news on where we had been—also a night in town to dinner is an *event* to them with their husbands away all the time. Mrs. Kennedy[1] and a Miss— (Captain's wife daughter—husband to be recently killed in aircraft) also attended.[2]

Ladies all on hand 5 minutes before seven—5 minutes ahead of time—Were they anxious to get the *news*—Told them the whole story—after a cocktail (2) at North British went to Aperitif for dinner[3]—Fine party—left at 2130—back to hotel—caught 2200 train for London and to bed.

Called London—asked Bill Ammon to send a cable to Dolly—Good Morning, Happy Birthday, feel fine—Love—felt happy after sending telegram. Hope Dolly receives it today.

25 April—Good nights sleep on train—very fine sleeper—arrived in London at 0900. Went immediately to Embassy had breakfast sent up to me—office expanded more than ever—more people—more work, more confusion.[4] Found orders waiting to send me to Liverpool, but Ad. Ghormley said that something had just broken and that I would not go—Conference with him and four others for an hour. Only 3 letters from Dolly—kind of disappointed—first mail for 2.5 months. Captain Lockwood[5] new attaché away on trip. *No orders home* as I expected after message at Scapa. Stayed at New Pipers . . . talked and read a special report until 0130 . . . .

---

[1] Wife of *Birmingham*'s navigator, Lcdr. A.R. Kennedy.

[2] The Captain's wife had brought along her son's fiancée. The son had been killed in an air battle 4 months earlier.

[3] Cost of dinner for seven persons, £4 15/-.

[4] During 1941, the total number of naval officers enlisted and civilians assigned to the U.S. Naval Establishment in London rose to 364 from a total of 59 in 1940. See Naval Historical Center, Washington, D.C.: Typescript History, Europe, Naval Forces, "Office of the United States Naval Attaché, American Embassy, London England, 1939-1946," p. 14.

[5] Charles Andrews Lockwood, Jr. (1890-1967). U.S. Naval Academy, 1912; U.S. Naval Attaché, London, 1941-March 1942. Later Vice Admiral; Commander, Submarine Force, Pacific Fleet, 1943-45.

Letter to Mrs. Wellings, 25 April 1941

. . . I was very keenly disappointed when I arrived in London to have confirmed the rumor I heard up north that my orders were not waiting for me. I found the office twice as large & twice as many officers and everything in a turmoil—at least I thought so . . . .

Letter to Mrs. Wellings[6]

. . . I was having breakfast in the office [25 April] . . . sent in from a restaurant next door—when Admiral Ghormley came in and said—"Wellings I have been looking for you." I went to see him after breakfast and he told me of what he wanted me to do. I told him about my orders to Liverpool and he said he would have them cancelled . . . . The next morning I saw the captain—who had returned about 10 minutes before—he said he wanted me to go to another city[7] instead of Liverpool. I told him about Admiral Ghormley and he said he knew nothing about it as he had just returned—After he saw the Admiral he cancelled my orders. I then went down town to attend a conference[8] and when I returned I learned that the cable just announced my orders home . . . .

Personal Diary, 27 April-7 May 1941

27 April . . . What excitement—Reopened letter written to Dolly last night and had given to Comdr. Dow sailing at 1300—told her the good news—believe I sounded disappointed in my letter at no orders and little mail.

Worked until 1800 at Embassy then back out to New Pipers for the weekend. Stayed in at night working on reports . . . .

28 April—Sunday—Stayed up last night until 0100—Up at 0800—Breakfast and a cab to 0900 mass at Egham. Walked home—½ hour. Took a nap—played badmington—then captains luncheon at New Pipers—All our officers plus Under Sec. of Navy, Forrestal,[9] Harriman,[10] Admiral Horton,[11] Ghormley and one or two others—A very fine luncheon—They all left by 1700—Worked at night.

29 April—In town again via cab with officers from Ranleigh. Worked on reports all day—lunch with Marshall Gaffney[12] & his boss Mr. Munroe. We talked shipping and shipping[13]—New Pipers at night.

---

[6]Letter of 29 April 1941.

[7]Londonderry, Northern Ireland, where a new naval base had been constructed.

[8]The conference was held at 1000 at the Admiralty and concerned closer U.S.-U.K. cooperation following the announcement of the neutrality patrol. See James Leutze, ed., The London Journal of General Raymond E. Lee, 1940-41 (Boston: Little, Brown, 1971), p. 257.

[9]James Forrestal (1892-1949). Later Secretary of Defense, 1947-49.

[10]William Averill Harriman (1891-   ). Special representative of President Roosevelt in Great Britain with the rank of Minister.

[11]Sir Max Kennedy Horton (1883-1951). Flag Officer, Submarines, 1940-42; Later CinC., Western Approaches, 1942-45.

[12]John Marshall Gaffney (1907-1967). Later Vice President and regional director of European general operations, United States Lines.

[13]"Following my daily visit to the Admiralty the morning of April 29th, my normal embassy routine was altered by a two-hour luncheon with Mr. Marshall Gaffney and his immediate superior, Mr. Munroe. Mr. Munroe was the senior United States Lines Representative for all of Europe. Mr. Gaffney was a former neighbor and boyhood sailing companion of mine at the Cottage Park Yacht Club in Winthrop, Mass.; he was

30 April-2 May—Continued work on reports. Lived at New Pipers. Had the duty on the 2nd at New Pipers—Wrote all my thank you letters plus reports. Gradually absorbing the London and attaché's atmosphere—Quite interesting. Read all Ghormley's dispatches—how interesting.

3 May—New Pipers filled up so I stayed in town—Had a tour of London from 1430 to 1830 with Bill Headden,[14] Capt Duncan[15] & Mrs. Ziegler. They went back to the country—I took a room at the Connaught.—Dinner at Embassy—sent in—worked on reports until *0100*—

The sight seeing trip was most interesting—visited West Minister Abbey, Parliament, St. Thomas Hospital—London Bridge—the old city of London etc. The bomb damage was quite extensive—

4 May—In town—Worked all day and night until 2400 at office on reports getting them squared away rapidly. Lunch with "Count" Austin at United Services Club—Met Comdr Currie—R.N. again—Had a cocktail in Counts apartment before dinner with a Comdr Griffen—R.N.—very brilliant.

5 May—Worked on reports—lunch with Capt. Moore & Comdr. Currie R.N.—Was in the *Hood* with them. They are now attached to Admiralty at United Services Club. Good to see them again—Out to country at night . . . .

6 May—Slept in country last night. Excellent sleeping but we never know when to go to bed. Captain Lockwood remaining in town until he sees his first air raid[16]—He can have it. Still working on reports and reading up letters and dispatches on operations. Left for country at 1800—Long hours these days—Called at 0645—Breakfast at 0730, Leave New Pipers 0810, arrive in office at 0900.—

Letter to Mrs. Wellings, 7 May 1941

. . . I am living out in the country at the same place as before . . . . Captain Lockwood the new naval attaché is also staying here, but he remains in town about half the time due to his official duties. He sends his official car out each night with his chauffeur. He has the same Buick 6 passenger '38 sedan with the two small seats between the regular front & back seats. We really ride in style to and from work.

Captain Duncan, a civil engineer (U.S.N.) Comdr. Lee, Comdr. Sylvester . . . . Comdr. Libbey, Bill Ammon (Lt. Comdr.) Bill Headden and I live in the big house which I have described in previous letters.—We also have the Captains (Lockwood) secretary—a *Miss* Ziegler. We had a Mrs. Ripman who was Capt. Kirks secretary but she has returned home and I believe is now Captain Kirks secretary in O.N.I. Miss Ziegler is quite an unusual type of girl. Very independent in her ideas, plain as can be and is more interested in the historical buildings, paintings etc than in anything else. She takes an awful kidding from the crowd of us but is a good sport.

---

the United States Lines Representative for Great Britain, with headquarters in London. We talked shipping—and more shipping—(plus a little yacht racing). Mr. Munroe told me that he had implemented my previous recommendation that all United States Lines controlled ships under 15 knots sail in convoys." JHW *MS. Reminiscences*, p. 146.

[14]William Ramon Headden (1902-). U.S. Naval Academy, 1925. Later, Rear Admiral. Retired 1955.

[15]Donald Bradley Duncan (1896-1975). U.S. Naval Academy, 1917. Later Admiral. Retired 1957.

[16]For Lockwood's comments on New Pipers and his decision to stay in London, see C.A. Lockwood, *Down to the Sea in Subs* (New York: Norton, 1967), pp. 234-235.

We also have two other houses in the same town—about a mile away. These are smaller houses, each one housing 5 officers. The government pays the rent, heat & light bills and we pay the servants and the food bill. Bill Ammon is house mother and has quite a job on his hands. However he will also be going home some time the latter part of this month. He has been here since a week before the war started. He came over as a regular assistant attaché expecting a quiet two years . . . . He is a grand man and I do not know what we would do without him.

. . . Bill Headden is a grand addition to our staff. He is full of life and fun. His stories of his meetings with English people are a scream . . . . Count Austin and MacDonald are still the same as ever. They retain their sense of humor and take everything in stride. Of course they have a grand example in Admiral Ghormley who is one fine man . . . .

Personal Diary, 7-8 May 1941

7 May—Same routine as yesterday.—Lunch with Marshall Gaffney . . . Caught train to New Pipers—arrived at 2020.—Admiral Ghormleys files are extremely interesting.

8 May . . . Reports are gradually getting completed. Grand sleeping in country . . . London has not had a raid since two weeks ago yesterday.

Letter from Rear Admiral Macnamara, RN,[17] 8 May 1941

Very many thanks for your letter and "The Bluejackets Manual," which arrived a couple of days ago.

It is quite the best [such] book I've ever seen, &, from what I remember, this edition—1940—is even better than its predecessor. I shall certainly use it a lot here—probably without giving due credit to its author, whoever he may be!

Sorry you didn't get any leave. This does not seem to be much about now-a-days. At least, I cannot find it if there is.

But, as a very different & poor alternative, come up here for another observation trip when you can. I doubt whether many changes and additions are apparent; but there are quite a lot. Again thanks.

Personal Diary, 9 May 1941

. . . All reports written two more to be typed.—Saw Capt. Lockwood and reported same to him. He asked me if my orders had been rec'd. Of course they had—He called the Admiralty and arranged tentatively for me to sail next Wednesday.—Was rather excited. Started to make plans—particularly shopping plans. Went shopping with Miss Ziegler—selected linens, gloves and sweaters—bought 24 yds of linens, 5 pr. of gloves & 4 sweaters—all the latter were baby sweaters. Glad to have this part of shopping completed. Had a try on for a new blue suit—Had my tweed inspected by Radford-Jones[18]—said it was O.K. Having it London shrunk.

Letter to Mrs. Wellings, 10 May 1941

Today is Saturday and your little boy has the duty out in the country. We still keep an officer here every day in order to keep an eye on our files, but of course we do not have anything out here that is too confidential. We are still ready to carry on business from

[17]Rear Admiral, Scapa.

[18]The tailor.

here should we be unfortunate enough to be bombed out of our offices at the Embassy. So far our luck has been very good.

I have just finished my lunch and will be alone until the officers return to the "country estate" later on in the afternoon. The duty out here gives me a chance to catch up on correspondence, reading, and in general a good day of rest. However the house seems like a huge barn with no one else around except the maids and cook. I have a fine fire in the fireplace which adds a little to the atmosphere as well as the warmth.

This morning was simply beautiful, but it is now beginning to become cloudy. The leaves of the majority of trees have been out for two weeks, the remainder are just about to burst forth. The grass is a beautiful shade of green and the areas under cultivation are just beginning to show the results of the farmer's hard work. From out in this area one would never know the greatest war in history is being waged to the limit of total destruction—except of course for occasional planes passing over head. These planes are all friendly during the daylight hours but at night the drone of the unsyncronous German motors is anything but musical.

London has not had an air raid for 17 days. The Wednesday before I arrived they apparently had one of their worst single raids. Compared to last fall when I first arrived and in Dec. the present raids on London are few and far between. Of course when the Germans do concentrate on London they do have a bad night. Naturally there is more evidence of bomb damage than when I left last Dec.—and in some areas it is quite severe. But nevertheless London is still going on determined to see this fight through. The trains are still running, buses, street cars and subways are still operating and in most cases with the same operating or running times as when the war started. Of course London is so large that the damage is spread out over a large area and is therefore not so noticeable.

I still maintain that it is poor policy to bomb large cities—or any city—at least wholesale bombing which is not confined to military objectives. Personally I believe the concentrated bombing of London was a vital error on the part of the Germans. True they have done considerable damage in some areas but not in the real military objectives. The Germans have paid heavily for their raids and worst of all the raids awakened the English people and solidified the classes and their determination to "carry on." Personally I also believed that the German raids on London were responsible for the increase in the public opinion of our country to do everything possible to aid England . . . .

Personal Diary, 10-14 May 1941

10 May— . . . completed last report—wrote remainder of letters to people in fleet— at night had dinner with Slim Hitchcock, Rudy S— and Lady Cunningham—at Slims house—Slim (Comdr.) is also due to leave with me—Quite an interesting evening. Returned to New Pipers at 2300—we started a political discussion which lasted until 0100,—Capt. Duncan, Comdr. Lee & Bill Headden plus yours truly. Discussion interrupted by going outside twice to see the show—London appears to be getting a good bombing tonight.—Could hear the night fighters—firing machine guns over head. Turned in at 0120 . . . .

11 May—Up at 0845—breakfast—drove to Egham to 1000 mass—walked home ½ hour walk.—Cycled down to village to get morning papers. Marshall Gaffney unable to come to lunch. Sorry—wanted him to see the house. Lunch . . . . Archer—Lt.— going home via air tomorrow . . . Had a nap—at night took a 45 min. walk.—to bed at 2300. London did have a terrific bombing last night. Comdr. Lee & Miss Ziegler went in to see the fires & damage—they said it was terrible—33 bombers brought down last night—31 of these by night fighters. Embassy O.K.—but some were quite close—one in the square in front of Embassy—Two incendiaries on Embassy.—

12 May . . . Today at office straightened out odds & ends and spent afternoon reading data on operations—wish I could write what I *think*— . . .

13 May . . . Getting things squared away in office—Reports all finished. Working for Admiral Ghormley[19]—very interesting work—At night read & do a little filing of reports—plus writing . . . We do not leave the office until 1800-1830 then it is 1930 before we return home. Definite arrangements made for me to leave via boat on 17 but this date may be postponed for 4 or 5 days. Getting a new blue suit made (civilian).

14 May . . . Quite a job getting things ready. Ordered a top coat to be made from tweed bought in Orkneys. Still working for Ad. Ghormley. Captain Baker[20] arrived. He will take over operations for Admiral Ghormley. Acquainted him with work to date. Lunch with him & Count Austin. Shopping with Miss Ziegler—bought peppermills, and nut trays—plus linen, hope Dolly will like them . . . .

Letter from Acting Commander S.J.P. Warrand, RN, H.M.S. Hood, 14 May 1941[21]

Very many thanks for sending the Plotting Sheets which are of great interest to me & I intend to do my best into spurring on our hydrographic department into producing something similar. In the meantime we, in *Hood* shall at any rate have your's to work on!

Another leaf that I have taken out of your book is to convert myself to the use of the new tables for working out sights: this also is due to your promptings. I had an hour or two to spare one day & so put in the time examining the new tables & found that it is possible to combine their use with the old system, so that one is spared the trouble of looking up & adding all the logarithms. It is a great saving of time.[22]

Life with us continues much as when you were with us except that the pace has sweetened up of late & for some weeks there was very little rest. As you know, I cannot give any details.

Eller[23] was on board this ship recently & I dined with him one evening when we had a

---

[19]"My assignment as a special liaison officer for Admiral Ghormley was merely a temporary one, pending the arrival of a Captain Baker, who was to be assigned to Admiral Ghormley's staff. I visited the Admiralty daily in connection with Admiral Ghormley's duties, as special representative of President Roosevelt. Among other subjects, Admiral Ghormley was greatly concerned with naval assistance to the British Commonwealth, including Lend Lease programs . . . . I merely handled odds and ends at the Admiralty for Admiral Ghormley, mainly with naval assistance pertaining to shipping, tactical matters, including convoy and anti-submarine operations . . . .

Now, twenty-eight years later, I will reveal one of my missions for Admiral Ghormley at the Admiralty, was to return to the United States with all the information and sufficient number of complete sets of tactical convoy and anti-submarine instructions, to permit our Admiral Arthur L. Bristol's entire Convoy Escort Task Force, (Task Force Four) then operating out of Newport, Rhode Island, to begin operating with British Royal Navy Forces immediately upon our entry into World War II." JHW *MS. Reminiscences,* pp. 144-45.

[20]Charles Adams Baker (1893-1970). U.S. Naval Academy, 1916; Naval War College, 1942; Later Rear Admiral, retired 1949.

[21]Warrand died exactly 10 days after his letter was written when H.M.S. *Hood* was sunk, 24 May. He was *Hood's* navigator.

[22]In 1936, the U.S. Navy Hydrographic office began to publish *Tables of Computed Altitude and Azimuth* (H.O. Pub. 214). The Admiralty began to publish similar tables in 1951.

[23]Lcdr. E.M. Eller, USN, previously noted.

cheerful party. He still retains that cheerful twinkle in his eye despite having been well bombed on one or two recent occasions.

Our leave period was a very pleasant interlude & flashed by all too fast. My own was broken with by having to return to the fleet in the middle for two or three weeks. I tried to get into touch with you but you were away all the time.

I hope for your own sake that your plans to return to the U.S. this week will materialize as you must be anxious to see something of your family once more. If, on the other hand, you find yourself remaining on this side I hope you will pay us another visit. We should all be delighted to see you again. Best luck.

Personal Diary, 15 May 1941

Ken Hartman arrived from Med. looks fine—He has had quite an experience—recommended for D.S.O. for his work in *Illustrious*.[24] New Pipers again at night.

Letter to Mrs. Wellings, 15 May 1941

. . . I am just marking time now—or almost marking time. An officer arrived yesterday who will take over my special job. The turnover is practically no work so I have spent most of yesterday and today clearing out my files, packing and shopping. Transportation has been requested and I believe I will sail sometime the latter part of next week. As usual—and rightfully so—I do not know the name of the ship or the port of arrival . . . .

Yes I received your letters about the china and silver. However I have not done any[thing] about it due to not only getting $6.00 for my last trip but getting checked $450.00 for my previous trips.[25] However I have enough money to get by on and perhaps a penny or a "ta-pence" to spare. I have bought a few odds and ends . . . Prices in London are much higher than they were last Sept. which is only natural when one considers that a 25% purchase tax has been placed into effect . . . .

Personal Diary, 16-19 May 1941

16 May . . . New blue suit completed. Rec'd definite information that I will sail from Gaurock (adjacent to Greenock) in the Clyde area on 21 May. Ship—*Brittanic*.[26] Making final preparations for leaving. Trying to get publications squared away so that I can take them home.[27]

Will have pouch mail with me—also Slims trunks—3, and Bill Ammon's—2, two boxes for Eller and 1 box for Vaughan Bailey—Pouch will be a large one. Quite a busy day—New Pipers at night.

17 May—Saturday . . . Technical section[28] gave Slim Hitchcock, Bill Ammon and

---

[24]Lcdr. K.P. Hartman, USN, previously noted. Served as an observer in H.M.S. *Illustrious* in the Mediterranean.

[25]The Comptroller has disallowed the payment of $6.00 per day for subsistence expenses to those officers on attaché duty who were serving on board ship. The amount which had been credited to JHW on this basis for service in H.M.S. *Eskimo, Hood,* and *Curacoa* was deducted from the total amount due to him.

[26]*Britannic*, built 1930, 26,943 tons. Owned by Cunard White Star Line, Ltd.

[27]British handbooks and procedures for Asdic and antisubmarine warfare, signaling, convoy procedures, German bomb fuse information, warship identification.

[28]Technical intelligence activities began in the U.S. Naval Attaché's office late in 1940. In January 1941 the office was reorganized on a functional basis with the Technical section headed by Cdr. Paul F. Lee.

I a luncheon at the Connaught—Captain Lockwood and Loftie also present. A very fine lunch—but too heavy—2 hour lunch—left for New Pipers at 1730. Captain had three English officers plus Slim for dinner—A very odd party—None of us were acquainted with the set up—I took a walk at 2300 and turned in at 2330. Party lasted until 0200.

18 May—Left New Pipers at 0830 with Comdr. Lee, Sylvester, and Libby plus Miss Ziegler for a tour of English countryside. Used car (Chev.) which Comdr. Lee can get when he desires. Beautiful day. Lunch at Stratford-on-Avon—Covered 202 miles. A grand day—My one and only opportunity to see the English countryside.

19 May—Ship now changed to *Rodney*[29]—leaving from Greenock at same time as *Britannic*—Even better for me as *Rodney* is due to call at Halifax, then proceed to Boston for refit.—Will leave tomorrow night for Glasgow at 2115. Completed shopping—top coat ready. Will have 11 boxes in official pouch—Will have a guard & a special bagge car—locked & sealed for trip to Glasgow—I will have a sleeper on same train. Practically all ready to leave—hope to get balance of publications tomorrow . . . .

Letter to Mrs. Wellings, 19 May 1941

Everything is rapidly drawing to a climax around here. My work is completed except for a few odds and ends . . . My special work for Admiral Ghormley is completed as the officer who will handle this has arrived and taken over. In other words I am a very short timer and ready to sign off from my duty in London and vicinity. Believe me it is a grand and glorious feeling to be a short timer, with all reports finished and plenty of time to make the last minute details including packing . . . .

When I first report [for duty in Washington] I am naturally going to ask for leave. However I will probably be in Washington a week before I can get away for leave. I also doubt if I will be able to get more than 10 days or two weeks at the most, if the stories the boys tell who have just come over are true. They say that the Navy Dept. is just wild with everyone working night and day . . . .

Personal Diary, 20 May 1941

. . . Drove in from New Pipers as usual. Completed final packing at office—Pay accounts squared away—Said goodbye to everyone—lunch with Comdr. Lee—Conrad[30] & Miss Ziegler at Claridge's. Had dinner at Calridge's with MacDonald. Close pouch—Brought gear & pouch to train at 1800—11 boxes—9 trunks 5 pieces of hand baggage. Saw all gear stowed in baggage car then turned it over to guard—bought own ticket—then back to town for dinner. Returned and said goodbye to London town as the train pulled out of station Kenneth Downey[31] from D.N.I. on same train, had one drink with him and turned in—On my way home to good old U.S.A. and my two little girls.

---

[29]Battleship H.M.S. *Rodney*, assigned as escort for *Britannic*.

[30]Robert Daniel Conrad (1905-1949). Lieutenant. U.S. Naval Academy, 1927; Later Captain.

[31]Kenneth Downey. Lieutenant, Royal Naval Volunteer Reserve.

CHAPTER EIGHT

BATTLESHIP *BISMARCK* AND BOSTON
21 May-12 June 1941

Personal Diary, 21-24 May 1941

21 May—Arrived in Glasgow at 0630. Arranged with R.T.O. for a truck to transfer baggage & pouch mail to Greenock. Very accommodating. Was also supplied with an auto plus a Wren chauffeur to drive *me* to Greenock. Had breakfast at Bay Hotel in Gaurock, then went to the F.O.I.C.'s office who told me where to unload baggage & pouch mail for the *Rodney*. Given a special boat. Arrived on board at 1145. Russell & Cooke[1] from *Eskimo* waiting for me. *Repulse, Exeter, Argus, Brittanic* plus 5 tribal DD's also in harbor. Nap in p.m. then over to *Eskimo* for dinner—good to see the DD crowd again stayed until 0200. Anne's birthday today—wish I were home.

22 May—Slept in until 0900. Exec.[2] quite concerned over keeping the boat late—apparently the *Eskimo* ordered a boat from *Rodney* to call for me and thereby interrupted their boat schedule. I knew nothing about it. Thought the exec. was a little too worried about the entire matter. Personally I think he used very poor judgment in making a fuss about it. *Underway* at 1230—Homeward bound. Speed 18, *Brittanic* astern 5 DD's as a screen. Passed through North channel at 1700. Course 300. Captain spoke over ships radio—We are due in Halifax on 29 May and perhaps sail for Boston same day. Have not met Captain as yet—it seems kind of odd.—Talked with Kenneth Downey & Captain Coppinger[3] new skipper of *Malaya* until 1030 p.m. then to bed. Have a comfortable cabin—inside one. All pouch material stowed away under lock and key plus sentry.

23 May—Underway with *Brittanic* and 4 DD's bound for Halifax. Weather overcast, sea fairly rough. Slowed to 13 knots at 0900—too rough for DD's. Talked with Miller and Herwitz our two C.P.O.s who are returning to U.S. in *Rodney*. Read & talked with Captain Coppinger after lunch. He seems to be a good sea dog but very odd in many ways. All hands asking me about Boston after Captain of *Rodney*, Darlrimple-Hamilton,[4] officially announced Boston as our final destination. At 2240 Captain announced over loud speakers that two German combatant ships had been sighted trying to break through between Iceland and Greenland.—Dolly & my monthly anniversary. Thought I would be home for this one.—Oh well it will not be long now.

---

[1]Lt. E.B.S. Russell, RNVR, and Engineer Lcdr. G.A. Cooke, previously noted.

[2]Executive Officer. John Annesley Grindle (1900-   ). Commander, RN. Later Captain, Commanded H.M.S. *Apollo, Glenearn, Victorious*; Deputy Chief of Combined Operations (Naval), 1946-48. Retired 1950.

[3]Cuthbert Coppinger was also a passenger in *Rodney*, en route to Philadelphia where he would take command of *Malaya*.

[4]F.G.W. Dalrymple-Hamilton, previously noted.

H.M.S. *Rodney*

Nelson-class battleship, launched 17 Dec. 1925 by Cammell Laird; length overall 710′; beam 106′; draft 28½′; speed 23 knots; displacement 33,900 tons; Armament: 9-16″, 12-6″, 6-4.7″ A.A., 24-2 pdr. A.A., 12-M guns, 2-24.5″ torpedo tubes, 2 aircraft. Served Home Fleet, 1939-42; Force "H", 1943; Home Fleet 1943-45. Scrapped 1948.

[Photo: Naval Historical Collection, W.L. Mullin Papers]

24 May—A little rough—Kenneth Downey & Gargon—Frenchman a little sick. We have a total of 512 passengers aboard. Contact last night was made by *Suffolk & Norfolk*. German ships are *Bismarck & Prince Eugen*. *Norfolk & Suffolk* still trailing. At 0553.5 this morning *Hood & Prince of Wales* engaged *Bismarck & Prince Eugen*. *Hood* sunk at 0600, *Prince of Wales* damaged slightly or perhaps more so. At 1200 *Rodney* left *Brittanic* and with 3 of the 4 DD's as screen changed course to the west ahead of the *Bismarck*. Everyone getting excited about possibility of making contact. I spent most of the day reading signals with Gallica.[5] At 2030 planes (9) from *Victorious*[6] made a torpedo attack on *Bismarck*—one hit which did not slow the *Bismarck*.

Naval Messages received in H.M.S. Rodney, 21-24 May 1941[7]

From	To	Time Sent[8]/Date	
Ad.[9]	CinC H.F.[10] & others	1603/21	Stated visual reconnaissance Bergen at 1330 on 21st reports two Hipper Class cruisers and 1 destroyer present.
Ad.	S.O.F. H,[11] Senior Officer Area A&B	1619/22	My 1717/21 Photos show BISMARCK Class BB in 60° 19' 48″ N., 5° 14' 48″ E., with 4 cargo ships in vicinity. Hipper Class cruiser and one DD in 60° 25' 16″ N., 5° 01' 20″ E., with 3 cargo and 6 auxiliary mine sweepers in vicinity. DD has oiler alongside. One merchant ship alongside Hipper Class cruiser.
Ad.	S.O.F. H, Senior Officer Area A&B	2320/22	My 1619/22 Reconnaissance at 1930/22 unable to locate units. No ships in anchorage.
CinC H.F.	Ad. and Home Fleet	about 2200/22	KING GEORGE V, GALATEA, KENYA, HERMOINE, AURORA plus 7 destroyers intend pass Hoxa at 2300 22 May through position 58° 45' N., 7° W.—thence course 273—speed of advance 16.
CinC H.F.	REPULSE	?/22	REPULSE join KING GEORGE V by noon 23— GALATEA and HERMOINE to patrol westward North Rona—Faeroe.

---

[5]Gaffney George Ormond Gatacre (1907-   ). Lcdr., Royal Australian Navy. Navigator, H.M.S. *Rodney*. Later Rear Admiral; Head Australian Joint Services Staff in United States; Flag Officer, Eastern Australian Area, 1962-64.

[6]*Illustrious*-class aircraft carrier.

[7]Enclosure B to JHW's Report serial F-1; x-27 dated 1 July 1941: "Operations and Battle of German Battleship Bismarck 23-27 May 1941." These dispatches were slightly paraphrased by JHW when he compiled them.

[8]*i.e.*, Time of Origination.

[9]Admiralty.

[10]Commander in Chief, Home Fleet, in H.M.S. *King George V*.

[11]Senior Officer, Force H.

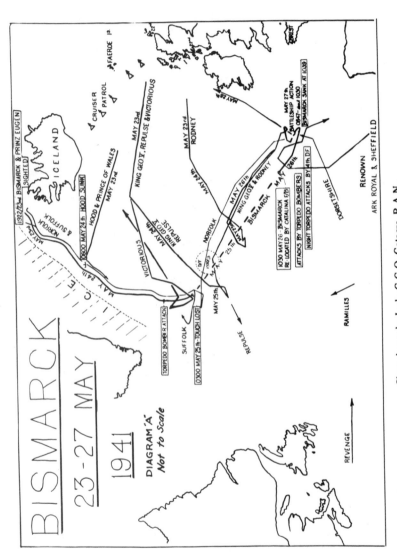

Chart drawn by Lcdr. G.G.O. Gatacre, R.A.N.,
The Navigator of H.M.S. Rodney, based on information available in H.M.S. Rodney, June 1941
Enclosure "G" to JHW's Report, serial F-1; x-27 of 1 July 1941.

From	To	Time Sent/Date	
CinC H.F.	B.C.1[12]	2207/22	Designated force with BC1 as Battle Cruiser Force with CinC H.F. as Battle Fleet. Both forces to cover possible breakout westward through Denmark Straits—Iceland—Faeroe Passage— Battle Fleet south of 62° N., Battle Cruiser Force north of 62° N.
C.S.2[13]	CinC H.F.	2215/22	BIRMINGHAM and MANCHESTER (CS18)[14] sailed Scapa 2200 speed of advance 21.
C.S.2	Ships indicated	2353/22	ARETHUSA, MANCHESTER, BIRMING-HAM to establish patrol of rectangle bounded by 320° 210 miles and 230° 30 miles from 61° 20′ N., 10° W.
A.C.W.A.[15]	N.O.I.C.[16] Iceland	1226/23	Reconnaissance of Denmark Straits to be given priority over all other commitments.
A.C.W.A.	CinC H.F. Ad. & others	1903/23	Denmark Straits reconnaissance was not—repeat not flown—cause weather.
SUFFOLK[17]	NORFOLK	1922/23	EMERGENCY—One battleship and one cruiser sighted in lat. 67° 07′ N., long. 24° 25′ W., course 240.
NORFOLK	Scapa Radio	2032/23	One battleship and one cruiser sighted 330°, 6 miles distance from 66° 43′ N., 25° 22′ W., course 240.
Ad.	All hands	2155/23	One BB and one cruiser reported by NORFOLK at 2032/23 in position 330° 6 miles from 66° 43′ N., 25° 22′ W., course 240.
NORFOLK	Scapa Radio	2145/23	Lost contact—visibility 8 miles—my position.
NORFOLK	SUFFOLK	2209/23	Lost enemy in rainstorm—believe he has resumed course. My position 66° 25′ N., 26° 24′ W.

[12]Commander, Battle Cruiser, Squadron One, in H.M.S. *Hood*.

[13]Commander, 2nd Cruiser Squadron.

[14]Commander, 18th Cruiser Squadron.

[15]Admiral Commanding, Western Approaches, at Liverpool.

[16]Naval Officer in Charge.

[17]"Captain A.J.L. Phillips of the *Norfolk* informed the author in Greenock after the *Bismarck* operation that the solid packed ice on May 23 extended southeasterly and east from the coast of Greenland to a line about 60 miles from the coast of Iceland. Clear visibility, however, over the 60 miles of open water between the edge of the solid packed ice and Iceland was only about three miles wide, beginning at the edge of the solid packed ice. The remainder of the 57 miles of open water toward Iceland was shrouded in fog, mist and rain . . . .

Captain Phillips of the *Norfolk* was also happy with the final destruction of the *Bismarck*. He informed me that Captain Ellis of the *Suffolk* said his first *Bismarck* contact on the evening of May 23 was by radar but he did not send his official sighting report to the *Norfolk* until he identified the two ships by visual sighting at 7:22 p.m. . . . "JHW MS. *Reminiscences*, pp. 163, 250.

From	To	Time Sent/Date	
NORFOLK	SUFFOLK	2311/23	I bear 142° 10 miles from you, my course 200 to cover move of enemy away from ice.
NORFOLK	SUFFOLK	2230/23	My position 66° 12' N., 26° 25' W. My course 250, speed 30.
Ad.	S.O.F. H	2253/23	Raise steam for full speed.
NORFOLK	Scapa Radio	0014/24	Lost contact. Visibility 3 miles. My position (garbled).
NORFOLK	Scapa Radio	0019/24	My course 180, speed 30.
Ad.	S.O.F. H	0050/24	Proceed when ready—join convoy WS8b after daylight 26 May. If reconnaissance today reveals one or both German cruisers have left Brest your instructions will be altered—keep destroyers with you or send them back to Gibraltar if they need upkeep—at your discretion.
NORFOLK	Scapa Radio	0055/24	Lost contact—last seen 57° 08' N., 36° 34' W., steering 165, speed 21.
S.O.F. H	Ad.	0141/24	Force H left port at 0200 today.[18]
NORFOLK	Scapa Radio	0145/24	My course 200, speed 29. My position 64° 49' N., 28° 16' W. Estimate enemy 269° 18 miles from me. Visibility 3 miles.
Ad.	C.S.2	0148/24	If not contrary to orders from CinC HF and in absence of other orders from him, GALATEA and HERMOINE should proceed with all convenient dispatch to 090 from Langanaes 30 miles.
Ad.	?	0220/24	Arrange for air patrol Denmark Straits—Iceland—Faeroe—Shetland Area, plus sending long range planes to Iceland.
SUFFOLK	Scapa Radio	0256/24	Two enemy ships detected by RD/F bearing 192° 9 miles from me on course 240, speed 28. My position 64° 39' N., 29° 22' W.
NORFOLK	SUFFOLK	0450/24	Lost contact.

---

[18] " . . . Force "H" was under the tactical command of Vice Admiral Sir James Somerville and normally consisted of his flagship the battle cruiser *Renown*, the aircraft carrier *Ark Royal*, the six inch cruiser *Sheffield*, plus six destroyers. Their regular mission was to control the western Mediterranean, and insure the safety of Gibraltar.

The two U.S. Naval officers assigned as observers in the battle cruiser *Renown*, namely Lieutenant Commander Dayton Clark and Lieutenant Commander James B. Clay, unfortunately were on shore leave in Tangier, Morocco when Force "H" received the unexpected orders to raise steam for full speed. They were unable to rejoin the flagship *Renown* before she sailed with Force "H" at 2:00 a.m. May 24. As a result of their having missed the *Renown*, Lieutenant Commander Joseph H. Wellings, U.S. Navy, the author, in the battleship *Rodney* was the only U.S. Naval officer to witness the sinking of the *Bismarck*." J.H.W. MS. *Reminiscences*, p. 166.

Chart drawn by Lcdr. G.G.O. Gatacre, R.A.N.,
The Navigator of H.M.S. *Rodney*, based on information
available in H.M.S. *Rodney*, June 1941
Enclosure "G" to JHW's Report, serial F-1; x-27 of 1 July 1941.

From	To	Time Sent/Date
C.S.1	Ad.	0615/24	HOOD blown up in position 63° 20′ N., 31° 50′ W.
C.S.1	DD's in company Ad.	0637/24	HOOD sunk in position 63° 21′ N., 31° 47′ W. —Proceed and search for survivors.
C.S.1	Scapa Radio	0720/24	At 0712 my position 63° 08′ N., 32° 12′ W— PRINCE OF WALES in company. PRINCE OF WALES has bridge out of action and "Y" turret temporarily out of action. SUFFOLK trailing from astern. Enemy bears 286° distance 18 miles from me. His course 205°, speed 28.
C.S.1	Ad.	0725/24	Information from PRINCE OF WALES states "A" and "B" turrets in commission, two guns in "Y" turret in commission. About 400 tons of water abaft armoured bulkhead. Compartments above steering gear compartment flooded but steering gear working, best speed of PRINCE OF WALES 27 knots. Above information received from PRINCE OF WALES at 0720/24.
NORFOLK	Scapa Radio	0745/24	My 0541—BB course and speed 210° 26 knots. BB bears 290° 17 miles from me. Cruiser appears to be opening and to starboard. My position 62° 56′ N., 32° 28′ W.
SUFFOLK	Scapa Radio	0757/24	Enemy BB has reduced speed. Appears to be damaged, on fire. My position 63° 10′ N., 32° 34′ W.
PRINCE OF WALES	CinC H.F. Ad.	about 0800/24	At 0553—30 PRINCE OF WALES opened fire, range 23,000. BISMARCK opened fire immediately on HOOD. HOOD opened fire just before PRINCE OF WALES. PRINCE EUGEN engaged PRINCE OF WALES. BISMARCK fire extremely accurate—straddling HOOD on second or third salvo. Fire immediately broke out in HOOD near after port 4″ A.A. twin mount, spreading rapidly to mainmast. At 0600 an explosion occurred between the after funnel and the mainmast in HOOD and she sank within 3 to 4 minutes. HOOD had fired 3 to 4 salvos prior to being sunk. Destroyer picked up only 3 survivors from HOOD, a midshipman, a signalman and a seaman. PRINCE OF WALES straddled on 6th. PRINCE OF WALES was astern of HOOD and had to maneuver to avoid parts of HOOD. BISMARCK immediately shifted fire to PRINCE OF WALES and almost immediately a violent explosion was heard in PRINCE OF WALES. At 0602-30 the bridge of the PRINCE OF WALES was hit, casualties, heavy, Captain unhurt. Same salvo placed both forward antiaircraft directors out of action. At this time only three of the ten 14″ guns of the PRINCE OF WALES were in action. "Y" turret would not bear. I decided to break off action and consolidate position and ship. I therefore turned away firing "X" turret in local control on the turn and making smoke— BISMARCK also turned to follow but

From	To	Time Sent/Date	
			immediately thereafter broke off the action. PRINCE OF WALES fired a total of eighteen 14″ gun salvos and three secondary battery salvos. PRINCE OF WALES then took station astern of trailing cruisers.
CinC H.F.	C.S.1	0824/24	My position at 0800—51° 17′ N., 22° 08′ W., am closing you at 27 knots. In company with me is Second Cruiser Squadron.
Radio Halifax	Ad.	0904/24	REVENGE to sail from Halifax at 1100 (zone plus 3)/24. In absence of other instructions will proceed to 43° 00′ N., 48° 30′ W.
NORFOLK	Scapa Radio	0900/24	My 0745—Enemy making large change of course.
PRINCE OF WALES	CinC H.F.	1007/24	Main battery control, secondary battery control and all secondary battery guns in commission. Nine 14″ guns in commission. Bridge badly damaged. The two forward AA directors out of commission. About 600 tons water in ship due to two or more hits at waterline aft. My estimated maximum speed 26. Have available 1600 tons of oil.
Ad.	RODNEY	1022/24	Enemy's position 62° 25′ N., 33° 00′ W., course 210, speed 26 at 0900/24. Steer best closing course.
Ad.	RODNEY	1026/24	If BRITTANIC can't keep up let her proceed alone with one destroyer.
NORFOLK	Scapa Radio	1057/24	Enemy BB and cruiser bear 273° 18 miles. Enemy zigzagging—mean course 220° speed 24. My position 62° 02′ N., 25° 21′ W.
Ad.	RODNEY	1116/24	If BRITTANIC is detached alter her course as follows to avoid U-boat---
RODNEY (visual)	ESKIMO	1124/24	At 1300 my position 55° 15′ N., 22° 15′ W.
Ad.	RAMILLES	1144/24	BISMARCK's position at 1100—62° 17′ N., 35° 00′ W., course 215°, speed 24. Adjust your movements to contact enemy from westward— which will place enemy between you and CinC HF.
Ad.	GALATEA & HERMOINE	1206/24	Unless otherwise ordered by CinC HF the following cruisers are to proceed to Faeroes to fuel *** ***
NORFOLK	Scapa Radio	1210/24	Visibility decreasing.
C.S.1	SUFFOLK	1216/24	If visibility decreases endeavor to maintain RD/F touch and inform me of enemy movements.
N.O.I.C. Iceland	CinC H.F.	1235/24	Plot of Sunderland on return appears to indicate NORFOLK's position accurate. BISMARCK leaving considerable wake of oil.

From	To	Time Sent/Date	
Ad.	General	1238/24	was an estimate of situation—Among which was EDINBURGH in 45° N., 21° W., has been ordered to close and take over standby shadowing —REVENGE about to leave Halifax under orders to close enemy; enemy battle cruisers in Brest on 23 May; At 1100 BISMARCK and PRINCE OF EUGEN in position 62° 17' N., 35° 00' W., course 215, speed 24—BISMARCK has received some damage.
Ad.	C.S.18[19]	1250/24	ordered CS18 in MANCHESTER to close enemy whose position at 1124 was 62° 02' N., 34° 58' W.,—mean course 220° speed 24—Reason, to take over relief shadowing if required. Conserve fuel while closing, suggest 25 knots. Once contact is made no consideration of fuel should cause you to lose contact.
NORFOLK	Scapa Radio	1314/24	My 0541—Lost contact with enemy low visibility.
RODNEY	DD's in company (visual)	1428/24	Am steering so as to intercept enemy, assuming his course 180, speed 20. Course will be adjusted as later enemy reports indicate.
C.S.18	Ad.	1430/24	Your 1250—My position 44° 17' N., 23° 56' W., course 320, speed 25, fuel on hand 57% and on contact at 1900 tomorrow 38%.
CinC H.F.	C.S.1	1455/24	Four cruisers plus VICTORIOUS have left my force to close enemy in order that VICTORIOUS may launch torpedo plane attack about 2200 today. At 1500 my position 60° 03' N., 27° 56' W., course 212, speed 26.
C.S.1	SUFFOLK	1546/24	My reference position at 1531—60° 29' N., 35° 45' W. Your reference position at 1531 based on my position was 60° 25' N., 36° 38' W.
SUFFOLK	Scapa Radio	1734/24	Enemy position—bearing 152°, 16 miles from 59° 43' N., 36° 15' W., enemy course 180, speed 24.
SUFFOLK	Scapa Radio	1839/24	Enemy course 240, enemy position is 342°, distance 20 miles from 59° N., 36° W.
ComDes Flot 6 (visual)	RODNEY	1901/24	Please confirm that as soon as enemy is contacted DD's are free to attain position for attack.
Reply (visual)			Yes—confirmed.
Ad.	C.S.1	1916/24	NORFOLK and SUFFOLK's shadowing has been admirable—keep it up and good luck.
Ad.	REVENGE	1917/24	ordered REVENGE to proceed at 14 knots to overtake HX 128.

---

[19]Commander, 18th Cruiser Squadron, in H.M.S. *Edinburgh*.

From	To	Time Sent/Date	
C.S.1	CinC H.F.	1934/24	At 1832 enemy turned away when engaged at long range. Engagement broken off to prevent forcing him further away from you. Am trailing enemy. 232° distant 18 miles. Enemy course 180. My position 58° 54' N., 36° 10' W.
NORFOLK	Scapa Radio	1957/24	One BB in position 241° 18 miles from 58° 45' N., 36° 15' W., course 180°.
Ad.	Ships indicated	2010/24	Unless otherwise ordered by CinC HF, BIRMINGHAM, MANCHESTER and ARETHUSA are to discontinue patrol and proceed to Iceland to fuel.
Ad.	General	2023/24	also a summary of present disposition of forces.
C.S.1	Scapa Radio	2106/24	Enemy speed appears to be 22 now. Enemy cruiser is probably to the westward of enemy BB. PRINCE OF WALES close astern of me. SUFFOLK on my starboard bow.
Ad.	S.O.F. H	2138/24	Send your destroyers back to port before it is necessary for you to fuel them. Your force may be required for extended operations.
NORFOLK	Scapa Radio	2151/24	My 1957—No change—Am still in contact—My position 58° 07' N., 36° 31' W. Enemy speed 22.
CinC H.F.	Home Fleet & Ad.	2156/24	Hope to engage from eastward the enemy about 0900/25.
A.C.W.A.	Home Fleet	2232/24	Cruiser LONDON is proceeding to vicinity of 25° 30' N., 42° 00' W., to search for enemy tanker.
Ad.	EXETER	2321/24	After you leave ARGUS she must proceed alone as it is not now possible to provide a cruiser escort.
NORFOLK	Scapa Radio	2329/24	Enemy course 160, speed 22.
Ad.	S.O.F. H	2331/24	Ordered him to steer so as to intercept BISMARCK from southward—enemy must be short of fuel and will make for a tanker—her further movements may guide you to this tanker.
Ad.	CHESHIRE	2338/24	My---Use your own judgment in carrying out previous orders.
SUFFOLK	Scapa Radio	2349/24	Enemy hidden in fog near ice—estimated course 200. My position 65° 56' N., 27° 50' W.

Individual Reports of Five Pilots from H.M.S. Victorious taking part in Torpedo Bombing Attack on German Battleship Bismarck at 2200-2400 24 May, 1941[20]

1. Take off 2220. Left Carrier 2225. Flew through bottom of clouds. At 120 feet steering 264 T. At 0010 changed course to 240 T. At 0025 entered cloud, first two of

---

[20]Enclosure "F" to JHW's Report, serial F-1; x-27 dated 1 July 1941.

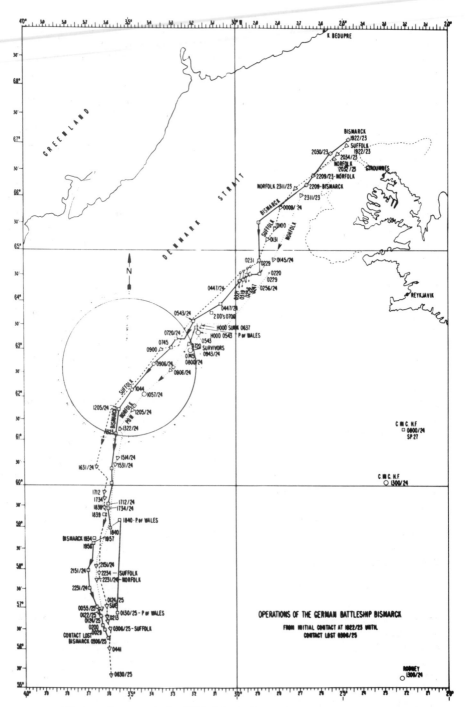

Redrawn from a tracing by JHW of the plot kept in H.M.S. *Rodney*, May 1941.

sub-flight turned starboard, 3rd straight ahead. Sighted American patrol boat, perhaps Coast Guard cutter, on course 000. At 0028 flew to starboard, altered course to 040 T, sighted BISMARCK off port bow at 0031 about 2000 feet. BISMARCK on course 270 T, speed estimated at 24 knots. Time 0038. Came clear of clouds about 3 miles to make certain of identification when she opened fire at 0048. Dropped to 100 feet altitude, saw first two flights attacking. 0115 asked for D.F., received three and a searchlight was visible at 0140. Landed aboard 0215. Visibility 2 miles, wind 20 knots, 330°, rain and ceiling going 1200 feet. Returning 1000 feet. Squalls rain. Observed one hit possible 3 huge mushrooms of black smoke. Pilots first operational flight day or night, 1st night DL has 280 hours total flying time, 3 hours 50 minutes. Ship was 20 miles out of position.

2. Took off 2220. First leg 2225. Altitude 1500 feet in the bottom of broken clouds approaching target. Went to 2200 feet. 2350 sighted target through hole in clouds, altered course to locate own forces—own forces astern of enemy—asked for bearing and distance, received same and by aldis lamp left own forces proceeding towards enemy and discovered an American ship what appeared to be a cable vessel at 0005. Located BISMARCK at 0010 who opened fire. Attacked at 0015. BISMARCK on course 180, sighted aircraft and altered course to 135 T. The aircraft arrived off beam #2 sub flight from dead ahead #1 30° port bow, #3 45° port bow. #1 sub flight leader had originally planned to attack the starboard bow but his right lower aileron carried away by shrapnel so he dropped on the port from between 800 and 1000 yards. The BISMARCK turned to starboard slightly. Attack completed 0017. Clear of short range fire at 0024. Other fire 0030. Returned to ship with DF 0130. Arrived 0215. Ship 20 miles out of position. Searchlight visible 35 miles. Cruised at 80 knots. Torpedo Mk. 12 aircraft, magnetic set for 48 feet. After sighting BISMARCK approaching head-on, Squadron went into line astern by Sub-flight and individual sub-flight went to line astern. BISMARCK turned to starboard putting up considerable fire. No. 2 sub flight were now abaft the port beam of BISMARCK and were endeavoring to get into position through the flak to attack from forward of the port beam. Flak forced us into cloud and the sub flight after splitting up reformed at water level some 3000 yards ahead of BISMARCK. Sub flight No. 2 went into line abreast at 300 yard intervals and went in to attack with BISMARCK turning to starboard and slowly opening up at a target. Sub flight ran into flak including from pom poms and tracers and dropped torpedoes inside 1000 yards using 24 knots sighting. Air gunner reported seeing two hits, there is no confirming this. Sub flight took urgent evasive action, accurate flak fire which continued until we were seven or eight miles away from BISMARCK's secondary armament. Only visual confirming of hits seen by pilot of G was large column of black smoke issuing abaft BISMARCK's "A" turret.

3. As we approached BISMARCK she started putting up a heavy barrage at the Swordfish. We came closer and suddenly noticed a large pall of smoke which had obviously been flown [thrown] into the air from the funnel as the result of an explosion. This was obviously not normal funnel smoke as the wind was strong at the time and the smoke would have remained low. The BISMARCK was taking avoiding action by turning hard to starboard and it appeared that she was not willing to be attacked from the starboard side. The attack appeared to be rather straggly and drawn out. BISMARCK fired a few rounds at us and we retired to shadow from about 10 miles astern having seen at least five Swordfish retire homewards. BISMARCK seemed to be in trouble for some time after the attack, her course was erratic and white smoke was issuing from the funnel. Eventually she settled down to a southerly course at about 15

knots speed, considerably less than that before the attack. The barrage appeared to be very heavy and she seemed to be firing everything she had. It was a very fine sight. After shadowing until almost dark we returned home.

4. 24 May—BISMARCK and HIPPER sighted and followed by the NORFOLK. PRINCE OF WALES and the HOOD steamed up and engaged the BISMARCK, HOOD sunk—three survived. The PRINCE OF WALES' bridge carried away and #1 turret out of commission. The BISMARCK was believed damaged but steaming away at 28 knots, zigzag course makes a good 24 knots. At 1500 VICTORIOUS received signal from Commander in Chief to detach from main body and proceed at full speed (31 knots) in company with one cruiser and four destroyers converging course. At this time VICTORIOUS was 300 miles away and closing at 10 knots. The BISMARCK changed course and the VICTORIOUS is now closing at 26 knots. Upon contacting launched 9 Swordfish as striking force to torpedo BISMARCK, 6 Fulmers will proceed as fighter protection and diversion for Swordfish attack. Upon completion of mission Swordfish will land aboard, reload torpedoes and attack the HIPPER—2 Swordfish took off at 1020, delivered attack at approximately 2330. One direct hit observed and possibly three, the BISMARCK damaged but still making 15 knots. Two Fulmers unaccounted for, all 9 Swordfish returned. Enemy delivered heavy A.A. fire before the aircraft had sighted her, using machine guns, multiple pom poms, 6″ guns and throwing 15″ shells in the water in front of the attacking aircraft. The aircraft joined up 7 miles from the BISMARCK after the attack and flak was still going through the formation. No direct hits. The Commanding Officer's ship had the starboard lower aileron carried away and 4.3.03 holes in the fuselage. Landed aboard 0230. Weather—visibility one mile, ceiling 1500 feet, 20 knot wind from 300°, heavy sea, VICTORIOUS pitching and yawing, spray over flight deck, light rain, temperature 50 F, scattered clouds at 1000, overcast solid 2000 feet. Swordfish took off at approximately 0000 to scout for enemy as the weather closed in during the night letting the BISMARCK escape.

5. Took off 1015. 31° variation. Formed up ahead of ship and steered 295 mag, speed 85 knots. 1120 turned to a course of 240 mag., and apparently flew nearly over BISMARCK in a cloud, whilst in the cloud we altered course to the North (1123) and intercepted PRINCE OF WALES, NORFOLK and SUFFOLK at 1130. NORFOLK passed a signal by light saying that enemy was on their starboard bow, 14 miles distance. 1145 left NORFOLK to intercept enemy. 1155 nearly carried out attack on American patrol boat; my own opinion that NORFOLK was shadowing this as a speck on the horizon, consequently reporting reduction of speed. 1215 sighted enemy on our port bow. Leader kept straight on, our sub-flight passed underneath him, trying to get ahead of the enemy. 1220 went into attack on her port bow, but found it too hot, also remainder of sub-flight had disappeared, so came out again, enemy thought we had dropped and turned toward us to comb the track. 1223 tried to get in again but gave it up and came right out. 1227 the pilot decided that our only chance was low on the water as we went in again this time with our sub-flight, which found us again just in time, in echelon to port about ½ mile away. We were approaching at about 6 feet over the water, right ahead of enemy. When we were about 2,500 yards away she started turning to port away from some other chaps who were dropping at the time. They did not see us until we were about 1,500 yards away as we were so low, carried on to 1100 yards and dropped at approximately 1231. Turned away and started to take photos about ½ minute later white cloud which may have been spray came up quickly followed by large black cloud which eventually rose to a height of 500 feet and then drifted away. They ceased fire with their pom poms and 4″ about 5 miles out but opened up again with

?″ at 7 miles keeping it up to 12 miles. We then turned to homeward course and led squadron until Commanding Officer caught us up.

6. Took off 1015, formed up with Commanding Officer sub flight and sighted the NORFOLK, SUFFOLK and PRINCE OF WALES at 1130. Cruiser flashed enemy 14 miles on starboard bow, took departure over fleet and onto a small vessel which appeared to be stationary. Retook departure and finally the BISMARCK which we saw through gaps in the cloud at approximately 1215. BISMARCK opened fire almost at once, bursts appearing very close to the squadron. The Commanding Officer climbed into cloud and we became separated from the sub flight. Came across B, the other machine in our sub flight, once but were separated again. Kept diving below cloud to observe BISMARCK and were fired upon with remarkable accuracy. Tried to work around to the starboard side of the enemy but she turned sharply to port. Went into cloud again and then dived steeply to attack the port side. Enemy appeared underneath us and we levelled out rather close at 8 or 9 hundred yards. Could not see any other machine attacking, released torpedo and turned away at about 500 yards. Fire from the enemy was very fierce and we zig-zagged continuously until we were about 2 miles away. Saw a large column of black smoke rising vertically above ship which was surrounded by an intense barrage of bursting shells apparently showing the attack of other machines. Saw machines coming out of attack and zig-zagging down wind to the rendezvous. Shells from the enemy dropping into the water near them, apparently of 6″ caliber. Joined up with Lieutenant Gich[21] as leader of squadron and made for home. Commanding Officer joined us later and took over command.

7. The attack as executed was quite dissimilar to the original plan demanding an instant reconsideration and fast execution of the new plan in order to still successfully coordinate. The squadron commanders intention of coming in from the starboard was thrown aside when he realized that his chances were very poor to arrive with his whole section and that three kippers from port might be better than one starboard. On accelerated take off southwest wingsfold—depth charges exploded. Landed aboard with three charges—gear collapsed—WOW. Took off 2215 for torpedo attack on the BISMARCK. My pilot was Carthwrite and we were in Gick's sub flight. For me this was an exciting trip for it was my first operation, the first time I'd flown from a carrier. So there was no gradual getting used to the enemy's actions on such occasions. We took off the deck with the "fish" and nearly went in the drink as a dripping night or of sight of those on the flight deck. We then formed up as a squadron and flew toward the enemy. The cloud, however, we got separated with one plane. We found the PRINCE OF WALES and the two 8″ cruisers and they gave us a bearing of the enemy. We kept on to a ship we found and to see it was a small white yacht. So into the cloud again . . . .

Naval Messages received in H.M.S Rodney, 25 May 1941

From	To	Time Sent/Date	
NORFOLK	Scapa Radio	0055/25	Lost contact with enemy BB—His last position 54° 08′ N., 36° 34′ W., speed 21, course 165.
SUFFOLK	Scapa Radio	0124/25	Surface craft by RD/F bearing 215° distant 11 miles. My position 57° 06′ N., 36° 05′ W.
C.S.2	CinC H.F.	0150/25	Attack completed at 0020. One hit observed—additional report later.

---

[21]Philip David Gick.

From	To	Time Sent/Date	
SUFFOLK	Scapa Radio	0228/25	Two ships bearing 192°, distance 20,900 and 25,500 yards. Enemy course 160, speed 20. My position 56° 44′ N., 36° 05′ W.
SUFFOLK	Scapa Radio	0238/25	At 0200 BISMARCK in 56° 40′ N., 36° 18′ W., course 160, speed 21.
SUFFOLK	Scapa Radio	0306/25	My 0228 no change.
RODNEY	ComDes22 Flot 6	0315/25	My speed 20 the initial course 262. Follow at your best speed under weather conditions.
SUFFOLK	C.S.1	0401/25	Enemy has either worked around to eastward under stern of shadowing ships or has turned westward—am acting on latter assumption.
SUFFOLK	C.S.1	0505/25	Lost contact with enemy at 0306.

Reminiscences, 25 May 1941[23]

When Lieutenant Commander Gatacre and I read the Suffolk 0401 message at about 4:20 a.m. saying she had lost radar contact with the Bismarck we became concerned over the Bismarck's probable course of action, and began immediately to make a summary of the situation. Captain Dalrymple-Hamilton arrived in the chart house shortly thereafter and called our full Operations Committee into session. Our summary of the situation indicated the Bismarck was headed for a Bay of Biscay port, probably Brest rather than St. Nazaire, because under the present unfavorable weather conditions Brest offered a much easier and safer entrance. Our decision was based on the following factors:

a. The *Bismarck* received some damage in her battle with the *Hood* and *Prince of Wales* as evidenced by her trailing oil, and a reduction in speed after the battle.

b. The hit by the *Victorious* torpedo aircraft may have compounded this damage.

c. A return to Germany via the Denmark Strait and Norwegian Sea, or via the Iceland Faroes Passage and the Norwegian Sea was too dangerous.

d. Repair facilities were available in the general Brest and St. Nazaire areas. In addition the overhauls of the battle cruisers *Sharnhorst* and *Gneisenau* at Brest were about completed.

e. German aircraft, submarines and surface craft (mainly destroyers) could easily provide air, submarine and surface protection to the *Bismarck* within about 400 miles of the western coast of France.

I remember distinctly my strong arguments in favor of the above decision. I believed without any doubt, the *Bismarck* was headed for a Bay of Biscay port, but I desire to reiterate that in many cases strategic decisions are not too difficult when you have all the factors bearing on the problem and the overall responsibility does not rest on your shoulders. Captain Dalrymple-Hamilton who bore all the *Rodney* responsibility listened to our discussions, asked several questions, and made the final decision to stay in the vicinity of our 0800 position for the time being and then act on the assumption the *Bismarck* was headed for a Bay of Biscay port if she were not sighted within the next two or three hours.

---

[22]Commander, 6th Destroyer Flotilla, in *Somali*.

[23]JHW, MS. *Reminiscences*, pp. 180-181.

I received an interesting side light on this decision as late as July 7, 1970 from our navigator, now Rear Admiral G.G.O. Gatacre, retired in New South Wales, Australia. He said in a letter, "Your probing discussions with me when *Bismarck* was 'lost,' undoubtedly contributed greatly to the conclusion we reached and shared—*COR-RECTLY!*—regarding the destination of *Bismarck*."

Personal Diary, 25 May 1941

. . . Still holding on to a westerly course. *King George the V* should be the one to make contact at 0900—At 0306 *Norfolk* & *Suffolk* lost contact. A search was organized. We changed course to about 060 to intercept if she headed for Brest. At 1330 D/F bearings gave an indication of *Bismarck*'s position. We steamed east (060) until we got on a line with this position and Brest then headed towards Brest (120). No further word of *Bismarck*. Will she get through. All kinds of excitement.

Naval Messages received in H.M.S. Rodney, 25 May 1941

From	To	Time Sent/Date	
C.S.1	Scapa Radio	0511/25	NORFOLK with PRINCE OF WALES in position 55° 52′ N., 36° W. at 0500—Close on port quarter of SUFFOLK. If visibility is good intend to work around to northward at dawn so that PRINCE OF WALES can join. If visibility poor shall keep PRINCE OF WALES to support me in maintaining contact at close range.
C.S.1	CinC H.F. VICTORIOUS	0522/25	In view SUFFOLK's 0441 request air search at dawn. Enemy speed has not exceeded 22 knots for some time.
CinC H.F.	C.S.2, VICTORIOUS	about 0600/25	Organize air and surface search northwest of the last reported position of enemy.
U.S.C.G MODOC	All Ships U.S. Coast Guard	0600/25	Cutter MODOC at 0600 GCT in 57° 40′ N., 38° 11′ W., searching for convoy survivors.
C.S.1	Scapa Radio	0605/25	Lost contact with enemy at 0306. SUFFOLK is searching to westward. At daylight NORFOLK to follow SUFFOLK, PRINCE OF WALES to join CinC HF.
C.S.1	CinC H.F.	0616/25	Enemy probably made a 90° turn to the west or turned back then and cut to eastward under our stern.
C.S.1	SUFFOLK	0630/25	Am searching now on course 285 at 25 knots. At 0600 my position 55° 30′ N., 36° 00′ W.
C.S.1	Scapa Radio	0704/25	At 0630 my position 55° 20′ N., 35° 54′ W.
PRINCE OF WALES	CinC H.F., C.S.1	0707/25	At 0700/25 my position 55° 12′ N., 35° 56′ W., course 205, speed 25.5.
S.O.F. H	Ad.	0800/25	My force consists of RENOWN, ARK ROYAL and SHEFFIELD. Destroyers have been detached. My position at 0730 40° 43′ N., 15° 50′ W., course 310, speed 22.
C.S.2	Scapa Radio	0800/25	VICTORIOUS position at 0800 56° 18′ N., 36° 28′ W., course 320, speed 24.

From	To	Time Sent/Date	
Ad.	General	0815/25	Weather forecast for various areas of operations within 200 miles radius of 57° N., 35° W.—Moderate to fresh west to northwest winds—rain and showers, visibility over 10 miles in northwest, but 3-7 miles in southwest.
Ad.	C.S.1	0829/25	Have you any evidence to confirm torpedo plane attack was successful?
Ad.	CinC H.F.	0836/25	Take all Home Fleet including RODNEY under your command.
Ad.	CinC H.F.	0855/25	From shortly after torpedo attack was supposed to begin until 0258 BISMARCK made a series of radio signals some of which were very long. A fair inference is that enemy has changed essential plans due to damage received.
RODNEY	CinC H.F.	0900/25	My position 52° 34' N., 29° 23' W. Have 3 destroyers as screen—Intend to stay in this vicinity to intercept enemy if he breaks through to southeast. Visibility here 10 miles.
PRINCE OF WALES	Ad.	0926/25	Have no evidence to confirm successful torpedo attack.
Ad.	General	0919/25	Summary of location of fleet units, among which were: Force H—ETP—39° 00' N., 18° 30' W; REVENGE 43° 30' N., 58° 00' W; LONDON 38° 40' N., 21° 00' W; CinC HF 55° 00' N., 35° 00' W; PRINCE OF WALES detached by C.S.1 to join CinC; RAMILLES—ETP—51° 30' N., 38° 00' W; EDINBURGH 49° 40' N., 30° 30' W; C.S.1 lost touch with enemy at 0306 in 56° 23' N., 36° 05' W., NORFOLK and SUFFOLK searching to westward.
C.S.1	Ad.	0943/25	Only evidence of successful torpedo attack is a message intercepted by NORFOLK from the aircraft to VICTORIOUS which stated that aircraft had attacked and only one hit observed.
Ad.	CinC H.F. and others	1030/25	D/F bearings on 7760 kcs at 0948/25 * * *
CinC H.F.	Home Fleet	1047/25	By D/F estimate enemy position at 0952/25 was 57° N., 33° W. All Home Fleet forces search accordingly.
Ad.	CinC H.F.	1139/25	D/F bearings on 7760 kcs at 1045/25. The signal was a repetition of signal made at 0948.

Reminiscences, 25 May 1941[24]

. . . We were very much surprised to read a message from the Commander-in-Chief Home Fleet shortly after 11:00 a.m. which said: "By radio direction finder bearings estimate enemy position at 0952/25 was latitude 57° north, longitude 33° west. All Home Fleet units search accordingly." This message had a time of origin of 1047/25. Our surprise, of course, was due to the fact our plotted position of the ship as indicated by the radio direction finder bearings was about sixty miles south of the position stated by the Commander-in-Chief Home Fleet. We checked the navigator's position and believed his position to be correct.

The Commander-in-Chief's Home Fleet message of 1047/25 was the unfortunate message which sent all the Home Fleet units except the *Rodney*, and perhaps the *Edinburgh* and *Norfolk* on the wild goose chase north and northwestward for about seven critical hours while the *Bismarck* was steaming southeastward toward Brest at 20-22 knots.

Captain Dalrymple-Hamilton thought the Admiralty would send a correction to the Commander-in-Chief's 1047/25 message.

The Commander-in-Chief's Home Fleet message of 1047/25 created a very difficult situation for Captain Dalrymple-Hamilton. Should he direct the *Rodney* to remain in the general area of our 0900 a.m. position? Should he order the *Rodney* to steer a course which assumed the *Bismarck* was returning to Germany via the Denmark Strait or the Iceland-Faroes Passage? Should he steer a course to arrive in the shortest possible time at the intersection of the track between the *Bismarck*'s last reported position at 02:00/25 by the Suffolk and Cape Finisterre? And if the *Bismarck* was not sighted within a reasonable time after passing through this intersection, then alter course to cross the *Bismarck*'s track in the shortest possible time, on the assumption she was headed for Brest from her last reported by the *Suffolk* at 02:00 a.m./25?

Captain Dalrymple-Hamilton's firm belief that the *Bismarck* was headed for a Bay of Biscay port resulted in his decision to leave our general area, and direct the *Rodney* to steam toward the intersection of the track between the *Bismarck*'s last reported position at 02:00/25 and Cape Finisterre. The *Rodney* altered course to 030° at 11:40 a.m., increased speed to 17 and then gradually to 20 and 21 knots. Captain Dalrymple-Hamilton, Lieutenant Commander Gatacre and I were extremely happy to receive an Admiralty message to the *Rodney* at 1158/25 which said: "Act as though the enemy is proceeding to a Bay of Biscay port."

The Admiralty also sent the following message to a number of shore stations at 1200/25. The *Rodney* intercepted and decoded this message which read: "The Admiralty believes the *Bismarck* is headed for Brest."

When the Bismarck was not sighted by 4:20 p.m.[25] Captain Dalrymple-Hamilton, after consultation with Lieutenant Commander Gatacre and Commander Grindle, altered the *Rodney*'s course to 055° in order to cross the *Bismarck*'s track in the shortest possible time on the assumption she was headed for Brest from her last reported position by the Suffolk at 02:00/25.

When the *Bismarck* was not sighted by 9:00 p.m. Captain Dalrymple-Hamilton ordered the *Rodney* to change course to 118°, as we headed toward Brest at a speed of 21 knots.

---

[24]JHW, MS. *Reminiscences.*

[25]"I believe, the best plot that can be made of the relative positions of *Bismarck* and *Rodney* shows that we missed intercepting *Bismarck* by no more than 25 miles!!" G.G.O. Gatacre letter to J.H. Wellings, 7 July 1970.

Naval Messages Received in H.M.S. Rodney, 25 May 1941

From	To	Time Sent/Date	
Ad.	RODNEY	1158/25	Act as though enemy is proceeding to a Bay of Biscay port.
Ad.	Shore Establishments (Plymouth, etc.)	about 1200/25	My *** not to all addressees—Admiralty believes BISMARCK is headed for Brest.
CinC H.F.	Ad.	1204/25	At 1100 my position 54° 40′ N., 36° 30′ W., course 055, speed 27. REPULSE detached to proceed to Conception Bay.
Ad.	CinC H.F.	1228/25	From D/F bearings position of enemy unit transmitting was approximately 55° 30′ N., and between 31° and 32° West at 1054/25. Longitude is unreliable.
Ad.	RAMILLES	1424/25	Ordered RAMILLES to escort BRITTANIC to Halifax.
PRINCE OF WALES	CinC H.F.	1540/25	At 1600 my course 080, speed 25.5, position 55° 20′ N., 34° 45′ W. Intend to proceed to nearest fueling port—Hvalsfiord, Iceland. At 2000 tonight speed 18 and zigzagging. Will have 6% fuel on arrival.
PRINCE OF WALES	Ad. CinC H.F.	1545/25	HOOD opened fire just before BISMARCK. The latter's opening fire range was 23,000. The BISMARCK's fire was immediately effective on HOOD. At 20,000 yards BISMARCK's secondary armament effective. Due to interference, probably by enemy, no results obtained on RD/F, types 281 or 284.
RODNEY (visual)	DD's in company	1605/25	My position at 1600 was 52° 58′ N., 28° 54′ W.
CinC H.F.	Ad.	1621/25	At 1600 my position 54° 54′ N., 33° 20′ W., course 080, speed 25. Your 1428 do you think enemy is heading for Faeroes?
C.S.2	CinC H.F.	1655/25	At 1700 my course 070, speed 27, position 57° 42′ N., 35° 40′ W. HERMOINE sent to Hvalfiord to fuel—VICTORIOUS, KENYA, AURORA in company. (C.S.2 in GALATEA). GALATEA and AURORA will leave for Hvalfiord for fuel at 0100/26. KENYA and VICTORIOUS will endeavor to locate and attack BISMARCK tomorrow morning if he is in the Iceland-Faeroe Area.
Ad.	N.O.I.C. St. Johns	1712/25	Informed addressee that REPULSE sent to Conception Bay to fuel and should arrive afternoon 26 May. A tanker and A/S escort should be sent to Conception Bay.
Ad.	RODNEY	1805/25	Cancel my 1428. Proceed on the assumption that the enemy's destination is a French port.

From	To	Time Sent/Date	
CinC H.F.	Ad.	1817/25	My position 54° 57′ N., 31° 53′ W., course 117, speed 24 at 1815.
Ad.	CinC H.F. and others	1824/25	Admiralty appreciation is that the BISMARCK is heading for a port on West Coast of France.
CinC H.F.		1912/25	Ordered Admiral in Charge of Destroyers to screen PRINCE OF WALES and VICTORIOUS as soon as possible.
C.S.1	CinC H.F.	2040/25	At 2100 my position 55° 50′ N., 31° 20′ W., course 120, speed 26. I had 50% fuel on hand at 2000.
CinC H.F.	Ad.	2200/25	My position 54° 07′ N., 29° 18′ W., course 117, speed 26.

Personal Diary, 26 May 1941

. . . Steaming as before looking for *Bismarck*. At 1030 Catalina flying boat sighted *Bismarck*—about 110 miles bearing 200 from *Rodney*. Continued on our course. At 1700 *K.G.V.* joined. *Ark Royal's* planes sighted *Bismarck*—torpedo attack at 1500 unsuccessful. Another attack at 2100 produced one & perhaps 2 hits. After this attack *Bismarck* made two complete circles then headed north, the only possible action she could take if we are to intercept. We headed south. Dark at 0100—C.in.C decided to wait until morning to attack.

Report of Ensign L.B. Smith,[26] USN, 26 May 1941

Report of Scouting and Search of PBY-5 No. AH545 "CATALINA" for BISMARCK 26 May, 1941.

1. Following 0325 take-off from Lough Erne, it was necessary to climb to 3000′ through overcast before proceeding to West Coast of Ireland. We took departure at 0430 from Eagle Island, altitude 500′ on westerly course. Weather conditions were undesirable, ceiling varying from 100′ to 1000′ and visibility ranging from 5 miles to zero. Wind 30-35 from N.W. which reduced ground speed to approximately 80 knots.

2. The plane carried four depth charges (500 lbs. each) and capacity gas load (1750 U.S. gallons) Aircraft at Lough Erne are always armored with depth charges and the British felt it a waste of time and effort to remove them before this flight. There was no special (ASV)[27] equipment aboard.

3. The trip to the assigned search area was uneventful other than several course changes which were necessitated by weather conditions. We arrived at our area at 0945 and immediately started search. Following is a diagram of sectors assigned to Squadrons 209 & 240 from Lough Erne.

---

[26]Leonard "B" Smith. This Report is Appendix H to JHW's Report serial F-1; x-27 of 1 July 1941.

[27]Aircraft/surface vessel.

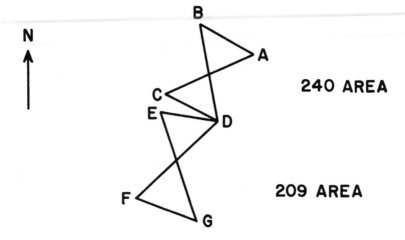

One aircraft from each squadron was to cover each sector, ours (209) being DEFG. I assume that similar areas were assigned to other groups in order to cover all western approaches of Europe. Upon examination, it will be found that in reality this area (DEFG) is two of our familiar "Pie shaped" Vectors joined at the vertex. Flight plan. Search leg DE; EG; GF; FD and repeat.

4. Weather at search area was somewhat better than that encountered on trip out. Horizontal visibility below 800' was good—up to 8-10 miles. Misty conditions prevailed between 800' and 2000' where cloud lane covered 5/6 of sky. Visibility between 800-2000 was about 4 miles and at 2000 about 1-2 miles.

5. We started leg EG of area at 1000 and at 1010 I sighted what was first believed to be BISMARCK, bearing 345° at 8 miles. Definite recognition was impossible at the time due to visibility. I immediately took control from "George" (automatic Pilot); started slow climbing turn to starboard, keeping ship sighted to Port, while the British officer went aft to prepare contact report. My plan was to take cover in the clouds, get close to the ship as possible; make definite recognition and then shadow the ship from best point of vantage. Upon reaching 2000' we broke out of a cloud formation and were met by a terrific antiaircraft barrage from our starboard quarter.

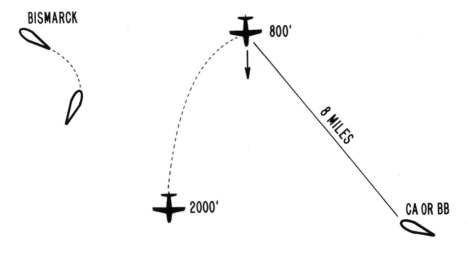

Immediately jettisoned the depth charges and started violent evasive action which consisted of full speed, climbing and "S" turns. The British officer[28] went aft again to send the contact report. When making an "S" turn I could see the ship was a BB and was the BISMARCK, which had made a 90° starboard turn from its original course, (This was evident from wake made by his maneuvering), and was firing broadside on us. The A.A. fire lasted until we were out of range and into the clouds. It was very intense and were it not for evasive action we would have been shot down. The barrage was so close that it shook the aircraft considerably—(one man was knocked from his bunk) and the noise of the burst could be heard above the propeller and engine noise. Numerous bursts were observed at close quarters and small fragments of shrapnel could be heard hitting the plane. The fitter came forward to pilots compartment saying we were full of holes. As soon as we were well clear of BISMARCK we investigated the damage, which consisted of a hole in after port hole (about 2″ in diameter) and one in bottom of hull directly below instrument panel (about 1″ in diameter). No other damage was visible at the time. I made short flight test (several turns, checked engines, etc.) and finding everything satisfactory returned to area to resume shadow of BISMARCK.

6. From this encounter it was obvious that there were two German warships in company on same course (140° true) and the leading ship was not identified but was of BB or CV class.

7. The 240 squadron plane had intercepted our contact report and set his course to intercept the ship from the position given in our contact.

8. As we had lost contact with the ship we returned to position of the BISMARCK. The navigation was somewhat in error, due to our evasive action, etc., and we could not find the ship the second time. According to reports that we intercepted from 240 plane, he was being attacked by enemy aircraft. We immediately set course to intercept him. We joined up with him and he was in contact with BISMARCK. We stayed in company for 45 minutes and then took departure for Lough Erne at 1530; the time specified by the Group Operations Officer.

9. We landed at 2130 with approximately 250-300 gal. of gasoline remaining.

CONCLUSION AND RECOMMENDATIONS.

10. On a mission of this nature, after contact has been made and reported, a torpedo attack by a patrol plane is entirely feasible. In any event, it would have been better to carry a torpedo in lieu of depth charges. The BISMARCK evidently had some type of aircraft detector device. This is evident by the fact that she had turned 90° and opened fire on us as we emerged from a cloud and had thus known our position before actually sighting us.

Naval Messages Received in H.M.S. Rodney, 26 May 1941

From	To	Time Sent/Date	
Ad.	C.S.2	0011/26	Unless otherwise ordered send one cruiser to guard Denmark Straits and two to the Iceland-Faeroe Passage.
Ad.	LONDON	0048/26	Cancelled LONDON's orders to search for German tanker. LONDON sent to help escort an SC convoy.

---

[28]Flying Officer Dennis Briggs.

From	To	Time Sent/Date	
Ad.	CinC H.F. & others	0109/26	Air searches beginning at 1000—Two cross-over patrols by Catalinas one from 50° 10′ N., 21° 00′ W., to 52° 20′ N., 19° 25′ W., the other from 48° 10′ N., 23° 30′ W., to 49° 50′ N., to 21° 10′ W.
C.S.1	S.O.F. H, CinC H.F.	0115/26	At 0100 my position 48° 54′ N., 15° 19′ W., course 150, speed 27.
A.C.W.A.	COSSACK, SIKH, ZULU, MAORI, PIORIN	0159/26	COSSACK, SIKH, ZULU join CinC HF immediately in position at 2200/25 54° 07′ N., 29° 18′ W., course 117, speed 26. MAORI and PIORIN join RODNEY in 52° 40′ N., 25° 45′ W., course 113, speed 20 at 0001/26.
Ad.	CinC H.F.	0340/26	My 2012/24 Patrol was flown—no results. Another patrol has been ordered to search today, 26 May. 400 mile square, the center is 43° N., 26° W.
SUFFOLK	CinC H.F.	0557/26	At 0500 my position 57° 51′ N., 25° 23′ W., course 060, speed 27.
RODNEY		0800/26	Destroyers of screen at 0800/26 had following fuel on hand—MASHONA 51%, SOMALI 48%, TARTAR 47.5%.
Ad.	General	0840/26	Weather report for area within 200 miles of 50° N., 20° W.—Strong northwest wind slowly slackening—backing in west—cloudy—squalls—occasional showers—visibility 8-12 miles—etc.
C.S.18	CinC H.F. Ad.	0940/26	Stated he was proceeding to Londonderry in MANCHESTER, would arrive with 13% fuel on hand.
A/C[29] "Z" (Catalina)	15th Gr.Hd.[30]	1030/26	One battleship latitude 49° 33′ N., 21° 47′ W., course 150°, speed 20.
CinC H.F.	Ad.	1051/26	The Catalina 1030 contact report—Request a check that contact was not RODNEY. I am in 51° 37′ N., 20° 42′ W., speed 26.
A/C "Z"	15th Gr.Hd.	1100/26	My 1030—Lost contact with enemy BB. Last position of enemy was 49° 22′ N., 21° 14′ W., at 1045.
ARK ROYAL A/C	A/C of ARK ROYAL	1114/26	One enemy battleship 292°, 83 miles from 49° N., 19° W.
A/C "Z"	15th Gr.Hd.	1114/26	Hull holed by shrapnel. Request instructions.
DORSET-SHIRE	Ad.	1130/26	Am with SC 74 and BULOLO, my position 44° 08′ N., 24° 50′ W. Intend to leave convoy now, steer 65, speed 25, to intercept and shadow enemy. I have 59% fuel on hand.

---

[29] Aircraft.

[30] 15 Group Headquarters, Coastal Command, at Liverpool.

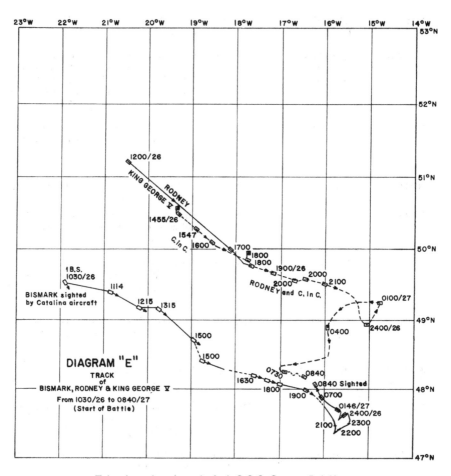

Taken from chart drawn by Lcdr G.G.O. Gatacre, R.A.N.,
The Navigator of H.M.S. *Rodney*, based on information
available in H.M.S. *Rodney*, June 1941
Enclosure "G" to JHW's Report serial F-1; x-27 of 1 July 1941.

From	To	Time Sent/Date	
RODNEY (visual)	MASHONA	1134/26	KING GEORGE V should bear 270° from me—distance about 20 miles. Search to westward, if contact made report my position—course 130, speed 21.5. Rejoin by 1500.
RODNEY (visual)	ComDesFlot 6 in SOMALI	1143/26	I will detach you at 1500.
15th Gr.Hd.	A/C "Z"	1150/26	Your 1114—search and trail as long as possible. Additional instructions later.
Ad.	CinC H.F.	1159/26	At least one Focke-Wolfe is proceeding towards the west from Bordeaux. At 1046 its positions- - -
A/C "Z"	15th Gr.Hd.	1200/26	Weather—type of "O"—amount of cloud cover 10/10—Height of bottom of clouds 1500.
CinC H.F.	Ad.	1210/26	ARK ROYAL A/C states BISMARCK in 49° 32' N., 20° 55' W., at 1114/26, course 110, speed 20. At 1100 my position 51° 30' N., 20° 43' W., course 150, changing to 130 at 1155, speed 26.
Ad.	SEVERN(SS)	1220/26	Ordered SEVERN to proceed to Gibraltar at maximum speed and establish an offensive patrol in Straits of Gibraltar. The tankers with SEVERN are to continue present duty (available to fuel fleet units at sea).
Ad.	CinC H.F.	1225/26	Your 1051/26—The enemy ship reported by A/C at 1030 is hostile.
Ad.	CinC H.F. S.O.F. H, and others	1244/26	By D/F on 7760 kcs enemy surface craft at 0954 GMT 26th (1154 of problem time) on following bearings—D/F stations and bearings stated, then followed: Estimated position within 50 miles of 49° 00' N., 21° 30' W.
S.O.F. H	Ad.	1301/26	Enemy BB estimated position, course and speed at 1215 as follows—49° 10' N., 20° 10' W., course 110, speed 20. A/C of ARK ROYAL in contact. My position, course and speed at 1248 as follows—49° 30' N., 19° 10' W., course 350, speed 15. Striking force of torpedo bombers will attack about 1500.
A/C "Z"	15th Gr.Hd.	1325/26	Your 1250—No holes can be plugged.
Ad.	VICTORIOUS	1328/26	Ordered VICTORIOUS to Clyde to fuel.
A/C "M"	15th Gr.Hd.	1330/26	One battleship 180°, 4 miles from 48° 12' N., 19° 50' W.
A/C "M"	15th Gr.Hd.	1340/26	Enemy course 140, speed 20.
Ad.	CinC H.F., S.O.F. H, and others	1343/26	This dispatch referred to Admiralty's 1244/26 and stated that fingerprint indicates transmitting unit at 0954/26 (GMT) 1154 of problem time—was the same unit which transmitted by being shadowed on 24 May and which transmitted at 0854 GMT on 25 May.

From	To	Time Sent/Date	
S.O.F. H	Ad.	1345/26	My position course and speed at 1345 as follows —49° 40′ N., 18° 53′ W., course 120, speed 18. SHEFFIELD detached to shadow. Enemy BB at 1315 position 49° 10′ N., 19° 45′ W., course 130, speed 21.
A/C "M"	15th Gr.Hd.	1345/26	Unknown A/C are attacking me.
RODNEY (visual)	ComDesFlot 6	1349/26	Please give me a check on CinC HF last reported position.
15th Gr.Hd.	A/C "M"	1350/26	Your --- check course stating whether course --- magnetic compass, gyro or true.
ARK ROYAL	ARK ROYAL A/C	1422/26	State your position in occasional reports. Use full procedure.
EDINBURGH	RODNEY	1440/26	Did you sight KING GEORGE V?
RODNEY (visual)	TARTAR	1446/26	I see EDINBURGH, is KING GEORGE V there as well?
ComDesFlot6	RODNEY	1448/26	MASHONA can stay another six hours. Would it be of assistance if he stayed with you?
RODNEY	EDINBURGH	1449/26	If you can see KING GEORGE V please report my position. My course is 130, speed 22. Also inform him that I am detaching SOMALI, TARTAR and MASHONA to Plymouth at 1700—PIORIN has not joined me.
ARK ROYAL A/C	A/C of ARK ROYAL	1454/26	Enemy altered course to about 110.
RODNEY (visual)	EDINBURGH	1456/26	KING GEORGE V bears 280° 15 miles from me now.
ARK ROYAL A/C	ARK ROYAL A/C	1500/26	Have regained contact. Enemy changed course to about 120.
RODNEY (visual)	ComDesFlot 6 in SOMALI	1501/26	Your 1448—Yes. I should like to keep the DD's as long as possible as I cannot afford to zigzag. Do you wish to amend your own time of leaving us? I had hoped PIORIN would be here by now.
ComDesFlot 6 (visual)	RODNEY	1511/26	Your 1501—TARTAR and SOMALI can remain until 1800—MASHONA until 1100.
ARK ROYAL A/C	ARK ROYAL A/C	1518/26	My 1454—Large oil track being left by enemy.
CinC H.F. (visual)	RODNEY	1519/26	Good luck, you may be there in time yet.
RODNEY (visual)	CinC H.F.	1527/26	Very much thanks. We are doing our best and much want to be with you.

From	To	Time Sent/Date	
S.O.F. H	Ad.	1520/26	At 1500 enemy BB position course and speed as follows—48° 24′ N., 18° 46′ W., course 110, speed 25. My position course and speed at 1515 was 49° 14′ N., 18° 19′ W., course 110, speed 26. Striking force left at 1500.
RODNEY	SOMALI	1523/26	My position at 1500—50° 25′ N., 18° 55′ W.
ARK ROYAL A/C	ARK ROYAL A/C	1524/26	Enemy battleship is 113°, 45 miles from 49° N., 20° W., making good 120°, speed 20.
ARK ROYAL A/C	ARK ROYAL TORPEDO A/C	1525/26	Enemy speed 22.
A/C "Z"	15th Gr.Hd.	1525/26	Lost contact. Enemy BB last observed position was at 1500 which was 47° 30′ N., 19° W.
ARK ROYAL A/C	ARK ROYAL TORPEDO A/C	1540/26	Enemy speed 25.
RODNEY (visual)	CinC H.F.	1544/26	My course 130, speed 22. SOMALI, TARTAR will remain with me until 1800. MASHONA until 2300. All going to Plymouth to refuel. I had 1600 tons of oil on hand at 1800.
CinC H.F.	Ad.	1551/26	Have engaged one aircraft. My position 50° 18′ N., 18° 45′ W., course 128, speed 26. RODNEY bears 100°, 11 miles from me.
ARK ROYAL A/C	ARK ROYAL TORPEDO A/C	1553/26	Still in contact. No change in situation.
A/C "M"	15th Gr.Hd.	1600/26	Have regained contact.
S.O.F. H	Ad.	1605/26	My 1520—Positions based on my fix at 1500.
A/C "M"	15th Gr.Hd.	1605/26	Enemy course 140, speed 20.
A/C "M"	15th Gr.Hd.	1615/26	Enemy course 140, speed 20.
ARK ROYAL A/C	ARK ROYAL A/C	1624/26	One light vessel bearing 060.
A/C "M"	15th Gr.Hd.	1630/26	Estimate position of enemy at 1610 was 47° 28′ N., 18° 15′ W.
ARK ROYAL A/C	ARK ROYAL A/C	1630/26	My 1615—Enemy course 140.
ARK ROYAL A/C	ARK ROYAL A/C	1630/26	So did we. Returning to base.
A/C "M"	15th Gr.Hd.	1632/26	Enemy A/C attacking me.
ARK ROYAL A/C	ARK ROYAL A/C	1640/26	Enemy BB position 159° 33 miles from 49° N., 18° W.
A/C "M"	15th Gr.Hd.	1655/26	Enemy changed course to approximately 125.
C.S.18 (EDINBURGH)		1656/26	Can make 27 knots until 2359 when I shall be forced to return for oil at 15 knots.

From	To	Time Sent/Date	
S.O.F. H	Ad.	1700/26	At 1630 enemy BB in position 48° 12′ N., 17° 34′ W., course 110, speed 25. My position at 1700 49° 00′ N., 17° 25′ W., course 140, speed 26. Striking Force now searching for enemy.
A/C "M"	15th Gr.Hd.	1700/26	My 1605 and 1655—Course was 140 true not 125.
ARK ROYAL A/C	ARK ROYAL A/C	1702/26	Enemy bears 110° distance 4 miles from me. My position at 1702 is 138°, 26 miles from 49° N., 18° W.
ARK ROYAL A/C	ARK ROYAL A/C	1715/26	Enemy bears 320° from me.
ARK ROYAL A/C	ARK ROYAL A/C	1717/26	Weather—visibility surface 10—sky 8/10—cloudy—base of clouds at 3000 feet.
CinC H.F. (visual)	RODNEY	1724/26	Have slowed to 22 knots to economize. Our only hope is for BISMARCK to be slowed up by torpedo bombers.
ARK ROYAL A/C	ARK ROYAL A/C	1725/26	Type 3019 effective.
ARK ROYAL A/C	ARK ROYAL A/C	1730/26	Enemy BB made good 110° distance 11 miles since 1700.
ComDesFlot4	CinC H.F. S.O.F. H Ad. SHEFFIELD	1730/26	At 1730 Fourth Flotilla plus PIORIN in 48° 43′ N., 17° 47′ W., based on my fix at 1515. Course 150 speed 27. SIKH reports periscope 5 miles back. No enemy in sight. Visibility 8 miles. Oil remaining 50% except for PIORIN which has 42%.
ARK ROYAL A/C	ARK ROYAL A/C	1735/26	My 1640—Enemy course 110, speed 22.
RODNEY (visual)	CinC H.F.	1735/26	Your 1714—Engine room conditions are quite severe but I do not wish to slow since you may go on and I get left behind.
S.O.F. H	CinC H.F.	1740/26	Request your course and speed. Shall I leave carrier and join you? If no reply shall remain with carrier.
SHEFFIELD	Scapa Radio	1740/26	One large vessel bearing 68°, 10 miles from a position 156°, 39 miles from 49° N., 18° W., course 120.
ARK ROYAL A/C	ARK ROYAL A/C	1744/26	My position 130°, 46 miles from 49° N., 18° W., enemy bears 090 five miles from me.
RODNEY (visual)	CinC H.F.	1747/26	Comdesflot6 in SOMALI now says he can remain with TARTAR until 2100 and MASHONA until 0200. Would you prefer them to leave now so as to be available again later?

From	To	Time Sent/Date	
CinC H.F. (visual)	RODNEY	1758/26	KING GEORGE V very probably will have to return for fuel at midnight. In case torpedo bombers get in another attack it is most important you should be able to continue steaming at not less than 20 knots.
A/C "M"	15th Gr.Hd.	1800/26	Lost contact—last observed position enemy was 47° 15′ N., 18° 23′ W. Am returning to base.
ARK ROYAL A/C	ARK ROYAL A/C	1800/26	Enemy made good 11 miles, course 113, since 1730.
S.O.F. H	Ad.	1800/26	At 1800 enemy BB in 48° 06′ N., 17° 02′ W., course 110, speed 22. At 1800 my position 48° 55′ N., 17° 18′ W., course 140, speed 29.
CinC H.F. (visual)	RODNEY	1820/26	What speed are you making good?
Reply (visual)			22 knots.
CinC H.F.	S.O.F. H	1821/26	KING GEORGE V reduced to 22 knots at 1705 to save fuel. At 1800 my position 49° 48′ N., 17° 33′ W., course 110. RODNEY is 132°, 4 miles distant on same course, her speed is 22. Unless enemy is slowed intend KING GEORGE V return to fuel at 2400/26. RODNEY will be able to continue chase but without destroyer escort. Recommend you stay with aircraft carrier.
ARK ROYAL	SHEFFIELD	1823/26	Striking Force which takes off at 1850 has orders to contact you before attacking.
S.O.F. H	Ad.	1825/26	Reports sent by SHEFFIELD and ARK ROYAL A/C are based on a dead reckoning position 20 miles north of position given in my 1520 and 1700 and 1800 which are based on a fix at 1500.
CinC H.F. (visual)	RODNEY	1829/26	On present course and speed how long can you continue and still have enough fuel to return to a fueling base at not less than 20 knots?
ARK ROYAL A/C	ARK ROYAL A/C	1840/26	Enemy made good 11 miles, course 110 since 1810.
ComDesFlot6 (visual)	RODNEY	1850/26	If TARTAR and MASHONA stay I would like to leave at 1930 so that I can make Londonderry if necessary.
Ad.	General	1850/26	Weather report from 2100/26 to 0900/27 Area 200 miles from 48° N., 17° W. Wind northwest, strong with squalls—cloudy—showers—visibility over 10 miles reducing at times to 3-7 miles.
Ad.	CinC H.F. S.O.F. H and others	1852/26	Stated that an enemy surface ship was D/F on 12040 kcs at 1625/26 (GMT) 1825 problem time—and was within 25 miles of 47° 40′ N., 17° 20′ W.

From	To	Time Sent/Date	
ARK ROYAL A/C	ARK ROYAL A/C	1854/26	Visibility decreasing in direction of 110° from BISMARCK.
SHEFFIELD	Scapa Radio	1859/26	My 1740—Position now 105°, 12 miles from a position 179°, 39 miles from 49° N., 17° W., course 110.
Ad.	All CinC's and others	1904/26	Estimated U-boat dispositions giving positions. This report indicated 20 German and 4 Italian U-boats on patrol in North Atlantic.
RODNEY (visual)	CinC H.F.	1911/26	Your 1829—RODNEY had 1600 tons of oil on hand at 1800. We use at present speed 23 tons per hour and 19 tons per hour at 20 knots. Clyde and Gibraltar are within my endurance if present course and speed are continued until 0800 tomorrow.
RODNEY (visual)	ComDesFlot6	1911/26	Tell KING GEORGE V your destination as I told him Plymouth. Very much thanks for your assistance.
ComDesFlot6 (visual)	RODNEY	1919/26	Very sorry to have to leave you at the end of the long chase. I still hope for your triumph.
SHEFFIELD	Scapa Radio	1937/26	My 1740—Position now 115° 9 miles from a position 158° 46 miles from 49° N., 17° W., course 115.
S.O.F. H	Ad.	1939/26	Position, course and speed of enemy at 1900— 48° 00′ N., 16° 28′ W., course 110, speed 22. My position, course and speed at 1900—48° 36′ N., 16° 54′ W., course 110, speed 29. Striking Force en route enemy. Above position based on 1500 fix.
RODNEY (visual)	TARTAR	1956/26	Station DD's on KING GEORGE V.
ARK ROYAL A/C	ARK ROYAL A/C	2000/26	My position is 148°, 54 miles from 49° N., 19° W. Enemy bears 110° 6 miles from me. Enemy course 110, speed 20.
RODNEY (visual)	TARTAR	2006/26	Tell CinC Home Fleet how long you think you can stay with us. Take note of strong headwinds.
CinC H.F.	Home Fleet	2024/26	Admiral's reference position at 2000—49° 34′ N., 16° 27′ W.
CinC H.F. (visual)	RODNEY KING GEORGE V	2028/26	Accurate station keeping not necessary in order to save fuel.
RODNEY (visual)	CinC H.F.	2029/26	KING GEORGE V's 22 knots is a bit faster than RODNEY's and we are dropping distance.
ARK ROYAL A/C	ARK ROYAL A/C	2030/26	Enemy BB in position 140°, 60 miles from 49° N., 19° W., course 111, speed 20.
ARK ROYAL A/C	SHEFFIELD	2049/26	If Striking Force not met D/F them in ---- Call sign ----

From	To	Time Sent/Date	
CinC H.F.	S.O.F. H	2054/26	Request aircraft give Destroyer Flotilla 4 visual link with enemy.
ARK ROYAL	All ARK ROYAL A/C	2100/26	My course 020, speed 12.
ARK ROYAL A/C	ARK ROYAL A/C	2100/26	Have attacked enemy with torpedoes. Estimate no hits.
ARK ROYAL A/C	ARK ROYAL A/C	2103/26	Enemy changed course to port.
ARK ROYAL A/C	ARK ROYAL A/C	2109/26	Enemy changed course to starboard.
ARK ROYAL A/C	ARK ROYAL A/C	2111/26	Enemy changed course to starboard.
ARK ROYAL A/C	All ARK ROYAL A/C	2111/26	Enemy changed course to starboard.
SHEFFIELD	ARK ROYAL A/C	2113/26	My 1740—Position now 140°, 8 miles from a position 68°, 12 miles from 48° N., 16° W., course 340.
ARK ROYAL A/C	ARK ROYAL A/C	2115/26	Have attacked enemy with torpedoes. Estimate no hits.
ARK ROYAL A/C	ARK ROYAL A/C	2115/26	Enemy course 090.
ARK ROYAL A/C	ARK ROYAL A/C	2122/26	Enemy course 000.
ARK ROYAL A/C	ARK ROYAL A/C	2128/26	Enemy changed course to port.
ARK ROYAL A/C	ARK ROYAL A/C	2130/26	Enemy course 340.
ARK ROYAL A/C	ARK ROYAL A/C	2130/26	Enemy laying smoke screen.
ARK ROYAL A/C	ARK ROYAL A/C	2135/26	Enemy course 330.
ARK ROYAL A/C	ARK ROYAL A/C	2136/26	Return to base by 2230.
ARK ROYAL A/C	ARK ROYAL A/C	2140/26	Enemy course 020.
SHEFFIELD	Scapa Radio	2140/26	My 1740—Position now 130°, 5 miles from a position 38°, 12 miles from 48° N., 16° W.
S.O.F. H	Ad.	2145/26	Estimate enemy position, course and speed at 2130 as follows—47° 45′ N., 15° 25′ W., course 330, speed 22. My position, course and speed at 2100 48° 17′ N., 15° 50′ W., course 020, speed 20.

From	To	Time Sent/Date	
ARK ROYAL A/C	ARK ROYAL A/C	2153/26	Enemy course 290.
CinC H.F. (visual)	RODNEY	2156/26	Have changed course toward enemy who is steering North.
ARK ROYAL A/C	ARK ROYAL A/C	2158/26	Enemy course 340.
S.O.F. H	CinC H.F.	2205/26	After one more small torpedo bomber attack tonight all torpedoes will be expended.
ARK ROYAL A/C	Designated A/C of ARK ROYAL	2213/26	Carry out trailing.
CinC H.F.	Ad.	2215/26	At 2215 RODNEY with me. My position 49° 10′ N., 15° 29′ W., course 170, speed 21.
CinC H.F. (visual)	RODNEY KING GEORGE V	2222/26	If concentrated gunfire use G/C disregarding sectors except first double after a signal G/C. Fire control frequency ----.
S.O.F. H	CinC H.F.	2225/26	Results torpedo bomber attack—One hit amidships, one possible hit starboard quarter.
ComDesFlot4	ARK ROYAL A/C	2229/26	Report course of enemy.
C.S.1 (in NORFOLK)	CinC H.F.	2230/26	My position 49° 48′ N., 16° 25′ W., course 130, speed 30. Have 30% fuel on hand. Can operate with RODNEY or Force H.
CinC H.F.	Ad.	2238/26	Request a destroyer screen be made available to rendezvous with KING GEORGE V. Lack of fuel may make it necessary for KING GEORGE V and RODNEY to reduce speed on 27th Tuesday in the morning.
S.O.F. H	CinC H.F.	2250/26	Lost touch at 2200.
ZULU	Scapa Radio	2251/26	One battleship bearing 115° 9 miles from 47° 40′ N., 15° 38′ W., course 110.
ZULU	Scapa Radio	2258/26	Enemy changing course to port.
ZULU	Scapa Radio	2259/26	Enemy course 020.
COSSACK (ComDes Flot4)	Ad.	2300/26	Enemy battleship bearing 115°, 7 miles from a position 242°, 19 miles from 48° N., 15° W.
COSSACK	Scapa Radio	2309/26	Enemy course 020.
S.O.F. H	Ad.	2310/26	My 2250—ZULU and COSSACK now in contact. Enemy course 060.
ARK ROYAL A/C	SHEFFIELD	2314/26	Enemy course 025.
COSSACK (D4)	SHEFFIELD	2315/26	Enemy changing course to port.

From	To	Time Sent/Date	
ZULU	Scapa Radio	2315/26	Enemy changing course to port.
COSSACK (D4)	Ad.	2322/26	My 2300. Enemy battleship bearing 70°, 7 miles from a position 233°, 21 miles from 28° N., 15° W., course 340.
ZULU	Scapa Radio	2331/26	Enemy changing course to starboard.
CinC H.F.	ZULU COSSACK	2337/26	EMERGENCY—Fire starshell.
ZULU	Scapa Radio	2338/26	Have lost contact.
A/C "O"	15th Gr.Hd.	2344/26	On large vessel bearing 270°, 2 miles from 47° 45' N., 14° 48' W., course 110.
S.O.F. H	CinC H.F.	2345/26	My 2205 cancelled. Not possible to deliver third torpedo attack tonight. Will deliver dawn torpedo attack tomorrow by 12 aircraft. Am turning west to clear you. My position 48° 42' N., 15° 17' W., based on a fix at 2000.
CinC H.F.	S.O.F. H Ad.	2347/26	My position 48° 46' N., 15° 20' W., course 30, speed 21.
COSSACK (D4)	Ad.	2400/26	Enemy battleship bearing 315°, 6 miles from a position 215°, 18 miles from 48° N., 15° W.
SIKH	Scapa Radio	0001/27	Enemy course 335, speed 12.
SIKH	Scapa Radio	0003/27	Enemy changing course to port.
SIKH	Scapa Radio	0005/27	Enemy changing course to starboard.
SIKH	Scapa Radio	0007/27	Enemy course 350.
CinC H.F.	S.O.F. H Ad.	0009/27	Plan to engage BISMARCK at dawn. He appears badly damaged.
COSSACK (D4)	Scapa Radio	0014/27	Enemy battleship in position 264°, 13 miles from 48° N., 15° W.
MAORI	Scapa Radio	0025/27	Enemy course 230.
CinC H.F.	S.O.F. H	0022/27	Request that you take position not less than 20 miles to southward of BISMARCK. I intend to be westward of him at dawn.
CinC H.F. (visual)	RODNEY	0030/27	Steam at 19 knots.
CinC H.F.	S.O.F. H	0045/27	Report estimated bearing and distance of enemy from you at 2345. Force H proceed southward of enemy.
S.O.F. H	CinC H.F.	0046/27	After BISMARCK was torpedoed she made two complete circles and reduced speed.
MAORI	Scapa Radio	0110/27	Enemy course 040.

From	To	Time Sent/Date	
A/C "O"	15th Gr.Hd.	0115/27	Am still in contact—47° 20' N., 13° 30' W.
CinC H.F.	RODNEY	0121/27	Change course to 270.
ZULU	ComDesFlot4	0122/27	Have completed torpedo attack.
ZULU	Scapa Radio	0127/27	My position 47° 50' N., 15° 32' W. Enemy bears 120°, 3 miles from me. Enemy course 040.
MAORI	ComDesFlot4	0128/27	Attack completed. Enemy was making smoke.
MAORI	ComDesFlot4	0140/27	One hit confirmed. Fire on forecastle.
COSSACK (D4)	DesFlot4	0141/27	COSSACK completed attack—claims one hit.
C.S.1	CinC H.F.	0210/27	Your ---- Will keep to northward in order to flank mark for you. What frequency?
Ad.	CinC H.F.	0213/27	Weather report Bay of Biscay Area—Strong and fresh NW winds—sky cloudy—visibility 12 miles with 1 to 3 miles in showers. Sea rough. Outlook —wind moderating slowly.
SIKH	ComDesFlot4	0234/27	Enemy appears stopped.
SIKH	ComDesFlot4	0235/27	Am in touch by RD/F.
CinC H.F.	ComDesFlot4	0235/27	EMERGENCY—Send your call sign on 210 kcs. Use power.
CinC H.F.	ComDesFlot4	0236/27	Fire starshell every half hour after all destroyer attacks are completed in order to indicate position of enemy. Report by radio when about to fire starshell. My position 49° 09' N., 15° 21' W., course 220, speed 19.
A/C "O"	15th Gr.Hd.	0300/27	Unable to obtain enemy course and speed. Position ----
DORSETSHIRE		0300/27	My position 46° 05' N., 15° 58' W.
COSSACK	Scapa Radio	0340/27	Enemy battleship 284°, 24 miles from 48° N., 15° W.
S.O.F. H	CinC H.F.	0335/27	My position 47° 48' N., 16° 29' W. Starshell bears 100°. At 0500 aircraft for KING GEORGE V will take off. Call sign ---- frequency ---- . This plane will spot for KING GEORGE V.
SIKH	CinC H.F.	0340/27	About to fire starshell. My position 47° 47' N., 15° 25' W.—doubtful.
ComDesFlot4	CinC H.F.	0353/27	The enemy made good between 0240 and 0340 a distance of 8 miles and is still capable of heavy and accurate fire.
A/C "O"	15th Gr.Hd.	0404/27	Have lost contact. Last enemy position observed was 47° 52' N., 12° 50' W., at 0236.

From	To	Time Sent/Date	
ComDesFlot4	CinC H.F.	0415/27	This time I am going to fire a round of high explosive in the approximate position - - the other (corrupt) is not good enough.
CinC H.F. (visual)	RODNEY	0421/27	Give me any bearings of ComDesFlot4 received.
CinC H.F.	DesFlot4	0459/27	Any DD in contact with enemy send call sign on Fleet wave—Use sufficient power for homing.
C.S.1	CinC H.F.	0502/27	My position 48° 24′ N., 15° 19′ W., moving to westward.
RODNEY (visual)	CinC H.F.	0514/27 and 0534/27	Gave D/F bearings of C.S.1—112° at 0511 and 091° at 0529.
C.S.1	Scapa Radio	0515/27	At 0508 detected a possible SS in 48° 26′ N., 15° 30′ W.
CinC H.F.	Scapa Radio	0520/27	Reduce to an absolute minimum retransmission on Fleet wave.
RODNEY (visual)	CinC H.F.	0539/27	Stated A/C from ARK ROYAL calling CinC H.F. on 348.4.
RODNEY (visual)	CinC H.F.	0546/27	SHEFFIELD bearing 255 at 0543.
MAORI	Scapa Radio	0550/27	BISMARCK's position 10°, 24 miles from 48° N., 16° W.
MAORI	Scapa Radio	0604/27	My 0550—Enemy course 260, speed 7.

NOTE: Above message rebroadcasted by Admiralty which said the course was 160°.

From	To	Time Sent/Date	
RODNEY (visual)	CinC H.F.	0606/27	MAORI bore 156 at 0604.
MAORI	Scapa Radio	0618/27	My 0550—Enemy changing course to starboard.
S.O.F. H	CinC H.F.	0620/27	Striking Force expected to arrive at 0715.
MAORI	Scapa Radio	0621/27	My 0550—Enemy course 320.
MAORI	Scapa Radio	0630/27	Enemy battleship 354°, 23 miles from 48° N., 16° W.
C.S.1	Scapa Radio	0632/27	MAORI at 0614 was 187° from me. At that time my position 48° 38′ N., 15° 37′ W.
S.O.F. H	CinC H.F.	0633/27	My 0620—Due to low visibility attack postponed.
RODNEY (visual)	CinC H.F.	0635/27	MAORI bore 148° at 0632.
MAORI	Scapa Radio	0649/27	Enemy course 000, speed 7.
ComDesFlot4	CinC H.F.	0649/27	In contact with enemy.
ComDesFlot4	CinC H.F.	0655/27	Enemy battleship position 286°, 32 miles from 48° N., 15° W.

From	To	Time Sent/Date	
CinC H.F. (visual)	RODNEY	0655/27	At dawn I intend to close and look for enemy.
SIKH	ComDesFlot4	0700/27	Enemy lost in rain squall.
S.O.F. H	CinC H.F.	0700/27	At 0650 MAORI bore 002° by D/F. Bearing second class. At that time I was in 47° 10' N., 15° 45' W.
ComDesFlot4	CinC H.F.	0701/27	Enemy has opened fire.
ComDesFlot4	CinC H.F.	0702/27	Enemy course 340.
Ad.	CinC H.F. A.C.W.A.	0707/27	Stated a number of U-boat signals made during the night. One could have made all the signals. Best guess is that 4 U-boats made signals. Message referred to a previous report which supposedly pertained to SS in general area of BISMARCK.
S.O.F. H	CinC H.F.	0707/27	My 0633—Have cancelled attack due to difficulties in identification of own ships in low visibility.
MAORI	Scapa Radio	0708/27	Enemy bearing 000, distance 12 miles from a position 345°, 26 miles from 48° N., 16° W.
CinC H.F. (visual)	RODNEY	0708/27	Am changing course to look for enemy. Keep station 1200 yards or more as you desire and adjust your bearings. If I do not like the first set-up I may break off the engagement at once. Are you ready to engage?
COSSACK (D4)	CinC H.F.	0711/27	Enemy bearing and distance 302°, 12 miles from —(corrupt groups followed).
ZULU	Scapa Radio	0715/27	BISMARCK's position 48° 13' N., 16° 14' W.
Ad.	CinC H.F. and others	0717/27	Weather report based on 0700 information. Wind NW strong in east, fresh in west. Sky cloudy. Visibility 8-12 miles. Outlook—wind moderating.
COSSACK (D4)	CinC H.F.	0720/27	Enemy changing course to starboard.
CinC H.F. (visual)	RODNEY	0725/27	If opportunity permits fire your torpedoes.
ZULU	Scapa Radio	0730/27	Enemy course 030°.
ZULU	Scapa Radio	0739/27	Enemy course 080°.
ZULU	Scapa Radio	0741/27	Enemy changing course to port.
SIKH	Scapa Radio	0744/27	Enemy course 330°.
COSSACK (D4)	CinC H.F.	0745/27	Enemy making good 330°.
SIKH	Scapa Radio	0746/27	Enemy changing course to port.

From	To	Time Sent/Date	
SIKH	Scapa Radio	0747/27	Enemy course 240°.
NORFOLK (C.S.1)	Scapa Radio	0753/27	EMERGENCY—One enemy battleship in --

Narrative of Action Between H.M.S. Rodney and German Battleship Bismarck on the Morning of Tuesday 27th May 1941[31]

(0737)	(c.080)
(0751)	(c.140)
(0800)	(105)
(0805)	(085 - 7 cab.)
(0826)	(wind 320—force 6-7) (Heavy N.W. swell) (Sun. 0650) (KGV—190°-8 cab.) (Norfolk—093-9.5 mls)
(0827)	(c.175)
(0834)	(c.110)
(0843)	(Sighted Bis.—bearing 122—dist. 12.5 miles steering towards)
0844	Green 005 degrees. Enemy in sight.
0847	Rodney fires first salvo.
0848	King George V fires first salvo.
0849	Enemy replies, 1000 short of Rodney.
(0850)	(Bis. opened fire)
(0851)	(Rodney straddled)
(0851)	(over)

---

[31]This narrative was recorded by a Paymaster Lieutenant, RN, located in the lookout platform above the bridge in H.M.S. Rodney. His only assignment during the action was to record the narrative. This narrative was Enclosure "C" to JHW's Report serial F-1; x-27 dated 1 July 1941. The narrative has been published with commentary from the German perspective by Baron Burkhard von Müllenheim-Rechberg, Battleship Bismarck: A Survivor's Story (Annapolis: U.S. Naval Institute Press, 1980), Appendix "E." The entries in parentheses are additional notes made by JHW in 1941, but not included in his report.

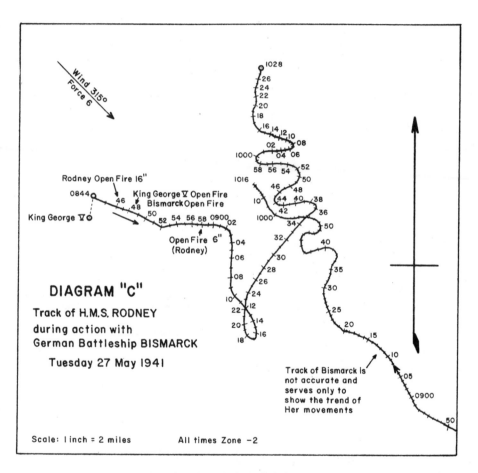

Adapted from chart drawn by Lcdr. G.G.O. Gatacre, R.A.N,
The Navigator of H.M.S. *Rodney*, based on information
available in H.M.S. *Rodney*, June 1941
Enclosure "G" to JHW's Report serial F-1; x-27 of 1 July 1941.

0852	Enemy shell 1000 over
0853	Enemy shell just short starboard side
(0853)	(Turn together 085)
0854	Enemy shell just over port side
(0854-0857)	(Over-range closed rapid -)
0856	Enemy salvoes over
0857	Enemy salvoes over
0858	*Rodney* straddled Enemy, firing steadily, beam on crossing *King George V* bow *Rodney's* secondary armament in action (6″) Main and secondary armament engaging enemy port side.
0902	Hit on *Bismarck's* upper deck (A&B turrets out of action. En. fire erratic) Enemy salvoes short (6 Torp - 11000 - no hits obs)
0905	Enemy shell 1000 over
0906	Enemy shell 300 over
0910	Our salvoes falling well together on astern of *BISMARCK* Enemy turning away firing at *King George V*
0913	Good straddle on *Bismarck* which was completely obscured.
0914	*Rodney's* shots falling well over
0915	*Bismarck* passing down *Rodney's* port side
0916	*Rodney* turning hard to starboard, enemy ship passing under *Rodney's* stern.
0917	Good straddles on *Bismarck*, one hit observed, enemy firing very intermittently and inaccurately.
0919	Salvo from Bismarck's after turrets. (Steady on 350—opened fire to stbd. *Bismarck* on same course range 8,600 yds.—*Bis.* shifted to *Rodney*—only X turret in action.)
0921	Good straddle on *Bismarck*

0922	BISMARCK fires after turrets at *Rodney*. Near miss on *Rodney's* starboard side.
0923	*Bismarck* hit (- run to Northward—range closed frm 8- to 4000 yds. En. ceased fire. large spread)
0924	Enemy still firing after turrets.
0924	Enemy turning towards RODNEY.
0926	BISMARCK straddled.
0927	Salvo from enemy's forward guns.
0928	Enemy turning towards RODNEY Enemy hit abaft funnel.
0929	BISMARCK on parallel course hit again.
0930	Another hit.
0931	Enemy fired after turrets.
0932	Enemy still on parallel course to RODNEY range 2 miles.
0937	Green 040 degs. Ship, probably DORSETSHIRE in sight opens fire.
0938	BISMARCK passes astern and comes up on port side distance still two miles.
0940	Enemy on fire fore and aft.
0941	Enemy hit again forward turning towards RODNEY.
0942	BISMARCK's "B" turret on fire.
0944	Enemy passes astern of RODNEY. RODNEY turning to starboard engages enemy starboard side.
0946	BISMARCK hit at least four times during this run on starboard side and has not herself fired.
0948	Old tactics. Enemy passing astern of RODNEY. Two more hits seen during last two minutes.
0949	RODNEY turning hard to port. Enemy engaged port side.
0951	Engagement continuing port side.
0955	Torpedo fired port side. No results observed.

0957	Torpedo fired port side and seen to leap out of the water two-thirds of the way across.
0958	Torpedo hit BISMARCK amidships starboard side.
0959	Enemy turning to starboard.
1000	Engagement on starboard side, enemy turning away.
1002	County Class cruiser, perhaps NORFOLK on RODNEY's starboard bow attacking enemy. DORSETSHIRE(?) on RODNEY's port bow.
1003	Lull in action. BISMARCK well alight, clouds of black smoke from fire aft.
1005	BISMARCK has been slowly turning around and is now passing down RODNEY's starboard side 1½ miles away smoking heavily.
1006	Enemy hit starboard amidships. KING GEORGE V, 5 miles astern, firing as opportunity offers.
1007	BISMARCK passes astern. RODNEY turns hard to port engagement continuing on port side. Much black smoke from the enemy.
1011	Salvo from RODNEY blows pieces off stern of BISMARCK and sets up a fire with greyish white smoke.
1012	KING GEORGE V ahead of BISMARCK.
1013	Salvo from RODNEY explodes amidships enemy.
1014	Big flames for three seconds from enemy "A" turret. Flash of exploding shell on enemy spotting top.
1016	KING GEORGE V approaching RODNEY on port bow, turns on parallel course and fires at BISMARCK from "Y" turret.
1019	Enemy smoking heavily. RODNEY's guns will not bear.
1021	BISMARCK dead astern of RODNEY.
1023	Red 145 degs. Six aircraft. Driving rain from port bow. Red 145. An unidentified ship firing at aircraft.
1026	Green 130 degs. County Class cruiser (DORSETSHIRE). BISMARCK still smoking heavily passing to port well astern.
1027	Sudden red flash visible from enemy's stern.

1028	Enemy ship now about five miles astern.
1029	Enemy a smoking mass bows on, DORSETSHIRE crossing her bows.
1038	BISMARCK disappears in a cloud of smoke, sinking, bow or stern visible momentarily sticking out of the water.
1039	BISMARCK sank.

Naval Messages Received in H.M.S. Rodney, 0900-2400 27 May 1941

From	To	Time Sent/Date	
Ad.	CinC H.F. and others	0907/27	A heavy enemy air attack is anticipated.
Ad.	CinC H.F.	0920/27	Roof of BISMARCK turrets and gun shields painted bright yellow.
S.O.F. H	CinC H.F.	0922/27	Striking Force has just left.
C.S.1	CinC H.F.	0940/27	Have stopped flank marking—RENOWN is coming up from the southward.
S.O.F. H	CinC H.F.	0947/27	ARK ROYAL and SHEFFIELD detached. I am heading for enemy from the southward. What is your position, course and speed? Mine is 47° 20′ N., 15° 53′ W., course 350, speed 17.
S.O.F. H	CinC H.F.	0953/27	In view of Admiralty's 0909 I have rejoined ARK ROYAL.
CinC H.F. (visual)	RODNEY	1011/27	Course 27, speed 19.
S.O.F. H	DORSETSHIRE	1022/27	Torpedo BISMARCK at close range.
S.O.F. H	CinC H.F.	1025/27	My 0922—Have you disposed of enemy?
CinC H.F.	S.O.F. H	1028/27	Have had to suspend for fuel.
DORSET-SHIRE	CinC H.F.	1034/27	BISMARCK is sinking.
DORSET-SHIRE	CinC H.F.	1039/27	Enemy is sunk.
C.S.1	CinC H.F.	1042/27	Am trying to pick up survivors.
CinC H.F.	S.O.F. H	1045/27	Cannot get her to sink with guns.
DORSET-SHIRE	CinC H.F.	1056/27	Am picking up survivors. Too rough to lower boats. Hundreds of men in the water.
CinC H.F.	Ad.	1101/27	BISMARCK sunk in 48° 09′ N., 16° 07′ W. My position 48° 23′ N., 15° 58′ W., course 027°, speed 17, no destroyers in company.[32]

[32]"From the time the Battle Fleet left Scapa (2300/22 May) until the sinking of the *Bismarck* (1100/27 May) about 380 cypher messages (including both routine & operational signals) were received in H.M.S. *Rodney*. This amounts to a total of about 25,000 groups." Note by JHW, June 1941.

From	To	Time Sent/Date	
DORSET-SHIRE	CinC H.F.	1107/27	I torpedoed BISMARCK on each side before she sank. She had stopped but her colors were still flying.
CinC H.F. (visual)	RODNEY	1110/27	Change course to 230°.
DORSET-SHIRE (visual)	CinC H.F.	1146/27	While picking up survivors a suspicious object was sighted which might have been an SS. I therefore proceeded with MAORI to rejoin you.
Ad.	A161 (122A)	1316/27	BISMARCK sunk at 1101.
C.S.1	CinC H.F. Ad.	1345/27	Seems fairly certain as established from independent witnesses that three German ships were in company when originally sighted. Rear ship smaller, likely a destroyer, which turned northeast parallel to NORFOLK. Definitely only two German ships present when BISMARCK engaged HOOD.

Personal Diary, 27 May 1941

. . . DD's attacked (3 DD's made independent attacks) 2 hits claimed. At sunrise—weather cloudy. DD's still shadowing. At 0708 we headed for *Bismarck*. Sighted *Bis* at 0843 At 0847 we opened fire. 1-15" later *K.G.V.* opened fire. *Bismarck* & ourselves closed 27 minutes later *Bismarck*'s fire erratic. We closed to 2750 yds. & continued to fire silencing *Bismarck*. At 1039 *Bismarck* sank. *K.G.V.* & ourselves headed north—Big show over. Second *Bismarck* salvo fractured hull above armor plate and at superstructure just forward of bridge particularly the forward anti-aircraft control area. Fortunately no one injured. How lucky we were if the second salvo landed about 20 yds. further aft our entire bridge structure would have been pierced & probably wrecked with the captain and other key personnel . . . .[33] The executive officer would be C.O. & yours truly . . . would assist him in accordance with Capt. Dalrymple-Hamiltons desires.

Captain Dalrymple-Hamilton presented me with *Rodney* plaque . . . in afternoon saying many thanks Wellings for all your assistance during an eventful week.

H.M.S. Rodney *Preliminary Gunnery Report of Action, 27 May 1941*[34]

NOTE: The RODNEY has three 16" triple gun turrets. All 16" turrets are located in the forward part of the ship and are named "A," "B" and "X" turrets in order from forward to aft. "B" turret is the high turret. The secondary battery consists of three 6" twin turrets on each side. The twin turrets are numbered from forward to aft on each side as follows: Port side—P1, P2, P3; Starboard side—S1, S2, S3. The long range A.A. guns consist of three 4.7" single mount guns on each side. These guns were not fired during the action with the BISMARCK.

---

[33]"Immediately after the Bismarck sank I inspected the damage from the shell fragments of the Bismarck's second salvo when two 15" shells landed in the water about twenty yards short of the Rodney on our starboard bow. I was certain we were indeed most fortunate to have received so little damage from these two 15" shells . . . . " JHW MS. *Reminiscences*, p. 233

[34]Enclosure "E" to JHW's Report, serial F-1; x-27 dated 1 July 1941.

1. Total number of rounds of 16″ fired—378.

    Total number of rounds of 6″ fired—706.

(a) "A" turret fired a total of 104 rounds.
        Left gun fired 36,
        Centre gun fired 46,
        Right gun fired 22.

(b) "B" turret fired a total of 144 rounds.
        Left gun fired 45,
        Centre gun fired 44,
        Right gun fired 52.

(c) "X" turret fired a total of 130 rounds.
        Left gun fired 44,
        Centre gun fired 42,
        Right gun fired 44.

(d) Each 6″ twin turret fired the following number of rounds:
        S1 - 128,   P1 - 93
        S2 - 154,   P2 - 97
        S3 - 160,   P3 - 74

2. In salvo fire the RODNEY fires double salvos. The first salvo consisting of 5 guns—wing guns of "A" turrets plus the center gun of "B" turret, the second salvo consisting of 4 guns—the center guns of "A" and "X": turrets plus the wing guns of "B" turret. In broadside fire all guns of all turrets that are loaded and can bear on the target fire simultaneously.

    (a) A summary of the 16″ rounds fired by the salvo method and by the broadside method is as follows:

    Salvo firing:—

        Number of single gun salvos - 6
        Number of two gun salvos - 22
        Number of three gun salvos - 41
        Number of four gun salvos - 28
        Number of five gun salvos - 6
        Number of six gun salvos -   1
                            Total - 104

    Broadside firing:—

        Number of eight gun salvos - 1
        Number of seven gun salvos - 3
        Number of six gun salvos - 1
        Number of five gun salvos - 2
        Number of three gun salvos - 1
        Number of two gun salvos - 1
                            Total - 9

NOTE: Since double salvos are used in broadside firing 5 and 4 gun salvoes should be fired alternately provided all turrets can bear on the target and all guns in each turret are ready to fire. Under the same conditions in broadside firing each salvo should consist of 9 guns. In the action with the BISMARCK "X" turret could only bear on the target on 6 out of the first 25 salvoes. After the 25th salvo "X" could not bear on 9 occasions, making a total of 28 salvoes or broadside that "X" turret could not bear on the target.

3. At the end of the action the following guns were out of action: Right gun of "A" turret completely, caused by a jammed tilting tray. Left gun of "B" turret very temporarily, caused by the lower cordite hoist being "double loaded" when loaded cage was lowered. Center gun of "B" turret temporarily, due to two shells and no cordite.

* * * *

Statement of Chief Petty Officer Miller, USN.[35]

ENEMY ACTION

The ship received four (4) hits—all 5.9″ shells.

Damage from these hits were very minor, no structural damage being sustained whatsoever.

One (1) hit in H.A. Director, causing a small hole in the bulkhead—no damage.

One (1) hit in the starboard Marine compartment, causing a 6″ hole in the starboard side of the ship—above water line—no damage.

One (1) hit in a stateroom just abaft of the conning tower, causing a small hole by splinter—no damage.

One (1) hit in the CPO mess, starboard side, causing a 6″ hole, above the water line—no damage other than to three lockers containing personal clothing.

OWN ACTION

Damage sustained from contusion of broadsides was very considerable, causing undue discomfort to the personnel and much work on their part to make compartments habitable.

Tile decking in washrooms, water closets and heads were ruptured throughout the ship. Urinals were blown off bulkheads, water pipes broken, and heads flooded.

Longitudinal beams were broken and cracked in many parts of the ship having to be shored. (Note: ship constructed with longitudinal beams instead of athwarthships as is the case in practically all ships.) The overhead decking ruptured and many bad leaks were caused by bolts and rivets coming loose. All compartments on the main deck had water flooding the decks. The British navy does not use swabs but wet rags to mop up any excess water, not only requiring considerable more man hours but also not accomplishing an efficient job as a swab.

Cast iron water mains were ruptured and in many instances broke, flooding compartments.

Electric lighting in compartments was left on during the action. All electric lights were disintegrated and bulbs and sockets snapped off the leads causing live wires to be existent throughout the ship.

Bulkheads, furniture, lockers and fittings were blown loose causing undue damage to permanent structures when the ship rolled.

---

[35]Miller was a passenger in H.M.S. *Rodney* returning to the United States.

Personal Diary, 28 May 1941
. . . Headed for Greenock. Two air attacks during day.—Were not pressed home.— Still talking about the big battle. What an event!! Certainly had my ring side seat. Collecting data. Should have a good story.

Naval Message, H.M.S. Rodney to CinC, Home Fleet, 28 May 1941
The Captain Officers and Ships Company of *Rodney* would like to congratulate their Commander in Chief on the very successful termination of a long and at times disappointing hunt. They are very glad to have been snatched back just in time to take part in the operation which entirely makes up for the *GNEISENAU* disappointment.[36]

Naval Message, CinC, Home Fleet to H.M.S. Rodney
Thank you very much for your message which I appreciate deeply, the sinking of the *Bismarck* may have an effect on the war as a whole out of all proportion to the loss of the enemy of a battleship. No one was more pleased than myself that the *Rodney* had the opportunity to play such an effective part in the operations. It was only what I expected but the *Rodney* like all units of the Fleet did exactly what I wanted them to do without signalled instructions from me. The hits scored with your torpedoes must have much encouraged *Bismarck*'s sinking feeling and I think it is the only case of effective use of torpedoes by a capital ship. I congratulate your Engine Room department on their extremely fine work in maintaining such high speed over so long a period and under such difficult conditions.

Naval Message, H.M.S. Rodney to CinC, Home Fleet, 28 May 1941
. . . Thank you very much for your signal which I have read to the Ships Company and it is very highly appreciated. We all feel it was most fitting that the *Rodney* should have been in action for the first time under the eye of her former Captain.[37]

Report of Commander L.P. Skipworth, R.N., Commanding Officer, H.M.S. TARTAR[38]
I have the honour to submit the following letter of proceedings covering the movements of H.M. Ship under my command from 0720 on 27th May 1941 until 1545 on 29th May and those of H.M.S. "MASHONA" until her loss on 28th May.

2. At 0720 on Tuesday 27th May on receipt of instructions from Commander-in-Chief, Home Fleet to proceed in execution of previous orders I took H.M.S. "MASHONA" under my orders and altered course to the Eastward with the intention of fuelling at Plymouth.

3. At 0745 it was seen that H.M.S. "KING GEORGE V" and H.M.S. "RODNEY" had turned to the Eastward and it was realized that action with BISMARCK was imminent. Accordingly course was altered so as to keep to the Northward of the action but in V/S touch in case we were required. Both ships were maneuvered so as to keep clear of H.M.S. "NORFOLK" and remained in that area until the action was broken off at 1024.

---

[36]Between 8-10 October 1939, *Rodney* with other ships of the Home Fleet attempted unsuccessfully to intercept *Gneisenau* when she appeared to be making a break out into the Atlantic from the Kattegat.

[37]Sir John Tovey commanded H.M.S. *Rodney*, 1932-34.

[38]Dated 31 May. Addressed to "Commander-in-Chief, Home Fleet, thro' Rear Admiral (D) Home Fleet. Copy to Captain 6th D.F."

4.   At that time course was altered to the North Eastward. At 1730 it was decided to proceed to Londonderry instead of Plymouth, the former being only eighty miles further.

5.   At 0830 on 28th May a four-engined F.W. Condor was sighted astern evidently shadowing. Other aircraft appeared almost immediately and the first attack took place at about 0840.

6.   Avoiding action was taken on each occasion but the shortage of fuel rendered high speed for long periods impossible.

7.   Aircraft taking part with H.E. III's and the majority of bombs appeared to be of about 250 lbs.

8.   At 0839 the first enemy aircraft report was originated.

9.   There were seldom less than five aircraft in sight at a time. Attacks continued and at about 0915 "MASHONA," a mile on my starboard beam, was straddled and received a hit port side abreast the bridge.

10.   At about this time two Town Class Destroyers were seen to the Westward and were ordered to close.

11.   At about 10 o'clock an aircraft was being engaged on the port beam flying from right to left when one round from the 4" mounting scored a hit. Pieces were clearly seen to fall from the aircraft also a trail of smoke. The aircraft flew on for half a minute before she dived towards the sea, the volume of smoke increasing. On striking the sea there was a large amount of smoke in the middle of which one wing of the aircraft could be clearly seen.

12.   Details of attacks . . . are contained in Appendix II.

13.   There was a pause in the attacks from about 1030 until 1230 during which period rescue operations were carried out. Shadowing aircraft were, however, still in attendance and a renewal of attacks were expected at any time.

14.   "MASHONA" commenced abandoning ship at about 1030, conditions of Sea and Swell 22. Wind from N.E.

15.   A separate report on the life saving operations containing recommendations based on experience is attached (Appendix I). [not printed].

16.   In all the following numbers were rescued: —

TARTAR	7 Officers	120 ratings.
SHERWOOD	2 Officers	54 ratings.
ST CLAIR	4 Officers	8 ratings.

In addition one officer and ten ratings died from exposure after rescue and were buried at sea.

17.   Rescue operations were completed by 1150 and after a torpedo fired by "TARTAR" had missed "ST CLAIR" was ordered to sink her. "MASHONA" had by now capsized and was lying bottom up with about 3 feet freeboard.

18.   "SHERWOOD" was stationed one mile on the Port beam of "TARTAR" and course was shaped for SLYNE HEAD.

19.   Air attacks were renewed at 1330 and continued on a heavy scale until 1700. At about 1615 an aircraft was seen to come down in flames about 10 miles astern. This was presumably the one shot down by our own fighters. No fighter aircraft had been seen up to this time.

20.   "ST CLAIR" rejoined at 1715 after sinking "MASHONA" and was stationed one mile on Starboard beam of "TARTAR."

21.   At about 1700 heavy rain commenced accompanied by thunder and these conditions assisted materially in keeping enemy aircraft away.

22.   At 1915 the first Hudson arrived and all was quiet until 2230 when an H.E. III was sighted approaching from astern. The Hudson was informed by Aldis Lamp and immediately gave chase. The enemy turned away and was eventually lost over the land.

23.   There were no further incidents.

24.   A signal T.O.O. 2305/28 to N.O.I./C Londonderry reporting our E.T.A.[39] and requesting the hospital drifter, water and provisions on arrival was passed to Whitehall W/T at 0130, but was not received at Londonderry and no arrangements were made for the transfer of the wounded to hospital.

25.   At 0620/29, "TARTAR," "SHERWOOD" and "ST CLAIR" secured to the oiler "PETROPHALT" at Moville. Survivors were then transferred to "TARTAR" for onward passage to Greenock and the wounded to "SHERWOOD" who was ordered to proceed to Londonderry to land them, there still being no signs of a hospital boat.

26.   At 1100/29 "TARTAR" proceeded at 30 knots securing at Gourock Pier at 1545 where survivors were landed.

27.   The bearing of the Ship's Company throughout these attacks was in keeping with the best traditions of the Service.

H.M.S. TARTAR'S APPENDIX II TO LETTER OF PROCEEDINGS DATED 31st MAY, 1941

. . .

2.   Owing to the frequency and intensity of attacks this report is of necessity made largely from memory, no one having the time to record details while they were taking place.

3.   Weather conditions were as follows. Wind force 3 from North East. Sea and swell 23. Cloud conditions varied considerably, the sky at times being clear and at others heavy cloud down to about 4000 feet.

4.   In the majority of attacks aircraft approached from astern, quarter or beam. No attacks were made from before the beam. Attacks were either level bombing or shallow dive bombing, bomb-release height being about 3,000 feet.

5.   It is believed that all attacking aircraft were H.E. III's. Occasionally a F.W. Condor was seen shadowing astern. It is estimated that about 50 aircraft took part in the attacks over a period of 13 hours.

6.   It is not possible to say how many bombs were dropped altogether but 160 bombs were dropped close to "TARTAR," of these two sticks of five each failed to explode. One of these sticks was within 20 yards of the ship's side.

7.   Bombs were mostly dropped in sticks of five. They exploded on impact.

8.   Full speed and full helm was used to confuse bomb aiming, the helm being put over just before bomb release position was attained. At least 5 sticks were avoided in this manner which would otherwise have fallen dangerously close.

9.   Every gun was used, the 4.7" in controlled fire and the 4" and close range weapons firing independently. 290 rounds of 4.7", 255 rounds of 4", 1,000 rounds of pom pom and 750 rounds of .5 machine gun ammunition were fired.

10.   No damage was caused to "TARTAR."

11.   The following points of interest which have already been communicated verbally to R.A.D.[40] were noted:

a.   There was a tendency for bombs to be released late. Most misses were overs.

b.   Attacks were all from abaft the beam.

---

[39]Estimated time of arrival.

[40]Rear Admiral Destroyers.

c.   Attacks were **well pressed home despite heavy fire.** Very few aircraft were turned away though the gunfire evidently upset their aim.

d.   There was a tendency to open fire too soon, although the aircraft were in range. In a prolonged attack of this nature ammunition must be husbanded to avoid running out. This tendency was checked in the later attacks.

12.   At about 1000 "TARTAR" was engaging one H.E. III on the port beam at about 3,000 yards range when one round probably from the 4 inch mountings was seen to hit. Pieces could be seen falling away from the machine and a trail of smoke was noticed. This machine flew on for about half a minute when it was seen to dive towards the sea, the smoke increasing. On striking the water a large cloud of smoke appeared and one wing could be seen sticking up. None of the crew bailed out. This aircraft was originally reported as having been shot down at 1025 but subsequent investigation shows that the time was nearer 1000.

13.   Several other machines were thought to have been hit but there is insufficient evidence to justify claiming any of them as "damaged."

14.   The following remarks from the Commanding Officer, H.M.S. "MASHONA" are of interest.

15.   The report by "TARTAR" . . . is the collated report on both ships.

16.   Similar avoiding action to that taken by "TARTAR" was taken in "MASHONA."

17.   With reference to paragraph 5 the following difference was noticed in the attack made on MASHONA in which the ship was hit.

18.   The stick dropped consisted of six bombs, the centre two of which appeared to be about 250 lbs. the remainder about 100 lbs. The 4th bomb, which hit, came down approximately 200 feet out of the line of the remainder and in the direction of the ship's turn. The flight appeared normal and the impression gained was that it was "aimed off" at the last moment as the flight appeared normal.

19.   The deflection may have been due to a bent fin but it is suggested that a pattern of this kind with a deliberate "aim off" would be extremely difficult to avoid.

Personal Diary, 29 May-6 June 1941

29 May—Arrived at Greenock at 0310—Stayed up until we anchored. Ashore at 1400 called Embassy said I was O.K. Back to ship at 1530. Went aboard *Neptune*[41] at night for 1½ hours. Turned in at midnight. Heard lots of stories. Wonder when we will get home.—I want to get started. However doubt if we will for a few days.

30 May—At Greenock—visited DD *Tartar* also heavy cruiser *Norfolk* heard more good stories. Decided to go to London tonight from Glasgow at 2130. Made all arrangements. Caught train on time. Doubt if ship will leave before Tuesday—3 June—. . . .

31 May—Arrived at London at 0800. Breakfast at Embassy. All the officers glad to see me back—safe & sound. Told my story to Capt. Lockwood & Ad. Ghormley, plus most of the staff in Ad. Ghormleys office. Very busy. Hair cut at Selfridges. Lunch at United Services Club with Jack Griffin, Capt. B.L. Moore (RN)[42] and Comdr. Currie

---

[41]*Leander*-class cruiser, 7175 tons, built 1933, lost 19 December 1941. She had also participated in the *Bismarck* operation.

[42]Barrington Lungley Moore.

(RN). At club saw Vice Admiral Whitworth, Admiral Little[43] & Ad. Pound[44]—One first Sea Lord & Two second sea Lords. They listened very carefully to my story of the chase & battle. Ad. Whitworth had left *Hood* only three days before it sailed on the fateful trip. Dinner with MacDonald at Connaught—Left London on 1915 train for Glasgow. Have two more pouch boxes—total now 13+3 trunks. Capt. Lockwood sent a dispatch to Navy Dept. saying that I had been in the final engagement with *Bismarck* and that I would have a full report of the operations.—Sent a cable to Dad—"Cheerio, feel fine, expect arrive home second week of June."

1 June—Arrived Glasgow at 0715—breakfast at station hotel (90 cents) for coffee, toast, one egg, & 1 piece of bacon. Truck met me to carry the two extra pouch boxes to Greenock—put same aboard drifter & arrived at *Rodney* at 1100. Just in time to see the First Lord come aboard & listen to his speech to the crew of *Rodney*. He had dinner in Wardroom & left immediately afterwards—his name—Alexander[45]—looked like a typical American politician of the organization class. Nap in p.m.

2 June—Greenock—aboard in a.m.—Ship still having trouble getting all its replacement ammunition—16" cordite due to arrive this afternoon. Went ashore at 1545 walked to battery park to see Catalinas—Met Ens. Robertson, USNR, a flyer—talked with him, then went to the Bay Hotel for a drink. Met Mrs. Madden, Abercrombie, Meyerick & Bird. Took them to dinner at the Bay. *Birmingham* due in tonight. Funny how the buzz gets around. Caught 2300 boat back to ship & bed.

3 June—Greenock—*Birmingham* at anchor close aboard. Went over at 0820 & told officers where wives were located. John Dathan invited me to lunch. Returned to *Rodney* at 0900. Sent Miller to *Tartar* to get official report of bombing of *Tartar* while enroute to Greenock after the battle. Luncheon in *Birmingham*. Glad to see them all again. They are about to make another WS convoy trip. Ad. & Mrs. Little, Air Vice Marshall Harris,[46] Mrs. Harris & 20 month old baby, Captain Au—Ewing & Capt. Morgan,[47] Comdr. Blamy[48] & Capt. .... of the Army arrived for transportation to the states. We sailed at 2030. Hope we will get across this time. Speed to be 19 knots, making good 17 with zigzagging. Distance to Halifax by route ordered *2750 miles*.[49] Estimated time of arrival 1200—10 June. Farewell to the British Isles.

4 June . . . sea calm—sky overcast. Steamship *Windsor Castle*[50] in company—screened by four DD's—one of which is *Eskimo*. All distinguished guests in Wardroom

---

[43]Sir Charles James Colebrooke Little (1882-1973). Second Sea Lord and Chief of Naval Personnel, 1938-41; Head British Joint Staff Mission in Washington, 1941-42. Little was relieved by Whitworth as Second Sea Lord.

[44]Sir (Alfred) Dudley (Pickman Rogers) Pound (1877-1943). First Sea Lord and Chief of Naval Staff, 1939-1943.

[45]Albert Victor Alexander (1885-1965). First Lord of the Admiralty, 1929-31, 1940-45, 1945-46. Minister of Defence 1947-50; Later, first Earl Alexander of Hillsborough.

[46]Arthur Harris (1892-   ). Head, Royal Air Force delegation to the USA, 1941. Later Commander in Chief, Bomber Command, 1942-45. Marshall of the RAF, 1945; Baronet, 1953. See his comments on this journey in Sir A. Harris, *Bomber Offensive* (London: Collins, 1947), pp. 59-62.

[47]Llewellyn Vaughan Morgan (1891-1969). Later Admiral; Admiral Superintendent, H.M. Dockyard, Portsmouth.

[48]Glendenning Blamey, Paymaster Commander.

[49]The distance by the most direct route between the Clyde and Halifax is 2,419 miles.

[50]*Windsor Castle*, Built 1922; 19,100 tons. Union Castle Mail S.S. Co.

before lunch for cocktail & to meet the officers.—Quite strange to see a 20 month old baby in the wardroom of a BB during wartime—or any time. On bridge part of morning—worked on report in afternoon—plus a 1.5 hour nap—on bridge at night. Cocktails with Air Vice Marshall Harris & his wife before dinner.—All is well so far—*Nelson* overhauled a German merchant ship which scuttled itself—*Nelson* north of Azores with a SL convoy.

5 June— . . . DD's still acting as A/S screen for us—*Windsor Castle* astern—All is well—No sign of submarines. Still considerable talk about the battle. Again had cocktails with Air Vice Marshall Harris & his wife plus a Capt. Morgan[51] who is going to Halifax to take command of *Revenge.* Sea calm.

6 June . . . Sea increased but far from rough. Destroyers left at dark today. We were in 25 West [longitude] when they left. Will be about 29 West at 0800 tomorrow. Submarines not concentrated near us according to reports. At our speed—19 knots & zigzagging it will be difficult for any of them to get in an attack. Hope to start work soon on report of battle—waiting for ship to decide just what happened.

Naval Message from H.M.S. Eskimo, 6 June 1941
We all wish you a well earned leave and are very glad you saw the kill after the best hunt of the season. (1944)

Naval Message to H.M.S. Eskimo
Appreciate your 1944. Till we meet again Au Revoir and best of luck to all the Bangor Boys. (1959)

Personal Diary, 7-12 June 1941
7 June . . . Sea moderate. Got assembled the various letters—notes—cables & pictures. Spent considerable time on bridge getting information on battle. Talked with captain of *Rodney* who promised me a copy of his official report & gave me permission to read & copy all the dispatches . . . nap in afternoon.

8 June . . . Went to mass. Ship has a catholic chaplain & a Church of England Chaplain. Worked on reports & scrap book. Sea moderating.

9 June . . . All is well due in Halifax tomorrow. Worked on reports—getting excited over thought of calling Dolly and home on the phone. Worked on reports.

10 June . . . Ship made a perfect landfall. Arrived Halifax at 1330. Quite a thrill but not half as great as when we will arrive in Boston. Took a nap in p.m. Went ashore at 1830 walked to Nova Scotia hotel. At 1900 put in a call to Boston for Dolly & home—. No trouble getting through . . . Had dinner at Lord Nelson hotel—a grand meal. Walked back to Nova Scotia Hotel—Saw the Captain, Nav. & Mr. Downey and walked back to ship with them at 2210. After a drink in the Wardroom—turned in—but too much excitement—Had trouble getting to sleep.

11 June—At Halifax—Went ashore at 1230 with the idea of getting a haircut & calling Boston to arrange for pouch mail to be sent to Wash. . . . & to straighten out the question of anchoring at 2200 Boston time in President Roads which the captain does not like—neither do I. After talking with American consul decided that the phone censor would not let me carry on my business. However I did call the Navy Yard at Boston, Captain Roland Grady[52] from East Boston, and hope I squared away the pilot question without revealing anything. Called at the dockyard for a half hour—Saw

---

[51]L.V. Morgan, previously noted.

[52]Ronan Calistus Grady (1883-1945). U.S. Naval Academy, 1906; Naval War College, 1927. Captain of the Boston Navy Yard.

Comdr. Carney[53] & Woodbridge[54] plus a Captain McHenry[55]—All U.S.N. All they wanted to hear was my story of the battle.[56] Back in *Rodney* at 1545—ship sailed for Boston at 1630. At 1845 I talked to the crew via ship's radio—on Boston—I hope it was O.K.—(a 15 min. talk) . . . .

OFFICERS LISTENING TO THE RADIO IN H.M.S. *Rodney,* 1941
[Photo: Imperial War Museum: A2129]

Remarks on the Ship's Radio, 11 June 1941

. . . I am very pleased that you and other ships are refitting in American ports. First of all it will relieve the work load in your own dock yards and second it will give you an opportunity to see and know at first hand the American people at work and at play. It will also give them a chance to know you. I am sure they will, as I do, like you and admire your courage and determination. Such visits as the RODNEY's to U.S. ports will create a mutual understanding and respect between the people of our respective countries that will endure long after Hitler has been defeated.

In conclusion I wish to express my sincere appreciation and the appreciation of both the U.S.N. CPO's on board for the many kindnesses we have received since we came aboard the RODNEY for a quick passage home. I was particularly fortunate to be with

---

[53]Robert Bostwick Carney (1895-   ). U.S. Naval Academy, 1916; Later Admiral; Chief of Naval Operations, 1953-55.

[54]Edmund Tyler Wooldridge, U.S. Naval Academy, 1919. Later Admiral; Commander, Second Fleet, 1954-55; Commandant, National War College, 1956-58.

[55]Harry Dickson McHenry (1889-1969). U.S. Naval Academy, 1911; Naval War College, 1936.

[56]All three men were assigned to the staff of Radm. A.L. Bristol, Commander, Support Force, Atlantic Fleet. They were in Halifax to study convoy procedures.

you in the chase and battle with the BISMARCK. My cruise with your navy is just about over—your cruise in the U.S. is about to begin. When you leave I hope you will be, as I am tonight—sincerely sorry to say goodbye and best of luck.

Personal Diary, 11-12 June 1941

[11 June] . . . Turned in at 2200—As tomorrow will be a big day.

12 June—Up at 0630—to mass at 0645—Holy day—Ascension day—cleared up paper work in a.m.—haircut—which I did not get yesterday. Suits pressed, etc. All ready for Boston.

Note from Lieut. Comdr. G.G.O. Gatacre, Navigator, H.M.S. Rodney, 12 June 1941

America in sight!!

Cape Cod lighthouse and the Pilgrim's monument at Provincetown were picked up at 25 miles. Can't make out your lady yet!!

Vice Admiral Sir Frederick Dalrymple-Hamilton, RN, greeting
Captain J.H. Wellings, USN, in Pearl Harbor, Hawaii, 1949.

"When Captain Russell Grenfell's book *The Bismarck Episode* was
published in 1948, I received a copy with this handwritten inscription on the inside cover.
To Captain J.H. Wellings, U.S. Navy
In gratitude for his assistance during an eventful week..
From F. Dalrymple-Hamilton."

J.H.W. MS. *Reminiscences*, p. 235.

Reminiscences, 12-14 June 1941[57]

... When we sighted Boston Lightship, Graves Light and Boston Lighthouse, followed by Captain Ben Smith, the Boston Navy Yard Pilot, boarding the *Rodney* from a Navy Yard tugboat just before we entered the Boston Harbor main ship channel, I really became homesick. I knew every buoy in the channel, and almost every rock on the bottom from my younger days sailing and racing sloops in Boston harbor years before I entered Annapolis.

Shortly after 11:00 p.m. the *Rodney* was berthed very snugly and quickly without any difficulty by Captain Ben Smith at the South Boston Annex of the Navy Yard. I was not surprised to see Mrs. Wellings looking radiant and beautiful on the pier at the foot of the bow, when the navy yard workmen moved it into proper position after the *Rodney* secured her engines and mooring lines.

Mrs. Wellings, our three year old daughter Anne and I enjoyed tea the following day with a group of *Rodney* officers aboard ship. A marine security detail from the Boston Navy Yard assumed custody of all my thirteen large boxes and three trunks of confidential and secret material from the time the seal was broken on the doors of the *Rodney* storeroom, until they arrived in the office of Naval Intelligence in Washington, D.C.

I said goodbye to the *Rodney* and to His Majesty's Service when Captain Dalrymple-Hamilton and all the *Rodney* officers aboard the ship came to the gangway to bid me farewell on the afternoon of June 14, 1941. As I walked down the gangway of the *Rodney* I knew in my heart that one of the most instructive and happiest highlights of my navy career had come to a conclusion.

---

[57]JHW, MS. *Reminiscences*, pp. 254-55.

INDEX

Part I: Ships' Names

Part II

General Index

A

Abercrombie, G.F. 101, 150, 181, 239
Aircraft
  British 17, 55, 57, 62, 63, 93, 95, 104, 105, 114, 115, 117, 122, 123, 128, 140, 141, 173, 193-95, 197, 198, Attack on *Bismarck* 199-203, 204, 206, Catalina sighting of *Bismarck* 209-12, *Bismarck* action 215-224, 236-37, 239
  German 17, 31, 33, 57, 74, 93, 105, 116, 167, 185, 214, 216, 236, 237
  Vichy 127
Alcock, Mr. & Mrs. 33
Alexander, A.V. 239
Ammon, William B. 26, 32, 33, 70-73, 81, 82, 89, 101, 181, 183, 184, 187
Anti-Submarine Warfare, see also Convoy
  ASDIC 39-41, 46, 62-63
  Screen 37, diagrams 38, 41, 53, 54, 56
  Zig-zag plans 20-21, 42-43, 55-56, 58-59, 62, 105, 107, 113, 119, 140, 154, 156, 161, 169, 170-71
Austin, Bernard L. 26, 31, 33, 89, 183, 184, 186

B

Bailey, Sir Sidney 33, 76
Bailey, Vaughn 26, 187
Baker, Charles A. 186
Bennett, Geoffrey M. 124
Binnington, David L. 65
Bird, F.D.G. 101, 150, 181, 239
Blackman, C.M. 100
Blamey, Glendenning 239
Bluejacket's Manual 184
Books read by JHW, authors of
  K. Coyle 122
  Kenneth Edwards 145, 150
  C.S. Forester 116, 119
  Mrs. H.M.W. Morrow 117
  C.V.R. Thompson 117
Boston, Massachusetts 1, 11, 240-43
Boutwood, John W. 93
Brest, France 54, 57, 198, 204, 205
Briggs, Dennis 211
Broadhurst, Joe 77
Browne, R.H.P. 85

C

Cape Town, South Africa 104, 145, 146, 147-150
Cape Verde Islands 118, 153
Carney, Robert B. 241
Carthwrite, Pilot 203
Cartwright, T.D. 88
Caslon, Clifford 35

Chapman, Alex Colin 98
Churchill, Winston 13, 14, 82, 83, 91
Clark, A. Dayton 33, 113, 123, 194 fn. 18
Clay, James B. 194 fn. 18
Cleary, James Sidney 135
Clothing and Uniforms 2, 47, 69, 81, 82, 85, 87, 93, 105, 115, 116, 118, 121, 163, 186, photos of JHW's version of tropical white, 119
Cockrane, Edward L. 30, 31, 32, 72, 73, 82, 89, 91
Communications
  Dispatches, deciphered 63, 107, 109, 111, 113, 115, 117, 120, 121, 122, 123, 128, 129, 142, 146, 147, 167, 171, 231 fn. 32
  Procedures 104, 107, 108, 110-11, 157, 158
Conrad, Robert D. 188
Convoy
  Formations 5, Diagram 6, 125, 129, 146, 163-65
  General Procedures 3, 5, 17-24, 74-76, 102-05, 115, 141-42, 162, 168, 170, 178-79, 186 fn. 19
  Groups
    Bermuda 10, 17, 61
    Halifax 61
    Sydney, N.S. 9, 17
  Numbers
    HX 84   51, 52, 53, 75
    HX 128   198
    SC 26   154
    SC 74   212
    SL 67   143
    SL 68   143
    SL 69   168
    SL 70   153-180
    WN   94
    WS   239
    WS 6   102-148
    WS 8b   194
Cooke, Godfrey A. 64, 67, 189
Coppinger, Cuthbert 189
Cotton, Miss 70, 89
Crawshaw, Stoker 136
Cross, W.K.R. 78, 84
Currie, R.A. 84, 183, 238

D

Dalrymple-Hamilton, F.H.G. 98, 112, 189, 204, 207, 232, 235, 243, photo with JHW in 1949, 242
Dathan, J.H. 98, 117, 150, 152, 239
Destroyers-for-bases Agreement 8, 9
Dodson, Edward Ney, Jr 100
Downey, Kenneth 188, 189, 191
Duncan, D.B. 183, 185

E

Edinburgh, Scotland 48, 69, 88, 181
Eire 54